THE MOTHER/DAUGHTER

PLOT

THE MOTHER/DAUGHTER PLOT

Narrative, Psychoanalysis, Feminism

MARIANNE HIRSCH

INDIANA UNIVERSITY PRESS
Bloomington and Indianapolis

Manufactured in the United States of America

Library of Congress Cataloging-in-Publication Data

Hirsch, Marianne.
The mother/daughter plot: narrative, psychoanalysis, feminism / Marianne Hirsch.
p.   cm.
Bibliography: p.
Includes index.
ISBN 0-253-32748-2.—ISBN 0-253-20532-8 (pbk.)
1. Fiction—Women authors—History and criticism.
2. Fiction—19th century—History and criticism.   3. Fiction—20th century—History and criticism.   4. Mothers and daughters in literature.   5. Fiction—Psychological aspects.   6. Feminism in literature.   7. Sex roles in literature.   8. Narration (Rhetoric)
I.   Title.
PN3401.H57   1989
809.3'9352042—dc19   88-46043
                                                                                      CIP

2 3 4 5 93 92 91

For Lotte
and for Rose

CONTENTS

ACKNOWLEDGMENTS

This book was written over a period of years during which feminist scholarship, and feminist literary criticism in particular, developed and changed tremendously. It therefore benefited greatly from the dialogues and debates that shaped this development. Much of this book was actually written with specific audiences in mind. These ranged from classrooms at Dartmouth College to feminist study groups, research institutes, conferences, and lectures. The conventions of acknowledgment do not suffice to convey the distinctive kind of feminist discussion that helped me to give shape to this argument. I therefore give in the introduction a fuller narrative of the intellectual context in which this book was written.

Some specific debts need to be acknowledged here, however. A full-time teaching job and a family do not leave much time for the writing of books. I am therefore grateful for the grants I have received and which have given me time not only to write, but to read in new fields. I thank Dartmouth College for a Junior Faculty Fellowship, a Senior Faculty Grant, and for its generous research support. I wish to thank the Wellesley Center for Research on Women for a year's grant, and the members of the 1979/80 Mellon Seminar there for their encouragement during the initial stages of this project. I am especially grateful to the Mary Ingraham Bunting Institute for its grant and for its unique way of fostering women's work. The 1984/85 Bunting Fellows know how much this book owes to them. Those who generously offered specific help were Teresa Bernardez, Judith Lewis Herrmann, Susan Strasser, Irene Sosa Vasquez, Jaimie Gordon, Kate Daniels, Margaret Carroll, Elaine Spatz-Rabinowitz, and especially and continuously Gail Reimer and Valerie Smith. I also want to acknowledge the immensely supportive role played by Margaret McKenna, the then Director of the Bunting Institute, and Ann Bookman, the Assistant Director. During my year in Cambridge I benefited greatly from discussions at the Harvard Feminist Theory Group, and I would like to thank the members of that seminar who commented on my work and whose influence helped to shape its pages, especially Patsy Beaudoin, Joseph Allen Boone, Marjorie Garber, Margaret Higonnet, Alice Jardine, Barbara Johnson, Ruth Perry, Susan Rubin Suleiman, Carolyn Williams, Susan Winnett, and Patricia Yaeger. I would also like to thank the members of the "Mothers' Group" in Cambridge: Mieke Bal, Teresa Bernardez, Carol Gilligan, Amy Lang, Evelyn Fox Keller, Ruth Perry, Gail Reimer, and Susan Rubin Suleiman. Each one of them has had a considerable influence on this book and I thank them for their example, their encouragement, and their constructive criticism.

I have greatly appreciated the strength and encouragement of the feminist community at Dartmouth College; my work is marked, I believe, by the collaborative spirit in which Women's Studies and feminist inquiry have been conceived here over the last fifteen years. A number of colleagues at Dartmouth have been extremely faithful and helpful readers and supporters of my work in its myriad stages over many years. I would like to thank in particular Faith Beasley, Lynda Boose, Mary Childers, Jane Coppock, Carla Freccero, Colette Gaudin, Mary Jean Green, Lynn Higgins, David Kastan, Audrey McCollum, Stephen G. Nichols, Neal Oxenhandler, Ivy Schweitzer, Christian Wolff, Nancy J. Vickers, and Susanne Zantop. And a very special thanks to Brenda Silver who has generously read every page several times, offering detailed and invaluable comments.

Much of this book came out of the experience of teaching a course on *Mothers and Daughters* in Comparative Literature and in the MALS Program at Dartmouth. Team-teaching with Mai-Lan Rogoff on two occasions was tremendously instructive and I thank her for her knowledge and help. I also thank all my students for their enthusiastic interest in this topic and their willingness to explore its various dimensions in both conventional and less conventional ways. Every one of them has contributed to this book.

Several others have generously read sections of this book and have offered bibliographic help, incisive suggestions, as well as inspiring examples. I thank, in particular, Elizabeth Abel, Helene Foley, Jane Gallop, Judith Kegan Gardiner, Joan Lidoff, Nancy K. Miller, Marta Peixoto, Mary Helen Washington, and Linda Williams. A very special thanks goes to Toni Morrison for an illuminating conversation about writing and motherhood in Afro-American culture.

For their research help, I would like to thank Emily Wheeler, Caroline Danielson, Jessica Seessel, Sabine Engel, and Gail Patten for helping me to prepare the manuscript.

There are other kinds of help that make the work of writing possible: I would like to thank the day care workers at Hanover Day Care, Norwich Day Care, La Petite Creche, and the Radcliffe Child Care Center for caring for my children so that I might have the time to write. I also wish to thank Peggy Kendall for her work in our household.

The conventions of the acknowledgment cannot do justice to the personal debts incurred throughout the work on a project such as this one. I thank, first, my children, Alex, Oliver, and Gabriel, for all that they have taught me about childhood and motherhood and about myself, and for being willing to live with a mother who is also a writer. My parents, Lotte and Carl Hirsch, as well as other members of my extended family, Rose Spitzer, Carl Spitzer, and Jane Coppock, have provided care, both physical and emotional, for us all.

This book could never have happened without the support and the assistance of Leo Spitzer, who not only shares the work of parenting with me, but who also has supportively read and commented on every page of this book. His example has been inspiring and his confidence in me has dispelled many discouraging moments.

In dedicating this book to my mother, Lotte Hirsch, I wish to recognize a bond that is unlike any other. My second dedication, to the memory of my mother-in-law, Rose Spitzer, commemorates someone whose friendship has been special in my life. I wish she could have read this book. Both have made me understand the importance of female transmission and of generational continuities among women.

The cover photograph depicts my maternal grandmother, Cäcilie Rubel Gottfried, and her older daughter, Friederike Gottfried Bong. It was taken in Czernowitz, Austria-Hungary, around 1909, shortly before, as Virginia Woolf remarked, "human character changed."

Versions of some parts of this book's chapters have been previously published, in somewhat different form. Two parts of chapter 1 appeared as "Female Family Romances and the 'Old Dream of Symmetry,' " in *Literature and Psychology* 23, 4 (1986), 37–47; one additional section of chapter 1 appeared as a part of "Spiritual Bildung: The Beautiful Soul as Paradigm" in *The Voyage In: Fictions of Female Development*, ed. Elizabeth Abel, Marianne Hirsch, and Elizabeth Langland (Hanover: University Press of New England, 1983). Part of chapter 5 appeared as "Maternal Anger: Silent Themes and 'Meaningful Digressions' in Psychoanalytic Feminism" in *minnesota review*, n.s. 29 (Fall 1987), 81–87.

Permission to reprint Muriel Rukeyser's "Myth" was granted by Random House. Parts of Cherríe Moraga's "For the Color of My Mother" are reprinted with permission from the author and Kitchen Table: Women of Color Press, PO Box 908, Latham, N.Y. 12110.

INTRODUCTION

UNSPEAKABLE PLOTS

> I am a white girl gone brown to the blood
> color of my mother
> speaking for her through the muzzle
> part of the mouth
> the wide-arched muzzle of brown
> women
>
> —Cherríe Moraga,
> "For the Color of My Mother"

> Long afterward, Oedipus, old and
> blinded, walked the roads. He smelled a
> familiar smell. It was the Sphinx. Oedipus
> said, "I want to ask you one question.
> Why didn't I recognize my mother?" "You
> gave the wrong answer," said the Sphinx.
> "But that was what made everything
> possible," said Oedipus. "No," she said.
> "When I asked, What walks on four legs
> in the morning, two at noon and three in
> the evening, you answered, Man. You
> didn't say anything about woman."
> "When you say Man," said Oedipus, "you
> include women too. Everyone knows
> that." She said, "That's what you think."
>
> —Muriel Rukeyser, "Myth"

Why didn't I recognize my mother?
(Or, Why didn't my mother recognize me?)
(Or, Why didn't I recognize my child?)

Muriel Rukeyser's 1968 revision of the Oedipus story anticipates more recent feminist questions and reflections about women's relations to men's plots. Rukeyser's poem "Myth" provides the Oedipus story—the classic and paradigmatic story of individual development in Western civilization—with a different female-centered ending. Unequivocally female, in possession of a voice and a plot, a subjectivity of her own, and a sense of irony, Rukeyser's Sphinx refuses to be included in the universal heading 'Man'. She poses the question of sexual difference and asserts the

1

particularity of women. Whereas Sophocles erases the figure of the Sphinx from his play, subsuming her questions within Oedipus's own questioning of his origins, Rukeyser has her speak out for women and, thereby, for herself.[1] Re-writing a classic plot motivated by the mechanisms of masculine desire, she begins to answer the question posed by Teresa de Lauretis in *Alice Doesn't:* "What became of the Sphinx after the encounter with Oedipus on his way to Thebes? . . . No one knows offhand and, what is more, it seldom occurs to anyone to ask. . . . Medusa and the Sphinx, like other ancient monsters, have survived inscribed . . . in someone else's story, not their own; so they are figures or markers of positions—places and topoi—through which the hero and his story move to their destination and to accomplish meaning."[2]

Both Rukeyser and de Lauretis have chosen the Oedipus story as the story through which to explore the relationship between plot and gender. By focusing on the Sphinx—the figure who is entirely absent from Sophocles's play and from Freud's developmental paradigm—both revise the conventional plot structure, in which men are central and women function as objects or obstacles. But what happened to Jocasta, the "other woman" in the tale? Virtually silent in Sophocles' play and present only as object of desire and exchange in Freud's theory, Jocasta is virtually ignored in feminist revisions as well. In de Lauretis's account she appears only in a parenthesis, to signal a parallel between the ending of her plot and the supposed ending of the Sphinx's: "The questions we might ask are obvious. Why did the Sphinx kill herself (like Jocasta)?" (p. 110). Although there are two female plots inscribed and silenced in the Oedipus story, de Lauretis is curious only about one. Both she and Rukeyser are attracted by the enigmatic, powerful, monstrous, and terrifying Sphinx; both omit the powerless, maternal, emotional, and virtually silent Jocasta. So that, while Rukeyser's Oedipus wonders why he did not recognize his mother, no one asks why—in spite of clearcut indications ranging from oracular predictions to swollen feet—his mother did not recognize him. Even Hélène Cixous, who devotes an opera to the story of Oedipus and Jocasta, casts Jocasta as the lover and clearly not as the mother of Oedipus.[3] No one imagines a Jocasta who wonders why she did not recognize her child.

This book foregrounds the "other woman," the mother, in relation to the "other child," the daughter. The myths we read and take to be basic determine our vision of how individual subjects are formed in relation to familial structures. Freud's optic was determined by the story he took to be central, the story of Oedipus. Other mythologies, the stories of Iphigenia, Electra, and Clytemnestra, of Demeter and Persephone, or of Antigone, for example, suggest alternate economies which may shape different plot patterns. They revolve around mothers and daughters as well as around brothers, sisters, and fathers. Even here, however, as we turn from the story of mother and son to the stories of mothers and daughters, Jocasta's silence is not radically reversed.

This book takes as its point of departure the intersection of familial structures and structures of plotting, attempting to place at the center of inquiry mothers and daughters, the female figures neglected by psychoanalytic theories and submerged in traditional plot structures. It concentrates on novels by nineteenth- and twentieth-century women writers from the Western European and the North American traditions, reading them with psychoanalytic theories of subject-formation in the context of the narrative conventions of realism, modernism, and post-modernism. Thus its aim is to reframe the familial structures basic to traditional narrative, *and* the narrative structures basic to traditional conceptions of family, from the perspectives of the feminine and, more controversially, the maternal.

By way of introducing the territory to be mapped in the course of this book, two stories will serve as paradigms—Jocasta's missing story in the Oedipus narrative, and a very recent black feminist re-vision of that story in Toni Morrison's *Beloved*. In one, we find a silenced mother who remains the object of the child's process of subject-formation and the ground on which the conflict between father and son is played out. In the other, a mother emerges who attempts to speak for herself even while she knows that her story is unspeakable—"not a story to pass on."

What earns the Sphinx, the non-maternal woman, privilege over Jocasta, the mother? Why do even feminist analyses fail to grant Jocasta as mother a voice and a plot? An earlier poem of Rukeyser's, "Private Life of the Sphinx" (1948),[4] suggests the advantages, for a feminist perspective, of distinguishing between these two female positions. In that poem, the Sphinx is actually conflated with Jocasta and presented as maternal:

> Simply because of a question, my life is implicated:
> my flesh and answer fly between chaos and their need. . . .
> My questions are my body. And among this glowing, this sure,
> this fact, this mooncolored breast, I make memorial.

Sharing Jocasta's powerlessness, this Sphinx clearly has a maternal and bodily identity. She questions not Oedipus, who never appears in the text, but herself, her own legendary status as Mother and Poet in the story of Man. Compelled to respond to man's "need" and "babble of demand," this earlier Sphinx *embodies* Truth and "set[s][her] life among the questioning." Resisting the power projected onto her and the misconceptions circulating about her, she conveys the personal bodily cost of the terrible knowledge she possesses about life and death. She dreams of a listener, of someone who will understand the meaning of her name and who will listen to her song. Whereas the later, non-maternal, extra-bodily Sphinx of "Myth" can challenge Oedipus's self-confident answer "Man," the earlier maternal Sphinx is resigned to accept it: "the answer must be 'Man.' " While the later Sphinx can devastate her opponent with one ironic comment, the earlier figure agonizes about being known and recognized for herself. We can understand Rukeyser's eagerness to revise her own revision in the 1960s, to eliminate the Sphinx's vulnerability, and to claim power and equality for women. Yet her shift away from the maternal and bodily identity of women in "Myth" is symptomatic of the moves of North American and European feminist writing and theorizing in the 1970s and 80s. This feminist tradition can succeed in inscribing the female into the male plot only by further silencing one aspect of women's experience and identity—the maternal.

In wondering why the Sphinx is more interesting, more worthy of having her story rewritten than Jocasta, in asking where the story of Jocasta is in the story of Oedipus, I am asking not only where the stories of women are in men's plots, but where the stories of mothers are in the plots of sons and daughters. I am asking that we try to imagine those stories. What can we say about Jocasta? In *Oedipus Rex* she appears only to attempt to discourage Oedipus from his questionings; yet she barely succeeds in delaying the terrible revelation. About herself she merely says: "Have I not suffered enough?" (l. 1059).[5] After announcing her eternal silence—"O lost and damned./ This is my last and only word to you/ For ever!" (ll. 1070–72)—she kills herself.

From sources beyond the Sophoclean trilogy, we do find the antecedents to this moment: Laius's homosexual rape, his marriage to Jocasta, and his refusal to sleep with her after the oracular decree. We find her ruse—getting him drunk to conceive Oedipus.[6] We do not discover her feelings about handing her child over to die, except in Oedipus's own exclamation: "The child she bore!" (l. 1178). Beyond this Jocasta is represented by silence, negation, damnation, suicide. The story of her desire, the account of her guilt, the rationale for her complicity with a brutal husband, the materiality of the body which gave birth to a child she could not keep and which then conceived with that child other children—*this* story cannot be filled in because we have no framework within which to do it *from her perspective*. She remains, in Oedipus's words, "That wife, no wife of mine—that soil/where I was sown and where I reap my harvest" (ll. 1258–59).

Harold Stewart asks why Oedipus survives although he committed two outrages, while Jocasta has to die for committing only one.[7] Jocasta, he speculates, actually engineered the destruction of Laius as a revenge for his homosexuality. I would argue that such a reading cannot be valid, given that Jocasta's motives and desires are not only absent from the text, but also absent from the very framework upon which Sophocles' and Freud's texts are built.[8]

Inasmuch as Cixous grants a voice to Jocasta in *Le Nom d'Oedipe: Chant du corps interdit*, it is the voice of Oedipus's lover and wife, the voice of the woman whose body is the home of man, but who herself experiences that home as lover and not as mother. Cixous tells the story of two lovers tragically separated by their fate and their past—a tragedy which leads

Jocasta to kill herself. Significantly, some of Jocasta's speeches echo her sparse dialogue, her call for silence and ignorance in *Oedipus Rex*: "Forget the world/ Forget the city/ Stay here. . . . Do not search for it/ Do not go out. Stay here" (p. 14, 26; my translation). Clearly, to know Jocasta's maternal story, we would have to rewrite completely the story of Oedipus and of the child's development: we would have to *begin* with the mother, not the son or the father. If masculine plotting is to be rethought from the perspective of the feminine, such rethinking needs to include Jocasta as well as the Sphinx, Jocasta the mother as well as Jocasta the wife and lover, and to reject the distinction, upheld even in recent feminist writing, between maternal and non-maternal women. For such a reframing, we have to go beyond classic texts to the work of women writers, who, as Rukeyser's poem demonstrates, have revised those texts, and to feminist revisions of psychoanalytic paradigms. But, as Cixous's play demonstrates, we also need to evaluate the process of revision and to determine whether and to what extent a mere repetition and reproduction of classic conceptions can indeed be transcended.

Alternate women-centered mythologies—the story of Demeter and Persephone, for example—are available to women writers, such as Toni Morrison, who wish to re-write the story of mother-child relations from maternal perspectives and, in particular, from the perspective of the mothers of daughters.[9]

The differences are telling. Unlike the Oedipus story, Demeter and Persephone's tale is told from the perspective of a bereaved Demeter, searching for her daughter, mourning her departure, and effecting her return through her own divine power. A breech caused by rape and death is undone by the mother's power to fulfill a mutual desire for connection. The compromise solution achieved by Demeter is that Persephone will spend three quarters of the year with her and one quarter with her husband in the underworld. Loss itself provides the occasion for the story's inception. In this case, the story of mother and daughter depends on Hades, the male figure whose intervention constitutes the disruption which prompts the narrative. It is only when Hades abducts Persephone that mother and daughter enter time: Demeter becomes an old woman as Persephone reaches maturity. Simultaneously, seasonal growth and agriculture begin for humans. Loss is presented as inevitable, part of the natural sequence of growth, but, since time is cyclical, mother-daughter reunion forms a natural part of the cycle. In ancient times, the mysteries at Eleusis celebrated this mother-daughter connection as the union of light and darkness, life and death, death and rebirth.[10] The hymn itself, however, grants legitimacy to the mother's feelings of bereavement, anger, and wild desire, even as it insists on the inevitability and the necessity of separation. Its cyclicality offers an alternative to oedipal narratives structured according to principles of linear repetition. The "Hymn to Demeter" thus both inscribes the story of mother and daughter within patriarchal reality and allows it to mark a feminine difference. Hades occasions both the separation and a narrative which will repair the breech.

Toni Morrison's Sethe, the maternal protagonist of her 1987 novel *Beloved*, is neither the silent Jocasta nor the powerful Demeter.[11] Like the Oedipus story, however, Morrison's novel is about the murdered child, a daughter, returning from the other side to question the mother, and, like the story of Demeter and Persephone, it is about a temporary, perhaps a cyclical, reunion between mother and daughter. Yet Morrison's novel, unlike the Oedipus story, *begins* with the mother, and allows *her* to *tell* her tale, to attempt to explain her incomprehensible act.

Like the "Hymn," the mother-daughter story in Morrison's *Beloved* depends on male intervention to occasion the narrative. Returning after an eighteen-year absence, Paul D. disrupts the uneasy household in which Sethe, the mother, and Denver, the daughter, coexist with the ghost of Sethe's murdered baby daughter. His presence makes it possible for Sethe to tell the story of motherhood under slavery, a story by which she has been obsessed for the eighteen years following her escape.

Familial structures in this novel are profoundly distorted by the institution of slavery. The action begins in 1871 in Cincinnati, and returns, through flashbacks, to the Mississippi slave plantation ironically called "Sweet Home." Sethe herself spoke to her own mother only once, and, when she saw her hanged one morning, was not allowed to check for the mark by means of which she might have been able to recognize her definitively as her mother. Sethe is permanently separated from her husband Halle and separates herself from her own children when she sends them ahead to freedom. In a slave economy in which even one's own body is not one's property, the white masters can rob Sethe of everything, including her mother's milk. It is no surprise, then, that the inhabitants of 124 Bluestone Road do not constitute a nuclear family that might fit Freudian paradigms. Morrison underscores this incongruity when she insists on the 124 (the novel's first words): triangles are repeatedly broken up as a *fourth* term either supplements or replaces the third. Sethe, her daughter Denver, and the grandmother Baby Suggs are joined by the ghost; after the grandmother's death, Sethe, Denver, and the ghost are joined by Paul D.; and, after the ghost is chased off, Sethe, Denver, and Paul D., whose shadows on the road do form a triangle, are quickly joined by the ghostly Beloved who thoroughly disrupts any possible nuclear configuration.

In Morrison's novel, the economy of slavery circumscribes not only the process of individuation and subject-formation, but also heightens and intensifies the experience of motherhood—of connection and separation. It raises questions about what it means to have a self and to give that self away. It raises questions about what *family* means and about the ways in which nuclear configurations (dominant in the master culture) prevail as points of reference even in economies in which they are thoroughly distorted and disrupted. If mothers cannot "own" their children or even themselves, they experience separation and loss all the more intensely.

Largely female, Sethe's family is determined by the dynamics of the relationships among the women: the husband Halle never makes it to freedom and the two boys leave before the novel begins. The passionate interaction is between the mother and the two daughters, one of whom is killed while the other survives, and between the sisters, one of whom drank the other's blood with her mother's milk. The intensity of the women's passion becomes so stifling as to threaten paralysis. At such moments, Paul D. comes in to make the story move along, but, until the last scene, he is consistently excluded from the power of their interconnection.

Sethe's murder of her as yet unnamed baby girl (whose milk had already been taken by the white masters at "Sweet Home" and who, along with her three siblings, was about to be returned into slavery), and Sethe's own attempts to explain it—to Paul D., to herself, to Denver, and to Beloved—are at the core of the novel. "The truth was simple," Sethe insists. "I took and put my babies where they'd be safe." Sethe's own insistence that "she had done right because it came from true love" (p. 251) and other characters' judgments of her mother-love as "too thick" or "wrong" suggest the moral complexity of the act, and demand that we examine our notion of mother-love, along with the value of life and self-possession.[12] The novel contains more than judgment: it contains the stories that precede and follow judgment, the stories that form and surround the relationship of mother and daughter during slavery and in post-abolition times. It contains stories both of maternal sorrow, guilt, and pain and of maternal joy and pleasure. As long as she can continue telling her stories and explaining her actions, the relationship continues: "It was as though Sethe didn't really want forgiveness given; she wanted it refused. And Beloved helped her out" (p. 252).

But, just as for Demeter and Persephone, separation and loss are inevitable; Beloved must return to the dark side from which she came. The doubly bereaved Sethe, nursed back to life by the other daughter Denver, is ultimately comforted by Paul D. who "wants to put his story next to hers" (p. 273). In response to her self-effacing "She was my best thing," he insists: "You your best thing, Sethe. You are." Holding her fingers, he enables Sethe to see herself as a subject, as a mother and a subject both. Her own subjectivity had been nurtured for a brief moment only (between her escape to freedom and the murder which was meant to preserve that freedom) and then abandoned by the shocked and disappointed mother-in-law, Baby Suggs. Now, holding Paul D.'s fingers, Sethe tentatively says "Me? Me?" Allowing a maternal voice and subjectivity to emerge, she questions, at least for a moment, the hierarchy of motherhood over selfhood on which her life had rested until that moment. The novel both explains and challenges that hierarchy.

Sethe's story, like Jocasta's (and like the story of slavery itself) is, as Morrison insists, "not a story to pass on," yet this novel does allow the mother to speak for herself, to speak her own name and the daughter's, to speak, after eighteen years, her unspeakable crime to her daughter. It allows Beloved to return, like Persephone, so that mother and daughter can speak to each other. And, it allows Sethe both to recognize Beloved as her child and to begin to recognize herself as "Me? Me?"

My book traces the transformations, within narrative conventions, psychoanalytic theories, and feminist thinking, which enable the silent Jocasta gradually to give way to the vocal Sethe. Through the voices of daughters, speaking for their mothers, through the voices of mothers speaking for themselves and their daughters, and, eventually perhaps, through the voices of mothers and daughters speaking to each other, oedipal frameworks are modified by other psychological and narrative economies. Thus the plots of mothers and daughters do not remain unspeakable.

Mothers, Daughters, and Narrative

This book is about Woman and about women, about the constructions of femininity in discourses of motherhood and daughterhood. In it I explore those discourses within the contexts of patriarchy as it "exists concretely, in social relations, and [as] it works precisely through the various discursive and representational structures that allow us to recognize it" (*Alice Doesn't*, p. 165). In particular, I am interested in the texts of women writers who write within this Euro-American patriarchal context of discourse and representation and, more specifically, within a sex-gender system which, during much of the period this book covers, identifies writing as masculine and insists on the incompatibility of creativity and procreativity. These women write within literary conventions that define the feminine only in relation to the masculine, as object or obstacle. Female plots, as many feminist critics have demonstrated, act out the frustrations engendered by these limited possibilities and attempt to subvert the constraint of dominant patterns by means of various "emancipatory strategies"[13]—the revision of endings, beginnings, patterns of progression. This process of resistance, revision, and emancipation in the work of women writers is, as Nancy K. Miller has argued, a *feminist* act defining a *feminist* poetics and it needs to be identified as such.[14] In Miller's terms, then, the writers I study here are not only women writers marked biographically, by their biology and psychology, but *feminist* writers who define themselves by their dissenting relation to dominant tradition. Although I find Miller's definition of strategies of dissent extremely helpful, I prefer, in this book, to reserve the term *feminist* for an aesthetics connected to the feminist movement of active social resistance in the 1970s and 80s. For the earlier writers I discuss I use the less explicit terms *women's* or *female*, but would include in those terms the self-consciousness and resistance Miller identifies as feminist.[15] Because the writers I study are, for the most part, canonical and not forgotten women writers, they can illustrate the multiple and conflicting identifications engendered by women writers' place in hegemonic tradition—their predicaments of marginality and aspirations to centrality.[16] Yet that choice also erases other forms of difference—class, for example, certain racial differences, and generic differences, such as autobiography or popular fiction.

That choice is motivated by the fact that the novel is the optimal genre in which to study the interplay between hegemonic and dissenting voices. In recent years, narratologists have analyzed the novel's polyvocality, revealing the conflicting discourses that make possible, within the structures of the novel, the interrogation of dominant cultural codes and assumptions. Thus, the novel is at once, as Rachel Blau DuPlessis finds, "the place where ideology is coiled" (p. x) and the place where it can be called into question. I use the term ideology in the Althusserian sense of "the system of representations by which we imagine the world as it is."[17]

Especially in the nineteenth century the plot of heterosexual romance and marriage structures the novels of women writers, even if its conventional sequence is variously subverted.[18] By concentrating on the relationship between mothers and daughters, I interrogate and reframe these plot patterns in particular ways, discovering not only certain ideologies of maternity embedded within them, but also narrative patterns which call the more conventional constructions of the love plot into question. I have decided to use Freud's notion of a "Familienroman"—a "family romance"—as a controlling figure in these analyses.[19] In Freud's terms, the family romance is an imaginary interrogation of origins, an interrogation which embeds the engenderment of narrative within the experience of family. Through fantasy, the developing individual liberates himself from the constraints of family by imagining himself to be an orphan or a bastard and his "real" parents to be more noble than the "foster" family in which he is growing up. The essence of the Freudian family romance is the imaginative act of replacing the parent (for boys clearly the father) with another, superior figure.

In using the term family romance, I retain Freudian definitions as reference points but reframe them to be more broadly applicable. My aim is to focus at once on the discursive and imaginative role that the family plays in our narratives and the particular shape and nature of familial structures in particular narratives and social contexts. The family romance describes the experience of familial structures as discursive: the family romance is the story we tell ourselves about the social and psychological reality of the family in which we find ourselves and about the patterns of desire that motivate the interaction among its members. The family romance thus combines and reveals as indistinguishable the psychological subjective experience of family and the process of narrative. As Julia Kristeva says: "Narrative is, in sum, the most elaborate kind of attempt, on the part of the speaking subject, after syntactic competence, to situate his or her self among his or her desires and their taboos, that is at the interior of the oedipal triangle."[20] The family romance is a structure of fantasy—the imaginary construction of plots according to principles of wish fulfilment. The notion of family romance can thus accommodate the discrepancies between *social reality* and *fantasy construction*, which are basic to the experience and the institution of family.

Although Freud defines a particular shape of the family romance as universal, I find biases, both androcentric and ethnocentric, in his definition. I argue that patterns of family romance can and do vary, for male and female writers, during different periods and for different cultural traditions.[21] This book traces some of the variations family romances have undergone in a number of nineteenth and twentieth-century texts. Yet, even the variations I have found follow certain circumscribed patterns. By replaying classic mythic paradigms which serve as their models (Electra, Antigone, and Demeter), and which I discuss in some detail in the book's Prelude, these alternate plot patterns go beyond Oedipus, yet show that variations of the family romance in the Western European and North American novel are, in many ways, still classic ones. If the Freudian family romance reflects not only psychologically valid patterns but also, as I argue, the patterns of nineteenth- and twentieth-century fictional plots, then female and feminist family romances necessarily situate themselves in a revisionary relationship to the Freudian pattern, with the fictional heroine often having to occupy both the position of subject and that of object in the narrative. Revisions reframe the basic paradigm to include the stories of daughters and eventually also the stories of mothers, but, ultimately, they do not entirely reframe the basic conception of family as static structure, of the relationship of familial patterns and narrative patterns, of triangles as fundamental figures in familial interaction. This book explores, then, both the potentials and the limitations of certain psychoanalytic terms and concepts for a feminist analysis of women's writing and the persistent adherence of women's plots to the terms identified in classical mythology and psychoanalytic theory.[22]

By using the notion of family romance, I treat both motherhood and daughterhood as *story*—as narrative representation of social and subjective reality and of literary convention. I would argue that in conventional nineteenth-century plots of the European and American tradition the fantasy that controls the female family romance is the desire for the heroine's singularity based on a disidentification from the fate of other women, especially mothers. In modernist plots, this wish is supplemented by the heroines' artistic ambitions and the desire for distinction which now, however, needs to include affiliations with both male and female models. In post-modernist plots, other fantasies of a more multiple relational identity emerge, including the stories of mothers who by definition are entangled in relations which define and circumscribe all further desire. All of these variations, however, are based on the heroines' refusal of conventional heterosexual romance and marriage plots and, furthermore, on their disidentification from conventional constructions of femininity. Mothers—the ones who are not singular, who did succumb to convention inasmuch as they are mothers—thereby become the targets of this process of disidentification and the primary negative models for the daughter. At the same time, however, mothers and other women increasingly appear in these novels as alternate objects of desire, suggesting other possible subjective economies based in women's relationships. Eventually, mothers begin to appear as subjects.

The notion of family romance, extrapolated from Freudian definitions and extended beyond them, can account for the ambivalences and duplicities contained in the fantasy of difference and singularity, the pull toward complicity, and the difficulties of dissent. It accounts for the process of "becoming-woman," of en-genderment, which is intimately tied to the process of transmission and the relationship to previous and subsequent generations of women. It traces both the story of women's "consent to" and dissent from "femininity" [de Lauretis], and the process of what Althusser has called "interpellation"[23] and the process of conscious resistance against it. And, as subsequent chapters will demonstrate, the structure of family romance, with its conjunction of desire and narrative, is operative both in fictional and in theoretical writings, including, of course, my own book.

I realize that my own relationship to psychoanalytic terms and concepts, and to certain familial patterns and fantasies, is an ambivalent one. Although I question the flexibility of psychoanalytic frameworks, I do so, for the most part, from within them, keenly aware of their compelling usefulness for feminist analysis of femininity as culturally constructed and internalized by individual female subjects. This section's very subtitle, for example—*Mothers, Daughters, and Narrative*—repeats the triangular structure of the nuclear family, with narrative occupying the place of the paternal. The book's structure is also tripartite. At the same time, the book longs for other economies and other figures. It longs for a space in which maternal subjectivities could be articulated and for the means of politicizing the psychological and the familial; both of these goals conflict with some basic psychoanalytic assumptions. I believe that the tension introduced by this ambivalence motivates the book's dynamic progression in ways that are both conscious and unconscious. The strategy of reading theoretical texts as fictions and of reading theoretical fictions along with literary ones, moreover, has the effect of allowing them to illuminate each other so that they can reveal deeper cultural desires in given historical moments.

It is essential for feminists to be aware of the pervasiveness of familial metaphors and of the family as vantage point in our culture and in its analytic methodologies. Whether feminist theorizing should go beyond the family to other relational models is a question of crucial importance. I am well aware that this book remains firmly rooted within familial ideologies. I believe that before the familial can be transcended or left behind, all positions within the family must be probed from all directions, including that of mothers and daughters. Yet, the fundamental question that under-lies these individual analyses is whether it is possible to arrive at a genuine critique of psychoanalytic assumptions and of familial ideologies from a vantage point which, of necessity, shares even some of these assumptions.

In this book these questions are posed in relation to maternal discourse. I believe that a thorough transformation of basic conceptual paradigms from a feminist perspective needs to include all women, mothers as well as daughters. Yet I find that while psychoanalytic feminism can add the female child to the male, allowing women to speak as daughters, it has difficulty accounting for the experience and the voice of the adult woman who is a mother. Like all psychoanalyses it is so profoundly child-centered that it has difficulty, even more generally, theorizing, beyond childhood, the experience of adulthood. But, so long as the figure of the mother is excluded from theory *psychoanalytic feminism* cannot become a *feminist psychoanalysis*.

Because of its concentration on mothers as well as on women and daughters, my argument offers a particular vantage point within the cur-rent debate among feminists about the female subject and the meaning of femininity.[24] First, by distinguishing between female positions—childless woman and mother, mother and daughter—it challenges the notion of woman as a singular, unified, transparent category. The multiplicity of "women" is nowhere more obvious than for the figure of the mother, who is always both mother and daughter. Her representation is controlled by her object status, but her discourse, when it is voiced, moves her from object to subject. But, as long as she speaks as mother, she must always remain the object in her child's process of subject-formation; she is never fully a subject. Second, the figure of mother is determined by her body more intensely than the figure of woman. By taking on the notion of essentialism so directly—maternity, inasmuch as it is represented as biological, poses the question of the body as pointedly as is possible—this book is able to look again at what feminists have hidden from view in both assertions and rejections of essentialism. It is easy to grant that neither sex nor gender can be invoked as fixed or unproblematic categories. It is more difficult to assert that reproduction provides a radical arena of *difference*—and more than merely biological difference—and that it thereby challenges a positional, destabilized view of sex and gender more than perhaps anything else. The perspective of the maternal makes it difficult simply to reject the notion of biology and forces us to engage both the meaning of the body and the risks of what has been characterized as essentialist. This is equally true for adoptive mothers whose bodies, I would argue, are equally engaged in the process of mothering although they have not given birth to children. Third, the focus on mothers and daughters redefines the notion of difference. Difference here is not merely gender difference. It encompasses the (maternal) difference within the feminine and the multiple differences within the maternal, the differences among women, the individual woman's difference from Woman and even from other women, and the difference of maternal plots and stories from conventional romance plots. *What is a mother?* and *what is maternal?* are questions that underlie every page of this book without ever being answered directly. In fact, I generally prefer the adjectival term "maternal" because it signals that there is no transparent meaning of the concept. In the chapters that follow, moreover, I take neither the notion of "experience" nor that of "identity" as given, but find that the focus on the maternal makes it imperative to use and to attempt to theorize both.

These questions of definition—of motherhood, experience, and identity in relation to sex and gender—have acquired particular urgency throughout the time of my work on this book, and especially recently, in connection to the feminist debates over reproductive technologies. I believe that feminists need to clarify their positions on motherhood, particularly at a moment when science and the legal system are themselves engaged in a process of charting the definitions and rights of children, fathers, and mothers. The Baby M case, for example, has forced feminists to scrutinize their most fundamental assumptions as they confront impossible decisions: between Mary Beth Whitehead, the birth mother (or the surrogate, the natural, the contract mother, depending on which position one takes) and Elizabeth Stern, the wife of the biological father (the adoptive mother, or the surrogate mother); between the rights of biological mothers and of biological fathers; between the "best interests" of children, or the "best interests" of mothers. The questions raised by this one case represent the most basic clash between biology and law, essentialism and constructivism. And as we begin to take into account the economic conditions of the Sterns and Whitehead, and of the lawyers who benefit from the legal confusions concerning the definition of maternity, we confront the variables of income level and class as they impinge on conceptual systems and social realities.[25] As feminists try to decide about more complex technologies, such as in vitro fertilization, other variables intrude and other forms of oppression and appropriation become possible—poor and third world women renting their wombs to rich, first world women, for example. What does the term *mother*, what does the term *father* mean in this context? And how do these terms relate to bodies which are being transformed through technology, to laws which displace those bodies, to experiences displaced by these laws? Although it is unlikely that feminists will reach a comfortable consensus on these issues, it is crucial that we understand the terms of the argument, and to do so we must scrutinize motherhood from personal, subjective, legal, psychological, biological, economic, historical, and technological vantage points.

After a discussion of mythic "Origins and Paradigms" in the book's Prelude I start my analysis with the work of nineteenth-century women writers because I believe that motherhood as a concept is historically determined in ways that are parallel to the notion of childhood. As Ann Dally argues: "There have always been mothers, but motherhood was invented."[26] She cites 1597 as the first entry for "motherhood" in the *Oxford English Dictionary*, and then only as fact rather than ideology. The ideology of motherhood as the ideal of femininity coincides with the institutionalization of childhood during the eighteenth and nineteenth centuries. As representations of the child's vulnerability and need for nurturing and protection became more prominent, motherhood became an "instinct," a "natural" role and form of human connection, as well as a practice. As the private sphere was isolated from the public under industrial capitalism, and as women became identified with and enclosed within the private sphere, motherhood elevated middle-class and upper-class women into a position of increased personal status, if decreased social power. In a largely technological and impersonal public world, motherhood came to represent, as Elisabeth Badinter puts it, "a repository of society's idealism" (p. 180); it became the force of conservation of traditional values. The focus of this ideology of the maternal, however, was not the *mother* but the *child*, that delicate and vulnerable organic being who required complete devotion and attention. Theories of child development and education, from Rousseau's work on, contain conflicting notions of the child's "best interests"— on the one hand, the "natural" mother-child connection, on the other, professional, often male-devised, educational strategies. In either case, however, the maternal role was figured in ways that are ultimately debilitating to women—equally so to those women who could afford to try to live up to the social ideal of maternity and to those who because of economic necessity could not. The mother became either the object of idealization and nostalgia or that which had to be rejected and surpassed in favor of allegiance to a morally and intellectually superior male world.

What interests me in Part I of this book is how, within this ideological context and within the context of the conventions of realism, mothers and maternity are represented in the work of women writers who stand both inside and outside those conventions. Not surprisingly I find, in chapter 1, that mothers tend to be absent, silent, or devalued in novels by Jane Austen, Mary Shelley, George Sand, the Brontës, George Eliot, and Kate Chopin. The conventions of realism, resting on structures of consent and containment, shut out various forms of indeterminacy, instability, and social fragmentation, including, I argue, maternal perspectives and experiences. The repression of the maternal leads women writers and fictional heroines to construct the "female family romance," based on fraternal rather than maternal attachments. I illustrate this pattern in a close reading of Austen's *Emma* in relation to Freud's "Family Romances." The chapter proposes that the nineteenth-century heroine, determined to shape a different plot for herself, tends not only to be separated from the figure and the story of her mother, but herself tries to avoid maternity at all costs.

Chapter 2 extends the analysis of the pattern of fraternal attachment to George Eliot's *Daniel Deronda*, the text I believe to be at once its ultimate illustration and its most devastating critique. Although mothers occupy a more central position in this novel, the primary nurturing activity is exercised by the male, fraternal/paternal characters, Daniel and Mordechai. Gwendolen's own "will to difference" is structured—both enabled and limited—by her fraternal attachment to Daniel, and not in relation to any of the novel's mothers.

Part II moves from realism to modernism, from the nineteenth-century cult of "true womanhood" to post World War I emancipation. It moves as well to a social context in which, because of significant medical advances in birth technology and contraception, motherhood is less life-threatening and more of a choice for women. Chapter 3 traces the emergence of the mothers as central figures in the daughter-artists' texts and the contradictions in the women artists' liminal position between maternal/female and paternal/male affiliations. Freud's essays on femininity and the importance of pre-oedipal mother-daughter connection, published during the 1920s, and Virginia Woolf's analysis of the position of the woman writer in *A Room of One's Own* form the background to readings of Woolf's *To the Lighthouse*, Colette's *Break of Day*, and Edith Wharton's *The Mother's Recompense*. These novels conjoin, uneasily, the narrative of mother-daughter attachment and the plot of heterosexual romance. The chapter explores some connections between gender and modernism, suggesting that for women writers contradiction and oscillation, rather than repetition, bind the modernist plot.

Part III moves from the 1920s to the 1970s and 80s and from modernism to post-modernism. Chapter 4 looks at feminist fictions and theories emerging in the 1970s and at their representations of female subject-formation in relation to mother-daughter relationships. Adrienne Rich's essay "When We Dead Awaken: Writing as Re-Vision" serves as a paradigm for this feminist relation to the past. What I call the "feminist family romance" appears in psychoanalytic re-visions of Freudian paradigms, which highlight mother-daughter bonding as a basis for a vision of gender difference and female specificity. This family romance pattern takes on different, less idealized shapes and valences in fictional texts which are more specifically contextualized and historical situations. Margaret Atwood's *Surfacing*, Marguerite Duras's *The Lover*, and Christa Wolf's *Patterns of Childhood* form the subject of textual analysis. The fictional and the theoretical texts I discuss in this chapter feature mothers prominently, and displace fathers, brothers, husbands, and male lovers. The texts themselves, however, are still written from daughterly perspectives.

Chapter 5 specifically explores points at which feminist discourse situates itself at a distance from the maternal and points at which a maternal discourse emerges. The feminist reliance on psychoanalytic frameworks begins to seem particularly problematic in relation to the feminist silencing of the mother. In analyzing the confrontation of maternal and daughterly voices in Toni Morrison's *Sula* and Alice Walker's "Everyday Use," and in coming back to Morrison's *Beloved*, I perceive a discourse of identity and subject-formation which goes beyond oedipal patterns and the terms of psychoanalytic discourse. Such a discourse might be able both to reverse the erasure of the mother and the daughterly act of "speaking for her" and to create the conditions in which mother and daughter would each be able to speak for themselves as well as for and with one another. It is significant, I believe, that I find examples of this discourse in the texts of American women of color, writers who clearly identify themselves as a new feminist generation in relation to the maternal tradition of the past, writers for whom fathers, brothers, and husbands occupy a less prominent place, writers who are in a more distant relation to cultural and literary hegemony.

Cherríe Moraga's "For the Color of My Mother," whose refrain forms one of the epigraphs for this introduction, defines this racial difference even as it carries the emotional weight of the unspeakable plots that connect mothers and daughters.[27] The poem centers on the act of speaking, speaking for *the mother: to her*, as addressee, *in place of, instead of*, or *on behalf of her* to the world, and *in honor* or *in celebration of her*.

To speak for the mother, as many of the daughters in this book do, is at once to give voice to her discourse *and* to silence and marginalize her. In repeating the act of speaking *for her*, Moraga's poem highlights a complex process of identification and distanciation, recognition and appropriation. The poem's refrain in itself contains a narrative sequence—"a white girl gone brown"—one traced more fully in the rest of the poem from the speaker's age of two to five, and fourteen to forty-five—the point at which mother and daughter merge in common wounds, gashes, barely stitched together by white doctors in alienating hospitals. What, in mother-daughter identification, makes the "white girl go brown to the color of [her] mother?" Is it that this relationship propels her to reverse a sequence of social assimilation through which the brown girl would go white, but only after leaving her mother behind? The poem ends with a communal affirmation of maternal silence which could be read, at the same time, as an invitation to the daughter to speak: "dark women come to me/ sitting in circles/ I pass through their hands/ the head of my mother/ painted in colors/ touching each carved feature/ swollen eyes and mouth/ they understand the explosion the splitting/ open contained within the fixed expression/ they cradle her silence/ nodding to me." The daughter's speech, the poem itself, thus appears as the result of the mother's silence and does perhaps depend on that silence to come into existence. Yet in speaking *for* her mother, the daughter "goes brown" affirming a maternal allegiance, as well as an allegiance with her racial and ethnic past, above other affiliations and assimilations. It is this complex process of identification and disidentification, this slow emergence of maternal speech from silence, that I trace, within specific contexts, throughout the novels that form the subject of this book.

The Location of the Critic

The story of this book's production and my own formation and "location" as a feminist critic within the context of the rapidly expanding field of psychoanalytic feminist theory can perhaps help articulate some of the assumptions that underlie the analyses to follow and the shifts that these assumptions have undergone since the project's inception. I am inspired in this effort by Adrienne Rich's call for a "politics of location," reframed by Nancy K. Miller as a "poetics of location,"[28] by the consciousness that I have been writing this book as a woman, a teacher, a daughter, a mother, a feminist (should I add a heterosexual, a Jew, an immigrant, middle class, an only child, a mother of sons?), within the institutions of patriarchy, of motherhood, of literary studies, of feminist studies, of the university in the United States (should I add of marriage, of divorce, of the Ivy League, of Comparative Literature and French Studies, of the development of Women's Studies?). If I present the theoretical assumptions underlying this project as a narrative, it is both to describe my own location(s) within the history of the emergence of feminist literary criticism in the last decade and to trace the dominant trends within that history.

In 1977, pregnancy and nursing afforded me the time to read "for myself."[29] Given my beginning efforts to join my political and personal engagement in the feminist movement with my work as a literary scholar, efforts aided by a collaborative project undertaken with two colleagues, Mary Jean Green and Lynn Higgins, on the work of Christiane Rochefort,[30] and given my new motherhood, it is not surprising that I should have turned with particular enthusiasm to Adrienne Rich's *Of Woman Born: Motherhood as Experience and Institution*. There I was to find not only a model for feminist writing, an alternative to the writing I had learned in graduate school—Rich's unusual combination of autobiography, incisive analysis, scholarly research, and poetic expression—but I was also to discover the statement of a lacuna that would serve as the inspiration for this project: "This cathexis between mother and daughter—essential, distorted, misused—is the great unwritten story. Probably there is nothing in human nature more resonant with charges than the flow of energy between two biologically alike bodies, one of which has lain in amniotic bliss inside the other, one of which has labored to give birth to the other. The materials are there for the deepest mutuality and the most painful estrangement. . . . Yet this relationship has been minimized and trivialized in the annals of patriarchy."[31] It occurred to me that the growth of feminist consciousness through the consciousness raising movement of the 1970s, combined with the methodological developments of feminist literary criticism and psychoanalytic feminism, might make it possible to reverse that silence, to write that absent story. Reading, during that same period, Dorothy Dinnerstein's *The Mermaid and the Minotaur: Sexual Arrangements and Human Malaise,* I came to understand more about the profound imbalances in male and female development and personality caused by the fact that human culture leaves the rearing of young children to women.[32] Dinnerstein's analysis goes further. She examines the devastating and potentially lethal consequences of an unacceptable division of labor, namely our attitude of mastery in relation to nature. What I could not yet see at the time was that the profound and pervasive cultural fear and devaluation of the figure of the mother was not only stated by Dinnerstein but was also reinforced and acted out in her account. Dinnerstein's vivid representation of the mother's powerful effect on the child, in the absence of an historical analysis, obscures mothers' and women's actual powerlessness in society. Inflating maternal influence has the effect of blaming mothers, rather than the culture, for the monstrous asymmetries Dinnerstein finds.[33] Reading Dinnerstein, however, did make it obvious that any approach to the subject of mother-daughter relationships in literature would have to include a psychoanalytic perspective which could illuminate the psychic complexity of the interaction and suggest the effects of that complexity on the construction of literary plots. It also became obvious that such a perspective would not be unproblematic.

Although during the early 1970s feminist writing and thinking had set itself in reaction against and in critique of psychoanalytic thought, by 1977, and largely as a result of intense work by feminists to explicate and appropriate psychoanalytic texts, it had become clear to many that psychoanalytic paradigms offered invaluable insights. Juliet Mitchell, in her 1974 book *Psychoanalysis and Feminism: Freud, Reich, Laing and Women,* presented the most convincing rationale for the incorporation of psychoanalytic thinking into feminist thinking. She insisted that "the way we live as 'ideas' the necessary laws of human society is not so much conscious as *unconscious*—the particular task of psychoanalysis is to decipher how we acquire our heritage of the ideas and laws of human society within the unconscious mind, or, to put it another way, the unconscious mind *is* the way in which we acquire these laws."[34] Psychoanalysis, in other words, can show us how we become gendered subjects within culture, thereby giving us the category "woman" or "the feminine" basic to any feminist analysis and giving us an analysis of the functionings of patriarchy within the individual psyche. As Teresa de Lauretis has since insisted, "Freud . . . does account for the continued existence and the functioning of patriarchy as a structure of subjectivity; in the same way as Marx accounts for the socioeconomic relations of capital that inform patriarchy in our times" (*Alice Doesn't,* p. 165).

A clearer sense of purpose and approach emerged for my own projected book with the appearance of Nancy Chodorow's *The Reproduction of Mothering: Psychoanalysis and the Sociology of Gender* in 1978 and my attendance at the Barnard Conference on *The Future of Difference* in 1979.[35] As gender difference became the focus of much feminist scholarship, and as that focus came to acquire different valences in American and French feminist inquiry, I began to imagine a book that would examine the specificity of female identity and experience through the lens of the most private and the most formative of women's relationships, the relation between mother and daughter, a book informed by my own situation between American feminism and French Studies.

The initial reading and thinking for this book was undertaken during a year as a fellow in an interdisciplinary faculty development seminar at the Wellesley Center for Research on Women in 1979/80. The discussions at the seminar convinced me both of the importance of interdisciplinary perspectives for the study of women's experience in culture and society and of the increased time such a redefinition of my own "field" would take. Freudian psychoanalysis and its feminist revisions provided, I believed, the most promising theoretical framework for the study of mothers and daughters. Clearly, my own focus at that moment was first on mother-daughter relationships—literature seemed a privileged locus for the representation of familial structures—and second on the conjunction of gender and literary form. Clearly also the focus was on *daughters* rather than *mothers*, on female development as the daughter's process of apprenticeship to the mother. This particular focus, I have since found, served as a screen, obscuring maternal subjectivities, not only for me, but for feminist criticism more generally, as I show more fully in chapters 4 and 5.

My perspective was marked by another book, *The Voyage In: Fictions of Female Development*, which I edited in collaboration with Elizabeth Abel and Elizabeth Langland. Intended to integrate gender with genre, this book studies the specificity of female formation as represented by novels that could fit a categorization of *Bildungsroman* only if that category was redefined to account for female difference of experience and representation.[36]

In 1981, I published a review essay on "Mothers and Daughters." Only five years after Rich's statement of absence, the popular and scholarly material on the topic not only had reached almost unmanageable proportions, but also had established a centrality in feminist analysis that I attempted to explain in the review essay: "There can be no systematic study of woman in patriarchal culture, no theory of woman's oppression, that does not take into account woman's role as a daughter of mothers and as a mother of daughters, that does not study female identity in relation to previous and subsequent generations of women, and that does not study that relationship in the wider context in which it takes place: the emotional, economic and symbolic structures of family and society."[37] Most of the pertinent works I reviewed were psychoanalytic, based on Freudian, Jungian, object-relations, and Lacanian models, and revised from the perspective of a feminine subject. For my own purposes, I came to see the pre-oedipal period as a determinant of women's difference. Because of maternal dominance in early childhood, and mothers' closer identification with daughters than with sons, women acquired a characteristically feminine, affiliative, and relational sense of self. Adopting the language of feminist object-relations theory, I saw female development as the gradual and not always successful process of identification with and differentiation from a mother who remained an important inner object for the maturing daughter, a process shaped by the fluctuations of symbiosis and separation. I posited then that "women's basic and continued relatedness and multiplicity, the mirroring of mothers and daughters, influence[d] women's writing in important ways."[38]

It is with this hypothesis in mind that I supplemented my reading of feminist object-relations theory with Lacan and feminist revisions of Lacanian psychoanalysis. In the writings of Irigaray, Cixous, and Kristeva, I found a greater focus both on language and the unconscious and a different framing of the question of difference—not as identity but as relation to language. Lacan's Imaginary and Symbolic took Freud's Pre-oedipal and oedipal out of a temporal, developmental sequence. Kristeva's notion of the "semiotic" and Irigaray's "parler-femme" came to supplement the notion of feminine specificity in language. Their writings transcended a definition of feminine as the negative pole in relation to masculine. Not satisfied with Lacan's assertion that "Woman does not exist" (except as constituted in phallic representation as absolute Other) and with the glorification of woman's silence and marginality,[39] they posited instead a notion of femininity as positive difference. My review essay included the first literary analyses based on some of this theory, as well as on a more traditional analysis of images of women in literature. The first book on the topic, *The Lost Tradition: Mothers and Daughters in Literature*, edited by Cathy N. Davidson and E. M. Broner, had just appeared.[40]

In my essay I attempted to account for the far-reaching implications of a psychoanalytic analysis that treated women's mothering as a "social structure which affects all other structures,"[41] and for the intersections between American and French trends within these theories. At the same time, I deplored what I perceived as the inherent limitation of their perspective: "at the source of each of these important and useful feminist analyses we find not only a male theorist but a developed androcentric system, which, even if deconstructed and redefined, still remains a determining and limiting point of departure" (p. 205). The essay ends with a call for a transformation of "the paradigms in which we think" and the invention "of theoretical frameworks that allow us, in our study of the relationships between women, to go beyond patriarchal myths and perceptions" (p. 221). Two texts that depart from strictly psychoanalytic frameworks, Sara

Ruddick's "Maternal Thinking" and Adrienne Rich's "Compulsory Hetero-sexuality and Lesbian Existence," were to serve as models for such a reconceptualization.[42] Both focus on women's relations with each other yet both insist that those relations are not and cannot be separate from rela-tionships between women and men. Yet, whereas Rich sees heterosexual-ity as compulsory, Ruddick envisions a world in which women and men, either together or separately, can do the work of mothering. Both of these essays have remained central to my conception of this book, yet the kind of reformulation I had envisioned, although it remains a preoccupation throughout these pages, has come to appear even more utopian as I explore the patterns of repetition, contradiction, revision, and transforma-tion throughout the texts covered in this book.

I wrote my first literary discussion of a mother-daughter text, "The Mother's Discourse: Incorporation and Repetition in *La Princesse de Clèves*" in the very particular context of the work of editing, in collaboration with six women colleagues from my department, a special issue of *Yale French Studies, Feminist Readings: French Texts/American Contexts* which appeared in 1982.[43] The essays in the volume and its collaborative introduction repre-sented an attempt to explore the connections and disconnections between French and American feminisms, to bring French theories of textuality together with American methods of textual reading. My own reading of the *Princesse de Clèves* was based on Adrienne Rich's notion of "reading as re-vision" and the notion of female subplots that palimpsestically underlie conventional plots in which women are but objects in the economy of male desire. Thus I argued that the submerged plot—the mother-daughter dyad—and not the surface plot—the love triangle—dominates the struc-ture and language of Lafayette's novel. In the essay I studied the effects of this re-reading, using the paradigm of pre-oedipal mother-daughter trust and closeness, external to the world of the court, as a counterpart of the heterosexual economy of exchange that characterizes the life within the court. I argued that the mother's early death and death-bed admonitions to the Princess, as well as the expectations of utter honesty and sincerity nurtured in the "pre-oedipal" moment prior to marriage and external to its institutions, ultimately constitute a debilitating force locking the Princess into a pattern of repetition from which she cannot emerge and which precludes further development and progression.

Although my analysis in that essay focused almost exclusively on the Princess's development, I was already interested in the mother's own discourse and in *her* motivations as they could perhaps be deduced from the scant information imparted within the novel. But the psychoanalytic model I had adopted as a lens, and the language of object-relations, with its central image of mirroring, emphasized for me the mutual dependency between mother and daughter rather than enabling me to see them as subjects exercising any independent control over their own plots. I con-cluded the essay by reiterating the importance of mother-daughter symbiosis in Lafayette's novel: "an early erotic attachment between mother and daughter which remains permanently incorporated into the daughter's psyche, a need to recreate the quality of that bond in adult heterosexual relationships which promise to duplicate but ultimately threaten the principal loyalty to the mother, all in the context of a society in which women are subjected to male inconstancy and betrayal" (p. 86).

I consider the writing of this essay a crucial moment in my thinking about mothers, daughters, and narrative. Since it stands outside of the historical framework of this book, however, I could not reprint it here, although in many ways it continues to inform my thinking. As I reread it now, I stand by my reading of the novel and its outline of limited choices offered to women.[44] What I would most wish to rethink, however, is my own relation to the pattern of mother-daughter dependency that I identify and which, clearly, fills me with ambivalence. Jane Gallop has pointed out the contradiction between the celebration of collectivity and intersubjectivity in which I participated as I coedited the journal and collaborated on the introduction, and its presentation as a largely negative force in my own essay.[45] I wish I had been more aware of the interaction between the work on the journal and the essay itself. The Dartmouth Collective did perceive its work as an alternative to institutional pressures and competitions, a haven to which we could retreat and through which we could experience a semblance of "pre-oedipal closeness" or of "life outside the court." Gallop, in her critique, fails to address the crucial issue of tenure which dominated, implicitly, our collaboration and which was a central preoccupation and concern among feminist scholars in the academy during the 1970s and early 80s. Later, of course, we came to see how much that work itself was implicated in the very structures to which it wished to offer an alternative. I wish I had been able to perceive this then and had taken that lesson to my reading of the novel. In so doing I would have avoided a certain amount of idealization and denigration that necessarily comes with positing for the mother-daughter relationship a separate pre-oedipal space external to the ideologies defining the heterosexual world of the court.

This narrative would not be complete without an account of my teaching about mothers and daughters in three different courses at Dartmouth College, one in Comparative Literature, one in Women's Studies and one in an interdisciplinary Masters degree program, team-taught with psychiatrist Mai-Lan Rogoff. It is through this teaching and team-teaching experience that I have become increasingly conscious of the limitations of models and paradigms in the discussion of familial relationships, as well as of the richness of individual literary texts as documents of personal interaction. With careful reading and rereading, my students and I were able to discover dynamics to which we were blind when we approached these works solely through the lenses of psychoanalysis. It took several repetitions of these courses for me to begin to uncover some of the biases of my own perspective, shaped by psychoanalysis, and by its feminist revisions. My students and I came to see that, although we could tease out the intricacies of various theoretical languages and the dynamics of various literary texts, we still lacked a language with which to describe some of our most fundamental and quotidian experiences of mother-daughter connection and separation. *Maternal experience,* in particular, appeared absent from scholarly accounts and external to our operative paradigms which were focused almost entirely on the perspective of the child. What is unique about the attachment between mothers and daughters? Do cultural, ethnic, and class differences, and differences in sexual preference, shape the details of their interaction? Do historical, cultural, and psychoanalytic assumptions about development and maturity correspond to our own experiences? And where are the voices of mothers, where are their experiences with maternal pleasure and frustration, joy and anger? What explains the fact that in fiction and theory we find only rarely the most common aspects of mother-daughter interaction, anger for example? These and similar questions emerged on the margins of my syllabi and became more dominant through the years, affecting not only the organization of and my approach to the material but also my pedagogy in these courses. Students were allowed to write one paper of a more creative or unconventional sort and all of us found ourselves more drawn to those assignments; I found that the discoveries they contained were fresher and less circumscribed by classic patterns. Some of these discoveries, confirmed by my own experiences as a mother (at this point of two sons and a step-son), gave me the courage to call into question patterns of representation that I had been taught to accept as given and to experiment with styles of pedagogy and writing that might be capable of giving speech to silenced voices.

Teaching alone did not comprise my professional activities throughout these years. This narrative needs to include, in particular, the administrative work relating to the beginnings of the Dartmouth Women's Studies Program—the collaborative participation in the Steering Committee and the work of cochairing the Program during two years—as well as the scholarly exchange offered by Dartmouth's interdisciplinary Feminist Inquiry Seminar and other more informal study groups. The activist struggles within an institution that, even during the process of co-education, preserved its largely male character are also an important part of this story which, like the story of feminist studies more generally, combines theory with practice, and individual scholarship with collective engagement, in ways that cannot easily be articulated.

It was a year-long break from teaching, however, that enabled me to start writing the chapters that follow and to reconceptualize this project, integrating the theoretical shifts in orientation that have marked feminist analysis as well as my own processes of revision. I spent the 1984/85 academic year as a fellow at the Mary Ingraham Bunting Institute of Radcliffe College: the experience of working in a women's research institute and in the context of the feminist community in Boston and Cambridge has shaped this book profoundly. At first the interdisciplinary context of the Bunting Institute seemed daunting—quite different from the seminar at Wellesley six years earlier. Disciplinary perspectives were much more specialized and less accessible, and their discourses seemed incompatible. Literary criticism, in particular, was received with skepticism by scholars from other fields who resented the exclusionary character of its language. Too, the feminist community in the area had grown to unmanageable proportions—the meetings of the newly-formed Harvard Feminist Literary Theory group were attended by 50–100 people, who all too easily assumed a shared perspective which often obscured important and telling differences. And, not all the scholars at the Bunting Institute were feminists; some had serious questions about the applicability or the benefits of feminist perspectives to their work. It took a great deal of time and work to discover what interdisciplinary and collaborative contexts could be achieved in the mid-1980s. This process of discovery is reflected in this book, although not in any obvious way.

The Feminist Theory Group some of us organized at the Bunting Institute quickly came to reflect tensions that had begun generally to challenge the fundamental assumptions of the feminist community in the United States.[46] The challenge came, primarily, from women of color in the group, who brought to the discussions perspectives and experiences that feminist theoretical paradigms, and the feminist rhetoric of collectivity, seemed incapable of addressing. The analysis of the interconnections of race, gender, and class oppression, the exploration of racism within feminist discourses began for that group at that moment and continued through the year. I want to emphasize here that an institution such as the Bunting Institute seems to me to be the optimal place for such a painful and far-reaching, such a personal and communal exploration. This is so, I believe, because of the time afforded by a year away from teaching responsibilities; because of the lack of overt competition and hierarchy within an institution which has already awarded each of its members all it has to give; because of the supportive atmosphere and the valorization of women's work, to which the Bunting Institute is committed, combined with the acceptance of the diverse and unconventional forms that work might take; because a small, continuing group could build at least some of the trust necessary to confront the process as well as the content of the discussions; and because of the minimization of territoriality in a genuinely interdisciplinary community. Still, the discussions were painful and perhaps incomplete, the affiliations and allegiances often took forms that were, for some of us, difficult to accept; the splits made some of us rethink many of our feminist assumptions about the benefits of collective process, the benefits of community, and the benefits of theory.[47] At times during the year the common dreams of feminism in the 1970s seemed irrevocably lost; the splits, insurmountable. At other times we were able to envision areas of union and issues around which coalition-building was absolutely crucial. My chapter 5 is the particular result of these discussions about issues of race in which I participated and which prompted me to put to the test some of the assumptions and models, psychoanalysis in particular, with which I was working. Arguments about difference and female specificity came to seem more problematic in the context of these discussions: the category "woman" assumes a certain commonality of experience and construction which no longer held. Thus "woman" had to be replaced by "women" and the construction of femininity could no longer be discussed in opposition to the construction of masculinity but both had to include the variables of race, culture, class, ethnicity. The contradictions thus introduced into feminist analysis are well summed up by Joan Scott in a review of a volume, edited by Teresa de Lauretis, which confronts the conflicts within feminism I have tried to outline above: "the differences and variability of any female subject's sense of self is in contradiction with the political activist's appeal to a unitary Woman with fixed interests and needs; and the relativism about knowledge introduced in some feminist critiques of the canons of traditional knowledge is in tension with the implicit moral certainty of feminist politics, which asserts the 'truth' of women's subordination as a way of justifying the demand for a more just and equitable organization of social life."[48] At this moment, "women" and not "woman" appears as the more politically powerful notion—"woman" is too much tied up in debilitating structures of representation. And "women" as a category itself needs to be put in question.[49] .

Issues of race did not constitute the only divisions in the community of fellows at the Bunting Institute; others concerned an important, though perhaps predictable, split between theory and praxis and, for me, a much more surprising split between the women who were mothers and the ones who were not. In the many discussions at colloquia, lunches, and study groups this division seemed to me to grow, to inform the perspectives and reference points of those participating in ways I had not expected and around topics that did not obviously lend themselves to such distinctions. This difference in perspective, combined with my own and others' awareness that much of feminist theory situates itself in the position of daughter and at a distance from the maternal, led to the formation of another discussion group, informally called a "mothers' group," which met periodically for two years in Cambridge.[50] Although the group did on occasion discuss some readings, its main purpose was to formulate a language with which to discuss maternal *experience*—what is left out of all that we had read—without, however, being naïve about what that notion means or facile about its discursive character. The members of the group, all mothers and scholars whose work touched on mothering in various ways, struggled primarily with the loose definition of the group's purpose: none of us felt comfortable with the open-endedness of this formulation, although we all recognized that the topic demanded a certain amount of risk-taking, and we all felt committed to the process of discovery, as well as somewhat curious about its results. The object, then, became to theorize from the place of "experience"; the process was similar to that of consciousness-raising in the early 1970s, although in the 1980s the activity of consciousness-raising necessarily had to take different shapes, shapes we ourselves would have to define.[51] The group's discoveries were as exhilarating as its difficulties were significant and, to a large degree, unresolved, perhaps even unspoken. We discovered important differences in maternal experience and discourse between those who had grown children and those whose children were still at home, between those who were single mothers and those who had partners, between those whose partners were their children's fathers and those whose partners were not, between those whose own mothers were alive and those whose mothers were not, between those who had siblings and those who did not, between those who had only children and those who had several, between those who had sons and those who had daughters. We felt strongly, moreover, the limitations imposed by the group's composition—a class and racial homogeneity (not offset by some national differences) which made a more probing analysis of the issues that came up virtually impossible.

Although these difficulties were telling and significant, they did not constitute the group's major stumbling blocks. Those emerged, first, around the tone we used to discuss our experiences as mothers and the limited range of voices culturally available for such a narrative. Thus some of us were bothered when others sounded too positive, too celebratory about their maternal feelings and accused them of idealizing these and fitting them into narrow cultural stereotypes; whereas others sounded much too negative and despairing, incapable of expressing maternal pleasure along with the pain, and again the pain came too close to cultural stereotypes. More serious still were a painful set of divisions which emerged between the discourse of mothers and that of daughters, opposing voices we each in various ways contained and could not combine. We found, in retrospect, that when we spoke *as mothers*, the group's members were respectful, awed, helpful in the difficulties of formulating maternal experiences. When we spoke *as daughters* about our own mothers, however, the tone and affect changed and we all giggled knowingly, reverting back to old stereotyped patterns of discussing a shared problem—our "impossible mothers." The sympathy we could muster for ourselves and each other *as mothers*, we could not quite transfer to our own mothers. Although as mothers we were eager to tell our stories, as daughters we could not fully listen to our mothers' stories. This inability, this tragic asymmetry between our own two voices, was so pervasive as to be extremely difficult to discuss. It revealed the depth and the extent of the "matrophobia" that exists not only in the culture at large, but also within feminism, and within women who are mothers. It was as though we were each wearing glasses with two different colored lenses, making it impossible for us to see anything but a blur when we looked out of both eyes at once. For me this was the most poignant discovery of the group, and increased my own determination to concentrate in some detail in this book on the perspectives of mothers and on the difficulties feminists have in sympathizing with those perspectives. The group itself did address this issue; tragically, it did so most successfully in one session that followed the deaths of two members' mothers.

The "mothers' group" had a profound impact on this book because it challenged me, for the first time, to translate my *experience* as a daughter and a mother into discourse, to theorize on the basis of my experience. It allowed me to perceive the evolution of my own thinking about mothers and daughters: while I had at first envisioned this book as a study of the daughter's developmental process, her female development as an apprenticeship to her mother, I now began to see it as a book about mothers *and* daughters, and about the narratives that connect or separate them. I became more aware of maternal silences and the ways in which they are perpetuated in feminist discourse. While I began with a book which had meaning for me as a daughter, I ended up with a book which also had meaning for me as a mother. The fact that my children are sons does make my own experience with mother-daughter relationships one-sided. Through the work on this book, however, through the process of writing it and talking about it with students, friends and colleagues, and with my family, I have been able to imagine other maternal and daughterly positions and to make them a part of my life and my work. It is from my own immediate and extended family, however, that I have learned about childhood, and about myself as a child. It is from them that I have learned about masculinity, and therefore about femininity. It is from them, moreover, that I have learned about the *experience* of family, about maternal and paternal, filial and fraternal roles and positions, and about the tremendous difficulty faced by all who want to reframe those positions.

Finally, this book is, in ways I cannot articulate directly, about my mother. In speaking to her I aim to show that what is unspeakable may nevertheless be heard, read, and spoken.

PRELUDE

ORIGINS AND PARADIGMS

> With some additions or subtractions, our imaginary still functions according to the patterns established through Greek mythologies and tragedies.
>
> —Luce Irigaray

> It was for Greece you gave me birth, not for yourself alone.
>
> —Euripides

> Our family is in fact constituted by and in the general movement of History, but is experienced, on the other hand, as an absolute in the depths and opaqueness of childhood.
>
> —Jean-Paul Sartre

"When Freud describes and theorizes, . . . in *Totem and Taboo*, the murder of the father as the foundation of the primitive horde," says Luce Irigaray, "he forgets a more archaic murder, that of the woman-mother, necessitated by the establishment of a certain order in the city."[1] For Irigaray, this mythic matricide, represented by the murder of Clytemnestra in Greek mythology, is the founding moment of civilization under paternal law. This moment is still timely today, she insists, for "mythology has not changed" (p. 17).

It is significant that Freud chose Oedipus as the privileged paradigmatic representation of individual maturation in the context of familial structures—as the paradigm for his family romance. The Oedipus story is the story of the *son's* relation to father and mother, male and female origin. To find the story of the *daughter* and the *mother*, alternative mythologies—female counterparts to Oedipus—with equal power and resonance, with equal presence in the work of modern writers, can indeed be discussed. And they do suggest alternate patterns of development, as well as alternate narrative patterns. Electra and Antigone, for example, function as particularly vital models for nineteenth-century representations of female development and female heroism. In the modernist period, the story of Demeter and Persephone enables the outlines of a different female family romance. And the figures of Jocasta, Clytemnestra, and Demeter suggest some reasons for the absence of a maternal subjectivity in contemporary feminist fiction. They begin to clarify the complicated shapes of a feminist family romance that moves only with difficulty from a daughterly to a maternal focus.

The classical paradigms I discuss briefly in this Prelude belong firmly to the tradition of Western patriarchy. To place them in such a prominent place in relation to fictions written by women writers many hundreds of years later, in cultures structured both similarly and differently from the ones that produced them, might seem to grant them too great an influence. It might seem, moreover, to predetermine the outcome of my exploration into feminocentric plot patterns, just as Freud might be said to have predetermined his theory by highlighting Oedipus. Yet I find not only that certain limited familial and narrative patterns do tend to predominate and to continue to inform modern writing, but also that they help to explain how, on the one hand, female difference is inscribed and attempted, and how, on the other, it can easily be subverted by a repetition of the same. The following discussion of classical texts, then, is both my recognition of their hegemonic power, their delimiting force, and my tribute to their explanatory potential. At the same time, these classic myths are seriously insufficient as paradigms for female and feminist plotting, especially as far as post-modernist fiction is concerned. As the book progresses, for example, I find a greater focus on women's relations to one another, on the relations of mothers, daughters, sisters, and friends, and much less emphasis on fathers, brothers, and husbands. Whereas the classical texts I analyze can illuminate some aspects of those female relationships, they are totally irrelevant to others. As I discuss the works of Afro-American women writers, in particular, the classical frameworks become more problematic. The familial structures which emerge from African traditions and from slave economies and which develop in the contexts of urban and rural poverty in the United States create different inflections in the plots of writers such as Toni Morrison and Alice Walker.[2] Yet, surprisingly, classic Western structures still serve as frames of reference even here, if only to be modified, reconstructed, and transformed; Morrison's play with oedipal triangles in *Beloved* is a good example of the power of classical paradigms. My intention is to let this discussion of origins stand here as a pre-text, a pre-figuration of the book's argument, a moment to return to and to depart from in the search for a female/feminist textuality that struggles toward and begins to define difference. Having it here, at the beginning, permits me to confront in a very direct way the problematic nature of "the classics" and "the tradition" in relation to a group of women writers who stand both inside and outside it, who both collude with it and contest it to various degrees.

Two classical Greek paradigms, the story of Clytemnestra and Electra and the story of Antigone, can help to define the parameters of the Victorian heroine's female family romance. Both are stories of daughters and fathers, sisters and brothers. Whereas Electra underwrites paternal law, Antigone rebels against the personal consequences of paternal and patriarchal identification and seems to uphold an alternative value structure. On closer analysis, however, it becomes obvious that both of these family romance models are based on maternal and sisterly repression and that Electra and Antigone represent not opposing but structurally quite similar options. And both had particular resonance during the Victorian period, offering models of female heroism at a moment of restricted social and economic opportunity and of severely limited legal rights for women.

For Luce Irigaray, the murder of Clytemnestra is the mythic representation of the mother's exclusion from culture and the symbolic order. Clytemnestra, Irigaray suggests, must be killed because she is not the virgin mother who had become a cultural ideal: she is passionate and sexual, she is guilty of having murdered her husband, and, worst of all, she is politically active and aware. In Aeschylus's *Oresteia*, the son who kills her is acquitted. With Athena's help Apollo denies the mother's procreative role: "The mother is not the true parent of the child / which is called hers. She is a nurse who tends the growth / of young seed planted by its true parent, the male."[3] Although Orestes, the son, actually commits matricide, and although he does so by the command of another son, Apollo, whose oracle Orestes has no choice but to obey, the passion and energy behind both the murder and the judgment belong to daughters, Electra and Athena. Both identify with and uphold a paternal law; both are, as Clytemnestra asserts in Euripides' *Electra* "daughters of the father." In fact, Electra, becomes heroic by conceiving and participating in an unspeakable crime—matricide.[4]

Whereas Athena, daughter of a divine father, exemplifies both the power that can come to the daughter from paternal identification—wisdom and victory in war—and the price—virginity and childlessness—Electra, the human father's daughter, suffers instead the ambiguities that come with paternal allegiance.[5] Electra's participation in her mother's murder is motivated not by an oracular decree but by an intense personal hatred of Clytemnestra and by an undying loyalty to Agamemnon. As Virginia Woolf suggests, "Clytemnestra and Electra are mother and daughter and therefore should have some sympathy, though perhaps sympathy gone wrong breeds the fiercest hate. E. is the type of woman who upholds the family above everything; the father. She has more veneration for tradition than the sons of the house; feels herself born of the father's side and not of the mother's."[6] In Sophocles' *Electra*, especially, the scenes between mother and daughter highlight their lack of sympathy. Electra accuses Clytemnestra of sexual betrayal, of hunger for power manifested in her marriage to a weaker man, and of non-maternal behavior toward herself and Orestes. She presents herself as everything her mother is not: she is a virgin, she is maternal to her brother, even while remaining submissive to him. Yet this polarity and this antagonism cannot disguise the profound similarity between mother and daughter, the strength of character and the rebelliousness they share. Equally similar are the conflicts they initially face—between *oikos* and *polis*, between familial values and allegiances to the state. As Woolf suggested, however, filial piety and official loyalty are indistinguishable in Electra's allegiance to her dead father. The need for loyalty to Clytemnestra has been eliminated: the agent of death, she is no longer maternal; as ruler of Athens and wife to Aegistus, she no longer represents the private. The two sides of Electra's dilemma have been subsumed into one: Agamemnon and Orestes have absorbed her divided loyalties erasing the influence of her mother and sister in the process.

Electra's lack of sympathy for the mother's choices and values emerges most clearly in relation to Clytemnestra's justification for the murder of her husband, i.e., vengeance for his sacrificial killing of her oldest daughter, Iphigenia. Electra, like Iphigenia herself, accepts this murder as necessary for the state, identifying completely with her father's discourse. In failing to understand her mother's outrage, and in justifying her sister's murder, Electra underwrites paternal law and male supremacy, as well as female antagonism, competition, and powerlessness. In planning the murder of her mother, in refusing to bond with her more conventional sister Chrysothemis, Electra eliminates the possibility for women to challenge the paternal order and perpetuates a sexual division of labor by which she can act only through her brother.

Electra may plot, but it is Orestes who commits the murder. He stands trial, is acquitted, and goes on to found a new public order. In both Sophocles' and Euripides' plays, Electra is featured on stage as her brother commits the murder off-stage. The emotion is hers; the action, his. In order to live her choice of paternal allegiance, Electra needs her brother to complement her intention, to carry out her plan, and to fulfill the emotional needs that result from her repudiation of mother and sister. Condemned to virginity, Electra needs Orestes to function in the roles of both lover and child; only with him can she act out the familial implications of the female posture she has adopted. Thus her fraternal love isolates her, excluding her from the possibility of becoming a mother and from any possible continuity.[7] Irigaray suggests that while the son/brother is saved from his madness, the daughter/sister is destined to remain mad (*Le corps-à-corps*, p. 17). Although Euripides offers Electra a future in the marriage to Pilades, this different ending fails to present an alternative to what Irigaray calls Electra's "madness."

Euripides' *Electra* does contain a subtext of mother-daughter sympathy, a brief moment of caring and understanding between them and a moment of regret on Electra's part: "Weep greatly for me, my brother, I am guilty./ A girl flaming in hurt I marched against/the mother who bore me . . ."(ll.

1183-85). Unlike Sophocles' Electra, Euripides' perceives the tragedy of her separation from her mother; as she kneels to cover her mother's dead body, she exclaims: "Behold! I wrap her close in the robe,/ the one I loved and could not love" (ll. 1230–31). Yet Pilades is Orestes' friend and, by marrying him, Electra further strengthens her alliance with her brother and her separation from sister and mother.

In her reading of the *Oresteia*, Mary O'Brien has argued that Aeschylus negates femininity in the motherlessness of Athena, in the transformation of Clytemnestra into an agent of death rather than life, and in the banishment of the Furies. Thus he can prove that male supremacy, that male control of law and property are both factual and just. Denying the maternal, she claims, enables man to circumvent the danger posed by the uncertainty of paternity and to found a "second-nature bond"—a new political fraternity "predicated on the equality of death and a high and rational ethics of giving one's life for one's polity." It is this bond which Athena upholds, which Clytemnestra threatens, and which Electra envies.[8] Through Orestes and fraternal allegiance, Sophocles and Euripides allow Electra to gain access to this powerful political arena, if only indirectly and vicariously. Electra's choices—maternal repression and fraternal alliance—produce a female narrative that remains deeply embedded in and intertwined with a dominant and oppressive male plot. Here the father and brother, equivalent figures, subsume what initially appeared to be conflicting choices and values, and female heroism precludes any continuing bonding among women.

Irigaray sees Antigone as the woman whose absolute rebellion threatens the paternal order of the state, even if that rebellion results in her ostracism and death. For nineteenth-century writers, especially Hegel and Eliot, the play's conflict, which they read as a conflict between right and right, made Antigone the most tragic of tragic heroes: "Here lies the dramatic collision: the impulse of sisterly piety which allies itself with reverence for the Gods, clashes with the duties of citizenship; two principles, both having their validity, are at war with each other."[9] According to Eliot, the struggle between Antigone and Creon amounts to a cosmic disorder, which leaves not only her culture but also Eliot's own in a permanent moral crisis, incapable of distinguishing between right and wrong. It is "that struggle between elemental tendencies and established laws by which the outer life of man is gradually and painfully being brought into harmony with his inward needs. Until this harmony is perfected, we shall never be able to attain a great right without also doing a wrong" (*Essays*, p. 264). It is important to note, however, that this nineteenth-century reading offers an unorthodox interpretation of Sophocles' play in which Antigone's act of loyalty to her brother is upheld even by Haemon, her rejected husband-to-be. Irigaray's reading, for example, constitutes a serious critique of Eliot's and Hegel's formulations: she finds that the particular way they state the conflict in itself exacerbates Antigone's dilemma. Having her actions reduced to *either* loyalty to the family *or* obedience to the state locks her into a vascillation between two institutions which are, in fact, irredeemably patriarchal and from which the only escape is the execution/suicide she eventually chooses. Hegel's formulation inadvertently clarifies this—Antigone's ethical decision to bury Polyneices makes her into a sister, a woman who acknowledges her highest duty to the irreplaceable brother. Her desire for him is pure, free, and submissive, Hegel insists.[10] The coincidence of the father and brother in the figure of Oedipus only underscores the closed system—the institutions of family and state—within which Antigone operates.

Unlike Electra, Antigone has no mother: her mother Jocasta killed herself after realizing that her husband was actually the son she had given away to be killed years before. Like Electra, Antigone rejects her more compliant and feminine sister Ismene. Unlike Electra, however, Antigone faces a choice: her brother and a seeming rejection of an autocratic patriarchal order, or her husband, the son of Creon, and an allegiance to the state. Antigone—daughter and sister of Oedipus whose exile she shares in *Oedipus at Colonus*, daughter and granddaughter of Jocasta—gives higher priority to her fraternal bond and to ancient burial laws. Her act amounts to a refusal of an exogamous marriage which could liberate her from the incestuous relationships within the family to which she remains undyingly loyal. In rejecting the laws of Creon's paternal state (Creon is the maternal uncle and thus the patriarch in the tale), and in affirming her familial/maternal bond, Antigone will not be an object of exchange. She will not open herself to the guilt of Jocasta, that is, to bear children and risk further incest. Like Electra and unlike her mother, Antigone remains a virgin. Her loyalty is with the past, with what Creon contemptuously calls "woman's law" (l. 524), with the brother she calls her "mother's son." "O but I would not have done the forbidden thing/ For any husband or for any son,/ For why? I could have had another husband/ And by him other sons, if one were lost;/ But father and mother lost, where would I get/ Another brother?"[11] Antigone's assertion of loyalty to Polyneices in *Antigone* follows her perfect fidelity to Oedipus in *Oedipus at Colonus*. Yet in what sense is this brother and this familial system truly an alternative to Creon's state?

Unlike Electra's action, Antigone's action in the play seems to present a serious challenge to the patriarchal state, an affirmation of past, familial, and private values over future and public ones, as well as a different narrative for women. It looks like an assertion of a female value system that stresses loyalty, fidelity, relationship over the expediencies demanded by Creon's politics.[12] Yet, as defiant as it might appear, and even though the play validates her choice, asserting that burial rites should not be legislated by the state, Antigone's bond with her brother does not pose an ultimate threat to a patriarchal order. That challenge can come only from the end of her tale, from the moment of her death, which motivates a succession of other suicides and spells the end of Creon's family. In reframing Antigone's conflict, in taking her position outside of the city walls to a place of what she chooses to see as potential female power, Irigaray wants to open the possibility of a new ethics among women, both vertically between mother and daughter, and horizontally among sisters, an ethics which for Antigone herself remains as unrealizable as it did for Electra (*Ethique*, pp. 113–15).

Electra and Antigone outline the bind in which the realist heroines I discuss in chapters 1 and 2 are caught, as opposite as their choices may seem, both remain locked into two patriarchal institutions and separated from their female kin as long as they are alive. The plot patterns of Victorian heroines range between the parameters set by these two mythic figures, both daughters of fathers and sisters of brothers. Family loyalty in female family romances is motivated by the attempt to imagine a different plot for the heroine, outside of an economy in which women cannot be more than objects of exchange. This attempt leads Victorian heroines to enact either the matricide of Electra in support of patriarchal power, or the refusal and challenge of Antigone, still based on maternal repression. Women writers' attempts to imagine lives for their heroines which will be different from their mothers' make it imperative that mothers be silent or absent in their texts, that they remain in the prehistory of plot, fixed both as objects of desire and as examples not to be emulated.Like Clytemnestra or Jocasta, the mothers of Victorian fiction are profoundly compromised, whether they are submissive victims of the paternal system or rebellious challengers of it. Only fraternal bonds can promise to substitute for maternal support and to protect from paternal authority. Yet they too ultimately fail to live up to the promise of an alternative to women's position as object of exchange among men. Allegiance to fathers/brothers has the advantage of protecting heroines both from marriage and from maternity; the quasi-incestuous bonds that tend to take the place of romantic love and marriage cannot result in pregnancy and childbirth. But as they ally themselves with fathers and brothers, rather than mothers and sisters, nineteenth-century heroines remain isolated—from female companionship, from previous and subsequent generations of women. And because their "brothers" sometimes turn into the patriarchs from whom they were supposed to offer a refuge, the heroines' fate actually ends up, in some ways at least, duplicating that of their mothers. This, in fact, constitutes the nineteenth-century's repetition of classical plots of tragic heroism. In attempting to construct/imagine a different plot and a different economy, nineteenth-century women writers still duplicate the traditional story of what Teresa de Lauretis has called "women's consent to femininity."[13] They thereby ally themselves with the "fathers" and "brothers" in their own literary tradition.

The emblematic example of the Demeter myth can serve to illustrate the complicated intersections of gender and plot exemplified in modernist fiction. This much earlier text, the Homeric "Hymn to Demeter," is indeed a mother-daughter narrative, not only the story of intense mother-daughter attachment and separation, but also the story of both the mother's and the daughter's reactions and responses. Its motifs—the pre-existence of timeless bliss vaguely identified with a matriarchal past, the descent to the underworld and the conflation of marriage and death, the connection of femininity with fertility and procreativity, the idealization of maternal power, the resolution of plot in cyclicity—carry a particular resonance for modernist writers. They connect to the images of Freudian psychoanalysis, such as the pre-oedipal, and to the anthropological and archaeological research of matriarchy theorists of the 1920s.

This unique mother-daughter narrative exists, however, only as a function of male intervention. Thus in the "Hymn to Demeter," a description of Persephone playing among the flowers precedes the actual inception of plot.[14] The narrative and temporality itself only begin with Hades' intrusion and rape, with the abduction of the daughter from the mother. This initial distance illustrates quite clearly a particular dynamic of plotting prevalent for female as well as male writers, and present also in women's modernism. Peter Brooks outlines it as follows: "plot starts (or must give the illusion of starting) from the moment at which story, or 'life' is stimulated from quiescence into a state of narratability, into a tension, a kind of irritation, which demands narration."[15] The hymn seems to corroborate this insight: narrative demands some form of breech, some space of anxiety and desire into which to inscribe itself. The perpetuation of infantile plenitude, the blissful play among the flowers, it seems to suggest, cannot offer a model for plot. The story of mother and daughter comes into being only through the intervention of the father/husband who, here, does not occasion an irreparable separation but offers the occasion for narrative itself.

Yet, the progression of the plot and the cyclic solution that mother and daughter work out together in response to the patriarchal reality in which they live resolves this plot in a way that is quite unique. Demeter tries to regain what she has lost, to repair the breech, both by living out several different powerless human plots and by asserting her divine power over humans, by denying them grain and by causing irreparable destruction and the end of plot. Neither of these opposing strategies succeeds. The compromise solution, however, differs significantly from the linear, repetitive, and ultimately self-defeating plot structures exemplified by the stories of Electra and Antigone. This mother-daughter narrative is resolved through continued *opposition, interruption,* and *contradiction.* As we follow Persephone's return to her mother for one part of the year and her repeated descent to marriage and the underworld for the rest, we have to revise our very notion of resolution. At the end of the story, Persephone is both alive and dead, both young and old, both above and below the earth. She lives both symbiotically united to her mother and ineluctably distant from her. Her allegiance is split between mother and husband, her posture is dual. The repeated cycle relies neither on murder nor on reconciliation, but on continued opposition—what in psychoanalytic terms might be called "bi-sexual oscillation"—to sustain and perpetuate it. The pomegranate seed Persephone eats signals her allegiance to her husband, while the ritual and seasonal celebration of her reunion with Demeter signifies her continuing attachment to her mother, an attachment which turns into identification in those representations in which Persephone is no longer the maiden but herself the mother of Triptolemus.

The story of Demeter and Persephone does not simply reverse heterosexual plots of disconnection in favor of a model of female connection. More complicated affiliative patterns are revealed here, patterns which describe the affiliative intricacies of female modernism. Still, Demeter's plot which progresses through *contradiction* offers an alternative to the limiting repetitions and deathly closures of Electra and Antigone.

The "Hymn to Demeter" does grant voice and legitimacy not only to the daughter's but also to the mother's story. Nowhere, for example, does the poem question Demeter's right to be angry. Zeus's compromise and the Eleusinian mysteries which celebrate the cyclic reunion of mother and daughter do recognize the needs of the mother as well as those of the child. In the hymn, sung to the mother-goddess, the poet identifies with the mother, he recognizes and legitimates her anger and its expression, as long as it can be properly channeled, contained, and ritually resolved. Still, maternal anger, maternal responses to the process of mother-child separation, to the loss of a child, are represented as terribly threatening in this story. Any discussion of maternal subjectivity—the subject of Part 3 of this book—has to take into account the pervasive cultural fears contained in the powerful and angry figures of Demeter and Clytemnestra. The threatening figure of the angry mother dominates even feminist writing about the maternal and creates particular conflicts for maternal self-representation, especially within the context of a feminist moment which values female consensus, eschews female difference, and is suspicious of women's power. As I will argue in Part 3 of this book, 1970s and early 1980s European and United States feminisms relate precisely in this manner to maternal subjectivity. A brief look at mythic representations of maternal power and maternal anger can set the stage for my later analysis of the peculiar distance between feminist discourse and maternal discourse.

Allowing us to see how Western culture imagines and represents the maternal, Clytemnestra and Demeter might serve as adult female counterparts to the oedipal narrative—the story of maternal attachment and separation. The story of Clytemnestra, even more than that of the at least partially powerful Demeter, illustrates how Western culture represents the mother's position in a familial and social configuration in which women carry children in their bodies, give birth to them, and then relinquish them to a world in which they themselves are powerless to determine the course of their children's development. Separation between mothers and children is provoked by murder, abandonment, and betrayal and Clytemnestra's angry response offers an emblem of how culture deals with maternal rage. For, if the anger of Menelaus and, by extension, of Agamemnon (based on male rivalry over woman and on male bonding, its underside), stands at the origin of the war with Troy that initiates the legitimate battle of culture, and if the deathly anger of Orestes and Electra is exonerated by Apollo and Athena as a legitimate expression of filial loyalty to the father, then Clytemnestra's anger remains at the edge of legitimacy and of representation. As the Furies, the fearsome subterranean representatives of maternal rage, are transformed into a new Athenian law upholding paternal right, the mother is supplanted and the father comes to control the laws of justice and discourse.

Euripides' *Iphigenia in Aulis* begins with Agamemnon's conflict between love for his daughter and loyalty to his brother, to the state, and to the gods who demand Iphigenia's sacrifice.[16] When the scene shifts to Clytemnestra, her manner of constructing her husband's moral dilemma gains our fullest sympathies. She is the mother who protects her child from the father's brutality and deceit. The child's loss is presented as a fate that cannot be evaded, but nonetheless it deeply wounds the deprived and abandoned mother. The bond between mother and child is subordinated to another order which has political primacy, but which is both emotionally and morally questionable. The mother herself is abandoned and betrayed by both husband and child: "Suppose, now, you're with the army, leaving me at home,/ And the slow months drag on, and you're still there at Troy,/ What thoughts do you imagine will occupy my heart,/ When every chair I see will be empty of her,/ Her bedroom empty; and I sit alone in tears/ Mourning for her, day in, day out? . . . / In the gods' name, my husband, don't force me to be/ A disloyal wife to you; nor be disloyal yourself" (ll. 1171-83).

Whereas Aeschylus's Iphigenia is gagged and "struggling for voice" (l. 241), Euripides admits us to her moving dialogue with her mother, in which the submissive daughter comes to see her own death as necessary and attempts to pacify the protective angry mother. Subordinating her own life to the good of Greece, Iphigenia embraces the father's logic and abandons the maternal value structure which raises life above death, private above public worth. She makes the shift to the father that is so central to Freud's vision of female maturity, even though that shift signals her death. "And indeed I have no right to cling to life so passionately,/ Since it was for Greece you gave me birth, not for yourself alone" (ll. 1384-85). The grieving mother is told to suppress her anger by the daughter who speaks in her father's name: "Mother, listen now to me./ Anger against your husband is beside the point" (ll. 1368–69). When Clytemnestra asks at parting "Is there some wish I could fulfill for you at home?" Iphigenia answers, "Yes. Do not hate Agamemnon. He is mine, and yours" (ll. 1450-51), again validating the father's values over the mother's.

Maternal anger in this play can be briefly expressed, only to be redefined and revalued by the daughter whose last wish is to silence her mother's grief at her death and at their separation: "What do you mean? Must I not grieve for your lost life? / No grief at all; and no grave shall be heaped for me" (ll. 1440-41). Although it cannot eliminate Clytemnestra's threatening anger, the play's ambiguous ending justifies Iphigenia's position: the daughter is saved from death by the gods and "survives," but she is forever separate from and unknown to her mother and other humans.

Iphigenia's position is, of course, confirmed in all of the later plays where Clytemnestra's anger, leading to adultery, violence, ambition, and murder confirms the worst unconscious fears of maternal omnipotence and destructiveness. Here, Clytemnestra's violent anger at Agamemnon appears self-serving and unnatural. In the conflict between paternal and maternal right, as Aeschylus presents it in the *Oresteia*, Agamemnon who performs the unnatural act of killing his daughter is vindicated, because he does so in the service of the state; but Clytemnestra's holding on to her child is presented as motivated by self-interest. That Agamemnon's violence and ambition should be more acceptable than Clytemnestra's says a great deal about gender distinction and about the distinction between paternal and maternal power. The perversion of Clytemnestra's maternity demonstrates the perceived dangers of maternal anger. Despite her repeated expressions of concern over the fate of her son Orestes, despite her reminder of the sacrifice of Iphigenia as the cause of her violent murder of Agamemnon, Clytemnestra continues to be seen as an "unnatural mother" who has abandoned all maternal activity and responsibility. In Aeschylus's *Oresteia*, in Sophocles' and Euripides' Electra plays, the anger that Clytemnestra experiences over the sacrifice of Iphigenia gets lost and perverted as a different range of ambitions take over in her. The physical sign of her maternity—the breast she bares to Orestes to show him the bodily tie that binds them—is also the place where he thrusts the knife that kills her. Maternal anger at separation and betrayal takes on deathly proportions; it must be domesticated or eradicated if the structure of civilization is to be maintained.[17]

Both Clytemnestra and Electra point to the incompatibility of maternity (the only legitimate form of adult womanhood in the culture) and action, of maternity and the expression of anger. And because their anger is not legitimatized, they also become incapable of experiencing love. The active, angry rebellious woman cannot be a mother; the mother can be neither active nor rebellious.

The Furies cult in Aeschylus's *The Eumenides* further demonstrates the altogether fearsome and dangerous character of maternal anger: the Furies have the power to leave "manhood unmanned," to "rain pestilence on our soil, corroding every seed/ Till the whole land is sterile desert" (ll. 797–99). Although superseded by Athena's new law, the Furies survive, giving lasting recognition, if not legitimation, to the maternal. Yet at the end of the play, as all sing together in a communal celebration, the Furies are placated and domesticated, robbed of their power, transformed into Friendly Goddesses and despatched to an underground home.

Iphigenia, Electra, Orestes—Clytemnestra's children—share in the fearful fantasy of maternal omnipotence, a fantasy which leads them to conspire in silencing maternal anger, and thus in erasing all other aspects of maternal subjectivity, including maternal love. The representation of Demeter as the powerful goddess who is capable of destroying the earth, the representation of Clytemnestra as the vengeful wife who can kill her husband and punish her children, these representations suggest how, as a culture, we imagine the mother's part in the child's development. In the context of a patriarchal culture in which mothers have little control over their children's paths to maturity, in a culture where children betray their mothers and abandon them, or are forcibly abducted, and where husbands act as enemies, maternal anger is depicted as powerful and threatening. Such figurations necessarily shape maternal representations and self-representations even within feminism. They explain why, even in post-modern feminist fiction, maternal stories are mediated and suppressed, especially if they involve anger. The last two chapters of this book outline these processes of mediation and chart the course of a maternal representation which seems still to be shaped by a cultural imaginary that participates in and underwrites unconscious fears of the maternal. Anger and fear insure that maternal plots will remain unspeakable; post-modern feminist narrative continues to be shaped by mythic taboos.

Underlying the discussion of maternal subjectivity in feminist fiction and theory is the crucial question of the discursive power of the mythic representations discussed in this Prelude. At the same time, this discussion is only partial: the novels discussed in these chapters outline a range of female relationships and narrative storylines that go beyond the paradigms charted here. Although anger does remain an object of fear as well as one of the primary markers of maternal subjectivity—a subjectivity that is in the process of being erased as it makes room for the emerging subjectivity of the child—the texts of post-modernist feminist fiction do present a greater spectrum of maternal experiences. They go beyond the narrow confines of a privatized maternal anger, suggesting possibilities of integrating anger with love and nurturance. Yet even here, in the absence of fathers, brothers, and husbands, some of the plots of mothers and daughters, especially the permutations of maternal subjectivities, remain fractured and self-contradictory—unspeakable. Yet the unspeakable itself acquires a different significance in texts that combine, without subsuming, the personal with the political.

I.

Realism and Maternal Silence

1

FEMALE FAMILY ROMANCES

A MORE ARCHAIC MURDER

> We had the self-same world enlarged for each
> By loving difference of girl and boy
>
> —George Eliot, "Brother and Sister"

> The phantom of the man-who-would-
> understand
> the lost brother, the twin—
>
> For him did we leave our mothers,
> deny our sisters, over and over?
>
> —Adrienne Rich, "Natural Resources"

Irigaray's definition of Western culture as inherently matricidal is particularly useful for an exploration of the realist novel in the European and American tradition.[1] In many nineteenth-century novels by women writers we perceive that, as Irigaray says, "verticality is in some ways always removed from the becoming-woman. The bond between mother and daughter, daughter and mother, must be broken so that the daughter can become woman. Female genealogy must be suppressed, in favor of the relation son-Father, of the idealization of the father and the husband as patriarchs. But without verticality, . . . the ethical order of love cannot take place among women" (*Ethique,* p. 106; my translation). This break in female genealogy determines most especially the lives of the realist heroines and describes nineteenth-century women writers' relations to the genealogical patterns that dominate the fictions of their period. In this chapter, I will examine structures of female plotting in several novels, accounting in particular for the repression of maternal bonds in favor of fraternal ones and tracing the emergence of what could be called a "female family romance."

43

What I have chosen to call maternal repression in fact includes a range of maternal representations—from dead mothers in *Emma, Persuasion, Wuthering Heights, Jane Eyre,* and *Villette,* to trivialized comic mothers in *Pride and Prejudice* and *The Mill on the Floss,* the malevolent yet inconsequential mother in *Valentine,* the miniaturized maternal portrait in *Frankenstein,* and ineffectual, silenced mothers in *Mansfield Park, Shirley,* and *Daniel Deronda.* Only at the end of the century, in *The Awakening,* do we encounter a protagonist who is herself a mother, who begins to act out in relation to her children the maternal absences other protagonists have experienced only as daughters.

Feminist critical interpretations and evaluations of these representations have ranged from celebrations to repudiations of mother-daughter connection. Sandra Gilbert and Susan Gubar in *The Madwoman in the Attic,* for example, see in motherlessness the emblem of female powerlessness in nineteenth-century society.[2] Maternal absence and silence, they argue, rob the heroine of important role models for her development, of the matriarchal power which could facilitate her own growth into womanhood. To forget the past is to ignore a matriarchal heritage that would enable the heroine to find her own "distinctive female power" (p. 59). The assumption is that even within patriarchy, women can be powerful if connected with each other. Adrienne Rich, in contrast, stresses the potentially debilitating effects of maternal identification. In her analysis of *Jane Eyre,* she applies Phyllis Chesler's formulation to the nineteenth-century novel: "women are motherless children in patriarchal society."[3] This means, Rich asserts, that women have "neither power nor wealth to hand on to their daughters . . . the most they can do is teach their daughters the tricks of surviving in the patriarchy by pleasing, and attaching themselves to, powerful and economically viable men" (*On Lies,* p. 91). Rich's essay argues that Jane is in many ways less constrained, more "unalterably herself," by being motherless and having a variety of maternal models and nurturing figures available to her, than she would be if she had just one. In this view, the Victorian heroine's motherlessness, like that of the orphan hero's, gives her the freedom necessary to circumscribe her own developmental course.[4]

Even more important than this notion of self-determination for the heroine, is the particular contradiction, pervasive in nineteenth-century fiction and ideology, between motherhood and authorship.[5] Although Victorian heroines are never writers, they do aspire to a singularity that is so clearly incompatible with motherhood as to preclude the possibility of the heroine's maternal identification, or of her potential maternity. Nina Auerbach defines the paradox succinctly in her gloss on Virginia Woolf's comment about the childlessness of several nineteenth-century women writers in *A Room of One's Own:* "Did the Brontës, Jane Austen and George Eliot write out of a thwarted need to give birth, sadly making substitute dream children out of their novels? Or did they produce art that allowed them a freer, finer, more expansive world than the suppressions of nineteenth-century motherhood allowed?"[6] Motherhood, in Victorian ideology—an ideology to which both Woolf and Auerbach do seem to subscribe—represents a confinement and potential destruction impossible to combine with the freedom and expansiveness seen as necessary to artistic creativity. The material conditions of the mother, even the middle-class mother, were certainly almost impossible to combine with a writing career. Even Mrs. Gaskell, herself the mother of four children and the author of numerous novels, reinforces this opposition, in her very attempt to resolve it. She suggested to younger novelists that, like her, they might wait to write until after they have raised their children. Thus, they might be able to use the morally redemptive qualities with which Victorian ideology endowed mothers to enrich an art that defines itself as separate from such qualities. But Margaret Homans, studying those strategies which allow some writers to define writing itself as a maternal activity thereby "neutralizing the conflict between writing and motherhood," demonstrates how easily such strategies can be appropriated so that they actually end up reinforcing the very ideology they were meant to overturn and to expose.[7] The heroine who wants to write, or who wants in any way to be productive and creative, then, must break from her mother, so as not to be identified with maternal silence. Like Electra and Antigone, she must find a male substitute for maternal nurturance, one that will aid her in gaining access to a more conventional definition of heroism. As with Electra and Antigone, that figure will be the "brother."

Margaret Homans's *Bearing the Word* explains the conjunction of the maternal with silence by invoking what she calls a "myth of language" prevalent during the Victorian period and later theorized by Freud and Lacan. According to this myth, Homans maintains, "language and culture depend on the death or absence of the mother and on the quest for substitutes for her. . . . Women are identified with the literal, the absent referent" (p. 4) which makes possible the (male) child's entry into the symbolic or Law of the Father. "Women must remain the literal in order to ground the figurative substitutions sons generate and privilege" (p. 9). Homans's book explores the existence of an alternative story in which women retain the pre-symbolic, literal relation to language, even while they are forced to conform to the father's law. "The daughter therefore speaks two languages at once" (p. 13), she concludes, though she finds that, in the Victorian period, what she calls the literal mother-daughter language exists only in brief moments of interruption and silence within the pervasive fabric of the symbolic, which tends to dominate the plots of realism. Homans's focus on and affirmation of a mother-daughter connection separate from simple assumptions about female power and powerlessness represents a significant shift in feminist criticism of the nineteenth-century novel.[8]

My own focus on the relationship of nineteenth-century heroines to their mothers and to their own motherhood alters in a somewhat different way the direction of feminist readings of the nineteenth-century realist novel. Whereas other studies take the heroine's orphan status for granted because it duplicates the hero's, I shall take a much closer look at the heroines' motherlessness, at their refusal of maternity, and at the portraits of mothers we do find in nineteenth-century realist fiction by women. Does the orphan status or the condition of motherlessness have a different psychological import for the heroine than it does for the hero? What is the relationship of maternal absence to the structures of desire that motivate the plots of these texts: the choice of fraternal allegiance, for example? In what ways does the childlessness of the nineteenth-century heroine qualify her relationship to marriage and the closure of her plot? Do the plots and structures of realism, rooted as they are in oedipal forms and preoccupations, rest on and benefit from the erasure, trivialization, or objectification of the mother? To what extent do women writers, having on the one hand to conform to the forms of nineteenth-century realism, and attempting on the other to imagine alternate plots for their heroines, find that they have to sacrifice the mother in this vacillation between resistance and compliance?[9] What textual model of the family romance emerges in these novels and in what ways, to what degree, does it lead to a redefinition of the nineteenth-century realist tradition?

Monstrous Mothers and Motherless Daughters

Adrienne Rich entitles her famous analysis of *Jane Eyre* "The Temptations of a Motherless Woman," seeing Jane as a representative of the nineteenth-century heroine who, in order to avoid succumbing to the "traditional female temptations" she encounters, needs to find a maternal figure, "the image of a nurturing or spirited woman on whom she can model herself, or to whom she can look for support" (*On Lies*, p. 91). Because of the difficulty the maternal role thus formulated poses for women in the Victorian period, multiple and surrogate mothers, like Jane Eyre's, are better able, at least in fictional representation, to help daughters avoid the traditional temptations of romantic love, of marriage, and of objectification than a biological mother might be. Jane's very motherlessness thus becomes the key to her success in Rich's reading. One mother, as Bertha Mason's story and the Reed sisters demonstrate, can have devastating effects on the life of her daughter, transmitting not the power to become "unalterably oneself," but madness, uncontrollable rage, intense competition, and frustration. The heroine, like the hero, is an orphan, attempting to cut herself off from a constraining past, to invent a new story, her own story, and eager to avoid the typically devastating fate of her mother. There are, of course, biographical correlates to the heroines' pervasive motherlessness: a number of the writers themselves, particularly, Mary Shelley, the Brontës, George Eliot, Elizabeth Gaskell, and Elizabeth Barrett Browning, lost their mothers either at birth or in very early childhood. But biographical parallels are not enough to explain the thoroughness with which the figure of the mother is silenced, denigrated, simply eliminated, or written out of these Victorian fictions. Maternal absence and silence is too much the condition of the heroine's development, too much the basis of the fiction itself; the form it takes is too akin to repression. In tracing a pattern of maternal repression through a number of representative novels from Shelley and Austen to Eliot, I would like to point to its pervasiveness in the first half of the century.

Mothers in these novels are either powerful and angry to the point of madness, like Mrs. Mason and Mrs. Reed, or they are frustrated, trivial, inconsequential, sometimes comic. Falling into neither of these categories, dead or absent mothers are, ironically, the only positive maternal figures we hear about. In Jane Austen's novels, for example, rich and powerful mothers control the novels' plots through anger and vindictiveness, often in an arbitrary and autocratic fashion. Lady Catherine de Bourgh and Mrs. Churchill pull all the strings from behind the scenes; since their own stories and their own subjectivity are never revealed, they can remain unambiguously unsympathetic. When Mrs. Churchill's illness is shown to have some basis in reality, she suddenly gains in human interest, even in sympathy, but she has to die in order to get someone to listen to her complaint. Invalidism invariably follows marriage and childbirth; it represents perhaps the greatest danger of adult womanhood in Austen's world. Not only mothers but also older married sisters who are mothers suffer from it, offering Austen's unmarried heroines the chance to demonstrate their superiority to their sisters. Thus, Emma invites her nephews for an extended visit when Isabella finds herself unable to cope, and Anne Elliott steps in for her incompetent and invalid sister Mary. Jane Fairfax's frequent headaches alert us to the impending danger she faces upon marriage to Frank; it is only a small step from headaches to the ailments which plague and finally kill Mrs. Churchill. As Gilbert and Gubar argue, Mrs. Churchill is "a double of what they (Austen's heroines) are already fast becoming" (*Madwoman*, p. 174). They suggest that Austen uses these nasty female characters to voice her own anger, thereby enacting a complicated dual identification both with the more compliant heroines and the subversive, capricious, powerful mothers, whom they in many ways resemble. Ultimately, of course, the novels tend to punish these mothers for their arrogance. Mrs. Norris, for example, is banished from Mansfield and from society itself to take care of the disgraced Maria Bertram, whose success she had meant to engineer.

In contrast to these powerful mothers, Mrs. Bennet and Miss Bates lack wealth and therefore influence. In their comic personalities we see the underside of the power of Mrs. Churchill or Lady Catherine; unable to control the plot, they can only impede its course ever so slightly through their seeming stupidity and empty babble. Like the powerful mothers, they can serve only as negative examples to the heroines even though, viewed from a different perspective, their babble does contain some of the most radical criticism of the system to which they are subject (for example, of the law of inheritance exclusively through male lines). Mrs. Bennet, like Mrs. Tulliver in *The Mill on the Floss*, becomes, in her silliness, a powerful fictional instrument of social criticism. Although fathers in Austen are also ineffectual, mothers are primarily responsible for the failed children. If mothers sometimes facilitate the plot, they do so only inadvertently. Mrs. Bennet's silliness, for example, makes Elizabeth more sensitive to Darcy's graciousness and more eager to leave her parental household.[10]

Dead mothers do elicit a certain nostalgia; nevertheless their absence invariably furthers the heroines' development. Emma's mother, we are told, was very much like Emma and was "the only person able to cope with her. She inherits her mother's talents, and must have been under subjection to her."[11] In contrast to her mother, Miss Taylor did not place Emma "under subjection," but, as Mr. Knightley insists, allowed her to participate in the process of her education. Thus, we surmise that Emma needed to grow up without her mother if she was to do "just as she liked." Like Emma's mother, Anne Elliott's stands outside of the novel's action. She represents no more than the title she acquired from her husband and the house she inhabited but did not own, accoutrements which did not help her to survive and which Anne, in spite of Lady Russell's injunctions, decides to do without. Her mother's actual life we know to have been loveless, unhappy, invisible, and clearly not to be repeated.

A similar pattern of maternal repression pervades the novels of other British and French women writers of the period. The mother appears as a miniature portrait in *Frankenstein*; crucial to the plot, an object of nostalgia for all the other characters, she herself can only reveal the powerlessness of her youth (repeated also in the story of Elizabeth's mother), a powerlessness that led her to marry her paternal guardian. In this "world abandoned by mothers" (Gilbert and Gubar), the mothers, themselves motherless, can only perpetuate a cycle of abandonment. The same is true of *Wuthering Heights*, where the death of Cathy and the birth of her daughter are told in the same sentence. Margaret Homans points out that the two Cathy's, unable to coexist within the space of the narrative, need to divide the novel between them. The other mothers, Frances and Isabella, also die shortly after the birth of their children, abandoning them to the powerful and manipulative Nelly Deane whose surrogate mothering of all the novel's children becomes more and more suspect in the course of the text. Although she has an important impact on the plot and on the lives of the novel's children, Nelly is not the mother, but the servant. Her tale is inscribed in Lockwood's, that is, the master's narrative.

In Sand's fiction, mothers are not so much absent as negative forces impeding rather than fostering the heroines' development; they tend to respond with great internal conflict, even revulsion, to the state of maternity. Valentine, for example, has three disastrous maternal models: a selfish and arrogant grandmother, driven by the love of luxury, a reluctant and hostile mother, driven by ambition, and a nurturing but competitive older half-sister, destroyed by love. As a result, Valentine is unmothered and fares no better than her sister, the motherless Louise. The story of Valentine's mother highlights the conflictual demands of maternity and selfhood, the sexual competition with her stepdaughter, and the social rivalry with her daughter, who only serves as a reminder of her own younger and more beautiful appearance and social success. Although the novel gives a full account of the countess's background, and of the political and social changes that altered her life and robbed her of her social position, it shows virtually no sympathy toward this stereotypic "terrible mother." Even the warm and nurturing Louise is devastated by the jealousy she feels toward the younger Valentine, as though "mother" and "daughter" could not co-inhabit the space of their fictional world but had to replace one another.

Mothers in the novels of Charlotte Brontë and George Eliot experience similar constraints and present similar obstacles to the developing heroines. *Shirley*, the only one of Brontë's novels in which the heroine is not totally motherless and in which a somewhat sympathetic mother is presented, offers perhaps the clearest articulation of the impossibility of motherhood in the context of the given social and familial structures. Both protagonists, Shirley and Caroline, grow up thinking that they are motherless. Not until the last sections of the novel does Mrs. Pryor reveal herself to Caroline as the mother who left her in her early childhood. Even this delayed revelation fills Mrs. Pryor with ambivalence; she seems more comfortable with the role of governess, or surrogate mother, both in relation to Shirley whom she raised and to Caroline whom she abandoned, because she could not tolerate her shattering marriage. She felt that the daughter was so totally connected to the qualities of that marriage that she had to declare: "I dared not undertake to rear you."[12] Mrs. Pryor can nurture a grown-up daughter, helping her to recover from a broken heart and virtual starvation, but she could not raise a child, could not undertake to protect her from the vicissitudes of the female plot. In the novel she stands as a warning, albeit not a successful one, to avoid the bondage and self-annihilation of the institutions of marriage and maternity.

Mothers in Eliot's work are perhaps more present than in the work of other writers, but even here maternity brings only frustration and powerlessness. *Daniel Deronda* will be discussed in the next chapter, but *The Mill on the Floss* can offer a brief example here. Mrs. Tulliver obviously belongs to the category of comic mothers whose complaints against their fate emerge as babble. Nevertheless, Mrs. Tulliver's initial failure to understand Maggie has quite harmful effects on the daughter, who ends up perceiving herself as a misfit and who draws all tenderness and support from her father and lavishes it on her brother. The Glegg sisters, in fact, represent the extreme conservative social forces to which Maggie cannot possibly conform. Aunt Moss, on the other hand, is more understanding,

but is socially and economically powerless. Again, the novel offers no
positive maternal figure and no model of maternity for Maggie or Lucy. It
does, however, qualify the negative judgment of mothers we might make,
when, in one of the novel's most moving moments, Mrs. Tulliver decides
to stand by the outcast Maggie, even though she fails to comprehend the
moral conflict that led to Maggie's ostracism. When Tom rejects the returning Maggie, Mrs. Tulliver simply offers "one simple draught of human pity
. . . more helpful than all wisdom": "My child! I'll go with you. You've got
a mother."[13]

Joan Manheimer argues that the rash of terrible mothers in nineteenth-
century novels should be read as social criticism, as a repeated and out-
raged critique on the part of both female and male writers of an impossible
social institution. "These women reveal terrible failings in their world, a
world in which activities are so codified that giving proper nurturance
drains the self of all possibilities of self-interest, sexuality and activity
outside the home." Urging readers to refrain from judging these characters
rashly, Manheimer concludes: "In their creation of Terrible Mothers,
nineteenth-century novelists leave an indictment, like an open wound,
pulsing against a society which is unable, without prohibitive cost, to
secure meaningful continuity for itself" (p. 545). Such an analysis of the
devastating maternal portraits in the works of nineteenth-century female
realism, while certainly valid, is only partial. For a fuller picture, we need
to look at the continuity between terrible and absent, or silent mothers. We
need to explore the role of surrogate mothers and the reasons for the
greater ease with which women characters can assume that particular
nurturing role. We need to look at what function the mother's absence,
silence, and negativity—the mother's repression—plays for the developing
heroine and for the structure of the fiction itself. We need to look at what
eliminating the mother makes possible for the heroine's development and
allegiance, at what fictional and social structures it supports. And we need
to evaluate the ways in which women writers compensate for their
heroines' maternal deprivation.

If we supplement Manheimer's social analysis with a psychoanalytic
perspective in relation to realist fictional convention, we see that maternal
repression stands at the very basis of the structure of plot. Moreover, the
thoroughness with which female realist writers eliminate mothers from
their fiction makes me wonder whether social critique is not at least in part
mixed with hostility, resentment, and disappointment on the part of these
writers themselves, as well as with their total self-identification as daughters.

Female Family Romances and the "Old Dream of Symmetry"

By naming the reluctant mother in her novel *Shirley* Mrs. Pryor, Charlotte Brontë suggests that priority and temporality, as well as the domi-

nance of origins and endings, are constitutive of the relationship between familial and narrative structures. Narratological analyses of nineteenth-century realist fiction tend to corroborate this conjunction. I will argue, however, that although recent narrative theories help to focus the psychological bases of plot construction—the parallels between how our lives are structured and how we tell the stories of our lives—they obscure the relation of plot and gender.[14]

Patricia Drechsel Tobin describes the genealogical structure of narrative thus: "By an analogy of function, events in time come to be perceived as begetting other events within a line of causality similar to the line of generations, with the prior event earning a special prestige as it is seen to originate, control and predict future events."[15] Realism, according to Tobin, rests on just such a conversion of randomness into necessity, defined by linear progression, causality, and therefore genealogy. Building on Roland Barthes's *Pleasure of the Text*, Tobin finds the "genealogical imperative" in every aspect of narrative structure: "The sentence, in other words, is a genealogy in miniature. At its origin it fathers a progeny of words, sustains them throughout in orderly descent and filial obedience, and through its act of closure maintains the family of words as an exclusive totality. The relations between the parts and the whole, which in narrative is the sign of its reality, in language is the sign of intelligibility. Thus, both life and thought are delivered to us with a paternal degree of their legitimacy" (p. 18).

Edward Said's *Beginnings: Intention and Method* employs a similar terminology of filiation to describe the engenderment of narrative. Not only the author, but also the novel itself and even the characters are presented in the role of paternal procreators: "the novel makes, procreates, a certain secondary and alternative life possible for heroes who are otherwise lost in society."[16] The narrative, then, acts as a "chiding father who has endowed his children with a patrimony and an abode he himself cannot ever relinquish. In being the author—and notice how this applies equally to the writer/author, the novel-father/author and the character/author—one engages oneself in a whole process of filiation not easily escaped" (p. 93). The very continuity of narrative, its potential to make sense, from syntax to plot structure, seems to depend on a relation to paternity, whether that relation be subordinate and obedient or rebellious. "The narrative represents the generative process—literally in its mimetic representation of men and women in time, metaphorically in that by itself it generates succession and multiplication of events after the manner of human procreation" (p. 146).

An interesting and symptomatic slippage has taken place in this brief critical survey: the exploration of origin and narrative, of its source and initial motivation, has moved almost immediately to a consideration of paternity, to an oedipal scenario of conflict between father and son. The paternal figure has not only appropriated the procreative act, engendering narrative without the help or the mention of the mother, but he has also usurped the conflict around which the narrative revolves—the conflict, in

Said's terms, between "authority" and "molestation," in Tobin's terms, between obedience and subversion, or, in Peter Brooks's, between the desire for closure and totality and the retard and postponement which alone can preclude ultimate closure and death.[17] Where is the woman, where is the mother in this narrative ordering? Said's genealogy and Tobin's is entirely male; Brooks's is predicated on woman's quiet participation as an object of desire.

Recent definitions of nineteenth-century realism also stress a continual and always unfulfilled struggle to contain excess, to create order and coherence out of looseness and chaos which can be, but for the most part has not been, seen in terms of gender. George Levine, for example, suggests that realist novelists in the Victorian period "wrote *against* the very indeterminacy they tended to reveal." According to Leo Bersani, "desire" is a threat to realistic fiction: "Realistic fiction serves nineteenth-century society by providing it with strategies for containing (and repressing) its disorder within significantly structured stories about itself."[18] Naomi Schor applies a similar vision of nineteenth-century realism more pointedly to the figure of Woman: "Realism is that paradoxical moment in Western literature when representation can neither accommodate the Otherness of Woman nor exist without it."[19] I shall suggest that the excess which must be contained, or the otherness that structures the fiction, is related more specifically to the figure of the mother. The work of women writers, moreover, participates in the process of placing the maternal into the position of silenced other.[20]

Psychoanalytic theories of creativity tend to identify the place of the mother as the very absence which lies at the point of linguistic origin. For Freud, for example, creative writing emerges from dissatisfaction and lack of fulfillment: "A strong experience in the present awakens in the creative writer the memory of an earlier experience (usually belonging to his childhood) from which there now proceeds a wish which finds its fulfillment in the creative work."[21] Similarly, for Lacan, language itself depends on a fundamental and irreparable breech, a primordial absence and loss which comes to be located in the space of the maternal. "It may be significant," Roland Barthes says rather tentatively, "that it is at the same moment (around the age of three) that the little human 'invents' at once sentence, narrative and the Oedipus."[22] For Barthes, then, the construction of the sentence and the ability to initiate and sustain narrative continuity are related to familial structures; the desire for the mother, the rivalry with the father, the anxiety about castration and the way that anxiety is overcome and transformed, all inform narrative design. "Doesn't every narrative lead back to Oedipus?" Barthes asks in *The Pleasure of the Text,* and he elaborates, "Isn't storytelling always a way of searching for one's conflicts with the Law, entering into the dialectic of tenderness and hatred? . . . As fiction, Oedipus was at least good for something: to make good novels, to tell good stories."[23] When Barthes says, for example, that the writer "is someone who plays with his mother's body" (p. 37), I think it is obvious that Freud, Lacan, and Barthes universalize an Oedipal textuality modeled on male sexuality and psychology.[24]

Peter Brooks's theory of plotting can serve as a symptom of recent theoretical preoccupation and procedure.[25] I concentrate here on Brooks's theory because I find his dynamic model of plot construction particularly appealing, but also particularly gender-blind. In the context of realism and modernism, narrative, as he sees it, charts the course of "the child become man" and "seems to turn on the uncertainty of fatherhood, to use this uncertainty to unfold the romance of authority vested elsewhere, and to test the individual's claim to personal legitimacy within a struggle of different principles of authority" (p. 64). Brooks insists that "narrative, like genealogy, is a matter of patronymics" (p. 302). Plot is a form of desire (Brooks uses Lacan's definition here), a dynamic force which carries us forward to the end, but it is a desire which is, by nature, unsatisfiable. The inherent temporality of plot, its duration, is also motivated by psychological forces: desire gone wrong but eventually cured, prohibited desire that gives way to legitimate desire. "The 'dilatory space' of narrative, as Barthes calls it—the space of retard, postponement, error and partial revelation—is the place of transformation: where the problems posed to and by initiatory desire are worked out and worked through" (p. 92). Citing *Beyond the Pleasure Principle*, Brooks sees repetition, which is basic to the dynamic of plot, as the movement "from passivity to mastery," but mastery itself—the end, meaning, truth, desire fulfilled—must be delayed, for it is coextensive with the death of the narrative and of the reader in the text.

According to Brooks, narrative repetition, the very binding of the plot, is based on the *fort/da* game in which the subject learns to cope with lack, namely the lack of the mother, in an elaborate process of substitution which is basic both to language and to the process of narration. Thus the drama of father and son, authority and legitimacy, is predicated on lack, on a fundamental breech as the initiating moment of the narrative—on the mother's absence, to be specific. "For plot starts (or must give the illusion of starting) from that moment at which story, or 'life,' is stimulated from quiescence to a state of narratability into a tension, a kind of irritation, which demands narration" (p. 103). And that initiatory moment gains significance only in retrospect as "prior events, causes, are so only retrospectively, in a reading back from the end" (p. 29). Inherently linear, moving inexorably toward an end which is both explanation and death, the structure of narrative can only be metaleptic, for "the beginning presupposes the end, since the concept of an ending is necessary to that of a beginning" (p. 93). If the ultimate goal of narrative is the act of transmission, the process of reading and understanding, the moment of contact without which no narrative can exist, that act depends on death. Brooks quotes Walter Benjamin who says that a man's life "first assumes transmissible form at the moment of his death" (p. 95).[26]

I would argue that Brooks's entire conception of narrative dynamic is based on a sexual and psychological model which is exclusively male and that similar limitations define all narratological theories which rely on models of authority and filiation. The language of male sexuality (*arousal, tumescence, delay, satisfaction*), the language of health and illness (*deviance, error, cure, working out* and *working through*), and the language of death (*lucid repose, rest in perspective*) reveal the value-laden and inherently gendered nature of the narratological project. Continuing to play out the drama of father and son, narratology has left aside the experience of the mother and the daughter and the work of women writers: symptomatically, Brooks's examples include no novels written by women.

How do women writers, and how do women's stories, relate to this conception of plot so fundamental to nineteenth-century realism? Can this plot pattern accommodate a female subject? Is there space for female difference here?[27] Focusing on maternal repression in the structures of plot, I shall now look at female revisions of oedipal plot patterns in which women writers try to imagine an alternative story to the classic "consent to femininity" and therefore a plot pattern that inscribes if not a radical departure, at least the will to difference.

The text that, in many ways, provides the basis for psychoanalytic narratological theories is Freud's 1908 essay "Family Romances."[28] A closer analysis of Freud's essay can provide a way to define and test the implications of oedipal narratology for women and to determine to what extent a "female family romance" might depart from the male prototype Freud outlines. By following out the implications of the Freudian model, it is possible to construct a paradigm of a "female family romance" which can clarify the structures of plotting in a number of nineteenth-century novels by women writers. Thus, one could say that both Freud's analysis and these novels themselves are subject to the same cultural and literary plots.[29] My argument here is that nineteenth-century women writers' resistance to those plots existed but was limited, indeed, that they, like Freud, saw the woman's story through what Luce Irigaray has called "the blind spot of an old dream of symmetry," that is, through a fundamentally male economy of desire in which the woman is other but cannot be different.[30]

If we read Freud's "Family Romances" in conjunction with Marthe Robert's gloss, *Origins of the Novel*, Freud's essay becomes the paradigm for a more extensive theory of fictionmaking.[31] The family romance, as Freud describes it, provides for the developing individual a necessary escape from the "authority of his parents," and it is this conflict over authority and legitimacy which becomes the basis for fantasy and mythmaking. "Indeed," Freud says, "the whole progress of society rests upon the opposition between successive generations" (p. 237). Two stages define this process of liberation. First, the child, feeling slighted and in competition with siblings, and seeing that his parents are not as unique and incomparable as he had at first supposed, imagines that he might be a step-child or an adopted child. He frees himself from his parents by imaginatively replacing them with other more noble ones. Marthe Robert calls this the "foundling plot" and discusses it as the basis for the fantastic narratives and romances of Chretien de Troyes, Cervantes, Hoffmann, Novalis, Melville, and Kafka. At this stage in his explanation of the "foundling fantasy," Freud finds it necessary to introduce a gender distinction, even though up to this point he has been discussing a neutral, and presumably universal "he." Thus, he argues that "a boy is far more inclined to feel hostile impulses toward his father than toward his mother and has a far more intense desire to get free from *him* than from *her*. In this respect the imagination of girls is apt to show itself much weaker" (p. 238). Clearly, for Freud, the fantasies surrounding the child's relation to his or her origin and the rebellious refusal of parental authority, processes intimately connected to the creation of fiction, are more available to the boy because they are embedded in the conflicts over authority between father and son. Because the girl fails to participate in the struggle over authority, or in the anxiety over legitimacy, she evinces, in Freud's terms, a weaker imagination. Significantly, Robert's analysis contains not a single woman writer or female plot.

At the second stage of the family romance *all* children's play and daydreaming is governed by the desire to replace the biological parents with others of higher social standing. Moreover, a beginning awareness of "the difference in the parts played by fathers and mothers in their sexual relations" begins to inform fantasy. When the child realizes that "*pater semper incertus est*, while the mother is *certissima*, the family romance undergoes a curious curtailment: it contents itself with exalting the child's father, but no longer casts any doubts on his maternal origin, which is regarded as something unalterable" (p. 239). The child's fantasies, Freud insists, become sexual at this stage and take the mother as sexual object— satisfying both the motives of sexual exploration and of retaliation against the father. Freud suggests that they have "two principal aims, an erotic and an ambitious one." Robert classifies this plot as the "bastard plot"—the origin of the realist fiction of Balzac, Dostoevski, Tolstoi, Proust, Faulkner, Dickens. Her male child—she never considers the possibility that all children may not be male—places the father alone into the realm of fantasy, while the mother remains firmly and certainly planted in reality, excluded from the process of what Robert calls fictionalization. While imagination can alter her status and explore her sexuality, it cannot replace her identity. This "real" mother does become the object of the child's manipulative fantasy, which turns her into an adulteress, the agent of his own social elevation. The mother needs to fall so that she can be redeemed; she needs to err so that she can be saved. Typically the mother falls in status while the father is elevated to royalty, and, ultimately, she is no more than an instrument in the central drama between father and son.

Neither Freud nor Robert explores the gender asymmetry of this model. If these daydreams and fantasies are the bases for creativity, what are the implications of this shift in the family romance for the girl, especially for the girl who also wants to develop her imagination and wants to write? I see several implications for the girl's relation to her mother, her father, and her own maternity. If the mother is *certissima*, then according to this model the girl lacks the important opportunity to replace imaginatively the same-sex parent, a process on which imagination and creativity depend. The father's presence, since his identity is *semper incertus*, does not preclude fantasies of illegitimacy, fantasies which can constitute a new self, free from familial constraints. The mother's presence, however, makes such fantasies impossible; therefore, we might extrapolate, in order to make possible the "opposition between successive generations" and to free the girl's imaginative play, the mother must be eliminated from the fiction. The Freudian family romance pattern clearly implies that women need to kill or to eliminate their mothers from their lives, if they are not to resign themselves to a weak imagination.*

Yet even eliminating the mother from her plots cannot offer the girl a story that is parallel to the boy's: the drama of father and son, so fundamentally a conflict about authority in the public world, could never translate into a drama between mother and daughter. However "excluded from fabulation" (Robert) the mother is in the boy's fantasy, in the girl's she is even more absent. Her plots, if they are to have any import, must, like the boy's, revolve around the males in the family who hold the keys to power and ambition. In his essay on "Creative Writers and Daydreaming," Freud corroborates this insight by insisting that men tend to dream of power and ambition, while women's fantasies are limited to the erotic, which, by being centered on only one figure—the father or brother—come also to absorb their ambitious wishes.[32]

While the boy uses the mother as an instrument in the conflict with his father, however, and ultimately replaces his erotic fantasies with ambitious ones, the girl's fantasies revolve around the father in at once a more direct and a more conflicted manner. Since the father is *semper incertus*, the girl's heterosexual erotic relationships, unlike the boy's, are always potentially incestuous. *All* men are possible brothers or fathers. For the boy this is true with sisters, but not with mothers, who are *certissimae* (Freud seems not to consider the especially unusual circumstances of Oedipus here). Thus, Freud's model implies that the danger of incest is more pronounced for the girl; the conditions for it lie at the basis of Freud's familial construction, making any marriage potentially incestuous and, conversely, any father or

*It is important to note that the mother is *certissima* only in certain cultural contexts. Slave mothers, for example, were often separated from their children and unknown to them. See my discussion of Toni Morrison's *Beloved* in the introduction and in chapter 5.

brother a potentially safe erotic and sexual partner.[33] In the female plot that can be extrapolated from Freud's argument, the paternal sexuality and power *are* the object; what is more, fathers, brothers, and husbands are, in this particular psychological economy, interchangeable. Their precise identity is *semper incertus*, even as their role is forever desirable. As Judith Herman and Lisa Hirschman say in their study on incest, "The girl's eroticized interest in her father does not develop out of an earlier bond with the father as caretaker. Rather, it is a reaction to the girl's discovery that males are everywhere preferred to females, and that even her mother . . . chooses men above women, her father and brother above herself. . . . In her imagination, her father has the power to confer the emblem of maleness (penis or phallus) upon her."[34] Unlike the boy who dreams of gaining the authority associated with the paternal position by taking the father's place, the girl, conflating eros and ambition, hopes to gain access to it by marrying him.

Thus the "female family romance" implied in Freud's essay is founded on the elimination of the mother and the attachment to a husband/father.[35] According to Freud's essay on "Negation," however, the elimination of the mother is only a recognition and corroboration of her overwhelming importance. Freud illustrates negation, the "intellectual acceptance of what is repressed" by quoting a patient who says: " 'You ask who this person in the dream may have been. It was *not* my mother.' We emend this," Freud explains, "so it *was* his mother."[36]

I would suggest that in nineteenth-century realist writing by women the maternal is located precisely in the interplay between absence/silence and determining significance. It is the mother's absence which creates the space in which the heroine's plot and her activity of plotting can evolve. We have already been able to appreciate the pervasiveness of absent, silent, or terrible mothers in nineteenth-century novels by women. Freud's essay, in all its implications, allows us to see that the maternal repression actually engenders the female fiction, a fiction which then revolves not around the drama of same-sex parent/child relations, but around marriage, which alone can place women's stories in a position of participating in the dynamics of ambition, authority, and legitimacy which constitute the plots of realist fiction.

If we look at the novels of nineteenth-century women writers, we find plots that both corroborate and call into question the female paradigm implied in Freud's "Family Romances," plots which explore the consequences both of maternal repression and of paternal alliance. Predictably, women writers do not simply hand their heroine from mother to father; they attempt to compensate for the loss of mothers by replacing authoritative fathers with other men who, endowed with nurturing qualities, might offer an alternative to patriarchal power and dominance. The female fantasy which emerges from this will to difference can be understood in Adrienne Rich's terms as the fantasy of "the-man-who-would-understand," the man who, unlike the father, would combine maternal nurturance with paternal power. Like Orestes, like Polyneices, the male object in this transformation of the marriage plot takes the form of a "brother" who can be nurturing even as he provides access to the issues of legitimacy and authority central to plotting. Most importantly, perhaps, his fraternal/incestuous status can protect the heroine from becoming a mother and can thereby help her, in spite of the closure of marriage, to remain a subject, and can help her not to disappear from the plot as the object of her child's fantasy. It is thus that women writers, in a gesture of resistance, revise a cultural plot leading, with certainty and inevitability, not only to marriage but also to maternity, a developmental plot Freud traces in his later essays on "Female Sexuality" and on "Femininity."[37] In these essays Freud asserts, of course, that mature femininity means not only the replacement of the mother with the father as libidinal object, but also the replacement of the wish for a penis with a wish for a child. In resisting this developmental course, women writers align their heroines with the classical heroic tradition of Electra and Antigone.

Yet, whereas the male foundling and bastard fantasies revolve around the self and guarantee the hero's agency, the revisionary fantasy of "the-man-who-would-understand" revolves around the attachment to another person and can at best promise only a mediated access to plotting. Moreover, as the stories of Electra and Antigone have shown, fraternal attachment ultimately offers the heroine only a potential or an extremely limited alternative to patriarchal power.

Emma and the "Man-Who-Would-Understand"

Jane Austen's *Emma* provides an excellent example of this female manipulation of the family romance. Emma's story emerges out of a double motherlessness—the death of her biological mother when she was still a child, and the marriage and therefore loss of her surrogate mother, Miss Taylor. The novel begins on the day of Miss Taylor's marriage and inscribes itself between this initial breech and what in a traditional plot signals the appropriate healing of the breech, Emma's marriage to Mr. Knightley. In the space between these two moments, Emma generates plots, for herself and for the women around her, plots following the conventional expectations of love and marriage. Thus, even though Miss Taylor acted not as a governess but as a friend, allowing Emma to do "just what she liked" (p. 1), the at least partial loss of her affection, companionship, and admiration is still a necessary condition for the emergence of the fictions that constitute Emma's active progression through her own story.

It is significant that Emma's plotting revolves around her friend Harriet who, unlike Emma herself, is a full orphan. Through Harriet, Emma can vicariously act out a different version of her family romance, one modeled on the male paradigm of illegitimacy. She imagines that Harriet's father was noble, that she is a gentlewoman, and that she must become the object of Mr. Elton's affection and proposal. Emma's activity of matchmaking/ plotting with Harriet as object allows her to express and try out her quite accurate perceptions of woman's position in society, perceptions which because of her own protected position in her father's house touch her only indirectly. Thus Emma sees the need for marriage as a form of protection and legitimacy, an inscription into the male plot: "A single woman, with a very narrow income, must be a ridiculous disagreeable old maid! the proper sport for boys and girls" (p. 58). But she also understands the terrible constraints of marriage for someone with her own imagination and creative talent: "I have none of the usual inducements of women to marry. . . . I believe few married women are half as much mistress of their husband's house, as I am of Hartfield; and never, never could I expect to be so truly beloved and important; so always first and always right in any man's eyes as I am in my father's" (pp. 57, 58). Here Emma has allied herself to power through her father, but with the difference that her refusal of marriage allows. Ultimately Emma learns the consequences and the limitations of Harriet's unprotected position, for if Emma can plot Harriet's many marriages, Harriet herself is free only to marry Mr. Martin.

Jane Fairfax functions as an even stronger reminder of how female dependency and subservience control plot. Jane suffers a triple breech, losing first her parents, then the grandmother and aunt who served as surrogate parents, and, at the novel's inception, the adoptive family who took her in to offer her the education of a future governess. The only options open to Jane in this extremely vulnerable position are to live as a governess, in "penance and mortification for ever" (p. 110), or to engage herself secretly to Frank Churchill and to suffer the humiliation he in his social advantage can inflict upon her. The dangers and vulnerabilities of the poor and dependent young woman are symbolized in the novel by Jane's dash from the boat (she is caught by Mr. Dixon) and by the attack on Harriet by the gypsies (she is rescued by Frank Churchill). Jane's unsettling reserve, her headaches, her secrecy, are all perfectly understandable responses to her utter vulnerability, but we cannot help but feel that they all prepare her for a life similar to that of her future mother-in-law, the bitter and controlling Mrs. Churchill who was also once an orphan and without means until Mr. Churchill married her. What this repetition suggests is that all women have a plot only insofar as it leads them to their eventual and inevitable marriages.

Emma's own boldness in the novel, then, stems from the unique combination of paternal protection and motherless freedom. This enables the intense and multiple plotting through which she can actively experiment with different female lives and destinies, yet keep herself out of the closure that marriage would entail. It is those lives themselves, and the economic conditions which determine them, that offer resistance to Emma's imaginative playfulness. By shielding herself from love, by enjoying the economic protection of her father and the freedom from maternal guidance, Emma can go too far: she leads Harriet to be deeply disappointed both by Mr. Elton and by Mr. Knightley, she deeply wounds Miss Bates with her thoughtless comment, and she becomes the object of Jane Fairfax's jealousy and the cause of her pain. Emma's undirected use of her imagination in a world that so strictly circumscribes what women are allowed to do, to invent, and to write, clearly cannot be allowed to continue. She must marry and insert herself into the proper place both in the social structure and in the structure of plot.

Ironically, Emma's transgressions resemble the excessive behavior for which she mocks the comic Miss Bates. In the game Frank invents for the amusement of the party, each guest is asked to say either one clever thing, two moderately clever things, or three dull things. When Miss Bates opts for the latter, Emma replies, "but you will be limited as to number—only three at once" (p. 254). Emma's own matchmaking games are similarly limitless, close to Miss Bates's chatter, beyond the scope of the circumscribed social game.[38] "If I thought I should ever be like Miss Bates! so silly—so satisfied—so smiling—so prosing—so undistinguishing and unfastidious—and so apt to tell every thing relative to every body about me, I would marry to-morrow" (p. 58). This ultimately is the choice open to Emma. In the economy Austen has constructed, female plotting is as meaningless and gratuitous, as excessive as Miss Bates's chatter.

Emma's engagement represents not only an imposition of limits, a recall to norm and convention, but also an inscription into the plot of authority and legitimacy—moral, social, and economic—represented by Mr. Knightley. The engagement takes place as a response to another experience of loss—Miss Taylor's pregnancy—but here loss leads not to an opening up of possibilities but to a closure which is marriage. One could argue that Miss Taylor's motherhood represents a more radical breech than her marriage— Emma will be replaced in Miss Taylor's affection by a sibling/surrogate daughter and is thus propelled into the limiting adult role she has been resisting with such determination. The account of the engagement best signals the closure and containment it represents. While Mr. Knightley is so agitated that for the only moment in the novel he loses control and actually stammers, Emma herself assumes perfect control, a control that the novel can no longer render because it stands too much inside convention and therefore outside of narratability: "She spoke then, on being so entreated.—What did she say?—Just what she ought, of course. A lady always does.—She said enough to show there need not be despair—and to invite him to say more himself" (p. 297). With her engagement to Knightley, Emma ceases to have things her own way, relinquishes the almost limitless freedom of her unmarried position and embarks on a straight path determined by the values and virtues of her husband. Mr. Woodhouse only agrees to the marriage because it offers protection, because he is worried about more loss and lawlessness after his poultry house was pilfered.[39] After trying to invent a plot for herself that would deviate from the plot of her mother and the other women she knew, Emma agrees to repetition, repetition of her mother's life, her sister's, Jane's, Harriet's. In D. A. Miller's terms, marriage provides an object choice for Emma's otherwise limitless non-objectal desire, thus allowing the dangerously unending narratability in which she is engaged to come to a necessary and comforting close (p. 20).

Emma's choice of Knightley, however, illustrates the revisionary pattern I see in so many women's novels of the period, a pattern that posits a husband who stands in a fraternal relationship to the heroine in order to maintain her position of difference in the plot. Emma and Knightley virtually admit to being brother and sister when they discuss whether they might dance together: " 'you know we are not really so much brother and sister as to make it at all improper.' 'Brother and sister! no, indeed!' " (p. 225). They are not literally brother and sister, of course, but Knightley is Emma's brother-in-law's brother. He watched her grow up, took charge of her moral education and, most important perhaps, offered an economic alliance, which combined the Donwell and Hartfield estates, thereby bolstering the alliance of Isabella and John Knightley and the inheritance of their children. As the older "brother," and unlike the ineffectual father, Knightley holds out to Emma moral goals and thus the prospect of actual growth.

Marriage to Knightley offers Emma the possibility of finding a place inside convention, inside a more meaningful plot but with a difference, a way to repeat her mother's life but possibly without the devastating results. Allegiance to "brothers" shields nineteenth-century heroines from the perils of exogamy. In remaining in their family and in their house, they can protect themselves from becoming totally subject to male power.

The pattern we have seen in *Emma* is greatly exacerbated in a novel such as *Mansfield Park*.[40] Not only are Fanny and her cousin Edmund virtually destined for each other as soon as it is decided that Fanny will leave her mother's house to be brought up at Mansfield, and not only does Edmund in numerous ways merge with Fanny's brother William, but Fanny must accept Mansfield as her true home before the marriage with Edmund can take place. Only when she realizes that she belongs wholly to the aristocratic, imperial, and patriarchal world of Mansfield can she gain Edmund as a husband. Yet this recognition of her unquestioning allegiance to Edmund and Mansfield is virtually the only development Fanny undergoes in the novel. Unlike Emma, Fanny is plotless; she silently and passively waits to step into the alternate plot Austen has written for her. She herself considers plotting and acting immoral.[41] The entire novel constitutes an indictment of exogamy for women and an explicit celebration of fraternal relation. Here, however, the identification of the fraternal and the patriarchal is made absolutely clear: "Fanny had never known so much felicity in her life, as in this unchecked, equal, fearless intercourse with the brother and friend, who was opening his heart to her, telling her all his hopes and fears, plans, . . . and with whom . . . all the evil and good of their earliest years could be gone over again, and every former united pain and pleasure retraced with the fondest recollection. An advantage this, a strengthener of love, in which even the conjugal tie is beneath the fraternal" (pp. 243–44). When Fanny, after her return to her biological family, finds that Mansfield is her true home, Edmund comes more and more to take the place of William. When Edmund provides the gold chain which enables Fanny to wear William's cross he strengthens the "fraternal" relation between them.[42] And when Fanny marries Edmund she is described as Sir Thomas Bertram's daughter, now fully occupying the place that was given to her at the novel's start. Unlike Emma, Fanny remains in that place throughout the entire novel, occupying it more and more firmly. The distance from her mother is still the precondition for the inception of the fiction, but here the immediate connection to the brother precludes the heroine's freedom to invent or to alter the plot.

In these novels brother-sister sexuality does, however, offer a potentially different mode of relation and, more important, a life free of the dangers of pregnancy and maternity. In *Literary Women*, Ellen Moers outlines the attraction of the sister-brother relationship for Victorian women: "Every reader of Dickens knows the importance of a sister to a brother struggling to resolve the extreme Victorian separation between the purity and the desirability of womanhood. But to Victorian women the sister-brother relationship seems to have had a different and perhaps even greater significance—especially to those women, so commonplace in the intellectual middle class, who in a sexual sense never lived to full maturity. The rough-and-tumble sexuality of the nursery loomed large for sisters: it was the *only* heterosexual world that Victorian literary spinsters were ever freely and physically to explore. Thus the brothers of their childhood retained in their fantasy life a prominent place somewhat different in kind from that of the father figures who dominated them all."[43] Moers refers to Maggie and Tom Tulliver's childhood games, to Christina Rossetti's goblins, to a passage from Alice James's diary, and to Catherine's desperately sexual childhood love for Heathcliff in *Wuthering Heights*. Eliot concludes "Brother and Sister" by saying: "But were another childhood-world my share,/I would be born a little sister there."

For an adult example, we might turn to the representation of the wedding night in Sand's *Valentine*, where two forms of sexuality, marital and "fraternal," are clearly juxtaposed.[44] Unlike Emma, Valentine does not marry the "man-who-would-understand" but remains passionately attached to him. Instead, she marries the man her mother has chosen for her, yet manages to delay the consummation of this doomed relationship and to retire to her room alone. But she is not alone: Benedict, the fraternal lover, has hidden in a closet of her room and watches the drugged and sleeping bride. In a brilliant analysis of this scene, Nancy K. Miller has identified a specifically "feminine/feminist" form of sexual pleasure, which values not possession through penetration but the moment which precedes and thus precludes possession.[45] Benedict watches Valentine, he takes her tresses into his mouth, kisses her hand, bites her shoulder, but, most powerfully, he "possessed [her] in [his] thoughts." Although she is drugged, Valentine is not unprotected, for Benedict in his "divine adoration . . . was her safeguard and defender against himself" (p. 193). Valentine herself half-participates in this scene of "possession": she is partially awake and in her drugged state she both invites and repels Benedict's caresses. This version of "fraternal" sexuality remains outside of the structures of marriage and legitimacy. As Miller points out, Valentine belongs to her husband legally, but spiritually and symbolically she belongs to Benedict. In splitting her attachment, Valentine insures both her continued virginity and her childlessness. In insisting that she needs to remain true to her "virtue," she also precludes the sexual fulfillment of her love of Benedict.

Valentine illustrates the liminal strategy of the female family romance: it enables the heroine to be both inside and outside of plot, both sexual and virginal, to be feminine without being maternal. As we see with Knightley, the fraternal husband does enable the heroine to remain within the structure of her family of origin and to remain childless, thereby increasing her self-determination, not to speak of her chance for survival. The fact that Knightley agrees to move into Hartfield after the marriage indicates both Austen's intent to construct a marriage of equality, and the possibility that the "man-who-would-understand" might actually compensate for the loss of the mother by taking her place in her house.[46]

Yet the "brotherly" Knightley emerges as a much more authoritative and repressive father than Mr. Woodhouse. At the end of the novel, Emma ceases to construct her own plots and begins to live the life he has outlined for her. In this way, Mr. Knightley exemplifies the fallacy of fraternal attachment; the brother may promise to be the "man-who-would-understand" but he quickly turns into the patriarch.[47] Ultimately, however revised the plot may appear, it remains fundamentally the same: marriage always brings an end to the woman's story. As Emma and Knightley enter their totally conventional roles, the narrative itself reaches closure: "What had she to wish for? Nothing but to grow more worthy of him, whose intentions and judgment had been ever so superior to her own. Nothing but that the lessons of her past folly might teach her humility and circumspection in the future" (p. 328). Knightley's moral goals only succeed in binding Emma to a plot from which she had been trying to escape. And Hartfield itself will soon be combined with Donwell, where Emma and Knightley will eventually live.

The Avoidance of Maternity in *Emma* and *The Awakening*

It is telling that when Emma re-imagines her future and decides to marry, she does not rewrite the plans she made early in the novel for a childless life which would insure the inheritance of her nephew: "I shall be very well off, with all the children of a sister I love so much, to care about. There will be enough of them, in all probability, to supply every sort of sensation that declining life can need. There will be enough for every hope and every fear; and though my attachment to none can equal that of a parent, it suits my ideas of comfort better than what is warmer and blinder. My nephews and nieces!—I shall often have a niece with me" (pp. 58–59). These plans are not altered when Emma marries; nowhere does she indicate that she intends to have children. In fact, Emma seems very well satisfied with the distribution of roles so common in Victorian fiction in which one sister leads the more conventional life so that the other may be free to break out of it. Transmission does take place at the end of the novel, but it is of a most indirect nature. Emma manages to reproduce herself with a little girl who is not her own daughter, but rather Miss Taylor's, a girl whose life Mr. Knightley outlines as a copy of Emma's: "She will be disagreeable in infancy, and correct herself as she grows older" (p. 318). As they discuss this little girl's life in relation to Emma's, it is implied that Emma and Knightley will not themselves have children, that their relationship is too much that of brother and sister to allow for reproduction. In fact, the little surrogate daughter becomes a common figure in nineteenth-century fiction. Another example is the little Valentine, daughter of Valentine's nephew Valentin, who, as the novel ends, plays on the double grave of Valentine and Benedict and will be the heiress of Valentine's chateau.

Unlike Valentine, Emma manages, in spite of her marriage, to survive and to construct a life outside of the debilitating dichotomies of the maternal and the sexual, the maternal and the creative. By not being a mother, she can avoid being eliminated in the service of her son's or her daughter's plot; by not having a daughter she need not herself perpetuate the repetitive cycle in which, in spite of her will to difference, she remains caught. As Nina Auerbach says, "In Austen's novels the consummately adult art of life may fulfill itself in marriage, but motherhood seems antithetical to it" ("Artists and Mothers," p. 9).

Only a fraternal marriage, however, can facilitate this solution and can offer an alternative to Valentine's, Catherine's, or Elizabeth's death. If Valentine and Elizabeth die so as to preclude maternity, Catherine, as we have seen, dies as an immediate result of it. Margaret Homans explains this seemingly inevitable conjunction in the imagination of nineteenth-century women writers and their characters: "Any literary woman of the nineteenth century would have assumed that marriage and motherhood would end her career. Further, the thought of the event of childbirth itself would have had highly ambiguous connotations for any pre-twentieth-century woman. In the nineteenth century, giving birth was not unlikely to be fatal to the mother or to the child or to both, and to fear childbirth or associate it with death would have been quite reasonable. . . . Women who become mothers in novels tend to die psychically if they do not die literally. . . . Within the conventions of fiction, childbirth puts an end to the mother's existence as an individual" (pp. 88–89). Adrienne Rich presents the contradiction between individuality and maternity as a more general and pervasive result of patriarchal social organization: "Typically, under patriarchy, the mother's life is exchanged for the child's; her autonomy as a separate being seems fated to conflict with the infant she will bear" (p. 166).

This is precisely the conflict illustrated in Kate Chopin's 1899 novel *The Awakening*, a novel which departs from and reveals as disastrous the model of female family romance prevalent in the novels of the first part of the century. The novel's atypical protagonist, Edna Pontellier, is already a twenty-eight-year-old wife and mother at the novel's inception.[48] Yet it is not as a mother that Edna has a plot. In fact, the novel begins as she tries to elude her identity as one of the "mother-women" who "esteemed it a holy privilege to efface themselves as individuals and grow wings as ministering angels" (p. 10). Instead, Edna learns to swim, discovers her inner strength and rich inner life and moves out of her husband's mansion into her own "pigeon house." It is this growing break from her husband and children and from her own maternity that occasions the inception of plot. She also falls in love with Robert, a younger man with whom she feels a spiritual and physical connection which makes him into what I have called the fantasied "man-who-would-understand." Furthermore, and perhaps most important, Edna is a burgeoning artist who, in the course of the novel, begins to take her painting seriously only to abandon it again.

Edna's process of "awakening" to a possible life beyond marriage and motherhood constitutes the novel's plot, but that plot is violently curtailed as the bonds of maternity reveal themselves to be more powerful and binding. That revelation occurs during a scene of childbirth in which Edna's friend Adèle, the mother-woman par excellence, suffers a "scene of torture" that makes Edna feel a "flaming, outspoken revolt against the ways of Nature" (p. 109). It is here that Edna is reminded to "think of the children," an admonition which will make her realize that the children to whom she had similarly given birth are now "antagonists who had overcome her; who had overpowered and sought to drag her into the soul's slavery for the rest of her days" (p. 113). Her only way to "elude them," the only possibility to step outside the non-life of the mother-woman is not to create the plot of the creative, sexual, and spiritual subject, but to step outside of plot altogether through the closure of suicide.

Edna's process of awakening, her brief attempt to envision an alternative to her plotless existence, is at once an attempt at plotting and a dangerous challenge to the only manner in which plot is conventionally perceived. Her attempt at plot is dangerously shapeless, dangerously non-linear, dangerously pro- rather than metaleptic: "But the beginning of things, of a world especially, is necessarily vague, tangled, chaotic, and exceedingly disturbing. How few of us ever emerge from such beginning! How many souls perish in its tumult!" (p. 15). Edna awakens not to outward possibility—in this world there is only "that outward existence which conforms"—but to an inner life of questioning, associated with the vastness of the sea which "invit[es] the soul to wander for a spell in abysses of solitude; to lose itself in mazes of inward contemplation" (p. 15). Fragmentation and discontinuity rather than progression define Edna's course through the novel. "The past . . . offered no lesson which she was willing to heed" (p. 46). The absence of plot and progression locks her into an endless moment from which she is incapable of emerging; beginning and end, origin and destination are identical.

The novel attempts to exchange formlessness for plot in two different ways: through the love and adultery plot offered by Robert and through the artist plot offered by Mlle. Reisz. Both fail. Although he seems to be the "man-who-would-understand," Robert can conceive of relationship only in terms of marriage and possession and therefore fails to offer an alternative to the identity of wife and mother. Mlle. Reisz, on the other hand, represents a life that is lonely, asexual, cut off from all human connection; in a traditionally masculine conception, the artist is described as the "courageous soul that dares and defies." Already tied to her children, Edna cannot contemplate such solitude. As she observes the birth, Edna comes to see herself as the originator of life; for her children, she is the ocean in which she herself longs to be immersed. Birth is separation and torture; suicide re-members the severed body. Edna eludes her children by becoming herself child and mother in her fusion with the ocean. As a *mother*, she enacts the breech, the maternal absence, that she and the other heroines we have encountered experience as *daughters*. But she enacts it in relation to sons. She has no daughters and refuses even to attend her younger sister's wedding. There is no female transmission in this novel.

Although her suicide provides the novel with a violent closure, its very form questions the notion of closure itself. As Edna swims out she is "thinking of the blue-grass meadow that she had traversed when a little child, believing that it had no beginning and no end" (p. 114). The suicide is described in highly ambivalent terms. Chopin juxtaposes the image of a "bird with broken wing . . . reeling, fluttering, circling disabled down, down to the water" with the contrary image of "some new-born creature, opening its eyes in a familiar world that it had never known" (p. 113). In overdetermining this moment, Chopin skirts the issue of whether the suicide is a triumph or a failure. What she does emphasize very clearly, however, is that it is a repetition and therefore a culmination of Edna's initial moment of awakening, a logical outcome of an inward growth which, because of her inescapable link to her children, and because of the absence of anyone who "would understand" her dilemma and help her resolve it, could lead nowhere.

The structure of Chopin's novel, whose end literally repeats its beginning without illuminating it, suggests both the inadequacy of the metaleptic conception of plot for women and Chopin's inability to imagine an alternative to closure in the form of death. Susan Winnett proposes the existence of patterns of plotting which might lie outside of the oedipal dynamic, "a representational economy grounded in female experience" ("Coming Unstrung"). If we envision narrative patterns based not on masculine arousal and discharge, but on female sexuality, birth and breastfeeding, we might find a narrative dynamics that is "radically prospective," Winnett suggests. We might concentrate on beginnings rather than middles and ends. Yet her suggestion is not worked out in Chopin's novel, where maternity still signifies a necessary death rather than a new beginning. If Chopin at first describes an alternate pattern of endless beginning, she ultimately abandons it for the suicide which, in the social context within which the novel is set and in the narrative tradition in which Chopin writes, becomes the only option for author and character alike.

In order to write, nineteenth-century women writers reenact the breech that, in the terms of culture and of the novel, alone makes plot possible. To do so they must separate their heroines from the lives and the stories of their mothers. Plot itself demands maternal absence. Ironically, however, that absence, the silence of mothers about their own fate and the details of their lives, insures that those lives, those stories will be repeated by daughters. Ultimately, then, the fantasy of illegitimacy offers male writers the freedom from familial constraint that enables the invention of plot and perhaps of a different story. However, for female writers, motherlessness means freedom not only from constraint but also from the power that a knowing connection to the past might offer, whether that past is powerful or powerless. Fraternal attachment cannot replace this power. Ironically, if daughters knew the mothers' stories, they might *not* repeat them. But for that suppressed mother-daughter connection to make its way into fiction, either the oedipal origins of plot would have to be reimagined and transformed, or oedipal paradigms abandoned altogether. Narrative itself would have to be enabled, at least in part, by maternal presence rather than absence. Birth rather than death would have to motivate the dynamics of plot; death would have to cease being associated with healing, and birth would have to cease being associated with fear and destruction. Beginnings and endings would have to stand in a more complex relationship to each other. Only thus could female plots get beyond the "blind spot of an old dream of symmetry." Some of these changes do begin to occur in the texts of female modernism and post-modernism.

2

FRATERNAL PLOTS

BEYOND REPETITION

> Exhalations laden with slow death
>
> —George Eliot

> She held the spindle as she sat,
> Erinna with the thick-coiled mat
> Of raven hair and deepest agate eyes,
> Gazing with a sad surprise
> At surging visions of her destiny—
> To spin the byssus drearily
> In insect-labour, while the throng
> Of gods and men wrought deeds that
> poets wrought in song.
>
> —George Eliot

With this reference to the ancient Greek poetess Erinna in a central epigram in *Daniel Deronda*, George Eliot explores the position of the female artist in relation to the world of male art.[1] As Eliot presents her, Erinna, self-conscious and aware of her fate, is destined to remain a distant observer of the realm of action and adventure which serves as the basis for artistic production. Her role is neither to act (she sits) nor to sing. Instead, she "gazes with a sad surprise" and she spins "drearily, in insect-labour." In the work of Victorian women writers, spinning, sewing, and weaving serve as traditional tropes for a subversively feminine self-expression: the female spider-artist inscribes her story into her web while seemingly complying with the sexual division of labor in which women spin "with the fingers," while men stud[y] or writ[e] poetry which is spinning with the brain.[2] In feminist literary discussion as well, the tales of Ariadne, Arachne, and Philomela have served as important and revealing parables not, as Eliot's excerpt seems to indicate, for women's silence, but for the specific difficulties and indirections—for the creative subversions—of women's writing.[3] Nancy K. Miller has called for a theory of reading women's writing that would be based on the story of Arachne, the woman-identified spinner who loses her head and is turned into a spider by the jealous and male-identified Athena. "Arachnologies" are readings of women's writing centered on the female signature, attentive to the representations of women's writing within the woman writer's text. Thus they would place in a central position the subject and the sex-gender system within which textual production takes place: one might say that they would insist on keeping in view the connections among the "gendered bod[y]" and the social reality of the spinner and the web she produces.[4]

Unlike Philomela, Arachne, and Ariadne who express, however indirectly, their plight and the plight of women artists within the texts they produce, Eliot's Erinna remains silent. It is significant that Eliot's epigram leaves unmentioned the poet Erinna's written work, her poem "The Distaff,"[5] and that, unlike other contemporary representations, she sees spinning as separate from and antithetical to writing (or singing). "The Distaff" itself is the poet's lament at the death of her childhood friend Baucis. In the poem, only fragments of which are extant, Erinna highlights not so much the contradiction between spinning and song as the opposition between different forms of female domesticity—Baucis's marriage, associated with her death, and Erinna's own virginity, associated with growing old at the loom. Both forms of domesticity are enforced rather than chosen: Erinna uses the image of the tortoise to allude to the punitive connection between the woman and her house[6] and presents herself as chained to the loom. This might explain why Eliot conflates these two options, concentrating on the distance between female domesticity and the potential for song. Whereas Erinna herself weaves her poem out of the domestic elements which constitute her life, thereby subverting an opposition that would leave women silent, Eliot associates poetry with the world of men and is unable or unwilling to envision a poetry so intimately tied to domesticity. In her own extensive use of spinning, weaving, and the web as images for the complications and entanglements of human lives, Eliot, characteristically ambivalent, does not align herself with the female origins of this metaphor but associates the weaving and unraveling of plot with its male appropriation.

The ambivalence about the possibility of combining domestic femininity with art may well be what fascinates Eliot about Erinna. Yet there is another element of the story, albeit a legendary one, that pertains to Eliot's allusion to Erinna in chapter 51 of *Daniel Deronda*. If Erinna sits by the spinning wheel gazing sadly, it may be because her mother has chained her there, causing her death. If Eliot sees spinning as contrary to singing, then this unmentioned mother functions as a screen between the daughter-artist and her potential art.[7] Familial relationships need to figure in any analysis of the sex-gender system of women writers and of their representations of women's writing. Eliot's novel focuses on these relationships, using the mother-daughter relationship as a central configuration which shapes the very process of male and female development in the novel, as well as Daniel and Gwendolen's versions of the family romance. In its implications about maternity, procreativity, and creation, the mother-daughter relationship informs, as well, the virtual emergence of the hero and the heroine as creators of plot.

Daniel Deronda, published in 1876 as Eliot's last novel, stands in an interesting relationship to the plot patterns discussed in the last chapter. First, mothers have a much more central position in this text than in most nineteenth-century novels by women. The heroine's developmental course takes its shape not so much against maternal absence as against a complex interaction of maternal speech and silence, mother-daughter connection and separation. Second, although Eliot still features the fantasy of "the man-who-would-understand" as a solution to the problems of female plotting, she constructs it with at once more caution and more far-reaching implications. The novel's double plot—Gwendolen's attempt to construct a life that is different from that of her mother's and other women's, and Daniel's search for his origins and the discovery of his mission—allows us literally to see the fraternal structure at work, as fictional "brother" and "sister" battle over textual ground, over the legitimacy of different versions of the family romance pattern. As "brother" and "sister" neither marry nor sustain a passionate attachment which could lead to the heroine's death, the novel's ending gains an unprecedented openness, suggesting at least the potential for a different resolution. Eliot's text can serve, then, both as a further illustration and affirmation and as a subtle critique of the patterns we have seen in women's novels from Mme. de Lafayette to Austen, Sand, Shelley, the Brontës, and her own earlier fiction. The double plot, moreover, offers a graphic enactment of Eliot's own male and female identification. Gwendolen and Daniel, both occupying (and competing for) the position of the novel's protagonist, enact the battle between Eliot's own self-representation as Marian and as George.[8]

Mothers and Daughters: Breaks and Genealogies

Mirah is the only motherless daughter in *Daniel Deronda*. Her tireless search for her lost mother is hampered not only by the greedy father who has abducted her, but also by her protectors, the Meyricks, who fear that her Jewish mother might disapprove of the new connections she has been able to make. As the Meyrick family, mother and daughters, discuss Mirah's future, their (and the novel's) profound ambivalence about the mother-daughter connection emerges. " 'It may be wicked of me . . . but I cannot help wishing that her mother may not be found. There might be something unpleasant.' 'I don't think it, my dear,' said Mrs. Meyrick. 'I believe Mirah is cut out after the pattern of her mother. And what a joy it would be to have such a daughter brought back again! But a mother's feelings are not worth reckoning, I suppose (she shot a mischievous glance at her own daughters), and a dead mother is worth more than a living one?' " (pp. 410–411). Mrs. Meyrick's speech, facetious as it is, reveals her deeply ironic understanding of the place mothers occupy in their daughters' plots. Maternal presence is indeed problematic, and in the novel's economy, where loss and gain are clearly calculated, it amounts to a liability. Mothers are both poor and powerless. They have nothing to hand on to their daughters that might provide valuable guidance or practical help in the process of constructing a successful life, whether that life is a domestic one or an attempt to break out of the bounds of domesticity. Mirah is indeed better off with a dead mother. She does not need to support her and thus can take her time getting married; she does not have to hear the stories of the mother's disastrous marriage and can thus proceed unquestioningly into matrimony and the conventional female plot. Mirah's "consent to femininity," her acceptance of Daniel's protection and proposal, is facilitated by her mother's absence from the fiction. Free of her mother, and caught between an evil father and a benign though distant brother, Mirah accepts her role as intermediary and instrument between two powerful men, Daniel and Mordecai.

Maternal absence makes possible the maternal idealization that propels Mirah into her allegiance with her brother. Indeed, what she remembers most strongly is the mother's voice calling Ezrah's name. Besides this one verbal memory, the mother remains enclosed in a pre-verbal idealized space. Mirah remembers only the Hebrew songs her mother sang to her when she was a baby, songs she can sing but does not understand—"lisped syllables . . . full of meaning" (p. 423), but indecipherable.

Daniel also felt more strongly connected to his mother when she existed only in his mind, as the object of his own speculations and fictionalizations, than when he meets her in person: "singularly enough that letter which had brought his mother nearer as a living reality had thrown her into more remoteness for his affections" (p. 681). In his fantasies she was like Mirah: "The agitating impression this forsaken girl was making on him stirred a fibre that lay close to his deepest interest in the fates of women—'perhaps my mother was like this one' " (p. 231). In contrast, her revelation carries with it only disappointments. In Daniel's response, her person is subordinated to her revelation: "But to Deronda's nature the moment was cruel: it made the filial yearning of his life a disappointed pilgrimage to a shrine where there were no longer any symbols of sacredness" (p. 723). Regardless of the unusual relation of the Princess to her maternity, no living mother could match the maternal image of deprivation, longing, and love Daniel had constructed, to which he brought his most pious feelings.

When we meet Gwendolen at the novel's inception, she is in the process of making precisely the break from family and genealogy that Mirah never attempts nor ever achieves, the break that Daniel spends his life trying to repair. The initial gambling scene which lets Gwendolen experience the extremes of gain and loss according to the laws of chance is strangely emphasized by the novel's irregular chronology. Although as readers we do not find it out until much later, after receiving the background to Gwendolen's flight to Leubronn, Gwendolen and her family lose all their financial assets just as this scene unfolds in the foreground of the novel. In fact, the initial scene of financial loss is framed by two moments of even deeper loss, both spiritual and monetary: the family's adjustment to the stepfather's death and their move to Offendene, "not the home of Miss Harleth's childhood, or endeared to her by family memories" (p. 50), and the ensuing loss of their small fortune, a loss which threatens to cause another move to even more modest and unfamiliar surroundings. Gambling, for Gwendolen, is an attempt to get the better of an economy in which property is handed down from father to legitimate son, and in which women are dependent and repeatedly dispossessed. As she attempts to enter an economy ruled by chance instead of the debilitating laws of inheritance and property, Gwendolen breaks from the familial ties that have taken her, her mother, and her half sisters close to poverty. If Gwendolen tries to revise the laws of transmission, to take them into her own hands, she quickly learns not only the futility but also the cost of the attempt. In order to pay her debts, she has to sell the necklace given to her by her father. When the necklace is bought back for her by the anonymous friend she knows to be Daniel, Gwendolen begins to understand the complex and inextricable laws of female dependence: her debt now is to Daniel, though it is a debt she is not even allowed openly to acknowledge.[9] Familial ties are reaffirmed and Gwendolen will continue to wear a necklace that binds her more firmly to the processes of transmission in which jewelry is handed down through women but is never theirs to hand down. Like Electra, she hated and feared her stepfather, and she will revere her adoptive brother Daniel, but Gwendolen does not share Electra's loyalty to her father.

The necklace does not mean much to Gwendolen, because she knows little about her father, and her mother has been virtually silent on the subject of both her marriages. Her silence is calculated: "the trials of matrimony were the last theme into which Mrs. Davilow could choose to enter fully with this daughter" (p. 342). In spite of her own marital difficulties, known about by the daughter but never discussed, Mrs. Davilow "could think of welfare in no other shape than marriage" (p. 127). Although Gwendolen, like most nineteenth-century literary heroines, repeatedly affirms that she desires her life to be different, and although she briefly contemplates the freer life of the stage artist, she soon comes to envision this difference within and not outside of the economy of the marriage plot: " 'Mamma managed badly,' was her way of summing up what she had seen of her mother's experience: she herself would manage quite differently" (p. 342). Marriage, never discussed between mother and daughter in any concrete detail, remains the only option in both their imaginations. In fact, the mother's silence about her own life assures

Gwendolen's eventual repetition of it: "For whatever marriage had been for herself, how could she the less desire it for her daughter? The difference her own misfortunes made was, that she never dared to dwell much to Gwendolen on the desirableness of marriage, dreading an answer something like that of the future Madame Roland, when her gentle mother urging the acceptance of a suitor, said, 'Tu seras heureuse, ma chère.' 'Oui, maman, comme toi' "(p. 126).

If marriage becomes the only option for the passionless Gwendolen, it is in large part out of an economic necessity that includes her mother and half sisters. Catherine Gallagher likens Gwendolen's marriage to Grandcourt to a form of prostitution in which Gwendolen is a commodity sold to the same party monthly, in return for the checks which support her mother. Through much of the novel, then, Mrs. Davilow is perceived by Gwendolen as a liability: she neither listens nor talks to her but must continue to support her financially. While the mother spends most of her time, as she puts it "in the dark," wondering what the daughter thinks, feels, and plans, the daughter confides in the male "fraternal figure" she has chosen as a maternal substitute. Daniel, who is not a real brother, provides fraternal nurturance even as he points to a way out of the family of origin which, in this case, is both impoverished and all-female. The best version of the "man-who-would-understand," he will ultimately provide an alternative to marriage as well.

Gwendolen's distance from the unconditionally supportive and adoring Mrs. Davilow is a measure of the self-centeredness and narcissism, the lack of nurturance and caring, with which she attempts to assert her difference from conventional women's plots and natures. She might have found out more about her father had she not silenced her mother's narrative with an unthinking reproach about Mrs. Davilow's subsequent marriage. Gwendolen's self-involvement, her plans and conceptions for her future, her will to a life different from that of other women, and her meager capacity to imagine such a life, her "passion to lead" (p. 69), make her very much like Austen's Emma. The difference in financial security is determining, however, and Gwendolen's imagination is even more limited than Emma's by the circumstances within which it is imprisoned. Even more than Emma, Gwendolen distances herself from the other women in the novel: she has nothing but contempt for her half sisters, breaks with her cousin Anna over Rex, and cannot truly befriend the distinguished Miss Arrowpoint. Her negative observations of matrimony and the lives of the women around her create in Gwendolen a struggle against female identification, and lead her to choose male friends and confidantes. She is horrified, for example, at the thought of working with her mother and sisters on embroidering a table cloth. Gwendolen's struggle for distinction is obviously doomed to failure, however, since the reason she so passionately scrutinizes women's lives is that on some level she knows that her fate is tied to that of the women around her.

That loyalty and friendship to women is not at all a priority for Gwendolen becomes obvious with her broken promise to Lydia Glasher. Their meeting illustrates perhaps most clearly Gwendolen's family romance—her doomed struggle against identification with women and female plots. Lydia represents everything Gwendolen has feared and stayed away from throughout the novel: dependence, abandonment, betrayal. And yet, when she meets Lydia face to face, the parallels between them are striking. Gwendolen looks at Lydia as though she were gazing into a mirror. Not only does she immediately recognize her as a lady and as one who "must once have been exceedingly handsome," but she also hears Lydia underscore the parallel: "You are very attractive, Miss Harleth. But when he first knew me, I too was young" (p. 189). The effect on Gwendolen is one of internalization as Lydia loses her material existence and becomes coextensive with the terror she evokes: "it was as if some ghastly vision had come to her in a dream and said, 'I am a woman's life' "(p. 190). What Gwendolen has not heard directly from her mother about the disappointments of marriage and the betrayals of heterosexual love, she learns unwittingly in this scene from another "maternal" figure, Lydia Glasher.[10]

The lesson is soon and irremediably reinforced with the package of Grandcourt's diamonds which Lydia sends to Gwendolen in what is surely a parody of mother-daughter transmission on the wedding day. Lydia absolutely insists on having the jewels delivered directly to Gwendolen—here again jewels belong to men but are given by women. With the diamonds, Lydia returns to the terms of their previous exchange, underscoring again and more forcefully the ties that bind Gwendolen to her and her fate: "These diamonds, which were once given with ardent love to Lydia Glasher, she passes on to you. You have broken your word to her, that you might possess what was hers." Whatever Gwendolen might desire in her marriage is already preempted by Lydia; whatever she might hope to achieve, could lead only to the end Lydia has already prescribed: "Perhaps you think of being happy, as she once was, and of having beautiful children such as hers, who will thrust hers aside" (p. 406). As Gwendolen reads Lydia's curse, the diamonds fall on the floor, creating endless reflections which Gwendolen still cannot bear consciously to recognize: "She could not see the reflections of herself then: they were like so many women petrified white" (p. 407). Still, the gesture of introjection is endlessly duplicated as "those written words kept repeating themselves in her," representing powerfully the economics underlying the plot of marriage and heterosexual romance. In understanding women's position in heterosexual exchange, Gwendolen has absorbed the "maternal" lesson. The identification with Lydia has already humbled and revised her will to a life different from other women. Contrary to her expectations during her engagement, the course of her married life with Grandcourt will only continue to solidify her recognition of the utter powerlessness she shares with Lydia and with her own mother. When she sees Grandcourt riding by the "Medusa-apparition" (p. 668) Lydia—the woman he once adored and their children—without a gesture of recognition, the distance and the difference between Gwendolen and Lydia has vanished. The secret knowledge they share robs Gwendolen of the possibility of rebellion and makes her position identical to Lydia's in dependence and submission. Speechless and paralyzed, she hysterically acts out Lydia's dependence.

The connection to Lydia, the diamonds they wear in common and all that those diamonds represent, also reinforces the connection between Gwendolen and her mother, a connection she has tried in various ways to break. "Her mother's dulness, which used to irritate her, she was at present inclined to explain as the ordinary result of women's experience. True, she still saw that she would 'manage differently from mamma'; but her management now only meant that she would carry her troubles with spirit, and let none suspect them" (p. 483). As soon as she actually marries Grandcourt and receives the diamonds and their message from Lydia, Gwendolen's lot is inextricably tied to that of the other women she knows and all possibility of escaping from the vicissitudes of female plot disappears. At the end of the novel, of course, Gwendolen will switch places with Lydia and end up living at Gadsmere.

Whereas gambling was meant to provide for Gwendolen a way out of unfair laws of transmission, the example of Lydia Glasher revealed it to be very much enmeshed in those laws. Both in the practice of gambling and in the conventions of inheritance one person's gain is another's loss. This is the lesson Deronda teaches Gwendolen, a lesson which becomes the source of her guilt and her atonement. On her wedding day Gwendolen "had wrought herself up to much the same condition as that in which she' stood at the gambling-table when Deronda was looking at her, and she began to lose" (p. 401). And after Grandcourt's death she tells Deronda, "I ought not to have married. . . . I wronged someone else. I broke my promise . . . I wanted to make my gain out of another's loss—you remember?—it was like roulette—and the money burnt into me" (p. 757). It is precisely this mathematical equation, the calculation of gains and losses and its moral implications, which cements the strong bond between Gwendolen and Daniel. In an easy adoption of the Freudian family romance pattern, both connect Lydia with Daniel's unknown mother and the fate of Lydia's children with that of the supposedly illegitimate and disinherited Daniel: "immediately the image of this Mrs. Glasher became painfully associated with his own hidden birth" (p. 489). If Gwendolen tries, throughout the novel, to explain herself to Daniel, it is at least in part an attempt to explain her action to Lydia's son and to ask his forgiveness.

In fact, of course, Daniel is not illegitimate. His mother is no more an adultress like Lydia than she is lost and powerless like Mirah. Like Lydia's children, however, Daniel too has in some way been robbed of his inheritance (not financial but spiritual) by his mother's actions. Although

Daniel's mother is unique among the women in the novel, her story, like the story of Erinna which introduces it, constitutes a crucial determining revelation about women's plots, female art, and their relation to maternity. Gwendolen never sees Daniel's mother and does not hear her narrative, but the Princess's story does represent one exceptional woman's attempt to rescript the female plot of daughterhood, marriage, and motherhood in which Gwendolen is caught. By implication, then, she serves as another maternal figure whose lesson is present albeit, for Gwendolen, unspoken.

There are, in fact, a number of parallels between Gwendolen and the Princess: their common interest in acting and singing as a possible alternative to the marriage plot (an interest Gwendolen, because of her lack of talent, cannot pursue, however); the distance they wish to establish from their past; their exceptional beauty, will, and imagination. When the Princess shows Daniel a miniature portrait of herself in her youth, she might, with some differences, be describing Gwendolen: "Had I not a rightful claim to be something more than a mere daughter and mother? The voice and the genius matched the face. Whatever else was wrong, acknowledge that I had a right to be an artist, though my father's will was against it. My nature gave me charter" (p. 728). The differences lie primarily in their education. Unlike Gwendolen who is educated by her mother to enter the marriage plot and lacks the ability truly to imagine alternatives, the Princess, whose mother was dead, was caught between a repressive father and an aunt whose example and whose training enabled her to embark upon an artistic career. If both women possessed a will to difference and tried, to varying degrees, to live it out, the disappointing result can be seen in the connection Daniel establishes between them. For him both represent "what was amiss in the world along with the concealments which he had felt as a hardship in his own life" (p. 685).

Alcharisi is the image of the female artist in the novel, of the demands, sacrifices, and contradictions Eliot inscribes into this quasi-autobiographical portrait.[11] Introduced by the epigram about Erinna and narrated in truncated and painful fashion to the son she could not see as anything other than an obstacle and a hindrance to her ambitions, the Alcharisi story is the story of the woman who would not be trapped in the marriage plot, the story of the woman who would not be domestic or maternal. It is a mother's story, finally articulated in the novel, and it contains all the frustration, pain, and rage Gwendolen so fears to encounter in the words of her own mother. Unlike Lydia's and Mrs. Davilow's stories, and as a complement to them, it is not a story of female suffering from male betrayal. Alcharisi is neither object nor victim; she is, she tries to be, the author of her own fate and Daniel's, to the point of leaving her son, of changing his patronym and his religion, and thereby freeing herself to "live out the life that was in me" without being "hampered with other lives" (p. 688). The theme that dominates her narrative is the desire for freedom from bondage—both the bondage of Judaism and the bondage of femininity. Both are enforced by a hated father who controls her years after his death, determining her life in a way that challenges and ultimately perhaps denies the authority she so desperately seeks. Freedom for Alcharisi is freedom from affection and love which, to her, are no more than forms of subjection: "I had not much affection to give you. I did not want affection. I had been stifled with it" (p. 688). Her story articulates a family romance more classically Freudian than other female versions—a romance which demands freedom from a family of origin and from familial bonds altogether.

In the economy of Eliot's novel, the life of the artist—synonymous with the ability to chart her own plot—is clearly and unequivocally incompatible with maternity. In her famous speech to Daniel, Alcharisi expresses the feelings which necessitate her ultimate removal from the novel, what Neil Hertz calls her "exorcism":[12] "Every woman is supposed to have the same set of motives, or else to be a monster. I am not a monster, but I have not felt exactly what other women feel—or say they feel, for fear of being thought unlike others. When you reproach me in your heart for sending you away from me, you mean that I ought to say I felt about you as other women say they feel about their children. I did *not* feel that. I was glad to be freed from you" (p. 691). Her sense of her freedom and her creativity necessitate a violent break from those with whom she is biologically and psychologically connected. Thus, her very meeting with Daniel is marked by her refusal of the mirroring Daniel longs for: " 'I am your mother. But you can have no love for me.' 'I have thought of you more than any other being in the world.' . . . 'I am not like what you thought I was' "(p. 687). We have already seen, of course, that she is neither like Mirah nor like Lydia.

When Neil Hertz discusses Alcharisi in relation to the author/reader who stands both outside and inside the text, he rightly wonders why the most genuine female artist in Eliot's work must be made a scapegoat and cast out of the novel. He concludes that she represents the pre-oedipal mother Daniel must leave when he enters the symbolic order dominated by Mordecai and his Jewish grandfather, emblematized by his acquisition of the ancestral trunk filled with his familial and national inheritance. More importantly, as the mother, she represents that "double darkness," that "abject," in Kristeva's terms, that "not yet object" who maintains the tenuousness of the not yet subject.[13] Daniel and the author herself can establish the stability of their subject position only by casting out the maternal figure, by refusing all identification with the one who threatens to blur boundaries and distinctions. Hertz's insight into the conflation of the "end of the line" moment with maternity is brilliant here, but needs, I feel, to be supplemented with some reflections about the relation of this figure to another authorial surrogate and fictional protagonist, Gwendolen.

What are the implications of the banishment and punishment of Alcharisi for Gwendolen's plot? For Gwendolen, as we have seen, Alcharisi completes the spectrum of maternal examples, from the meek, loving, and submissive Mrs. Meyrick to the proud, rebellious, and rejecting singer Alcharisi. Yet, unlike Daniel, Gwendolen has no access to Alcharisi's lesson. The consolidation of his subjectivity, made possible by his encounter with his lost mother and his knowledge of her story, is unavailable to Gwendolen. Their failure to meet and Gwendolen's lack of information perpetuate the feared connection between Daniel's mother and Lydia, and continue to cast Gwendolen not as a reflection of the Princess but as her hated antagonist. In spite of the important parallels between them, Eliot chooses to deprive Gwendolen of knowledge of a story which is of crucial importance to the novel's author and reader, thereby affirming even more definitively the novel's distance from Alcharisi's particular solution to the predicament of the female plot. The independent life Gwendolen briefly contemplates is not an option for her; she is not even allowed to envision it concretely by being privy to the Princess's version of that life. The figure of Mirah, moreover, represents a clear revision of the Alcharisi story, one that is acceptable to and rewarded in the novel. "I think her nature is not given to make great claims" (p. 728), Daniel affirms, describing Mirah's distaste for the stage performances his mother loved, and her love for the Jewish tradition his mother rejected.[14]

Gwendolen, then, is cut off from all the maternal figures in the novel: from her own mother by silence, miscommunication, and her will to difference, from Lydia by fear and shame, from Alcharisi by authorial decree. Gwendolen's inability to sympathize and identify with the mothers causes her violent rejection of the plots in which they are enmeshed. In psychological terms, she affirms boundaries through distance and separation and struggles against identification. This attempted break with female plot, however, only succeeds in enmeshing her more firmly within it. Not only does Gwendolen remain in the position of the child, always seeking nurturance and never able to give it,[15] but she also comes to live out the life of powerlessness and dependency she so firmly tries to reject. When she is finally able to understand what she calls her mother's "dullness," her education is almost complete. In fact, the goal of her education in the novel is precisely the recognition that "I think I am almost getting fond of the old things now that they are gone" (p. 508). Although Gwendolen returns home after Grandcourt's death, and although she eventually comes to appreciate her mother's presence more than anything else and is finally able to sympathize with her mother, Gwendolen's relation to Mrs. Davilow remains, at the end of the novel, as silent as it was before her marriage. Sobbing and crying instead of speaking, she retains the "determination to be silent about all the facts of her married life and its close" (p. 825). Again, only hysterical attacks allow the body to speak what the mouth will not utter. The knowledge and comfort mother and daughter share stand outside the confines of narrative and the symbolic, emerging only in moments like that of the night following Gwendolen's engagement when, full of dread, she is incapable of sleeping alone and asks to sleep with Mrs. Davilow: "She could bear it no longer and cried: 'Mamma.' 'Yes, dear,' said Mrs. Davilow, immediately, in a wakeful voice. 'Let me come to you'" (p. 356).[16] At the end of the novel, mother and daughter, like Demeter and Persephone, are reunited in physical closeness, even while they perpetuate a culture-wide silence about the female plot they have shared: "What wretchedness her child had perhaps gone through, which yet must remain as it always had been, locked away from their mutual speech" (p. 829). It is questionable therefore whether their reunion at the end constitutes the same kind of healing and repair that Persephone's return does, or whether it does not on one level perpetuate the breech between them while repairing it on another.

In the course of her development, Gwendolen, like Electra, chooses masculine instead of feminine identification, masculine instead of feminine power, masculine instead of feminine nurturance. In exploring the parameters of these choices, Eliot reevaluates the "female family romance" in which the mother is displaced by the "man-who-would-understand." But when the "brother" leaves to establish his own familial line and to claim his patriarchal heritage, Gwendolen ultimately affirms a unique physical and erotic, albeit nonverbal, bond with her mother. The novel does not explore the implications of this outcome.

The Brother Tongue

I have been discussing the families in *Daniel Deronda* primarily as mother-daughter families. The fathers are either absent or of relatively little import for the mother-daughter interactions.[17] Sons or brothers do, however, occupy a central place, competing with the mother for the primacy of affection and desire in the daughter's life. For Mirah, the father is identified with evil, while mother and brother together offer visions of solace and love: "That seems like heaven, to have a mother and brother who talk in that way" (p. 521). Her mother's voice, as I mentioned above, is primarily remembered as she calls the brother's name, "Ezrah." The brother's voice, his talk about their common past, is the discourse Mirah most fervently yearns for. We appreciate the strength of brother-sister bonding through its repetition as a paradigm in the novel: Rex, Hans, and, to a degree, Mordecai provide the solace of the brother tongue, suggesting that Lydia's son may do the same for his sisters. Anna is ready to give up her life for Rex, and the Meyrick sisters live a life that revolves around Hans.

Gwendolen has no brother, of course, and fails to understand the feelings of passionate affection that mark Anna's bond with Rex. Her own relationship to men is colored by the strong repulsion she felt toward her stepfather and by her lack of knowledge about her father. Her uncle never gains importance in her affective life. When Gwendolen marries Grandcourt, she does, as Dianne Sadoff has demonstrated, enter into a scene of oedipal seduction. Grandcourt and Lydia have a young child, evidence of recent sexual intercourse between them. Gwendolen hopes to be able to "manage" Grandcourt, yet the financial dependence that ties her to him, as well as his vast sexual experience and rich past make their relationship not one of equals, but one of repressive "father" and rebellious "daughter."

Cut off from her mother's body as well as from her speech and tied to a cold, unsympathetic "father" whom she must please and obey, Gwendolen comes to seek the solace offered by the brother, "the man-who-would-understand." She does not choose Rex, who loves her sexually and to whom she is actually related, but Daniel Deronda, who is inaccessible enough not to threaten the "fierce maidenhood" she maintains even after her marriage. As she tries to escape from Grandcourt to Deronda, Gwen-dolen plays out the conflict between paternal authority and fraternal nurturance that is central to the female family romance plot. Her hope is to replace her own feelings of rage, evoked by her powerlessness in relation to Grandcourt, with the broad-based affection taught by Deronda. With the strange and powerful connection that develops between Daniel and Gwendolen, Eliot envisions a different kind of heterosexual bonding, one that stands somewhere between the analytic relationship—Breuer and Anna O., Freud and Dora—and the infantile brother-sister eroticism we found in the last chapter. "He took one of her hands and clasped it as if they were going to walk together like two children. . . . That grasp was an entirely new experience to Gwendolen: she had never before had from any man a sign of tenderness which her own being had needed" (p. 755).[18] Standing outside of convention, their relationship is not only continually misinterpreted by others, but equally tenuous and incomprehensible to the two of them. Daniel always fears that he is promising more than he can intend; Gwendolen always wonders what his promises mean. As they work out the limits of mutual expectations, they could be said to be perfecting the relationship between analyst and analysand, with Daniel being as little aware of the depths of his involvement and attraction as Breuer is before he flees from Anna. In Eliot's work, this relationship is closest to the confessional pastoral bond between Janet and the Reverend Tryon in Eliot's *Janet's Repentance*, but Daniel is not a minister and he and Gwendolen do not eventually marry.

In the novel Daniel, like Tryon, represents the power and the seduction of what might be called a "brother tongue," a tender form of discourse which revises both the coldness of paternal authority and the rage or anxiety underlying maternal silence. It is Daniel who buys back Gwen-dolen's necklace, affirming the value of genealogy over exchange, of family over independence. It is through Daniel that Gwendolen comes to appreciate her need for affection and for her mother as a source of nurturance. Their discourse together is the discourse of confession, soon to become the discourse of analysis; Gwendolen bears her soul and Daniel listens, accepts, forgives, and nurtures better than any mother can.[19]

Daniel's own history describes perfectly the Freudian family romance in its most successful form. He grows up as an orphan, cared for by the loving and powerful Hugo Mallinger. In possession of the means and the freedom to explore various possible lives, he ends up choosing freely the one that is identical with his actual heritage, Judaism, but he does not find out about his heritage until after he has already chosen it himself. His mother reappears in his life, and although she disappoints his need for mirroring, she makes no demands that might limit his development. When he marries, he marries the woman who is like the mother he desired, rather than the mother he had. The combination of these circumstances create a man whose sympathies are vast, whose values are admirable and who is clearly the figure in this novel most capable of appropriating and fulfilling the necessary and absent function of "mothering."

Daniel's encounter with his mother constitutes perhaps the best illustration of Daniel's "brother tongue." Here he is more maternal, more feminine than the Princess: "All the woman lacking in her was present in him" (p. 723). Rather than being angry at her abandonment of him and at her concealment of his Jewish heritage, Daniel comforts her for her pain, forgives her and, most important, mediates between her rebellious point of view and her father's traditional one. He even justifies the rightness of his Christian education by stating that it will enable him to gain the breadth of vision to which he has always aspired. In this encounter, Daniel and the Princess reverse roles: her maternity is harsh, angry, self-absorbed; his is generous, self-less, forgiving.[20]

Daniel functions as "mother" in more literal ways as well. He saves both Mirah and Gwendolen from drowning, enabling them to be reborn out of river and sea, ready to face life in ways he suggests to them. For Mirah, he provides the physical care she needs to construct the life she has already earned morally. For Gwendolen he provides the moral education her own mother had not been able to give: he teaches her to consider others and to look beyond her own needs. He even teaches her eventually to notice him, to engage in a discourse which is more reciprocal than the confessionals they shared in the beginning.

The brother tongue is nurturing, sympathetic, accepting, and undemanding. As such it is much like the voice of Eliot's narrator, as Dianne Sadoff suggests, contrasting the sympathetic Daniel with the punitive Tom Tulliver (*Monsters of Affection*, p. 115). The brother tongue controls the voice and the moral topography of the novel. Not only is Daniel featured in the novel's title to the utter exclusion of Gwendolen, but he also owns the point of view of the novel's opening. It is through *his* eyes that the reader observes Gwendolen, and we are, in *his* mind, analyzing the disquieting effects she has on him: "Was she beautiful or not beautiful?" (p. 35).[21] His question literally engenders the fiction, and the quality of his perspective colors the rest of the narrative. We could say that Daniel both gives birth to the novel and nurtures it through its course.[22]

Yet unlike in the other novels that enact the female family romance pattern I have been discussing, Gwendolen and Daniel do not marry. Their relationship becomes more mutual at the end of the novel, but it never becomes passionate, never explicitly sexual. Although Gwendolen harbors hopes of marrying Daniel, unable to envision her life without him, she must learn, like a "daughter" or "sister," to incorporate his presence as a part of her emergent self. More and more, they affirm the fraternal quality of the relationship, clasping hands like little children. Yet unlike Maggie and Tom's, their clasped hands lead to life apart, not to death together. At the end of the novel, Gwendolen's life has an openness unprecedented in female plots: she is neither married, nor drowned, nor mad. Her future is open, calling into question even the possibility that marriage to the "brother," to the "man-who-would-understand," could, in its practice, ever be a marriage of equals. There certainly are no *fictional* precedents for such a marriage. Unlike Monsieur Paul in Charlotte Brontë's *Villette*, who must die in order to protect the *potential* of an egalitarian marriage, Daniel survives and the novel holds out no hope for a union of equals. Instead, Daniel marries the woman who makes no claims for herself and who is his fantasied mother. Gwendolen is able to accept the marriage. With the letter she sends him, she shows that she has indeed introjected some of his generosity and sympathy, that she has indeed learned to think of others more than of herself, and that she will not be "the victim of his happiness" (p. 877): "I only thought of myself, and I made you grieve. It hurts me now to think of your grief. You must not grieve any more for me. It is better—it shall be better with me because I have known you" (p. 882). With this letter, Daniel ceases to be a parent and truly becomes her "brother." On the other hand, one could also say, as Ellen Rosenman does, that with the letter she has learned to *mimic* the language of patriarchy, the "brother tongue."

"Brother" and "sister" undergo parallel developments in the course of the text, vying over fictional space and value. But the novel is profoundly unbalanced. If, as Daniel believes, life is like a roulette game, the novel itself conforms to the same economy, and Daniel's gain is Gwendolen's loss. Their division of labor falls into the most conventional categories: she fumbles, lost, while he always knows; she is the "spoiled child" who must be educated, while he becomes the agent of that education; she is guilty, while he has the power to absolve her; she is incapable of creating or procreating, while he creates her; and even when they become "equals," she returns home, while he goes off to found a new civilization. In addition, the values of selflessness that Daniel represents and that he wants to teach Gwendolen have radically different gender implications in the context of the culture represented in this novel. For Daniel, selflessness signifies a gain in vision and receptivity. For Gwendolen, conversely, selflessness amounts to an acceptance of cultural constraints on women's development.[23] It can take the form only of the Midrash tale Mordecai tells and Mirah interprets—of a woman's self-annihilation for the man she loves, either, as Mordecai sees it, out of love, or, as Mirah argues, out of the thirst for power. Either motivation leaves her dead, however; the only effect she can have is posthumous.[24] As Carol Gilligan has argued, selflessness may well be a lower moral stage for women than for men; for women, the goal of moral development is not to learn to be selfless, which is what the culture dictates for women anyway, but to learn to consider themselves in relation to others.[25] Eliot's novel does not perceive this distinction, however. The second half of the novel comes, more and more, to contain Daniel's story, as Gwendolen's selfishness and selfhood diminish.[26] In adopting the voice and the value structure of the brother tongue, the novel is able to create an artistic consciousness of tremendous suppleness, breadth, and generosity. But that consciousness is masculine, albeit "maternal," and its cost is a parallel female creativity.[27] The novel's inability to chart a creativity for women, moreover, calls into question its openendedness, since it contains no hint, no model for the shape Gwendolen's life might take in the future.

Childbirth without Pain: New Patterns of Transmission

When Grandcourt dies and his will is opened, everyone speculates about whether Gwendolen is pregnant, for it seems logical that after some months of marriage a young wife might be. We know, however, that Gwendolen has been living in dread of pregnancy: "Some unhappy wives are soothed by the possibility that they may become mothers; but Gwendolen felt that to desire a child for herself would have been a consenting to the completion of the injury she had been guilty of" (p. 736). Gwendolen not only deeply fears sexuality, as her repulsion of Rex and her hysterical attack on her wedding night demonstrate,[28] but she is also reduced to dread lest she should become a mother. "It was not the image of a new sweetly-budding life that came as a vision of deliverance from the monotony of distaste: it was an image of another sort" (p. 736). The images that actually haunt Gwendolen are images of vengeance, violence, and death. She comes to fear her own feelings of anger, to fear that her inner rage has usurped all creative force, resulting in the creation of death rather than life. Her dread of pregnancy clearly goes deeper than the desire to protect Lydia's son's inheritance.

For Gwendolen, the conjunction between angry feelings and violent action, resulting in the destruction of life, seems as inevitable as it is connected to the act of nurturing and maternity.[29] Violence is everywhere around and inside her, ready to erupt, as it did when she strangled her sister's canary as a child. I would argue that Gwendolen's fear of sexuality and pregnancy is represented by the images of enclosed boxes and cabinets, which contain the potential of violent eruption. Her father's emeralds and Grandcourt's diamonds are both delivered in boxes contain-

ing letters which evoke strong and violent emotions. The dagger with
which she contemplates killing Grandcourt is locked up in a cabinet whose
key she keeps, loses, and tries to restore, fearing and desiring the violence
that might erupt out of *her* if *it* were opened. Even the Princess is afraid of
all that is contained in the trunk she is transmitting from her father to her
son. All letters in the novel, except Gwendolen's last letter to Daniel, carry
news of loss, separation, and doom.

The range of emotions evoked by the moments during which such
messages are received is already represented during an early scene, when
Gwendolen, arriving at Offendene, first notices a small cabinet which,
when opened, "disclosed the picture of an upturned dead face, from which
an obscure figure seemed to be fleeing with outstretched arms"(p. 56).
Disturbed, Gwendolen is anxious to lock this cabinet once and for all, but it
comes back to haunt her violently when she stands on stage ready to act
Shakespeare's Hermione. When the panel opens in the midst of the tableau, Gwendolen cannot disguise her terror. For here the underside of
Hermione emerges. As Gwendolen attempts to portray the lost and mis-
treated mother, returned from the dead to forgive the betrayals per-
petrated upon her, she suddenly catches a glimpse of the murderous rage
that may be concealed beneath that role. In a reversal of maternal care, the
figure on the panel flees with outstretched arms from the terrifying dead
face, as Gwendolen will be tempted to flee from Grandcourt's dead face,
refusing to rescue him.[30]

Alcharisi demystifies the novel's conjunction between female anger and
destructive power. Surprisingly, Alcharisi's rage against her father and his
imprisoning force, and against the child who only hampered her progress,
does not have the murderous results all other characters, especially Gwendolen, desperately dread. In fact, her anger and frustration lead her to a
solution which she believes to be beneficial to her child. To her, if their
disconnection is violent it is only figuratively so. But Gwendolen, who
does not know about Daniel's mother, is unable to envision this kind of
resolution. The novel itself also punishes Alcharisi as an unnatural, power-
hungry, unnurturing mother, unable to recognize here a possibly non-
destructive resolution to female anger.

The unquestioned connection between enclosure and rage, disclosure
and death precludes any possibility of Gwendolen as mother. I would
argue that the anger and frustration she knows to have been her mother's
experience, the rage transmitted by Lydia with the jewels, and her fear of
her own uncontrollable rage, combined with her lack of access to Alcharisi's different resolution of female anger, create the firm connection for
Gwendolen between maternity and death we have encountered before.
When she tells Daniel of the boating accident, she insists that in seeing
Grandcourt's dead face, she sees her own creation: "I saw my wish outside
me" (p. 761). *Daniel Deronda* is haunted by the equation between heterosexual procreation through female birth and monstrosity, devastation, destruction. The novel's heroine can envision neither sexuality nor maternity;

she retains the "fierce maidenhood" which distinguished her as the young girl who could not imagine why women would fall in love with men. The attraction to Deronda may lie precisely in his sexual unavailability, in Mirah's prior claim. Similarly, the attraction of Grandcourt is his lack of passion; clearly, he is interested in power rather than love.[31]

By refusing pregnancy and maternity, Gwendolen, like Alcharisi, refuses to "consent to femininity," to perpetuate a system of transmission in which women gain nothing. As Gillian Beer puts it, outlining women's role in the process of natural selection as Darwin and other late nineteenth-century thinkers envisioned it, "Her triumph, therefore, must be her barrenness"(*Darwin's Plots*, p. 220).

As we have seen, however, procreativity and transmission are not absent from the novel. Like weaving, they have been appropriated and reenvisioned by the male characters.[32] While Deronda plays a maternal role in relation to Mirah and Gwendolen, Mordecai goes further by attempting to redefine the process of reproduction altogether. In a direct echo of Gwendolen's terrifying creation of death ("I saw my vision outside me") Mordecai creates the child who will liberate his "spiritual travail from oblivion, and give it an abiding place in the best heritage of his people" (p. 531). Mordecai's creation of his heir is at once reproductive and visionary: "He yearned with a poet's yearning for the wide sky, the far-reaching vista of bridges, the tender and fluctuating lights on the water which seems to breathe with a life that can shiver and mourn, be comforted and rejoice" (p. 537). A benign and rewarded Frankenstein, Mordecai succeeds, without the pain and the risks of pregnancy and birth, to create the being he has envisioned in his mind: "Obstacles, incongruities, all melted into the sense of completion with which his soul was flooded by this outward satisfaction of his longing. His exultation was not widely different from that of the experimenter, bending over the first stirrings of change that correspond to what in the fervor of concentrated prevision his thought has foreshadowed. The prefigured friend had come from the golden background, and had signalled to him: this actually was: the rest was to be" (p. 550). When Daniel disembarks, Mordecai surprises him by saying that he had been expecting him for five years, thereby announcing to him the new identity, that of Mordecai's creation and double, he is to assume. For Daniel is now "my (Mordecai's) new self—who will live when this breath is all breathed out."[33] Whereas Gwendolen's desire can only be fulfilled by death and whereas plotting, for her, means killing, for Mordecai dream and desire are realized by life and procreation.

The mysterious spiritual union between Daniel and Mordecai, a kind of birth as well as a kind of brotherly marriage, rests on the Cabalistic doctrine of the transubstantiation of souls, a revision of the process of transmission through women and heterosexual marriage: "You will be my life: it will be planted afresh; it will grow. You shall take the inheritance. . . . You have risen within me like a thought not fully spelled: my soul is shaken before the words are all there" (p. 557–59).

As (male) souls are reborn in new bodies, perfecting and purifying themselves evermore, the role of women is to create the bodies that can house these ever more perfect souls. Whereas women like Alcharisi and Gwendolen refuse to participate in the legitimate transmission of an intolerable system, men like Deronda and Mordecai appropriate the important and valued aspects of the process of transmission. They do so outside of law and outside of convention, but supported by a powerful spiritual and religious tradition. And as they do so, we begin to wonder about the implications of this burst of male procreativity for the women in the novel, and for the novel itself. The novel poses the question of femininity as a hysterical "spectacle" of procreation, only to subsume and resolve it by means of an elaborate gesture of masculine appropriation. As the masculine subject comes to control the processes of transmission, the text can relinquish some of the dread it evinces in its scenes of hysteria.

Endings and Beginnings

"Men can do nothing without the make-believe of a beginning" (p. 35), asserts the epigram of the novel's first chapter. As Gillian Beer says, "the paragraph initiates the novel by questioning the concept of beginning even as it enacts it" (*Darwin's Plots*, p. 188). And the novel, of course, begins not at the "beginning" but *in medias res*. Unique in her novels, Eliot's reversal of chronology in *Daniel Deronda* has elicited copious critical exploration. Its effects are crucial in this text, for this particular formal choice is part of a much vaster questioning of origins and endings, genealogy, narrative sequence, chronology, generation, cause and effect. The illusion of beginning is acted out not only in this scene, but in Daniel's story as a whole. Obsessed with his origins, he finds them only after already creating them himself, almost as an effect of that self-creation and not as its cause.[34] Even as Daniel and the novel's other characters try to escape from the determining forces of descent, they find themselves mysteriously and irremediably caught within those forces. Again and again, the novel poses the question of past and future, raises the possibility of novelty and rupture, without actually suggesting how such breaks might be effected. Although the novel plays with the possibilities of myriad selves for each character, identity is assigned and not self-created: Alcharisi refuses to be a mother and a Jewish woman and ends up as the progenitor of a large family; Daniel is raised as an English gentleman only to take on the Jewish destiny of his birth; Gwendolen fights for a different life, only to reproduce the plot of her mother and to return home at the end of the novel. All of this in spite of a narrative structure shaped by sudden turns, chance events, unpredictable reversals, losses of fortune, letters from lost mothers, chance encounters in synagogues and bookshops, drownings and rescues. At every turn, the novel seems to ask: Is change possible? What is the relationship of a temporality structured by unpredictability both to the fixity of identity and to the possibility of change?[35]

Although these questions are never answered definitively, the novel's ending does at least suggest the possibility of the new beginning for which the plot desperately calls. In *Daniel Deronda*, as George Levine has pointed out, "the world of the realistic novel is irrecoverably in fragments—the church turned stable, the American civil war commenting on Gwendolen's egoistic concerns, family ties shattered, English culture a mere facade of wealth and aristocracy" (p. 18). Novelty cannot be absolute, but it could, the novel suggests, emerge out of the individual and collective struggle with the past, with tradition and inheritance. As Mirah and Daniel marry, they receive new jewels containing no history of female suffering. The locket given by the Mallingers "to the bride of our dear Daniel Deronda" and the watch sent by the Klesmers with an inscription the novel does not reveal, constitute the beginnings of this new inheritance. The novel's only legitimate heir, the "unmistakably English," "mealy-complexioned" Grandcourt is dead, and the only representatives of the next generation are his illegitimate children and the upwardly mobile children of Ezrah Cohen. The Arrowpoint fortune will be inherited by the children of the Jewish artist Klesmer. Rex did not go overseas to participate in England's colonial ambitions. Instead, Daniel and Mirah, conveniently freed of the sick Mordecai, will go to Palestine in a journey the novel cannot narrate, but which could infuse the old world with new blood and new values.[36] Their journey, though not yet begun at the end of the novel, does signal change for Europe and for the Jews (inasmuch as Jews are represented as European), if not for woman's place in the marriage plot. For women, however, homelessness is not resolved; property is still the issue. While Gwendolen, her mother, and sisters live in the inferior Gadsmere, Daniel is given "the East" to explore and inhabit. The novel's ending, like the conversation at the "Hand and Banner," leaves open the question whether this change necessarily means progress. When Mordecai, citing *The Book of Ruth*, assures Daniel that "Whither thou goest, Daniel, I shall go. Is it not begun?" we wonder at the implications of a reversal in which the parent follows the child. Even more importantly, however, we note that in this revision a woman's story of parent-child reunion has been appropriated by a man.

Gwendolen, unlike a number of other nineteenth-century fictional heroines, is neither married nor dead at the end of the novel.[37] Instead, she asserts to her mother: "I shall live. I mean to live. . . . I shall be better" (p. 879). Her education is not finished, and her future life is not in any way foreseeable. Her determination to live is expressed in hysterical shrieks in the middle of the night. Her struggle with herself and with the vicissitudes of female plot is not over. Yet Gwendolen, back with her mother and sisters, does write to Daniel, in her own voice, her tenuous and provisional construction of present, future, and past: "It is better—it shall be better with me because I have known you" (p. 882). Her hesitant foray into the future tense in this sentence is the only promise the novel gives us for its heroine, and as I mentioned above, it could be mimicry, and what looks like novelty could be stagnation. The reunion between mother and daughter is, after all, but a consolation for the loss of Daniel. The novel's actual ending, which is much more conventional, is appropriated, in what has become a typical pattern by the image of the dead Mordecai.

Of all the novel's characters, it is Gwendolen who has changed most profoundly, who has felt most deeply, and who retains the capacity to change still more. It is she who has struggled most tenaciously with emotions for whose existence women's education does not prepare them, but whose intensity is shared by all those who are trapped in the female plot. Her anger, her dread of its eruption, the hysterical outbursts which alone help her control it (albeit through self-punishment), her guilt and atonement, the sympathy she learns to feel once the anger is somewhat controlled, form the emotional core of the novel. The vicissitudes of these emotions, the inner dialogue Gwendolen carries out, predicted in the novel's epigram, "Let thy chief terror be of thine own soul," punctuate her progress through the marriage plot. Her inner life gives an unprecedented richness and depth to the story of her moral development. As Gillian Beer suggests, her fear becomes a form of consciousness, in Daniel's terms "a safeguard" and "a faculty, like vision" that can be used. What Daniel, in his proto-analytic function, proposes to her is that she be the subject of her dread and not its object. As such, Gwendolen realizes that although she did not kill Grandcourt, her rage did affect the event of his drowning. She did, in her imagination, create Grandcourt's dead face.[38]

If the novel posits a new plot for women, it is a plot that is structured not by the outward unpredictabilities of chance events, but by the drama of emotions women—mothers and daughters—feel and cannot express in the plots and stories they have been handing down to one another through the generations. The challenge Eliot leaves to the novel of the future, a challenge to which her own novel only begins to respond, is to find a plot that, instead of repressing those feelings, will contain, acknowledge, and perhaps legitimate them. Such a narrative form would have to go beyond the confines of the brother tongue; it would have to contain the possibility of a female origin associated with life rather than death. Such a narrative would have to begin and end with the mother more than as a solace for the loss of the brother/lover. How such plots could emerge from the patterns of the realist novel, female modernism begins to ask.

Daniel Deronda, however, leaves us with the vision of an artistic sensibility that is freed from gender paradigms through a feminized male authorial persona.[39] The contradiction Eliot presents through the figure of Erinna— of a femininity trapped in domesticity and a creativity connected to deeds wrought outside the home—is provisionally resolved in the novel. The male artist is enriched with the values of home, as he weaves the plots in which both men and women will become entangled. But the future fate of his female counterpart is left uncharted.[40]

II

Modernism and the Maternal

3

THE DARKEST PLOTS

NARRATION AND COMPULSORY HETEROSEXUALITY

> The turning-away from her mother is an extremely important step in the course of a little girl's development.
>
> —Sigmund Freud

> Again if one is a woman one is often surprised by a sudden splitting off of consciousness, say in walking down Whitehall, when from being the natural inheritor of that civilization, she becomes, on the contrary, outside of it, alien and critical.
>
> —Virginia Woolf

> I am inclined to believe there is no such thing as repetition.
>
> —Gertrude Stein

Parables of Exclusion

In 1928, at the request of one of the women's colleges at Cambridge, Virginia Woolf gave the talks on women and fiction that later became *A Room of One's Own*, perhaps the most famous essay in feminist literary theory. Woolf's tone in this text is as modest as her argument is tentative: "All I could do was to offer you an opinion upon one minor point—a woman must have money and a room of her own if she is to write fiction. . . . I have shirked the duty of coming to a conclusion upon these two questions—women and fiction remain . . . unsolved problems."[1] At most, Woolf insists, she can show us how she arrives at her "opinion," thereby offering us not an essay but a narrative about her own involvement in the question of women's relation to fiction. The subject of that narrative, the speaking "I," moreover, is not Virginia Woolf, but "only a convenient term for somebody who has no real being" (p. 4).

Beginning with a walk through Oxbridge University, her trajectory is full of interruptions and false turns, one of which provides a convenient starting point for my own analysis of gender, writing, and modernism. Near the beginning, totally focused on her thoughts, Woolf finds herself walking across a college lawn. "Instantly," she tells us, "a man's figure rose to intercept me. Nor did I at first understand that the gesticulations of a curious-looking object, In a cut-away coat and evening shirt, were aimed at me. His face expressed horror and indignation. Instinct rather than reason came to my help; he was a Beadle; I was a woman. This was the turf; there was the path. Only the Fellows and Scholars are allowed here; the gravel is the place for me" (p. 6).[2] Woolf's narrator does not complain about her exclusion from the turf here—the only harm done, she remarks ironically, is that the Beadle's intervention caused her to forget her thought. When the exclusion is repeated, however, this time at the door of the library, the narrator reacts more directly—"Never will I ask for hospitality again, I vowed, as I descended the steps in anger" (p. 8). Resolved nevertheless to admire the famous buildings from the outside, the narrator resumes her meditation on her status as a woman writer and scholar, on what it means to tell the story of women's lives *as a woman*. Woolf's parable of interruption, exclusion, and writing—her marginal position in Oxbridge—illuminates the locus of femininity and women's discourse at the particular moment of her narration, the 1920s.

A Room of One's Own, like a number of women's *Künstlerromane* of the twenties, defines the liminal discourse of a female artist who stands both inside and outside of the library, both inside and outside of the structures of tradition, representation, and the symbolic. They do so by means of a particularly female and very private thematics—the mother-daughter relationship. This chapter analyzes this distinctive mapping of a territory through readings of Colette's *Break of Day (La Naissance du jour)*, Woolf's *To the Lighthouse*, and Edith Wharton's *The Mother's Recompense*. It interrogates the intersection of the sex-gender system of the woman writer, the narrative strategies she chooses, and the distinctive shift in cultural images of femininity which marks the modernist moment and which can be gleaned from psychoanalytic narratives emerging during the same period.

The difficulties Woolf's narrator encounters in *A Room of One's Own* can serve as parables for understanding the peculiar strategies devised in women's writing of the period. Faced with totally contradictory representations of "woman" in the books of male "experts" and forced to come up with some answers of her own, she oscillates, in her exploration, between the shelves of the British Museum and the dining rooms of a women's college. The same oscillation marks her thinking.[3] On the one hand, Woolf's text insists on a female difference which is and must be inscribed into women's writing: the sentence available is unsuited for a woman's use, she tells us, and must be transformed, adapted to the female body and to women's ways of working, which will always be subject to interruption and to inadequate concentration. On the other hand, she says that "it is fatal for anyone who writes to think of their sex" (p. 108). Criticizing Charlotte Brontë for letting a female anger contaminate her writing, she advocates the androgynous consummation of "some marriage of opposites": "It is fatal to be a man or a woman pure and simple; one must be woman-manly or man-womanly" (p. 108).

Critical assessments of these obvious contradictions in Woolf's text have varied. Jane Marcus, for example, asks: "How can she hold both views at once? . . . She is biased in favor of women."[4] Peggy Kamuf, on the other hand, sees Woolf's interruptions as providing her with a means to unravel the sexual opposition which has been the root of women's oppression and exclusion.[5] In contrast to both of these views, I see Woolf's text as offering her a way to address the contradictions of her gendered position within academic and literary convention. I would argue that Woolf's is a strategy of inconclusiveness—embracing rather than denying contradiction, lingering on process rather than rushing toward conclusion, zigzagging around Oxbridge and London rather than directly pursuing a destination—a strategy appropriate to someone who, having been represented as object, strains to define herself as subject. Woolf does so neither by insisting on a separate female culture nor by deconstructing gender dichotomies, but rather by walking both paths simultaneously, by affirming difference and undoing it at the same time.[6] The dialogic form of her essay/lecture, a dialogue not only with the "mothers" of past tradition and the "daughters" at Girton, but also with the fathers, brothers, and sons who, as Adrienne Rich suggests in her reading of the essay, are always eavesdropping, serves as a model of discourse available to the woman who is turned away from the steps of the library.[7] If Woolf's insights into women and writing are valuable, then, it is precisely because they subvert each other and lead, as one recent critic deploringly observes, to "a thicket of self-refutation."[8] This chapter argues that Woolf's oscillations in *A Room* ultimately do become her mark of gendered specificity, characteristic of the circuitous strategies of female modernism.

One of the protagonists of Woolf's narrative in *A Room* is Judith Shakespeare, the imaginary sister of William, and Woolf's emblem for the woman artist. Judith's story reveals a sexual division of labor which has disastrous results for women's artistic aspirations. Shakespeare's sister does not write, of course; her talents remain undeveloped, her hopes unfulfilled. Typically for a woman who is also an artist, she flees an arranged marriage, but ends up committing suicide as a result of an unwanted pregnancy by the man who had offered to aid her in her career. Woolf never suggests that William could have offered Judith access to his masculine creative world; she is less than sanguine about the fraternal

fantasies that marked female family romances in the Victorian period. As
Sara Ruddick suggests: "No matter how good a brother Shakespeare might
have been, he could not have offered his world to his sister. . . . there
would have been no place in his world for a person with a woman's body
who wished to practise a man's art" (p. 191).[9] And yet *A Room*, locating
itself at a different moment from that in which Judith Shakespeare was
thwarted, does propose the solution of androgyny in fraternal terms.

After engaging in painful thoughts about the separate realm of femininity, and after puzzling through Mary Carmichael's revolutionary female
sentence and broken sequence, Woolf's narrator finds refuge in the idea of
androgyny.[10] When she arrives at her emblematic vision of the young girl
and young man getting into the taxicab, she finds the "natural" quality of
the image of heterosexuality to be a great relief: "Perhaps to think, as I had
been thinking these two days, of one sex as distinct from the other is an
effort. It interferes with the unity of the mind. . . . some of these states of
mind seem, even if adopted spontaneously, to be less comfortable than
others. In order to keep oneself continuing in them one is unconsciously
holding something back, and gradually the repression becomes an effort"
(pp. 100–101). The idea of androgyny, of the "natural" cooperation of the
sexes, emerges for Woolf as one state of mind that requires no effort. And
the mind that emerges as most fully androgynous and, at the same time,
most clearly exemplary of the dangers of androgyny is the mind of Shakespeare himself. But there is a cost: his very androgyny may be what
prevents him from thinking of women, his sister for example. His lack of
thoughtfulness, Woolf's narrator maintains, takes on disastrous proportions in the modern era. If Shakespeare's sister is to be born in the
twentieth century, she tentatively concludes, it will be not as a result of her
brother's help, but instead with that of her sisters and mothers: "she would
come if we worked for her" (p. 117). Here Woolf reinforces the female line
of literary inheritance she refers to as "thinking back through our mothers": "For masterpieces are not single and solitary births; they are the
outcome of many years of thinking in common, of thinking by the body of
the people, so that the experience of the mass is behind the single voice"
(p. 69).

Just like androgyny, however, female assistance has its own grave
limitations. When Woolf's narrator compares the modest dinner in the
women's college with the elegant and filling meal at Oxbridge, we notice
the beginnings of her resentment against the mothers whose nurturing of
their daughters leaves much to be desired:[11] "What had our mothers been
doing then that they had no wealth to leave us?" (p. 21). Beyond failing to
provide the financial inheritance that would foster female education and
creativity, however, mothers have actively impeded the daughters' freedom to write. Woolf explains this most clearly with the figure of the angel
in the house in her 1931 essay "Professions for Women."[12] The maternal
angel is the figure who encourages the woman writer to "be sympathetic;

be tender; flatter; deceive; use all the arts and wiles of your sex. Never let anybody guess that you have a mind of your own. Above all, be pure" (p. 59), and who must be killed if women are to continue to create. "Killing the Angel in the House was part of the occupation of the woman writer" (p. 60), Woolf insists, in a tone that does not succeed in concealing her rage.

Both solutions—androgyny and male identification, on the one hand, and the act of "thinking back through our mothers," on the other—are frought with contradiction and ambivalence. I would argue that the process of oscillating between them, however, is attractive not only because it is the only course to take but because it suggests the possibility of a different construction of femininity and of narrative. In speaking about the split consciousness Woolf's narrator discovers in herself in the passage that serves as an epigram to this chapter, Mary Jacobus says: "To recognize both the split and the means by which it is constituted, to challenge its terms while necessarily working within them—that is the hidden narrative of the trespass on the grass."[13] This sort of double consciousness has, in fact, become a paradigm for the discussion of women's writing within feminist criticism. Sandra Gilbert and Susan Gubar have spoken of "duplicity" and a palimpsestic structure; Elaine Showalter has discussed strategies of submerged plots within dominant plots which create a "double-voiced discourse."[14] I would like to emphasize that the strategy that *A Room* allows us to define, and which will be evident in the novels discussed in this chapter, is one of contradiction and oscillation rather than submersion. Although the language of darkness and concealment is still used, the fictions themselves bring the "submerged" plots to the surface, thereby creating dual, sometimes multiple plots in which contradictory elements rival one another. DuPlessis's notion of a "female aesthetic" that embraces a "both/and" vision and for which Virginia Woolf is a "locus classicus" ("For the Etruscans," p. 149) seems to me most useful for a reading of modernist texts by women writers. If the strategy of oscillation and contradiction is still applicable beyond the moment of modernism, it is helpful to locate it firmly within what I see as its historical and cultural origins.

A Fictional World Where Boy Never Meets Girl

Woolf wrote *A Room of One's Own* at a moment at which both the shapes of literary plot and the shapes of women's lives were changing quite dramatically, and the questions she asks, the strategies of her argument, both reflect and map some of these changes. Suffrage in Britain and America, increased educational opportunities, women's increased independence as a result of World War I, and innovations in childbirth technology are but a few of the social factors altering women's lives. The changes in male/female relationships resulting from the first World War were drastic and pervasive: "When the guns fired in August 1914," Woolf asks "did the faces of men and women show so plain in each other's eyes that romance was killed?" (*A Room*, p. 15).[15]

In *Literary Women*, Ellen Moers defines an important shift of emphasis in modern fiction from the heterosexual plot of courtship, marriage, and adultery to the story of what she calls "maternal seduction."[16] For Moers, this movement of the novel "beyond courtship to a fictional world where boy never meets girl" finds its most salient examples in the women writers of the 1920s. Virginia Woolf, Gertrude Stein, Willa Cather, and Colette, Moers points out, all recount the female artist's story in relation not to a father or male lover, but to a powerful, seductive, traditionally female mother-goddess.[17] Woolf and her contemporaries thematize the relation of the process of artistic production to familial configurations and psychological structures. But their family romances differ radically from those that predominate in the Victorian period. Female *Künstlerromane* of the 1920s feature young and middle-aged women who renounce love and marriage in favor of creative work, who renounce connection in favor of self-affirmation. This rebellious choice is intimately bound up in their relationships with their mothers but often is in great conflict with the choices the mothers themselves have made. What emerges in Colette's texts and in Woolf's novels and essays of this period is an intense, passionate, and ambivalent preoccupation with the mother, which oscillates between a longing for connection and a need for disconnection.

Typically, Colette finds, in her explorations of female identity, that "at no time has the catastrophe of love, in all its phases and consequences, formed a part of the true intimate life of a woman."[18] Beneath the plot of love, adultery, and betrayal, Colette suggests, there are "other important and obscure secrets which she herself does not understand very well" and which, she suggests, explain the characteristically autobiographical nature of women's novels. Even if women write about love, they are still concealing their "darkest plots." Woolf, when calling for new fictional forms in her essay on "Modern Fiction" corroborates this insight in similar language: "the problem before the novelist at present, . . . is to contrive means of being free to set down what he chooses. He has to have the courage to say that what interests him is no longer 'this', but 'that': out of 'that' alone must he construct his work. For the moderns 'that', the point of interest, lies very likely in the dark places of psychology."[19] I would argue that for Woolf and Colette, and for female modernists more generally, those "dark places" contain the hidden narrative of the passionate attachment between mother and daughter. Moreover, modernist writing strategies, characterized by increased room for subjective representations of consciousness, allow this previously hidden narrative to come to the surface of women's fiction.

The conjunction of the refusal of heterosexual love and the romance plot and of a celebration of mothers is a pervasive feature of women's writing in the 1920s. Yet it is important to realize that this interrogation and celebration of maternity is in itself new for women writers and intimately tied to this moment of textual production. For Kate Chopin's Edna, maternity meant the denial of all artistic ambition. Woolf's Judith Shakespeare commits suicide rather than becoming a mother. The fourth Mary, missing from *A Room of One's Own*, is Mary Hamilton, who was tried and executed for infanticide. *A Room* makes clear that motherhood and achievement were utterly incompatible in previous generations; yet Woolf does begin to entertain the conjunction for the present and certainly for the future. I would suggest that interest in maternity, however limited, could emerge only at a time in history when motherhood had become less life-threatening and more of a choice for women. As Susan Gubar points out in her excellent discussion of the female *Künstlerroman*, the invention, improvement, and greater availability of contraception, the radically lower birth rate, and the significant decrease in mother and infant mortality, all of which occurred in the teens and twenties, made it possible for women writers to reimagine the maternal.[20] Significantly, however, they did so not for themselves but for the generation of their mothers, attempting to unite the disparate experiences of two generations separated by a remarkable shift in opportunity for women, to minimize the distance between the emergence of women as artists and the conventional femininity embraced by their mothers. Whereas in Victorian fiction the distance between the heroine and her mother needed to be maintained, here connection has become possible, even necessary. Even while the daughter-artist herself still does not become a mother, the mother's life can be and needs to be known and explored in its details, incorporated into the daughter's vision. Yet these texts about mothers are elegies;[21] they are not composed by the daughters until the mothers are dead. Only then can memory and desire play their roles as instruments of connection, reconstruction, and reparation. In fact, one might say that, in contrast to the Victorian examples, death here enables the mothers to be *present* rather than *absent*.

In Gubar's analysis, Katherine Mansfield's liberation from the fear of maternity and her ability to envision a form of art centered not in autonomy but in connection, not in a bodiless mind, but in a female body, was a direct result of her brother's death in the war. Mansfield is the sister who, freed both from fraternal fantasy and from sisterly subservience, can flourish: "Her brother's death liberates her to celebrate women's capacity to birth as an aspect of the artistry she enacts as a fiction writer," Gubar says ("Birth of the Artist," p. 34). While claiming to bring the dead brother back to life, however, Mansfield, like Woolf and Colette, creates a fictional world in which women and female relationships predominate. But as the rest of this chapter demonstrates, the break from the plot of romantic love and from the fantasy of the "man-who-would-understand" is never total; the mother coexists uneasily with the male figure—brother, father, heterosexual lover—who is always still part of the story and who, in fact, enables the story of mother and daughter to be told, who focuses the experience of connection and disconnection, passion and renunciation. In this period, then, the mother-daughter narrative tries to displace the narrative of heterosexual romance, tries to find its *own* language and expressive medium, but it cannot do so entirely. Mother-daughter narratives are still subject to what Adrienne Rich has termed the institution of "compulsory heterosexuality."[22] The term "oscillation" may serve here as well, to describe the complicated plots that emerge out of these shifting rivalries and competing affiliations.

Break of Day, To the Lighthouse, and *The Mother's Recompense* represent at once experiments with the composition of what Colette speaks of as "a book that isn't about love, adultery, semi-incestuous relations and a final separation" (*Break of Day*, p. 19) and experiments with novelistic forms that will accommodate that new story. Re-mapping the familial configurations which are the bases of literary construction, these novels demonstrate how circuitous women's efforts at writing and "thinking back through their mothers" have to be.

Discovering the Pre-Oedipus

"Ce n'est pas dans la zone illuminée que se trame le pire" ["It is not in the illuminated zone that the darkest plots are woven"] says Colette, using two centrally Freudian images for femininity, weaving and archaeology. Significantly, it is also in the 1920s that Freud, revising his developmental theory, comes to recognize the importance of the pre-oedipal bond between the girl and her mother, a bond that underlies and, in some ways, outweighs the formative power of the Oedipus complex. The archaeological image Freud uses to describe the discovery of the pre-Oedipus highlights its concealed and subversive power—it is, he says, "like the discovery, in another field, of the Minoan-Mycenean civilization behind the civilization of Greece."[23] Here Freud echoes, as well, the important archaeological discoveries and anthropological theories positing a matriarchal pre-history to patriarchy, theories much under discussion in the twenties. One of their prime proponents, Jane Ellen Harrison, makes a brief appearance in *A Room of One's Own* as "a bent figure, formidable yet humble, with her great forehead and her shabby dress—could it be the famous scholar, could it be the great J——— H——— herself?" (p. 17).[24] That name, and presumably the discoveries associated with it, signal for Woolf's narrator a mysterious unease: "All was dim, yet intense too, as if the scarf which the dusk had flung over the garden were torn asunder by star or sword—the flash of some terrible reality leaping, as its way is, out of the heart of the spring" (p. 17). Could the terrible reality be Harrison's discussion of a matriarchal past underlying the patriarchal present—and tearing its surface asunder?[25]

Freud stresses the almost total repression of the pre-oedipal stage of mother-love and the analyst's difficulty in reaching it. The pre-Oedipus, he surmises, has no narrative and no history: it can be reached only retrospectively, after it has already been abandoned, more or less successfully. Lacan's later reformulation clarifies that the pre-oedipal stage coincides with the pre-verbal imaginary stage which has to give way to the symbolic. As Freud envisions the story of female development, the mother-daughter bond must be abandoned in favor of a strong attachment to the father which, in turn, must be superceded by the adult love of another man and the conception of a child, preferably male. Freud's essays on femininity written in the late twenties attempt, in various ways, to motivate this shift away from maternal affiliation, a shift that is obvious for the boy threatened by castration, but not at all obvious for the girl.[26] Yet the girl's shift is utterly crucial for Freud inasmuch as the very idea of heterosexuality and his definition of adult femininity in culture depend on its successful completion; in his words, it demonstrates "how a woman develops out of a child with a bi-sexual disposition" ("Femininity" (1933), vol 21:116).

As Freud sees it, when the girl abandons her mother as libidinal object she transforms her sexuality from an active (masculine) to a passive (feminine) one. She transfers her attachment to the father and represses her love for her mother. And she has to accept the painful and humiliating "fact" of her castration. In view of the discontinuities that distinguish the female developmental course from the straightforwardly linear male one, it does not surprise Freud that this should be such a problematic moment for the girl, often leading to neurosis: "this phase of attachment to the mother is especially intimately related to the aetiology of hysteria, . . . in this dependence on the mother we have the germ of later paranoia in women" ("Female Sexuality," vol. 22:227). Further complexity in the identity of the adult woman derives from what Freud identifies as left-overs—the girl's inability to surmount either the pre-Oedipus or the Oedipus complex adequately, and thus to reach maturity in a smooth manner. Her difficulty may well derive from the fact that, for her, maturity is a passive subordination to male superiority, or what Teresa de Lauretis has called the girl's "consent to femininity," connecting the process and the narrative of that consent with the female Oedipal scenario.[27] Freud insists that the mother remains an important figure in the adult woman's life, often determining the nature and quality of marital relationships. Although teleologically determined, adult femininity, at its best, is the result of a long, conflicted, and discontinuous developmental course, marked by what Elizabeth Abel has termed "a series of costly repressions."[28] In fact, many women fail to complete these successfully, even at the enormous cost they exact, and end up either with "a general revulsion from sexuality," ("Female Sexuality," vol. 21:229) or the victims of a "masculinity complex" which can lead to homosexuality.

Where is the narrative of the repressed "pre-historical," pre-oedipal mother-daughter attachment for Freud and the analysts of the twenties and early thirties? As his argument evolves in the course of the essays he devotes to this topic, Freud himself not only views the female pre-Oedipus as more and more important, but he also describes it in more detail. However, the particulars he provides in "Femininity" (1933), his fullest account, are remarkably unimaginative. In fact, he seems to read mother-daughter relations from the retrospective point of view of the oedipal, father-daughter phase: "We knew, of course, that there had been a pre-liminary stage of attachment to the mother, but we did not know that it could be so rich in content and so long-lasting, and could leave behind so many opportunities for fixations and dispositions. . . . Almost everything that we find later in her relation to her father was already present in this earlier attachment and has been transferred subsequently on to the father" (vol. 22:119). Even the fantasy of paternal seduction is only a repetition of an earlier fantasy in which the seducer was the mother, he maintains. In this version of the developmental narrative, the drama of mother and daughter has no distinctive features. As Abel insists, "Prehistory is written from the vantage point of history" (*Virginia Woolf*, Introduction). It is as though the narrative of mother-daughter attachment can only be ex-trapolated from the later father-daughter bond, even though its impact is at least equally powerful.

In these later essays, Freud carries on a dialogue with a number of women analysts whose work touches on female development. He con-cedes, at one point, that female analysts have a clearer access to their patients' pre-oedipal content than he does (vol. 21: 226–227). In fact, the contemporary narratives of Melanie Klein, Karen Horney, and Helene Deutsch do provide a fuller account of the pre-oedipal phase and, in some cases, of mother-daughter attachments. For example, Melanie Klein, and later D. W. Winnicott, move the drama of development back to the first year of life and center it in maternal-child interactions. The breast and feeding are the prime elements of this pre-verbal set of object relations and the child's cognitive efforts are directed almost exclusively toward the mother—dealing with her contradictory influence, processing the anger that her power incites, protecting itself from the fear she elicits, making reparation for the aggressive impulses she unleashes in the child. Although Klein's narrative is not specifically gendered, it revolves, for children of both sexes, around the figure of the mother. The father merely allows the girl to repeat her earlier interaction with her mother and thus to deal with it more effectively. The mother remains an important psychic presence throughout life, motivating even the production of art and cul-ture. What is significant about Klein's work, for my purposes, is that she attempts to arrive at this pre-oedipal story not by way of the father but through observation of children—by means of its indirect expression in play.[29]

For Klein, as for Karen Horney and Ernest Jones, the transfer of affection from mother to father, which had caused Freud so much anxiety, is motivated through a "natural" and innate tendency toward heterosexual-ity. This hypothesis divorces sexuality from reproduction and grants women a primary sexual impulse. Karen Horney even suggests that

Freud's sequence might be reversed, and that this natural heterosexual attraction to the father and not envy of the penis or the rejection of her mother may be primarily responsible for the girl's interest in the penis.[30] Horney, unlike Klein, does not pay a great deal of attention to the mother-child bond or to maternal identification; instead she sees the father as a primary figure of desire and identification in the girl's developmental journey. Yet, that journey is also a conflicted and complicated one, moving to what she calls the "flight from womanhood"—the adoption of a fictitious male role, motivated socially by "the actual disadvantage under which women labor in social life." It is here that Horney's interest in a primary femininity, marked by vaginal sensations, genital anxiety, and reproductive pleasure, emerges, explaining her rejection of the central role penis envy plays in psychoanalytic theory: "At this point I, as a woman, ask in amazement, what about motherhood? And the blissful consciousness of bearing a new life within oneself? And the ineffable happiness of the increasing expectation of the appearance of this new being? And the joy when it finally makes its appearance and one holds it for the first time in one's arms? And the deep and pleasurable feeling of satisfaction in suckling it and the happiness of the whole period when the infant needs her care?" (p. 205). This remarkable passage comes early in Horney's essay, but its subversive message is quickly abandoned in favor of the long discussion of the "flight from womanhood." This ambivalence firmly places Horney in the modernist posture of duplicity and contradiction we encountered in *A Room of One's Own*. She embraces for women a passionate heterosexual orientation and an androgynous male identification. Yet, she affirms the pleasures and dangers of a primary femininity and tells the story of pre-oedipal mother-child attachment from the mother's own perspective. Horney thereby calls into question, albeit indirectly, some of the foundations of contemporaneous psychoanalytic thought and the sequential, teleological narrative of development. She fails, however, to draw out some of the potentially far-reaching implications of her series of open-ended questions.[31]

The language of Helene Deutsch is closest to the terms I have used to describe the conflictual femininity of *A Room*. Deutsch sees female development as a process of "bi-sexual oscillation between mother and father." "Thus the task of adolescence is not only to master the oedipus complex, but also to continue the work begun during prepuberty and early puberty, that is, to give adult forms to the old, much deeper, and much more primitive ties with the mother, and to end all bisexual wavering in favor of a definite heterosexual orientation."[32] Although she firmly upholds the Freudian telos, Deutsch's term "oscillation" adumbrates the forces of female identification and maternal attachment which continually undermine it.

What are the implications of these psychoanalytic debates in the 1920s and early 30s for the structures of narrative? I return here to my discussion of narrative structures in chapter 1. If narrative is indeed based in oedipal structures, as I argued there, and if the female Oedipus is perceived to take a different, more complicated, circuitous form, then narrative structures adopted by women writers should reflect some of these complications.[33] There are several suggestions of difference that we can glean from Woolf's outline of the sex-gender system typical for the modernist woman writer and from the period's psychoanalytic accounts of female identity. For example, we might conclude that the narrative of female development would not be linear or teleological but would reflect the oscillations between maternal and paternal attachments as well as the multiple repres- sions of the female developmental course. Pre-oedipal closeness to the mother, oedipal separation and attachment to the father, the subsequent transfer of that attachment to another male love object and the wish for a child, combined with the many forms of resistance against this course— continued female identification, or the "flight from womanhood"—all of these configurations do find their way into the narrative structures ex- emplified by Woolf, Colette, and their contemporaries. From this perspec- tive the story of mother and daughter needs to be told retrospectively, by way of the father. Melanie Klein's notion of reparation may also suggest why these texts are so pointedly oriented to the mother as addressee. Teresa de Lauretis's direct connection between narrative and psychology, her elaboration of the "duplicity of th(e Oedipal) scenario and the specific contradiction of the female subject in it" (*Alice Doesn't*, p. 157) is helpful here. Her book explores what she calls the "politics of self-representation" of the woman writing in these circumstances. In the oedipal scenario, de Lauretis explains, woman is not the subject but the object of desire; her story, still embedded in male desire, is the cruel tale of her eventual consensual participation in the male plot.[34]

However, it seems to me that Karen Horney's remarkable description of the sensations and feelings associated with reproduction also suggests a narrative pattern different from the dynamically temporal one outlined by Peter Brooks and discussed in chapter 1—"retard, postponement, error and partial revelation" leading to the end, meaning, and truth, that is, to death.[35] Horney's interrogative format in itself points toward the radically pro-spective and openended nature of maternal preoccupation and per- haps of maternal narrative.

The Demeter myth illustrates well the complicated intersections of gen- der and plot raised by these texts. Narratability itself, the Homeric hymn suggests, demands some form of breech, some space of anxiety and desire into which to inscribe itself. The perpetuation of infantile plenitude cannot offer a model for plot. The story of mother and daughter comes into being only through Hades' rape, through the intervention of the father/husband. The compromise resolution, however, again rests not on "retard, post- ponement" or "deferral" but on *continued opposition, interruption, and con- tradiction*. As we follow Persephone's return to her mother for one part of the year and her repeated descent to marriage and the underworld for the rest, it seems to me that we have to revise our very notion of resolution. At the end of the story, Persephone's allegiance is split between mother and husband, her posture is dual. The repeated cycle relies not on reconciliation, but on continued opposition to sustain and perpetuate it. Persephone literally enacts the "bi-sexual oscillation" of the Freudian female plot.

Some feminist critics have wished to substitute a female vision of plenitude, shared knowledge, connection and continuity for male narrative models based on lack and dissatisfaction. The emblematic example of "The Hymn to Demeter" conveys, I believe, that such a simple reversal fails to take into account the particular incongruities and multiplicities of women's affiliative patterns, and the ways in which women—even women who bond and identify with women—are implicated in heterosexual plots.

"An Open and Unending Book": Colette's *Break of Day*

Feminist critics in search of female specificity have privileged the relation between Colette and her mother, described in numerous autobiographical, semi-autobiographical, and fictional works. It seems that Colette's role in women's literary history is to signal an exception from a mother-daughter conflict that we have come to assume as inevitable, to sketch a mother-daughter relationship in which the daughter's "separate self develops within an unbroken stream of primary love."[36] It has become accepted to view Sido and the garden world of Puisaye as the source of Colette's creativity. Both Nancy K. Miller and Germaine Brée have used the example of Colette to expand our conception of the process of literary creation.[37] Revising Michel Beaujour's account of the poetics of the *autoportrait*, Miller asserts: "Thinking back through her mother, Colette's 'I' does not suffer the fate of the 'modern individual' whose 'curse comes from the simple fact of his *birth* rejected from the maternal breast, marked with the sign of the *ego*, condemned to wandering and conquest . . . or else to their obverse, interminable writing.' Unlike the male model of the genre, Colette's self-portrait is comfortably connected to the maternal body" (Eisinger, p. 173). Brée goes even further to suggest that "Writing for her (Colette) is released less by the fear of loss than by this secret knowledge. . . . Thus writing is the opposite of a breech, it is a rite of preservation" (Tétel, 112; my translation).

My reading of *Break of Day* finds such a revised theory—of writing emerging not from lack but from plenitude, not from disconnection but from comfortable connection—not to be borne out by the text. The story of mother-daughter love does allow us to revise our paradigm of what is narratable, does allow us to base it elsewhere than in the "catastrophe" of romantic love or the drama of ambition and possession, but such a revision, this text suggests, has serious limits. If the story of female development, as it is told in the modernist period, does not proceed inevitably from maternal to paternal/heterosexual attachment, as Freud would have it, neither can it remain immersed in primary love. It needs to situate itself in the liminal space between a passionate maternal eroticism and the anxieties which shape the heterosexual plot.

Break of Day is a story of renunciation. At middle age, "Colette" is faced with the prospect of a young love, Vial, and refusing his advances, affirms her independent life "outside of loving" to use the terms of George Eliot's Maggie Tulliver. This refusal is inscribed into a reading of her mother's letters and a reflection on her similarity to/difference from her mother. Yet the process of "thinking back through her mother," the impulse to "bring my mother close to me again" is far from comfortable. In fact, it is marked by conflict and anxiety. In its oscillation between Vial (love) and the memory of "Sido" (maternal attachment), between the narrator's youthful yearning for passion and the acceptance of middle age, the text pulls disquietingly in two different directions.[38]

The text begins with "Sido's" own famous letter of renunciation. An answer to an invitation to visit her daughter, it is written to Henri de Jouvenel, Colette's second husband. "I'm not going to accept your kind invitation. . . . The reason is that my pink cactus is probably going to flower. It's a very rare plant I've been given, and I'm told that in our climate it flowers only once every four years. Now, I'm already a very old woman, and if I went away when my pink cactus is about to flower, I am certain I shouldn't see it flower again" (p. 5). Triumphantly and lovingly, "Colette" defines her own identity in her lengthy reflection on this refusal: "I am the daughter of the woman who wrote that letter. . . . I am the daughter of a woman who . . ." (pp. 5–6). This mode of self-identification is prompted by a particular anxiety, a need for recognition and affirmation which structures the space of the entire novel: "Now that little by little I am beginning to age, and little by little taking on her likeness in the mirror, I wonder whether, if she were to return, she would recognize me for her daughter, in spite of the resemblance of our features" (p. 6). Throughout the text, "Colette" is eager to establish points of contact with her mother on every level: "Sido" is "my model," "you who are always with me"; "Colette" is "her own image, coarsened and impure" (p. 25). This anxiety is all the more surprising when we realize that "Sido's" initial refusal to see her daughter is Colette's construction. In her biography of Colette, Michelle Sarde quotes the actual letter on which the novel is based, which contains an eager, almost passionate acceptance of the invitation for a reason "I can never resist: seeing my daughter's face and hearing her voice."[39] Why the drastic transformation? Why begin her novel with a constructed separation which results in anxiety and discomfort?

Some critics have resorted to biography, suggesting that Colette transforms the letter because of her own guilt at not having seen enough of her mother shortly before Sido's death (Sido, in fact, never came for that visit).[40] Other more closely textual reasons are possible, however. I would argue that "Sido's" letter presents a model for the renunciation "Colette" herself needs to learn in the course of her non-affair with Vial—initial distance between mother and daughter paradoxically establishes a relationship of imitation. As they tell the story of child development, psychoanalytic theories traditionally cast the mother as the one who desires connection and the child as the one who struggles to separate; however, Colette invents a mother who desires separation, thereby making it easier for her to resolve the conflict between attachment and separation herself.

More importantly, this initial distance fulfills the same function as Hades' rape in the Demeter myth by creating the space that makes plot possible. "Comfortable connection" carries with it the danger of non-meaning, a sinking back into a night of non-differentiation, a night which will never turn into dawn. Colette dramatizes this danger when she outlines a story which, she says, she has always wanted to write, of a "family devoured, bones and all, by its parents" (p. 40). This text would suggest, then, that death and non-meaning, and *not* a different narrative model, emerge from the perpetuation of infantile plenitude. "Sido's" refusal, moreover, is addressed to the husband, who already stands as the disruptive presence between mother and daughter.

The anxiety that creates the impulse for this narrative is primarily sexual, implicating mother-daughter connection in the institution of compulsory heterosexuality. As Nancy K. Miller has shown, this novel is part of a group of women's novels which inscribe a maternal intratext of sexual renunciation.[41] Although "Colette," like her mother, is awake at break of day, she wears not a blue apron with pockets full of grain for the fowls, but is "half-naked in a fluttering wrap hastily slipped on, standing at my door which had admitted a nightly visitor" (p. 7). Throughout Colette's work, this male figure intervenes between "Sido" and "Colette." Whether it turns out to be Willy, Chéri, or Vial, the attachment to this figure creates the distinction between pure and impure, it separates her from the garden world of her childhood "of which I am no longer worthy." The story of "Colette" and "Sido" is inextricably connected to men. The husband is the addressee of the initial letter, while the young lover occasions the reading of the mother's letters and the complex process of identification between mother and daughter. As Colette places the mother/daughter plot within the tale of heterosexual love, it becomes clear that the story of renunciation can be realized on the level of represented experience, but not fully on the level of narrative, nor, for that matter, on the level of "reality."[42]

Nevertheless, the male presence in the text constitutes no more than an instrument which allows the story of mother-daughter love to be represented. While the scenes with Vial have been criticized as unconvincing, the mother/daughter plot contains the great passion and interest in this book. As she says no to Vial, "Colette" revises the conventional love story which leaves woman depleted, emptied of resources and creativity, addicted to giving with neurotic compulsion. Love thwarts development, limiting the woman who has lived for a single man to "the shrivelled innocence of an old maid" (p. 19). In her new-found freedom from this danger, "Colette" attempts to achieve the serenity she has seen in her mother and to copy "Sido's" calm self-enrichment that has taken the place of compulsive giving. This transformation and revision is aesthetic as well as experiential. Vial (or love) is not only dangerous; he has become boring; what is missing between them is desire, "that supreme intruder." Vial represents the "déjà-lu," a story that has been told too many times.

In Colette's text, "Sido" is at once absent (she said she would not come, she is dead) and present (in the text of her letters) Neither absence (loss) nor presence (fulfillment) are total—Colette alters the letters: "Sido" is gone but also is part of "Colette." What structures the narrative, then, is not an initial loss and the desire for restitution, not an insatiable appetite seeking gratification, but the paradox and contradiction emerging from the simultaneity of loss and gain, separation and closeness, difference and similarity. Applauding her distance from the time in her life "when I inclined only in one direction, like those allegorical figures at the source of rivers, cradled and drawn along by their watery tresses" (p. 31), Colette suggests a multiple narrative model based on substitution, alternation, and contradiction.

Taking "Sido" instead of Vial as the object and the model for love alters "Colette's" conception of loving altogether. She discovers, in her mother's letters, a life full of passionate attachments, but the passion "Sido" stands for is never single-minded, never oriented toward possession. From Sido, Colette learns to love through abstaining, to refrain from directly touching the butterfly's beautiful wing. The built-in distance and abstention seem to provide the possibility of a relation that would devour neither subject nor object but would still create the space necessary for narrative.

Sido's last letter makes this message clear in its very opaqueness.[43] The letter is the avant-garde text par excellence. The message "Colette" receives is that her mother no longer feels the obligation to use our language. The two sheets of the letter contain signs that seem joyous, arrows, small rays surrounding a word, two "yes yes" and a short "she danced." At the bottom, Colette finds the address "mon amour." In the process of reading this text and of transmitting it (because it no longer uses our language, it cannot be copied like the other letters but must be described, translated, interpreted, recreated in the medium of language), "Colette" must assume both the roles of receiver and sender; she must project herself into the very text of the letter. For "Colette," the letter conceals not a story but an image that she would rather not face, the image of the dying mother. The letter itself cannot be read for a clear significance—its message lies in its very resistance to interpretation, a resistance which Colette simply accepts. Instead of a "confused delirium," Colette finds in it "a new alphabet, . . . one of those haunted landscapes where, to puzzle you, a face lies hidden among the leaves, an arm in the fork of a tree, a body under the cluster of a rock" (p. 142). As she vacillates between figure and ground, Colette reassembles the maternal body which has been fragmented, dispersed, and transfigured, merging with the landscape. "Sido's" almost other-worldly maternal discourse is perpetually poised at the edge of non-meaning, only to be wrested from a submersion in the permanent darkness into which "Sido" herself has disappeared by "Colette's" own investment.

The end of the novel again finds "Colette" at break of day, suspended at the moment of differentiation, dawn barely "wrested from the night." Yet, as she lies there, she is no more comfortable than she was at the beginning. As Vial figures in her thoughts, she is impatient, eager, hungry. She knows that what is needed is a process of transformation, through which love would retain its formal properties but would abdicate its male object in favor of a cosmic content: "But I only have to help him and lo! he will turn into a quickset hedge, spindrift, meteors, an open and unending book, a cluster of grapes, a ship, an oasis. . . ." (p. 143). By imagining and announcing, in the future tense, the conflation of the male lover with the pink cactus, her mother's own object of passionate attachment, Colette finds a way to live with the contradictions in her life and in her text, to embrace the logic of "both/and." As we have seen, *Break of Day* is very much tied to love and to narrative as we conventionally know it. Sido's last letter may present a model for a different narrative, one about which "Colette" can fantasize at break of day, but Colette herself cannot write in the absence of some vestiges of conventional plot, vestiges she would like to and, to a degree, does transform into the elements of a new story, "an open and unending book."

The modernist form of her text participates in the duple logic she embraces at the end of the novel. It is multiple, containing the voices of "Sido" and "Colette," signaled by a mixture of italic and roman print. All roles get reversed when "Sido" is presented as a lover—"*Can it be then that, in my way, I am a great lover? That's a discovery that would much have astonished my two husbands*" (p. 23)—and a writer—"Between us two which one is the better writer, she or I?" (p. 141). Cause and effect, origin and consequence are frequently reversed, as "Sido's" letters move from being pretexts for the narrative to the central position as text. The novel hovers indefinably between fiction and autobiography: "You have sensed that in this novel the novel does not exist," writes Colette to a critic.[44] It announces a renunciation of love, just as Colette herself is about to marry for the third time. It is perhaps the most passionate story of mother/daughter attachment in literary history, yet that story is still inscribed in a conventional tale of heterosexual seduction. In the novel, the love plot, proceeding forward chronologically, rivals the mother/daughter plot, which proceeds associatively and retrospectively. These indeterminacies demand of the reader an acceptance and an acting out of contradiction, an oscillating reading similar to the one "Colette" herself demonstrates as she reads "Sido's" last letter. They chart the plot of mother-daughter love within the heterosexual institution of narrative which both silences and articulates it.

Dreadful Passages: Woolf's *To the Lighthouse*

At one point in *Break of Day*, "Colette" discusses what it took for her to acquire, "both legally and familiarly, as well as in my books, . . . only one name, which is my own" (p. 19). She associates that acquisition, of which she seems both proud and horrified, with the fate of those women who devote their entire lives to one man. Whether for her that one man is writing, the love plot to which her writing is so attached, or her father whose name she did indeed take, remains ambiguous. In her earlier book *My Mother's House*, however, "Colette" does identify her own writing with her father's failed attempt to write. Colonel Colette, it seems, left a series of empty notebooks on the top shelf of his bookcase and left his daughter as a kind of disciple who might fill those books with words and stories. "You represent what he would so much have liked to be when he was on earth. You are exactly what he longed to be. But he himself was never able."[45] Colette's adoption of writing as a career and an identity is thus as much tied to her relationship with her father as to her bond with her mother. In fact, it occurs in a typically triangular relationship, for the father's empty notebooks in which, figuratively, Colette writes, have only one full page: the dedication, "To Sido."

For Virginia Woolf, as well, writing involved a dual origin and a dual destination, both paternal and maternal. As Jane Marcus points out, however, Woolf's father did not leave her a series of empty notebooks; he left the text of patriarchal tradition itself.[46] It was he who initiated her into reading and writing, he who gave her books to read, and he who inspired her description of herself as "an educated man's daughter." Woolf first saw *To the Lighthouse* as a book about her father; only later does she clearly identify it with the memory of her mother. In a 1925 diary entry Woolf writes: "This is going to be fairly short, to have father's character done complete in it; and mother's; St. Ives; and childhood; and all the usual things I try to put in—life, death, etc. But in the centre is father's character, sitting in a boat, reciting, we perished, each alone, while he crushes a dying mackerel."[47] But when she writes about *To the Lighthouse* in retrospect, in "A Sketch of the Past," it is the figure of her mother which stands at the center of the entire project: "Until I was in the forties . . . the presence of my mother obsessed me. I could hear her voice, see her, imagine what she would do or say as I went about my day's doings."[48] It is *To the Lighthouse* that frees Woolf from this obsession: "I wrote the book very quickly; and when it was written, I ceased to be obsessed by my mother. I no longer hear her voice; I do not see her. I suppose that I did for myself what psycho-analysts do for their patients. I expressed some very long and deeply felt emotion. And in expressing it I explained it and then laid it to rest" (*Moments of Being*, p. 81). In the complicated genesis of this novel, then, the story of the mother displaces a projected story featuring the father. Later in "A Sketch of the Past," Woolf reevaluates yet again her father's role in relation to her mother and finds it to be more central than she had been willing to admit earlier: "Just as I rubbed out a great deal of the force of my mother's memory by writing about her in *To the Lighthouse*, so I rubbed out much of his memory there too. Yet he too obsessed me for years. Until I wrote it out, I would find my lips moving; I would be arguing with him; raging against him; saying to myself all that I had never said to him. How deep they drove themselves into me, the things it was impossible to say aloud. . . . But in me . . . rage alternated with love. It was only the other day when I read Freud for the first time, that I discovered that this violently disturbing conflict between love and hate is a common feeling; and is called ambivalence" (*Moments of Being*, p. 108). Woolf's novel acts out this alternation and ambivalence, this dual allegiance to mother and father, in its very structure and form. It thereby creates a distinctively modernist version of the female family romance. Although father, mother, brothers, and sisters all play archetypal roles, this family romance is capacious enough to include the mother in a position of centrality, to focus on her presence as well as her absence. Like *Break of Day*, it offers feminist critics a central text through which to explore the representation of mother-daughter relationships.[49]

   To the Lighthouse is propelled by a desire for understanding, by a series of questions which fit Peter Brooks's schema of the novel as explanatory narrative. The novel begins with Mrs. Ramsay's answer to James's implied question about the trip to the lighthouse: "Yes, of course, if it's fine . . ."Other questions, posed by different characters at different moments structure the novel's progression: "What was there behind . . . (Mrs. Ramsay's) beauty and splendor?" (p. 46); "But after Q? What comes next?" (p. 53); "What did it all mean?" (p. 159); "Would they go to the Lighthouse tomorrow?" (p. 173); "What does it mean then, what can it all mean?" (p. 217); "What's the use of going now?" (p. 218); "D'you remember?" (p. 254); "What does it mean, how do you explain it all?" (p. 266). The primary enigma in the novel is the figure of the mother—the beautiful and mysterious Mrs. Ramsay. Repeated, rephrased, reformulated throughout the text, the questions about Mrs. Ramsay, her life, and the lives of those who surround her are not answered but are confronted with a series of oppositions. Male and female, father and mother, life and death, light and darkness, affirmation and destruction, enclosure and separation, lighthouse and window—all appear to find in the text a third term of resolution. At the end of the novel, a form of closure and discovery seems to redeem the pervasive destruction of the novel's second part, "Time Passes." Critics often focus their analyses on Woolf's strategies for resolving opposites, for finding that "razor-edge of balance between two opposite forces," for creating in Lily the figure of the artist who is "woman-manly and man-womanly." They discuss the novel in terms of "equilibrium" (Corsa), "balance of forms" (Proudfit), the triumph of art over the "powers of darkness, dissolution and chaos" (Love); the process of maturation which depends on the integration of a male principle which will resist the engulfment that the maternal will commands (di Battista).[50]

Loss and longing mark the novel's very substance. We cannot deny that the trip happens too late, that nothing can compensate for the loss of Mrs. Ramsay, that the annihilation wrought by the war is impossible to redeem. Yet the economy of loss and recovery still operates in much of the novel, as the reader is repeatedly seduced by moments of harmonious resolution, moments which are implicit in the text's oppositional structure. Brooks emphasizes the necessity for delays and false turns on the road to healing and culmination, and it is precisely such a pattern that the novel at first seems to enact.

However seductive this sort of reading might be, it is my contention that the economy of loss and recovery and the aesthetic conceptions that accompany it are actually revised in the course of *To the Lighthouse*. I do not mean that the apparent resolution is simply ironic, but that it is left behind in favor of a different economy. My argument centers on the figure of Lily and on the relation between her work on her painting and her connection with Mrs. Ramsay.[51] In my reading, Lily's strategy is not the adoption of an androgynous artistic identity, but of a dual, perhaps duplicitous posture which, instead of resolving the differences between opposite forces, embraces contradiction as the only stance which allows the woman artist to produce.[52]

In the first section of the novel, Lily is unable to finish her painting or even to work on it productively. She is hindered both by Mrs. Ramsay's injunction that she should marry and by Charles Tansley's repeated judgement that "Women can't paint, women can't write . . ." In this period, painting is a very personal act for Lily: she describes it as a birth process in which the "passage from conception to work [is] as dreadful as any down a dark passage for a child" (p. 32). In this analogy, painting is both a way out of what she experienced as the wish for childhood fusion—during the dinner she can protect herself from the lure of the "we" by thinking about the picture and moving the salt-cellar on the tablecloth—and a way back into it, but differently, a way to know Mrs. Ramsay, to "spell out" the secret she locks up inside her, like "treasures in the tombs of kings, bearing sacred inscriptions." Sitting in the bedroom with Mrs. Ramsay, putting her head on Mrs. Ramsay's knee, Lily wonders how she can get closer, how she can know more about Mrs. Ramsay: "What art was there, known to love or cunning, by which one pressed into those secret chambers? What device for becoming, like waters poured into one jar, inextricably the same, one with the object one adored? . . . Could loving, as people called it, make her and Mrs. Ramsay one? for it was not knowledge but unity that she desired, not inscriptions on tablets, nothing that could be written in any language known to men, but intimacy itself, which is knowledge . . ."(p. 79).[53] Critics have read this passage as an indication of Lily's immature and self-annihilating desire for fusion with the mother, a desire she must outgrow, resolve, and reframe so as to separate from Mrs. Ramsay and finish the painting. Freudian telos would, indeed, emphasize the necessity for separation as a measure of maturity and would present Mrs. Ramsay's death as the essential rupture which occasions the mourning that allows Lily to grow.

The novel itself supports such a sense of progression. The moments between Lily and Mrs. Ramsay move gradually outward from the bedroom to the dining room and finally to the beach, which occasions a return to the steps and Lily's vision. Yet this spatial progression is not clearly mirrored in Lily's thoughts and feelings. In fact, she describes the process of painting not as an externalization but as a progressive movement inward, back into the past, back beyond the "illuminated zone" into the earliest feelings of longing and desire: "She went on tunneling her way into her picture, into the past" (p. 258); "She was not inventing; she was only trying to smooth out something she had been given years ago folded up; something she had seen" (p. 295). Lily's movement into (or out of) the picture, Lily's process of painting it, is a complicated one and cannot be encompassed by either a linear or a dialectical image. In fact, it does not conform to the conceptions and images of art and the artistic process on which the other characters agree. This may well be the source of Lily's problem, that in telling or painting the story of Mrs. Ramsay, the scene of mother and child, she must redefine the forms and the expectations of art: "for it was not knowledge but unity that she desired, not inscriptions on tablets, *nothing that could be written in any language known to men, but intimacy itself, which is knowledge . . .*" (my italics). If we read "men" not for its generic but for its specific meaning, we see that Lily searches for a different language, one that will not oppose knowledge and intimacy, but will allow for what we might call their tautological interrelation. In so doing, she refines the notion of modernist art, struggling painfully and against her own sense of culture and tradition, to introduce a mark of female difference.

Art, the characters agree, must last, a requirement which is distinguished from momentary enjoyment. Art must create order and understanding through its form. Like the sonnet it must be "beautiful and reasonable, clear and complete, the essence sucked out of life and held rounded here" (p. 181); "If only she could put them together, she felt, write them out in some sentence, then she would have got at the truth of things" (p. 219). More than anything, perhaps, art creates unity and harmony where before there was chaos, fragmentation, hostility and destruction. This could be the key to the success of Mr. Carmichael's poetry during the war. It is also the key to Mrs. Ramsay's very particular artistic creation: "That woman . . . made out of that miserable silliness and spite . . .

something . . . which survived . . . like a work of art. . . . In the midst of chaos there was shape; this eternal passing and flowing . . . was struck into stability" (pp. 239–41). As Lily sees and remembers it, Mrs. Ramsay creates harmony, Mrs. Ramsay brings people together and forms a communion which will survive her. This is what art must do, Lily thinks, recognizing Mrs. Ramsay as an artist, even though her media are food and community.[54]

When Lily works on her own painting, then, she too aspires to the criteria of permanence, harmony, and aesthetic balance as the measure of success. "It was a question . . . how to connect this mass on the right hand with that on the left" (pp. 82–83); "the question was of some relation between those masses" (p. 221). She feels that her painting must achieve a particularly difficult kind of artistic equilibrium: "the light of a butterfly's wing lying upon the arches of a cathedral" (p. 75). Where are her models for such a task? Lily does not work within a tradition; she does not benefit from the discussion about art and philosophy shared by Mr. Ramsay and Charles Tansley. Her talks with Mr. Bankes demonstrate how little encouragement she actually receives: he shakes his head with incomprehension at her irreverent interpretation of the mother and child theme. And Mr. Carmichael offers no more than a silent presence. Surrounded by a community of scholars and artists, Lily acutely experiences her distance from their exchanges.

Unlike "Sido," who does offer a model of both creativity and self-possession to "Colette," Mrs. Ramsay's stance as artist is, for women, a dangerous one to live up to because her aesthetic perfection is bought at the expense of her life. Her success at establishing harmony, permanence, and order, at resolving opposite forces, causes in Mrs. Ramsay a strain she cannot survive, precisely because her medium is interpersonal and not aesthetic. Her art of matchmaking, knitting, storytelling, cooking, and community building is a form of plotting not unlike Emma's; her plots are as ingenious and her solutions as creative. Yet while Woolf's novel validates the activity more than Austen's, it also clearly measures its costs. During the dinner and at the beach, the guests only come together because Mrs. Ramsay wills them to, because she can hide from them, and from herself, the irredeemable areas of contradiction and disconnection. She can do so, however, only by absorbing that discord, just as she absorbs the disagreements between herself and her husband.[55] Only later do we find out how provisional and fragile, how momentary and how costly the community and the marriage she creates really are. Mrs. Ramsay literally spends herself in order to sustain husband, children, and guests: "There was scarcely a shell of herself left for her to know herself by; all was so lavished and spent" (p. 60). "She often felt she was nothing but a sponge sopped full of human emotions" (p. 51). Even in the moments when she is alone and sees herself as a "wedge-shaped core of darkness" relating only to the beam of the lighthouse, we realize that the archetypal mother, presiding over the archetypal family, can claim for herself only silence, emptiness, and darkness, not presence and plenitude.[56] Mrs. Ramsay exists to reflect Mr. Ramsay's sterility, her son's anger, her daughters' desire, the existence of inanimate things. Her only moment of triumph is her ability *not* to speak—*not* to say to Mr. Ramsay that she loves him.

In substituting Lily's art for Mrs. Ramsay's, Woolf is not only substituting a woman's independent unmarried life for Mrs. Ramsay's compulsive and fatal life of "giving, giving, giving," but she is also calling into question the traditional standards of female artistic achievement represented by Mrs. Ramsay, those that are dependent on sacrifice and subordination, on a cruel "consent to femininity." Woolf speaks of this lack of full cooperation in *A Room of One's Own*, remarking on the anger of the gentlemen who are used to seeing themselves reflected in the female looking-glass at twice their natural size. Lily's refusal of marriage is her refusal of this role and a refusal, as well, of the economic and emotional dependence fostered by the institution of marriage. Yet her rejection of the course Mrs. Ramsay has taken cannot be total; against her will, Lily finds herself being nice to Charles and comforting Mr. Ramsay.

I see Lily's solution to what art should be and her completion of the painting as being made possible by yet another partial, modulated refusal. Presenting only a very provisional form of closure, one that can be read from within the pattern of Sido and Colette or of Demeter and Persephone, the painting itself ultimately refuses a notion of artistic permanence. In fact, in a clear reversal of the myth, Lily envisions the dead Mrs. Ramsay and Prue, the married women, walking through fields of flowers, just as Persephone does *before* her rape and marriage. For Lily, this repeated and dream-like vision gives rise to another vision—the apparition of an approving Mrs. Ramsay on the steps. The timeless vision of Mrs. Ramsay and Prue is a vision of death. Both married, mother and daughter are both dead. The married mother cannot offer a refuge from the underworld of marriage and the triangular structure of the nuclear family, represented in the vision by the third mysterious figure that accompanies them. Death, the novel implies, might result if Lily's desire for unity and intimacy could be fulfilled or, conversely, if she were willing to participate in Mr. Ramsay's and Mr. Tansley's male plot. Although there is no third option for Lily, she chooses neither of the two debilitating ones, or both.

The contradiction between the two options is not resolved in the novel, but its two sides are maintained in a state of perpetual tension. Thus the parallel plot of Part III, the male oedipal story of the trip to the lighthouse, offsets the threat of female dissolution, just as the female plot of mother-daughter reunification offsets the threat of marriage and appropriation. Gayatri Spivak has argued that Lily uses the men in the novel as instruments, to further her work—Charles Tansley's nasty comments are actually productive, and Mr. Ramsay's trip enables her to see Mrs. Ramsay. Charles Tansley is in fact the "brother" who, in *this* text, has become a useful antagonist: in the scene on the beach, for example, Lily and Charles act like a brother and a sister whose relationship is mediated and controlled by a tolerant and maternal Mrs. Ramsay. Again, as we have seen in *A Room* and *Break of Day*, male presence provides a mediating space which clarifies the liminal position of women's discourse and of female relationships in the realm of the father, thereby making possible the representation of mother-daughter love.

Significantly, the novel does not end triumphantly with the vision of Mrs. Ramsay come back to life. After the vision on the steps, Lily and the narrator turn to Mr. Ramsay's landing at the lighthouse and to Mr. Carmichael. Only then does Lily go back to the painting, only then can she think about how to complete it: "There it was—her picture. . . . It would be hung in the attics, she thought; it would be destroyed. But what did that matter? she asked herself, taking up her brush again. She looked at the steps; they were empty; she looked at her canvas; it was blurred. With a sudden intensity, as if she saw it clear for a second, she drew a line there, in the centre. It was done; it was finished. Yes, she thought, laying down her brush in extreme fatigue, I have had my vision" (pp. 309–310).

What does the painting, what does this line look like and what does it mean? Critics have assumed that the line is the textual equivalent of the lighthouse which connects the two disparate parts of the painting, but that assumption needs to be reexamined. Is the line horizontal, we might ask, connecting the masses on the right and left? Is it vertical, suggesting not unity but separation? Or does it radiate in different directions like the rays of the lighthouse? I would argue that the novel chooses not to interpret this crucial moment, but rather supports contradictory readings of it. This very undecidability makes it a rejection, or at least a revision of the aesthetic requirements to which modernist art still adheres and to which Lily has been trying to live up throughout the novel. Here is an acknowledgment that the masses on the right and left can neither be connected nor remain disconnected, but must be both. This reading is only possible, of course, because we have a verbal description of a visual image—it would not be possible were the image represented for us. This explains Woolf's choice of a visual rather than a verbal artist for the protagonist of this novel. The line is drawn in the space where Lily can be productive—between mother and father, between feminine and masculine; not meant as a connection, it marks the perpetual boundary of Lily's difference.[57] In this sense, Lily's solution—the line at the center—could be read as the equivalent of Mrs. Ramsay's shawl, instead of as a repetition of the lighthouse. When Cam is afraid of the skull on the wall and unable to go to sleep, whereas James refuses to go to sleep if the skull is removed, Mrs. Ramsay decides, brilliantly I think, to cover the skull with her shawl so that it can be present for James and absent for Cam. Similarly, the line can mean presence and absence, connection and disconnection for Lily, and the bodily gesture of painting it can both connect and separate her from the model of Mrs.

Ramsay. Unlike Cam, who continues to deal with the father's demand for sympathy, hating him, admiring him, relying on him to save her from drowning, and who continues to subordinate her own feelings to those of her brother James, Lily succeeds in breaking her own silence in the novel. The possibility of expression comes with her decisive drawing of the line, her acceptance of contradiction and of the boundary.

Woolf's modernist style, with its violent interruptions and alternations demonstrates the implications of such an aesthetic choice. The culmination of Part I—the dinner party, the silent expression of love between the Ramsays—is followed by the violent and devastating intervention of Part II—the destruction of the war, the dissolution of the house, the breaking of the mirror, the devastating effects of maternal death. This "Time Passes" section is itself full of shocking stylistic breaks and cuts, not the least of which is the parenthetical mention of the deaths of Mrs. Ramsay herself, of Prue in childbirth, and of Andrew in the war. This experiment with an impersonal representation of loss and mourning itself illustrates the aesthetic of "both/and": there is no writing without loss, and writing cannot quite constitute recovery. Loss is the pretext for a fictional attempt at recovery. Similarly, Lily's longing cry for "Mrs. Ramsay, Mrs. Ramsay," which eventually results in the vision, is immediately followed not by that vision but by the brief and bracketed chapter about fishing: "(Macalister's boy took one of the fish and cut a square out of its side to bait his hook with. The mutilated body (it was alive still) was thrown back into the sea.)" (p. 268). The reader, like Lily, must learn to adjust to such shocking cuts, to recognize and maintain contradictions rather than trying to subsume them into a false synthesis. At the end of Part III, Mr. Ramsay compliments James, they land at the lighthouse, Lily completes her painting. Yet the double plot does not merge and oppositions remain. Mrs. Ramsay remains potentially present (she did appear on the steps for a moment), but now the steps are empty. Cam, as Elizabeth Abel has pointed out, remains the silent victim of paternal filiation who can only "gesture toward a story she cannot tell."[58] Lily herself has learned to relinquish her demand for unity and permanence. Her "It would be hung in the attics, she thought; it would be destroyed," echoes Woolf's own predictions of the reception of *A Room of One's Own*: "I am afraid it will not be taken seriously. . . . I doubt that I mind very much. . . . It is a trifle, I shall say; so it is; but I wrote it with ardour and conviction."[59] Similarly Lily feels, "I have had my vision." The process of writing, the ardour put into it, and not the product or the response are the bases of Lily's and of Woolf's own aesthetic.

As she strolls through Oxbridge, Woolf muses about Milton's *Lycidas*, an elegy like *To the Lighthouse*, rethinking it as a work which is not venerable and whole like a religious object but the result of a process of creation and alteration. Such is Lily's painting: it need not last like Mr. Carmichael's poetry; she is content to see it "clear for a second," content to accept that "the vision must be perpetually remade" (p. 270). She is content to have had her vision, because it is the concrete and *bodily* process of having it that is important, and not the vision itself. In this conception of her art, Lily is not far removed from Mrs. Ramsay whose creative act is the "boeuf en daube," quickly consumed yet remembered by those who were present. In her new borderline language unknown to men, but in which men are also involved, intimacy redefines knowledge and constitutes art: not possession, it becomes a form of momentary contact, continually in need of being remade.[60]

Plots and Modernisms

For Peter Brooks, literary modernism is marked by a despairing feeling of belatedness and secondariness. There are no longer any primary narratives—stories have to be retold, repeated endlessly, like Mr. Ramsay's repeated "we perished, each alone." The modernist author—Conrad or Faulkner—is no more than a belated follower in the track of another, intent on recapturing a sense of primacy and fulfillment that has been lost. These are not descriptions of artistic production that apply either to "Colette" or to Lily. As Gilbert and Gubar describe it: "The son of many fathers, today's male writer feels hopelessly belated; the daughter of too few mothers, today's female writer feels she is helping to create a viable tradition which is at last definitively emerging."[61]

For Lily it is not a question of recovering a past she has lost—she is only a surrogate daughter and was never symbiotically fused with Mrs. Ramsay. Unlike Brooks's modernist protagonists, Lily is not destined to repeat interminably a story that has already been told. She ultimately understands that she is not in a relation of secondariness to Mrs. Ramsay, as she had thought in the first part of the novel. For "Colette," "Sido" does provide a positive and at times enviable model of passion and strength, yet it is not a model she aims simply to emulate. Much of her anxiety in *Break of Day* comes precisely from the difficulty of distinguishing identification from separation. Since "Sido" also writes, the sense of primacy and secondariness disappears as the daughter learns to see the mother as an artist like herself. For these daughters, it is rather a question of rewriting the past, of reframing the stories of "Sido" and Mrs. Ramsay, of refusing to repeat them, even while acknowledging the importance of maternal inheritance. Lily's story, "Colette's" story, the story of their generation of women, is located between *repetition* of past female plots and the possibility of *transformation*.

Unlike their Victorian predecessors, these protagonists do not begin their stories by affirming that their lives will be utterly different from their mothers'. Consequently, they allow themselves to know the mothers' stories and can, through knowledge and intimacy, transform them—they can both repeat and not repeat. In the Victorian novels I discussed, maternal inheritance was lacking—the jewels came down through fathers and husbands, never were they directly bequeathed by mothers. In *To the Lighthouse,* the brooch Minta loses when she agrees to marry Paul was her grandmother's; the novel she forgets is *Middlemarch.* Maternal inheritance is valuable here, but it is always in danger of being replaced by paternal heritage. Paul cannot replace the brooch, marriage cannot substitute for the all-female treasures of the pre-oedipal. Through her painting, Lily wants to keep, change, and incorporate all that Minta had to sacrifice. Mrs. Ramsay does allow her daughters to pick out jewels for her, yet Prue, who does, dies because she simply repeats Mrs. Ramsay's choices. Lily, on the other hand, does not simply lose herself in the space of Mrs. Ramsay's buried treasures; she reframes them on the canvas of her picture. Similarly, "Colette" needs to transform the pink cactus into a "book." Lily and "Colette" need both to accept and to reject the inheritance of a maternal tradition.

What visions of modernism and what kind of plot models can we glean from this reading of Woolf's novel and of Colette's? Glancing back to the text with which I began may provide some suggestions. I am interested in *A Room of One's Own* not for its points about women and fiction, but for its progression, through digression and contradiction, toward something that does not resemble a conclusion. Repetition, for Brooks, is more than a description of the modernist writer's relation to the writers of the past. As "a movement from passivity to mastery," repetition is basic to and "initiatory of narrative" itself. It relates to what Todorov speaks of as the basic constitution of plot out of the tension between two formal categories: difference and resemblance, or the "same-but-different." In Brooks's redefinition, based on a reading of Freud's *Beyond the Pleasure Principle* and the notion of repetition compulsion, the static and formalist model of the "same-but-different" is transformed into a dynamic model moving from beginning through middle to end. "Narrative always makes the implicit claim to be in a state of repetition, as a going over again of a ground already covered: a *sjuzet* repeating a *fabula,* as the detective retraces the tracks of the criminal" (Brooks, p. 97). In narrative we go "back over the same ground"; "an event gains meaning by its repetition . . . the concept of repetition hovers ambiguously between the idea of reproduction and that of change, forward and backward movement" (p. 100). For Brooks, repetition *binds* the plot, but the process of *binding*—postponement and delay—is painful and tense, urging us toward the end, an end which cannot, however, be reached too quickly and which, when reached, is a return to a "transcendent home" (p. 111).

Woolf suggests that repetition itself does not work for women writers of her age; its connotations are just too debilitating. Repetition is going into the library for research and finding no help in the texts of men. Repetition is the *déjà-lu,* the story that has been told too many times. Repetition, in the female plot, is the noise of the children which makes the air full of vibrations and prevents us from hearing clearly (p. 295). Repetition is the

Victorian mother/daughter plot, the daughter repeating a maternal story
that is unspeakable.

Woolf and Colette, it seems to me, suggest *contradiction* and *oscillation* as
alternate strategies to repetition, as ways to relate to the writing of the past,
to "think back through their mothers." They provide ways not to *bind* the
plot in order to make it progress, but to *bond* with it. Whereas binding
connotes constraint, bonding is a looser and more voluntary form of
connection. "In a question like this," Woolf says, "truth is only to be had
by laying together many varieties of error" (*A Room*, p. 109). But writing
through contradiction instead of repetition, bonding instead of binding,
will have the effect Woolf finds in her own reading of women writers of the
1920s. Mary Carmichael's first novel, for example, is upsetting to read.
"Mary is tampering with the expected sequence. First she broke the sentence; now she has broken the sequence . . . the expected order. Perhaps
she had done this unconsciously, merely giving things their natural order,
as a woman would if she wrote like a woman. But the effect was somewhat
baffling; one could not see a wave heaping itself, a crisis coming round the
next corner" (*A Room*, pp. 85, 95). This sense of discomfort and irresolution
does mark the plots I am discussing, in which the oscillation between
opposites, the shifting allegiances, the duplicitous posturing are not resolved into comfortable or harmonious ordering. No clearcut sense of
closure ensues and the narrative remains prospective and proleptic, poised
at break of day, or focused on the process rather than the product of vision.
Contradiction itself is not, of course, a total rejection of repetition; it is
merely one pole of it. If at one pole we have binding and the "same-but-
different," at the other, we have a refusal to return, a looking forward, a
bonding, which is implied in the idea of maternity and the experience of
reproduction.

From Daughter to Mother? Wharton's *The Mother's Recompense*

Break of Day and *To the Lighthouse* remain the narratives of daughters. The
discourse of the dead mother is mediated through the voice of the daughter-artist. The mother herself does not speak as subject and the woman
artist writes or paints as a daughter and not as a mother. This is true even
for Colette, who was a mother in life, although only rarely in her work. Are
there, in this period, more plural texts that are capable of including both
voices and perspectives, the mother's and the daughter's, thereby
transcending the elegiac structure of *To the Lighthouse* and *Break of Day*? To
what extent does the mother-daughter narrative depend on irredeemable
loss, on initial separation, and on male intervention?

One contemporaneous novel which does inscribe a maternal voice and
perspective, Edith Wharton's *The Mother's Recompense* (1925), seems to offer
a contrasting, perhaps inverse model.[62] Kate Clephane, the mother, is the

center of consciousness in this novel; Anne, her adult daughter, is seen only from the mother's perspective. Here, the initial separation, which predates the start of the novel by nearly twenty years, was the result of maternal and not daughterly abandonment. Desperately unhappy in her marriage, Kate left husband and child to run off with another man. In this reversal of the Demeter plot, the mother is abducted and, twenty years later, the daughter acts as the agent of their reunification. The blissful reunion of mother and daughter, their physical closeness, intuitive understanding, and uninterrupted happiness form the narrative of the novel's first part, marred only by Kate's anxiety about her past infraction. Here too everything seems reversed. Perfect, mysterious, and idealized by her mother, Anne is the Sido or Mrs. Ramsay figure. "It was from Anne's presence, her smile, her voice, the mystery of her eyes even, that the healing flowed. If Kate had an apprehension left, it was her awe—almost— of that completeness of Anne's" (p. 59). Anne takes care of her mother, nurtures and feeds her, supports her financially, and even tries to bequeathe to her the family jewels, her ancestral home, and her money. In fact, neither daughter nor mother want the material signs of conventional marriage and family life, inherited from the father. They try to give them to each other and to remain outside the weighty structures of tradition which Kate once fled. Living together in perfect happiness in this first section of the novel, they actually manage to stand outside of these potentially debilitating conventions. Anne paints, Kate watches, nurtures, and supports her daughter's artistic ambitions and achievements. As they get closer, Kate believes she has repaired the breech caused by her terrible abandonment. "But now, for the first time, love and security dwelt together in her in a kind of millenial quiet" (p. 119).

The second part of the novel reintroduces the breech, however, and in a form that proves to be irreparable. From the pre-oedipal plot of mother-daughter symbiosis, the novel moves to a prototypically and unalterably oedipal plot, which, contrary to the initial appearance, reinscribes the novel into the oedipal/pre-oedipal plot patterns we saw earlier in this chapter. Mother and daughter are separated again, and again as a result of male intrusion. The man is Chris Fenno, a young man with whom Kate had had a secret affair before the war. The only man she had ever loved, Chris was the agent of her sexual awakening. When Chris enters the story now it is to love and to marry Anne. Kate knows that if she is to retain the precious love of Anne, her own transgressive affair with Chris must remain a secret; but she also knows that as long as it does remain a secret, she will lose Anne to Chris in marriage. It becomes clear that, with Chris's appearance in the story, mother-daughter closeness is irredeemably lost, never to be regained.

Kate's choice is terrible: losing Anne by telling her or losing Anne by not telling her. What this novel makes utterly and starkly clear is that mother and daughter cannot coexist together as adult *sexual* women. The secret that forever divides them is the secret of maternal sexuality. Kate cannot imagine saying to her daughter about Chris: "Yes, I loved once—and the man I loved was not your father" (p. 105). Kate knows that, in her world, to be a "real" mother is to renounce her sexuality and her memory of Chris, to be content to recede into the background, perhaps to marry old Fred Landers and to become, as Demeter does, an old woman when her daughter reaches maturity. If mother and daughter are both sexual, what Anne calls their "experiment" to live together as "perfect pals" becomes revoltingly incestuous. When Anne cries out, repeatedly, "I want you both," she is uttering a plea for triangularity and bi-sexual oscillation; but so long as Kate insists on remaining sexual, Anne cannot have her wish.[63]

What separates mother and daughter in this second part is silence—the result of male interruption and intrusion in the oedipal plot. Sexuality is shrouded by secrecy. Anne's choice of Chris over her mother is her entry into the oedipal plot, and her development takes the predictable form. Kate's attempt to stop her is an illusory effort to remain in the realm of pre-oedipal mother-daughter bliss, a bliss that, because of her initial transgression, is already illusory. Mother and daughter have to live in the house and the world of the father, ruled by his property and transformed by his war, which, the characters emphasize, has socialized Chris into the man Anne wants to marry.

The novel's third part contains a resolution of sorts, one which is based on the model of oscillation this chapter has outlined. I would argue that, although *The Mother's Recompense* seems to offer a different maternal plot, it is as deeply implicated in oedipal heterosexual structures and models as the other texts discussed in this chapter. Separated from her daughter by her own self-affirmation, Kate herself invents a solution which, ironically, she describes as renunciation. She frees herself from the temptation of marrying Fred Landers and turning into the dull Enid Drover, her matronly sister-in-law, by confessing her sin to Fred, who cannot live with her and the knowledge. She leaves New York, goes back to the Riviera where she was at the beginning, and lives by letters—letters from Anne whom she will never see again, and weekly letters from Fred, repeating a marriage proposal he knows she will never accept. This repeated renunciation keeps Kate alive, lends her all of her self-esteem, her pride, her sense of self. "Nothing on earth would ever again help her—help to blot out the old horrors and the new loneliness—as much as the fact of being able to take her stand on that resolve, of being able to say to herself, whenever she began to drift toward new uncertainties and fresh concessions, that once at least she had stood fast, shutting away in a little space of peace and light the best thing that had ever happened to her" (p. 272). What she shuts away is both her preoedipal moment with Anne—a moment that can be preserved only by renouncing a continuing relationship which would wear away at what makes it best—and her affair with Chris. She can only have Anne by renouncing her. She can only be a mother, "what she was destined to be," by redefining the institution of motherhood, which traditionally demands an even more devastating renunciation of sexuality and selfhood.

If Kate's is a maternal story, it fails to redefine the terms of the daughterly and elegiac qualities of Colette's and Woolf's texts. Like them, *The Mother's Recompense* underscores the compulsory heterosexuality and triangularity to which women's narrative in the 1920s continued to subscribe.

III.

Postmodernist Plots/ Maternal Subjects

4

FEMINIST FAMILY ROMANCES
LIFE BEFORE OEDIPUS

> In prehistory there are no men.
>
> —Margaret Atwood

> Three women
> on a marriage bed, two
> mothers and two daughters.
> All through the war we slept
> like this . . .
> Later we fought so
> bitterly through the peace
> that father blanched in his uniform . . .
>
> —Olga Broumas

> Hating one's mother was the feminist
> enlightenment of the 50's and 60's;
> but it is only a metaphor for hating
> oneself. Female literature of the 70's
> goes beyond matrophobia to a
> courageously sustained quest for the
> mother.
>
> —Elaine Showalter

Writing as Re-Vision

In 1971, Adrienne Rich re-read *A Room of One's Own* as she was writing her own important essay about women and fiction, "When We Dead Awaken: Writing as Re-Vision."[1] Like Woolf, Rich presents herself as someone attempting to chart new territory, however tentatively: "For writers, and at this moment for women writers in particular, there is the challenge and the promise of a whole new psychic geography to be explored. But there is also a difficult and dangerous walking on ice, as we try to find languages and images for a consciousness we are just coming into, and with little in the past to support us" (p. 91). The thematics of Rich's essay are similar to Woolf's: the difficulties of writing as a woman in a tradition and a context dominated by men and by male institutions, the interruptions of housework, the lack of space, time, and freedom that stifle female creativity. Like *A Room of One's Own*, Rich's essay defines the place of women writers within a generation that is just in the process of coming into a "new" "feminist" consciousness and self-consciousness. Very much as it does for Woolf, that emergence takes place by way of a thoughtful consideration of the legacy of the past. Both Woolf and Rich find their respective generations hovering between a yet uncharted future and a no longer useful past. And still that past remains an important reference point. Where Woolf insisted that "We think back through our mothers if we are women," Rich defines all writing as a process of re-vision: "Re-vision—the act of looking back, of seeing with fresh eyes, of entering an old text from a new critical direction—is for us more than a chapter in our cultural history: it is an act of survival. . . . We need to know the writing of the past, and know it differently than we have ever known it" (pp. 90–91).

Re-reading Woolf's essay is, for Rich, such an act of re-vision, such a process of self-definition in relation/in contrast to the texts, the lives, and the stories of the past. (I'm finding it difficult to find terms for that relation since Rich insists that "we need to know the writing of the past differently than we have ever known it"). And just as Woolf criticized Charlotte Brontë for her anger, Rich criticizes Woolf for not being angry enough in *A Room*: "I was astonished at the sense of effort, of pains taken, of dogged tentativeness in the tone of that essay. . . . It is the tone of a woman almost in touch with her anger, who is determined not to appear angry, who is *willing* herself to be calm, detached, and even charming in a roomful of men where things have been said which are attacks on her very integrity. Virginia Woolf is addressing an audience of women, but she is acutely conscious—as she always was—of being overheard by men" (p. 92). Rich insists that this consciousness, this double audience, has begun to change in the 1970's. Although she is addressing a plenary session at the convention of the Modern Language Association, which she describes, in Woolf's terms, as a "procession of the sons of educated men," and in her own, as "both marketplace and funeral parlor for the professional study of Western literature in the United States," she is specifically talking not to the men but to those feminist scholars and writers who are working in the "interstices of these gentlemanly rites (or, in Mary Daly's words, on the boundaries of this patriarchal space)."[2] In so doing, she is both challenging and re-vising the "compulsory heterosexuality" of discourse, to use one of her own later terms.

Writing specifically for women and unconcerned about being overheard by men, then, Rich's voice is more personal, less artful; her narrative is more directly about her own writing, more straightforwardly autobiographical than Woolf's. Even as she traces her difficulty in coming to write poetry in the first person, and the effort it took to move from "she" to "I," she separates herself from Woolf by "us[ing] myself as illustration." Although the "I" is by no means unproblematic, Rich insists that, in comparison to Woolf, the contradictions she describes are more directly her own. Most importantly, she acknowledges the anger that accompanies the contradictions that have shaped female plot and the careers of women writers throughout this century. As she confronts her anger and stops trying for the "objectivity" and the "detachment" to which, she says, Woolf aspired, Rich can begin to map the newly emerging psychic geography of a *feminist* consciousness: "And this drive to self-knowledge is more than a search for identity: it is part of her refusal of the destructiveness of male-dominated society" (p. 90).

How can we characterize the relationship between Rich and Woolf here? The purpose, Rich says, is "not to pass on a tradition but to break its hold over us." What does it mean to "know" the texts of the past "differently than we have ever known" them? And in what ways does the commitment to female relationships affect what Woolf still experienced as the "compulsory heterosexuality" of academic and literary discourse? As Elaine Showalter has said, women's literature of the 1970s is based upon a "sustained quest" for the "mother,"[3] both the biological and the cultural mother. At this particular moment of women's writing—at the moment of an emerging political feminist movement, of a feminist literary consciousness and at the moment of a scholarship which explores gender difference in a number of academic disciplines—what plots become speakable between mothers and daughters, what developmental paradigms emerge for fictional heroines and for women writers, and how is female subject-formation represented? This chapter will address some of these questions.

While the ambition to present oneself as starting afresh is certainly in itself neither new nor different, it does acquire a particular valence for feminist writers of the 1970s who are, on the one hand, immersed in the post-modern sense of the "déjà-lu," the always already read, and, on the other, part of a feminist consciousness and a historical moment which wants to situate itself at a significant distance from previous generations. It is thus that the notion of revision becomes particularly significant. No new model—whether psychological or literary—emerges as definitive: the relation between past, present, and future is viewed as neither linear, causal, nor progressive. As we saw in the previous chapter, the women writers of Virginia Woolf's generation, whom writers of the 1970s regard as precursors, inscribed intense contradictions into their texts. The generation of Adrienne Rich, as we shall see in this chapter, tries not to resolve but to revise these contradictions in the process of creating a new feminist subject. Yet, as Rich suggests, "the new psychic geography" of feminist consciousness is treacherously unstable and those who explore it are "walking on ice." The process of charting it entails intense and repeated shifts and re-turns.

The history of "When We Dead Awaken: Writing as Re-Vision" itself provides an interesting illustration of the re-visionary pattern that defines much feminist writing in the 1970s. Rich initially gave it as a talk at the 1971 Modern Language Association Conference, then published it, unchanged, in a special issue of *College English*. With "a few revisions, mainly updating," it was then "reprinted" in *American Poets in 1976*. In 1978 this latter revised text appeared in Rich's own collection *On Lies, Secrets, and Silence*, supplemented by some introductory comments, and several footnotes marked "A.R. 1978." The content of the two revisions is significant.[4]

In lengthening the essay in 1976 and including more examples from her poetry to trace the development of her own poetic and political consciousness, Rich's speaker understands, first of all, that she had heretofore falsely represented the conflict of the woman poet as a conflict between " 'love'—womanly, maternal, altruistic love . . . and egotism—a force directed by men into creation, achievement, ambition, often at the expense of others, but justifiably so" (*On Lies*, pp. 46–47). It is perhaps this insight— "the word 'love' is itself in need of re-vision"—which leads Rich to change radically the ending of her piece. In 1971, she ended optimistically, anticipating "another story to be told," the story of masculine consciousness which, she felt, was also waiting to "gestate and give birth to his own subjectivity" and to the understanding that although "women can no longer be primarily mothers and muses for men, . . . we can go on trying to talk to each other, we can sometimes help each other, poetry and fiction can show us what we are going through" (p. 98). In contrast, in 1976, Rich ends her essay by asserting, Cassandra-like, that "the creative energy of patriarchy is fast running out; what remains is its self-generating energy for destruction" (*On Lies*, p. 49). Rather than "giving birth to" their own subjectivity, she feels men are "generating" destruction, in their sexual brutality against women and even in their consciously political poetry, their self-pitying condemnations of the Chilean junta or U.S. imperialism which refuse to recognize that the enemy can also be within. From a conciliatory position in 1971, Rich's feminism moves toward separatism in 1976: "A new generation of women poets is already working out of the psychic energy released when women begin to move out towards what the feminist philosopher Mary Daly has described as the 'new space' on the boundaries of patriarchy" (*On Lies*, p. 49).

But in her introductory comments added in 1978, Rich is already more cautious about idealizing the mutual love and celebration of women working together in this "new space." Here, she discusses two challenges confronting mainstream academic feminist literary criticism—the charge of black and lesbian feminists that their own work has failed to receive sufficient attention, and the reminder from the activist women's movement that academic feminism might be losing its necessary connection to the political movement. The enemy, certainly, is not safely contained outside the self. And, clearly, that "new space" on the boundaries of patriarchy is not a fixed territory but shapes and reshapes itself in response to shifting political and ideological contexts.

Rich's move into a female world, away from a reconciliation with "the male imagination," illustrates an important configuration in feminist writing of the 1970s: the death or elimination of the father, the brother, the husband, the male lover from feminist fiction and from feminist theorizing—from what I have come to call the feminist family romance and from the fictional heroine's developmental course. Whereas in the nineteenth-century novel, mothers had to be eliminated or disempowered so that heroines could have access to plot, in the texts of the 1970s, the elimination of fathers has become either a precondition or an important preoccupation of female plots. The liminal discourse of female modernism, embedded in shifting affiliations, gives way here to a more passionate embrace of female allegiance as the basis both of female plotting and of female subject-formation.

Another, seemingly minor, but extremely significant change occurs at the end of the 1976 version of "Writing as Re-Vision." Rich's 1971 metaphor of feminist self-birth—"both the victimization and the anger experienced by women . . . are our birth-pains and we are bearing ourselves" (p. 98)—is simply dropped from the revised essay which reads: "both the victimization and the anger experienced by women . . . will go on being tapped and explored by poets, among others" (*On Lies*, p. 49). Rich does not comment on this change in imagery, yet clearly the figure of feminist self-generation and self-birthing is important in the context of her own very concrete discussion, throughout the essay, of her motherhood and the barriers it posed to writing. And its omission becomes important in relation to the publication, also in 1976, of her ground-breaking analysis of motherhood, *Of Woman Born: Motherhood as Experience and Institution.*[5] A major split characterizes the voice of the speaker in Rich's 1971 essay; she presents herself at once as the poet who is also the caretaking mother of three small children within the patriarchal institutions of marriage and motherhood, as the poet who is the daughter of Virginia Woolf and other female writers of the past, and as the sister in a feminist movement which would help women free themselves from the shackles of motherhood and daughterhood in a gesture of self-birth. In exploring and validating the role of the mother and the daughter of mothers, *Of Woman Born* implicitly criticizes Rich's own self-representation as self-created feminist subject in the earlier essay.

In *Of Woman Born*, Adrienne Rich urges all women to accept and to acknowledge the fundamental role their daughterhood and their motherhood play in their identity and self-definition as women. And she urges women to recognize and to explore what she defines as the most formative relationship in their lives: "The cathexis between mother and daughter—essential, distorted, misused—is the great unwritten story. Probably there is nothing in human nature more resonant with charges than the flow of energy between two biologically alike bodies, one of whom has lain in amniotic bliss inside the other, one of which has labored to give birth to the other" (p. 225). With Rich's book, with numerous studies in psychoanalysis, sociology, religion, anthropology, and history, and with numerous fictional texts by women writers focusing on mothers and daughters, that relationship quickly becomes a central aspect of "the new psychic geography" of feminist consciousness. Moreover, most studies exploring gender difference, whether theoretical or fictional, come to locate difference within the quality of mother-daughter connection. Whereas only a few years prior, Rich found it necessary to cut herself off from her mother by "giving birth to [herself],"—the break from the mother becoming the token of a feminist rejection of female victimization—in *Of Woman Born* and the many novels, poems, and essays which come to dominate the feminist writing of the period, the figure of the mother becomes an important object of exploration in relation to the birth of the feminist daughter. Thus, the "new space on the boundaries of patriarchy" is inhabited by daughters and mothers, whose lives and whose roles, whose very selves are deeply intertwined with one another. As Rich says "We are, none of us, 'either' mothers or daughters; to our amazement, confusion, and greater complexity, we are both" (*Of Woman Born*, p. 253). It is this sense of fundamental interconnection, both exhilarating and terrifying, that motivates feminists of the present both to know *the past* differently, and to *know* the past differently "than we have ever known it." And that knowledge is located in a moment—the pre-oedipal or, as Luce Irigaray has termed it, "the dark continent of the dark continent."[6]—which for modernist fiction and classic psychoanalysis had been unavailable and unspeakable.

The rest of this chapter considers some representations of female/feminist subject-formation and mother-daughter relationships in feminist fictional and theoretical writings of the 1970s and early 1980s, looking at some parallels, and some extremely telling differences, between revisionary psychoanalytic paradigms and fictional plot patterns. Several elements of these representations emerge with particular force: the impetus to return to a pre-oedipal, pre-verbal moment of origin which, though virtually unavailable to language and memory, nevertheless is meant to provide an instrument for binding the fragments of self; the more or less successful displacement of fathers and other male figures from the "feminist family romance"; the ideological implications of the specificity of mother-daughter bonding as basis for a definition of gender difference; the continuous process of re-vision and therefore destabilization as a defining structure of both feminist plotting and subject-formation.

Feminist Family Romances: Psychoanalytic Revisions

During the early 1970s, feminist writing and thinking undertook a fundamental critique of psychoanalytic thought, viewing Freud and his system as enforcing the subjugation of women in culture (Millett, Ellman,

Janeway). Psychoanalysis began to seem useful, even necessary to feminist thought, only with the intense effort of theorists like Juliet Mitchell, who took pains to present the works of Freud and Lacan not as in themselves perpetrating a system in which women are oppressed, but as reflecting and describing the internal workings of a culture which is gendered in particular ways.[7] Even though apologists like Mitchell convincingly argued the usefulness of psychoanalytic paradigms for a feminist analysis, still, many texts illustrate some of the possible pitfalls of a psychoanalytic framework for feminist thinking. Thus, for example, writers as varied as Nancy Friday in the popular text *My Mother/My Self: A Daughter's Search for Identity*[8] and Marie Cardinal in her novel *The Words to Say It*[9] follow Freud in blaming the mother for the daughter's victimization and make mother-hate the condition of female liberation and self-determination. Interestingly, both show a strong reliance on the (male) doctor/(female) patient relationship. Compensating for failed maternal nurturance, the doctor can thus induct the woman patient into a system which will only separate her from other women.[10] Both books have struck an extremely responsive chord in a broad spectrum of women readers. Adhering to basic psychoanalytic assumptions, both value separation as a touchstone of adult womanhood. Cardinal's protagonist is "cured" only when her mother dies. She first perceives herself as an adult only when she can distance herself in disgust from her mother's sick, rotting body, only when she can contemplate the fixed grimace of horror on her mother's dead face, and when she can use that death for her own awakening.

Works like Friday's and Cardinal's, founded as they are on classic psychoanalytic paradigms, demonstrate the problems for a feminist perspective of turning to a system which supports the denigration of women and female relationships, if only by reflecting rather than openly underwriting cultural assumptions. Yet, during the same period, the revisionary efforts of Jean Baker Miller, Dorothy Dinnerstein, Jane Flax, Evelyn Fox Keller, Jessica Benjamin, and especially of Nancy Chodorow and Carol Gilligan in America, and of Luce Irigaray, Michèle Montrelay, Julia Kristeva, and Hélène Cixous in France, demonstrate the need for psychoanalysis as the instrument of a vision of difference, of a model of female subject-formation and of female specificity which might redefine the self-denigrating visions exemplified by Friday and Cardinal. It is in their work that we can find several particularly compelling and influential versions of what I have called "feminist family romances." I continue to use this formulation to signal in the very process of revision a continued reliance on classic psychoanalytic paradigms and the pitfalls they inherently contain.

Nancy Chodorow's psychoanalytic feminism is especially mother-directed, even if it is not mother-centered, as Jane Gallop has recently claimed.[11] Going back to Freud's "Minoan-Mycenean civilizations," she seeks to explore and illuminate what he merely discovered, yet she does so by relying on object-relations psychology more than on a classic Freudian model. For Chodorow, the basis of female identity, then, lies not in the oedipal but in the pre-oedipal period; here mother-daughter bonding, not phallic lack, connection, not castration, characterize female identity; here closeness to the mother and not shift of allegiance to the father defines the process of women's development in culture. In the work of Luce Irigaray, moreover, female silence and negativity in language is replaced by a "parler-femme," an other, specifically feminine speech.[12] For Julia Kristeva, women's psychosocial position facilitates the access to the pre-symbolic, to what she calls the *semiotic*, which challenges the primacy of the logos, while for Hélène Cixous, women's speech is located in the body which through its menstrual blood, its mother's milk, becomes the locus of an erotics of writing and speaking.[13] In identifying a characteristically female pattern of selfhood and relation to language, and in locating that pattern not in autonomy but in fluidity and connectedness, these theorists offer a psychoanalysis much more in tune with the ideals of the feminist movement and, despite significant divergences among their works, participate in creating a psychoanalytic feminism of enormous influence.

These psychoanalytic feminisms (the plural is meant to call attention to profound differences among these theorists) tell a revisionary story of female (and male) development. Whether their sources lie in object-relations or in Lacanian theory—that is, whether they posit at the beginning maternal presence or absence—psychoanalytic feminists take as their starting point the formative influence of the pre-oedipal period and the female parent's domination of that period. The belief in a unique bond between mother and female child leads, in every case, to a revision of their psychoanalytic sources. The consequence is a re-definition of maturity as different either from autonomy and separation or from self-division and alienation. Adult personality, embedded in connectedness, offers a picture of continued mother-daughter entanglement. The result is a theory of language founded not on lack but on a form of plenitude, a myth of a mother-tongue which affirms, or at least suggests, the existence or the possibility of constructing something outside the name-of-the-father. These writers all find the sources of a different adulthood in pre-oedipal mother-daughter connection and conflict. Here, too, can be found the potential for transformation, for the subversion of patriarchal (oedipal and logo-centric) structures and assumptions.

The "feminist family romance" that emerges in these revisions of psychoanalytic plots and patterns, then, diverges radically both from Freud's family romance and from its female revision, the fantasy of "the-man-who-would-understand." Where Freud posits, at the basis of all individual development, an opposition between successive generations and the child's break from his parents—a break which dominates the female family romances as well—feminist revisionaries allow for the possibility of a continued inter-relation. This continuity is defined not by repetition or contradiction but by an attempted re-vision of the past and of the individual's relation to the past. Whereas for Freud the process of imagination and the activity of fabulation are motivated by loss and by the longing for liberation from familial constraints, for feminist theorists and for some feminist writers of the 1970s, the imagination is fueled either by a longing to reexperience symbiotic union with the mother (by identification with her) or by a struggle against an identification which still reveals a profound and continued closeness. The content of plot is not a process of successive distancing but, rather, is a struggle with a bond that is powerful and painful, that threatens engulfment and self-loss even while it offers the very basis for self-consciousness. In these writings the pre-oedipal realm figures as a powerful mythic space, not irrevocably lost but continually present because it is recoverable in ideal(ized) female relationships. Presymbolic and pre-cultural, it points to an alternative to patriarchy and the logos—a world of shared female knowledge and experience in which subject/object dualism and power relationships might be challenged and redefined.

Whereas the female family romance prevalent in nineteenth-century novels revolves around the attachment to a male figure, the brother or "man-who-would-understand," and the female family romance of the 1920s subscribes to a reliance on the "compulsory heterosexuality" of discourse, the feminist family romance of the 1970s de-emphasizes the role of men: the retreat to the pre-oedipal as basis for adult personality, the concentration on mother-daughter bonding and struggle, and the celebration of female relationships of mutual nurturance leave only a secondary role to men. Although the Freudian shift in libidinal attachment from mother to father still figures in this schema, it is less definitive, more tentative. It is the connection to the mother that carries emotional weight, not the shift to father or husband. In Chodorow's analysis the father offers at best some protection, some relief from a mother-daughter connection that threatens to become too stifling, too overbearing. No longer central, the father's presence constitutes no more than an alternative to the mother's. Moreover, Chodorow presents the adult woman's relation to her husband as so fundamentally unsatisfying that it insures what she has called the "reproduction of mothering." Unable to relive with her husband the primal symbiotic connection she shared with her mother in infancy, the adult woman needs a child with whom she might relive that bond *as* a mother. Chodorow also implies, although she never clearly develops this aspect of her analysis, that for women, lesbian relationships—relationships among individuals raised with similar ego structures—are bound to be more satisfying.[14] Whereas the connection between mother and daughter is fraught with potential dangers, intragenerational friendships among women offer only the benefits and not the pitfalls of same-sex bonding.

Other theorists also downplay the place of men in the story of female development. Dorothy Dinnerstein argues, for example, that women's own collusion in the perpetuation of patriarchy is their reaction to an overpowering mother-daughter bond.[15] Maternal omnipotence is so great a threat, she suggests, that we are willing to acquiesce to male rule in adulthood; even to women, paternal authority looks like a reasonable refuge. But the primary involvement, the involvement that counts emotionally and that forms the content of imaginary projection, is the passionate connection to the mother. For Luce Irigaray, the father functions as obstacle, as the antagonist who makes the continued connection between child and mother impossible, whose law decrees the maternal body off-limits to her child. Irigaray identifies not castration but the cutting of the umbilical cord as the child's original trauma: the father and his "nom" merely function to cover over the "nombril"—the scar which is the first and foremost trace of identity and the perpetual reminder of an initial traumatic rupture.[16]

This separation from men and the creation of a would-be separate all-female realm on the borders of patriarchal culture is fundamental to this version of the "feminist family romance" and to the self-representation of feminist consciousness. Women's self-representation rests on a radical vision of gender difference resulting from social gender arrangements which make women primarily responsible for infant and child care. Nancy Chodorow characterizes these differences as follows: "Feminine personality comes to be based less on repression of inner objects, and fixed and firm splits in the ego, and more on retention and continuity of external relationships. From the retention of pre-oedipal attachments to the mother, growing girls come to define themselves as continuous with others; their experience of self contains more flexible and permeable ego boundaries. Boys come to define themselves as more separate and distinct, with a greater sense of ego boundaries and differentiations. The basic feminine sense of self is connected to the world, the basic masculine sense of self is separate" (*The Reproduction of Mothering*, p. 169). The theorization of such far-reaching differences in personality structure have the effect of distancing not only woman from man in individual heterosexual relationships, but also, much more generally, feminine from masculine cultural realms; they create a myth of female separateness which underscores values of empathy and connectedness, overturning traditional value structures and implying the superiority of women to men.

Jane Flax and Jessica Benjamin, among others, have identified far-reaching consequences for the gender asymmetry which lies at the basis of subject-formation and for the resulting conflation of individuality and masculinity.[17] According to Benjamin, "Selfhood is defined negatively as separateness from others" (p. 148). Because of the ways boys and girls relate to and differentiate from their mothers, they grow up to play different roles in the inevitable division between subject and object, domination and submission defining human interaction in Western culture. "The male posture . . . prepares for the role of master. . . . The female posture disposes the woman to accept objectification and control. . . . He asserts individual selfhood, while she relinquishes it" (p. 167). This division of roles, Benjamin insists, creates a false sense of differentiation which perpetuates, in our culture, a form of "rational violence" leading to sado-masochism in human relationships and to the possession and domination of nature.

The fact that theories arguing gender difference should emerge with such force and urgency during the 1970s is certainly not surprising. In the face of increasing threats of war and nuclear destruction, in both Europe and the United States, it might have seemed essential to imagine an alternative to what was perceived as masculine destructiveness.[18] The feminine, of course, presented only one of many possible "others" who could provide an alternative, a way out of Western phallogocentrism, one possible deconstruction and reconstruction of the masculine rational, authorial subject. The space of "otherness" located in the feminine is the pre-oedipal space of mother-daughter mirroring, which comes to replace the rupture between self and world implied in the destructiveness of war. American feminism, then, creates a fantasy of cultural survival through the dissemination of traditionally feminine values into the public world (*polis*), on the one hand, and through a reconstruction of the masculine by means of greater involvement in the home (*oikos*), on the other.[19] French feminism, operating in a poststructuralist context which has already challenged any notion of defined identity or ego and any unified transcendental subject, still views the notion of the "feminine" as the means by which to break out of phallogocentrism, through silence toward otherness. Whether based on the object-relations model of ego development or in the deconstructive vision of a split subject, psychoanalytic feminisms have engaged in a process of revision with global and visionary aspirations.

Both Chodorow and Dinnerstein conclude their books with a call for shared childrearing in early infancy and throughout childhood. If fathers shared in the all-powerful role of primary caretaker, they argue, a more balanced human race might develop, one whose attachments might be more flexible and varied. If we subscribe to their analysis of gender difference, however, we might wonder where the sympathetic, nurturing, and empathic men, eager to participate in child-rearing, would come from. The effort to bring men into the nursery, although convincingly presented as a desirable goal, emerges in Chodorow's book in a conclusion not supported by the persuasive argument of gender difference which pervades the rest of the book. Yet, in an important sense, it is the logical conclusion of her theoretical argument. This return of the father does not offset his displacement in her family romance. At best, paternal nurturance is presented as a potential, still primarily utopian solution, a conflation perhaps of what in Sara Ruddick's or Carol Gilligan's terms is a longer process of masculine re-education and transformation.

The feminist family romance of the 1970s is based on the separation not from parents or the past, but from patriarchy and from men in favor of female alliances. Yet, inasmuch as this romance is centered almost entirely on the experience of daughters, with mothers no more than objects supporting and underlying their daughters' process of individuation, this very rejection, this very isolation of a female realm creates an uncomfortable position for mothers themselves. It is the woman as *daughter* who occupies the center of the global reconstruction of subjectivity and subject-object relation. The woman as *mother* remains in the position of *other*, and the emergence of feminine-daughterly subjectivity rests and depends on that continued and repeated process of *othering* the mother.

Adrienne Rich identifies "matrophobia" as a predominant preoccupation of feminist women; I would suggest that it might be seen as the underside of the feminist family romance. "Thousands of daughters see their mothers as having taught a compromise and self-hatred they are struggling to win free of, the one through whom the restrictions and degradations of a female existence were perforce transmitted. Easier by far to hate and reject a mother outright than to see beyond her to the forces acting upon her. But where a mother is hated to the point of matrophobia there may also be a deep underlying pull toward her, a dread that if one relaxes one's guard one will identify with her completely" (*Of Woman Born*, p. 235). Clearly, daughters are at the center of the feminist family romance; clearly mothers remain in the position of dreaded other, of objects to the daughters' emerging subjectivity. Matrophobia, Rich reminds us, is "the fear not of one's mother or of motherhood but of *becoming one's mother*" (p. 235). Mothers are perceived as women whose allegiance is with the father rather than the daughters: "we thought she loved/that strange male body first/ that took, that took, whose taking seemed a law."[20]

Luce Irigaray's two short texts, "When Our Lips Speak Together" (1977) and "And the One Doesn't Stir Without the Other" (1979), clarify what I would identify as the ultimate shift in attachment that characterizes the feminist family romance, the compensatory shift from mother, not to father and husband, but to sister, female lover, or woman friend. In the first essay which constitutes the concluding section of *This Sex Which Is Not One*, Irigaray explores the territory of a "parler-femme"; the female labia, speaking together in what is either a dialogue between female lovers or the monologue of a double subject (I/you) make an effort to construct, through language, a different body and a different sexuality. From this celebration of the plurality and continuity of female subjectivity, from this experiment with dialogue and mutuality, the mother is excluded. The effort is to create a space of relation carefully situated outside of the family, that is, outside the structures of patriarchal institutions in which the mother is implicated: "I love you who are neither mother (forgive me, mother, I prefer a woman) nor sister. Neither daughter nor son. I love you—and where I love you, what do I care about the lineage of our fathers and their desire for reproductions of men? Or their genealogical institutions? What need have I for husband or wife, for family, persona, role, function? Let's leave all those to men's reproductive laws. I love you: Your body, here and now. I/you touch you/me; that's quite enough for us to feel alive" (p. 209). In the later text, "And the One Doesn't Stir Without the Other," Irigaray returns to the family and begins to explain the mother's exclusion from the "luminous mutuality" of the "I/you" she celebrated in the earlier text. Here the daughter speaks, pleadingly, to a mother trapped in the function of "maternage," trapped by her role in a script she has not written. The daughter/speaker pleads for liberation from the icy mirror of similarity where she finds her own image blended into her mother's and in which she finds herself frozen, petrified. She is at once filled, glutted by the mother's excessive nurturing and emptied by the mother's icy non-presence, by her absence as subject from their dialogue: "But we have never, never spoken to each other. And such an abyss now separates us that I never leave you whole, for I am always held back in your womb. Shrouded in shadow. Captives of our confinement. And the one doesn't stir without the other. But we do not move together. When the one comes into the world, the other goes underground. When the one carries life, the other dies. And what I wanted from you, Mother, was this: that in giving me life, you still remain alive" (p. 67).

The contrast between the two texts is striking. Whereas in the first we witness the formation and celebration of a double self, which in order to speak needs to undo subject/object division, in the second the positions of speaker and addressee remain painfully separate, even while the speaker senses and fears the blurring of boundaries between them. Daughter and mother are separated and forever trapped by the institution, the function and role of motherhood. They are forever kept apart by the text's daughter-ly perspective and signature: the mother is excluded from discourse by the daughter who owns it. Irigaray's texts of the late 1970s suggest that the fantasy of mutuality needs to exist outside the structures of family, that the mother and the pre-oedipal can perhaps be its source, its point of origin, but it can never be its destination.[21] In her poem "Sibling Mysteries," Adrienne Rich traces this evolution from father to mother, to a sister/lover characteristic of the feminist family romance:

> The daughters never were
> true brides of the father
>
> the daughters were to begin with
> brides of the mother
>
> then brides of each other
> under a different law.

In the next chapter, I will explore further the location of the feminist family romance in the position of daughterhood and sisterhood and its un-comfortable distance from the maternal.

When Adrienne Rich suggests, then, that "we need to know the writing of the past differently than we have ever known it" and that the goal, in this particular moment of emerging feminist consciousness, is "not to pass on a tradition, but to break its hold over us," she could be read as speaking of the feminist separation from patriarchal assumptions in which the mother, the woman of the past, is too profoundly implicated. What connects present to past, daughter to mother, then, is the "need to know"; what separates them is the impulse, the need, to break the hold of tradition, to break from the heterosexuality of discourse which the mother represents. Continued connection and partial separation coexist in this relationship, and the particular way in which they coexist makes this mother-daughter relationship different from any that have existed before.

The feminist family romance, as it is voiced in the texts of psychoanalytic feminism, is the romance of the daughter, entangled with her mother through identification and the struggle against it, increasingly distant from father, brother, and male lover, unproblematic only in the connection to her sister or female lover. It is located in the pre-verbal realm of the pre-oedipal, available to the writing consciousness not through memory but through fantasy and projection. The mother who possesses the recollection may well have to be eliminated as subject and maintained in the position of the object of a "sustained quest" if the feminist family romance is to maintain, through fantasy, its imaginative and subversive vision of gender difference.[22] It therefore moves only with extreme ambivalence toward the position of mother.

Postmodernist Plots

The fictions of women writers offer their own differently inflected and, in some ways, pointedly critical versions of this feminist family romance. Three novels from different traditions, written between 1972 and 1984, will serve to illustrate some of the trends I see as most striking and important: Margaret Atwood's *Surfacing*,[23] Marguerite Duras's *L'Amant (The Lover)*,[24] and Christa Wolf's *Kindheitsmuster (Patterns of Childhood)*.[25] Duras is the oldest of the three writers; the other two are more or less of the same generation. All three texts are situated quite specifically at the same historical moment, the 1970s and early 80s, looking back at the narrators' childhood and adolescent experience in the 1930s and 40s. All three texts portray the private relationships of several generations of female protagonists in relation to the public historical events which define their period and to the male figures who, more and more, are displaced from the foreground of their stories. As public and private merge, the protagonist herself is multiplied, split into several selves—mother and daughter, past and present, adult and child, autobiographical subject and fictional character, "she," "you," and "I." The process of subject-formation has become a major preoccupation for the narrator/protagonist who sees herself as part of a newly emerging feminist generation. Boundaries of selfhood are not only fluid, they become dangerously blurred. All three texts are structured around the motif of return, the process of memory, and the desire to come to terms with the past by integrating it with the protagonists' present self-representation, by attempting to find in the past an alternative to a present sense of complicity and alienation. And, in all three, the effort to connect past and present, to assemble a sense of self, is frustrated and ultimately redefined as the stories they try to tell seem more and more unnarratable—fragments virtually impossible to assemble into significant and meaningful narrative patterns, demanding to be ordered and reordered in a process of continual revision, requiring a language and narrative form that might accommodate the unspeakable.

What distinguishes these fictional "family romances" most pointedly from the theoretical paradigms outlined above are their more concrete and therefore more painful portrayals of mothers, as well as the virtual absence of sisters or other alternative maternal figures. Seen retrospectively from the vantage point of their daughters' memories, the mothers' lives are contextualized and historicized in these literary texts in ways that they are not in the theoretical ones. The lost and remembered realm of mother-daughter connection and the daughter's process of subject-formation are located in specific historical and political contexts—the period during and after World War II—which inform the authors' aesthetic choices. In calling these plots *post-modernist*, I want to highlight this contextualization and historicization of subjectivity. Although I identify in these texts some of the literary strategies we have come to identify as post-modernist—polyvalence, multiplicity, fluidity, indeterminacy, open-endedness, fragmentation—I do not connect them with what Lacan identifies as the slippage of the signified, the play of the signifier, or the irreducible, unbridgeable bar between signifier and signified.[26] I do not see here the indifference—the dissolution of all forms of difference—which characterizes poststructuralist theory and deconstructive practice. On the contrary, in my view of post-modernism, influenced by the analysis of Andreas Huyssens and Craig Owens and not by Jean-François Lyotard, the subject returns from its dispersal and disappearance in poststructuralist and deconstructive fiction and theory, but it returns to raise the political, historical, and social question of subjectivity.[27] It returns as a tool of social transformation, to shape what Hal Foster calls an "anti-aesthetic": a "critique of the world as it is," and a "counterpractice of interference."[28] Huyssens locates the break between modern and post-modern not at the moment of the subject's "death" but at the moment of its re-emergence in the writings of the 1960s and 70s. "The post-moderns . . . counter the modernist litany of the death of the subject by working toward new theories and practices of speaking, writing and acting subjects. The question of how codes, texts, images and other cultural artifacts constitute subjectivity is increasingly being raised as an already historical question"

(p. 44).[29] It is as a historical question that I wish to raise the question of the subject in my readings of these three novels which, I believe, also raise it in this manner. I also wish to bring the historical vision of the gendered subject to bear on psychoanalytic perspectives, in order to carry the psychoanalytic assumptions of feminist analysis to the point at which, I believe, they become problematic.

The novels I discuss here situate themselves self-consciously within a feminist fictional tradition. They thereby engage the period notion of post-modernism in the particularly politicized way suggested by Huyssens and Owens. Yet, at the same time, their questions remain more separate, less directly engaged with those raised by male post-modernist texts than the realist and modernist novels discussed in previous chapters. The aim of this analysis, then, is less to define a female as opposed to a male post-modernist practice, than to see the post-modern in relation to feminist ideology and practice.[30]

Life before Oedipus: Atwood's *Surfacing*

Margaret Atwood's *Surfacing*, published in 1972, presents perhaps the closest fictional analogue to the feminist family romance as outlined in revisionary psychoanalytic theories. Rapidly incorporated into the standard feminist literary canon, the novel has been read as a paradigmatic feminist tale of mythic dimensions.[31] The title (which alludes to mythic quest motifs of death and rebirth), the absence of the narrator's name, the story's location on a distant French-Canadian island, the oppositions between Canada and America, nature and civilization, silence and language, female and male, peace and war, and the fractured structure of the narrative which inscribes the difficulties of narration, all contribute to the novel's success in representing issues of central concern to the development of feminist consciousness throughout the 1970s. For example, Adrienne Rich reads *Surfacing* as the heroine's story of feminist awakening, highlighting her ability at the end of her mythic quest to point, through a return and reunification with her mother, "beyond patriarchy" (*Of Woman Born*, p. 242). My own reading examines Atwood's novel as the representation of female subject-formation, of a woman's "life before Oedipus," to play with her own later title, *Life Before Man*.[32] In structuring her narrative around a return to the isolated Canadian landscape and an examination of "civilization" and its problems from that distant vantage point, and in casting that return in familial terms (the heroine is always a daughter, a sister, a potential mother, and wife), Atwood's novel both exemplifies and puts into question what I have called the feminist family romance.

As she attempts to make her way back to the distant landscape of her childhood, the novel's nameless narrator realizes that "Nothing is the same, I don't know the way any more" (p. 15). Whereas the past is frozen in her memory and seems unrelated to present concerns, her present life is artificial and alienated. As a commercial artist, she is commissioned to draw according to her employer's conceptions instead of her own; as a lover, she finds herself in a relationship she did not actively choose and in which she is unable to feel. Her self-conception is largely mediated through visual images of confinement and fragmentation: photographs, films, mirrors, and drawings reflect parts of a self that can neither be unified nor accurately represented. The language she feels forced to use is foreign to her and she speaks only with reluctance: "Language divides us into fragments, I wanted to be whole" (p. 172). Her sense of fragmentation is pervasive: Anna asks her whether she had a twin who was lost; she depicts her "divorce" as amputation and she suffers from a split between her head and her body that caused her "atrophy of the heart." There is the sense that her public existence, corresponding to cultural constructions of femininity, has cut her off from what she posits as a hopelessly lost, authentic, private self: "Woman sawn apart in a wooden crate, wearing a bathing suit, smiling, a trick done with mirrors, I read it in a comic book; only with me there had been an accident and I came apart. The other half, the one locked away, was the only one that could live; I was the wrong half, detached, terminal. I was nothing but a head, or, no, something minor like a severed thumb; numb" (p. 129).

The return to the island and her search for her father, for her mother's legacy, and for her own purer origins there could be read as an effort to re-member that fragmented selfhood, to reach the "other half" that "could live." Clearly, it is an attempt to find at what point she had come apart and had become unable to feel. Her search comes to seem all the more necessary in the context of her present relationship with David and Anna, whose words and actions all seem drawn from comic books and television commercials, and with Joe who insists on using the word "love," a term she is incapable of uttering.

If that search for a lost authenticity is indeed the motivation for the novel's plot, its progress consists of repeated revisions which, even while holding out the possibility of successful reintegration outside the confines of a dying and degraded civilization, fails to reach such a sense of closure. The narrator's present sense of fragmentation rests on an image of a recent past which, as we find out two-thirds of the way into the novel, is false—a culturally acceptable construction designed to repress what she cannot bear to remember: "A faked album, the memories fraudulent as passports; but a paper house was better than none and I could almost live in it" (p. 169). The fraudulent story of her wedding, her motherhood, and the abandonment of her husband and child is revised, toward the end of the novel, to reveal the "truth": the story of her forced abortion. "I couldn't accept it, that mutilation, ruin I'd made, I needed a different version. . . . I was emptied, amputated; I stank of salt and antiseptic, they had planted death in me like a seed. . . . I could have said No but I didn't; that made me one of them too, a killer" (pp. 169–170). This is a radical revision of the narrative we have been reading so far, entailing a reassessment of many of the narrator's previous statements which had created a different plot about marriage and childbirth, and a different sense of guilt about abandoning her child and her husband. This revision does not, however, return her to the authentic self she believes she has lost; on the contrary it reveals her own complicity in the murderous life-denying civilization she would reject. It reveals, as well, a larger complicity in the killing of animals, in the wars and murders that define that civilization. As the lake triggers and admits the memory she had for so long repressed, it also comes to be filled with death and ceases to provide the safety and alterity she had expected and wished for. What the narrator loses in the course of the narrative, then, is not a protected innocent self, but her own dream of its ever having existed. She loses the devastating effect of the loss of that authenticity.

To assess *that* loss, she needs to recall and relive the experience of her childhood on the lake, an experience which seems to stand in complete contrast to the inauthenticity of the present and which seems to contain a unity and identity which, in the present, is no more than a nostalgic memory. In the protected garden world controlled by parents functioning as household gods, all seemed under control. Although she grew up during the war, it felt like peace. Her childhood drawings, unlike the violent drawings of her brother, were a series of smiling rabbits, "no monsters, no wars, no explosions, no heroism," revealing the powerful parental protection she experienced. Her rationalist father and naturalist mother, she feels, were "from another age, prehistoric, when everyone got married and had a family, children growing in the yard like sunflowers" (p. 169). This particular vision of parental order and childhood perfection is revised at several points in her story and it is this process of gradual revision that enables her to remember the abortion and to accept her own participation in it.

Neither the father nor the mother retain their initial characterization, but it is the father who, in the narrator's vision, changes most profoundly. As she searches for traces of him throughout the house and the island, she realizes first that Goldsmith and Burns, the enlightenment writers he admired, were actually alcoholics and madmen. Then she finds the mysterious drawings he left behind, drawings she later discovers to be copies of underwater prehistoric cave paintings depicting hands, unformed antlered figures, childish bodies with neither hands nor feet, all somewhere between human and animal. These drawings testify to the father's transformation, to what she calls "the failure of logic" which must, at first, have terrified him ("it would be like stepping through a usual door and finding yourself in a different galaxy, purple trees and red moons and a green sun" [p. 171]) but which must have opened another aspect of existence to him. This profound paternal transformation culminates in her final vision of her father as a wolf, an "it" ready to abolish mental categories and to relinquish his "gods of the head" (p. 179), ready for "the forest to flow back into the places his mind cleared: reparation" (p. 218). It is at this point, when he sheds his human, masculine form, that she can identify and merge with him, recognizing that the "wolf's" footprints are actually her own.

The father's metamorphosis is a crucial step in the narrator's own evolution in the novel. Making her aware of a prehistoric existence, antecedent to recent categories dividing human and animal, child and adult, male and female, matter and spirit, the father's drawings prompt her to dive into the lake to discover an illuminating vision: "It was below me, drifting towards me from the furthest level where there was no life, a dark oval trailing limbs. It was blurred but it had eyes, they were open, it was something I knew about, a dead thing, it was dead" (p. 167). This vision—either the father's or the little brother's drowned corpse, or the aborted foetus— enables her to remember the abortion and to revise the story she has been telling. More importantly, it motivates her to displace the search for her father from the center of her plot and to supplement it with the search for her mother. Finding the father's corpse frees her to search for a maternal legacy.

The narrator's obsessive desire to make epistolary contact with her mother, dating from the mother's death when she began to check the mailbox every day for a letter, motivates a reassessment of the mother's life. She discovers first a diary that meticulously records the weather, day after day, but includes nothing about the narrator herself, nothing about feelings or states of mind. It is as though language itself were insufficient to express anything beyond such a straightforward seasonal record. The diary is not a message, because it refuses to signify. During her recollections, the vision of the mother as "mistress of the animals" (Rich's term) feeding the jays, is offset by another image—as a child, the mother attempted to fly off the roof of the barn and broke both her ankles, a disappointment the narrator considers unbearable. These memories and found objects all constitute a form of maternal legacy, but one drawing does come to assume the status of a message addressed specifically to the surviving daughter. It is the narrator's own childhood drawing of a woman "with a round moon stomach: the baby was sitting up inside her gazing out. Opposite her was a man with horns on his head like cow horns and a barbed tail" (p. 185). The narrator knows that the drawing represents herself as a foetus in intimate relation to her mother and a male figure, both her father and a patriarchal god; however, it also represents her own aborted foetus still inside her body, their relation dominated and mediated by the powerful male who is present even in the pre-natal state of undifferentiation. While her father's drawings take her to a cultural prehistoric existence, this drawing takes her to her own personal prehistory; both reveal identity to be tenuous and relational. Thus, the drawings are comprehensible only when taken together: at the point of pre-identity both mother and father preside powerfully over the child; their relationship is both necessary and complementary. Here the father is no longer the rationalist, residing solely in the head; he is no longer the powerful male who had the authority to decide the fate of her child. He has been transformed into an antlered god who participated in the creation of life. The father's transformation enables the narrator to contemplate motherhood, to conceive a child with Joe even while she refuses to tell him she loves him, to participate briefly in his conventional romance plot. Thus, contrary to what she asserted in the beginning of the novel, she *can* take her mother's place: although it constitutes the mother's legacy, the drawing she finds is after all her own and not the mother's.

Surfacing is a novel about a heroine who first, like so many fictional heroines before her, is unable to become a mother, but who revises that inability and finally embraces her own potential maternity. In part, that process of revision rests on a search for a lost authentic self, outside of the institutions of civilization. Following her parents to their afterlife, she needs to "die" like them. Her "death" consists of a ritual stripping of her civilized self (clothes, food, house, reason, and language) to the point where she becomes animal-like, merging with the setting ("I lean against a tree, I am a tree leaning. . . . I am not an animal or a tree, I am the thing in which the trees and animals move and grow, I am a place"). As she remains on the island, protected by a mystical power derived from the memory of both parents and finally able to mourn their death, to reunite with them in a form of death, the narrator creates yet another, more mystical, family romance, another alternative to a degrading civilization. The parents have become animal-like, she herself has relinquished the need for anything artificial. Most important, she has relinquished the need for language: "The animals have no need for speech, why talk when you are a word" (p. 212). When the dead parents speak to her it is in "the other language" (p. 220). In this family romance both parents are present and both have protective powers that far outweigh the powers they had in her childhood. But both are profoundly transformed; they have relinquished gender, oppression, and power as bases for their relationship. The father has recognized the failure of logic and has become vulnerable, scared, feeling; the mother quietly feeds the jays and becomes one of the jays she has been feeding; no longer afraid of dying in the hospital, no longer disappointed in her inability to fly, she has regained the natural power she had during the narrator's childhood. The brother who represented the violent and evil "American" in the family cannot be transformed and remains absent. Other men are absent as well: the novel's alternative "pre-oedipal triangle," existing in a timeless pre-oedipal moment, remains invulnerable to external pressure.

If, at the end of her story, the narrator is ready to have a child, to become a mother, she first envisions that possibility in nature, outside of civilization and away from men. She conceives the child out of her own choice, using Joe to give her "part of myself," and she imagines birthing it: "The baby will slip out easily as an egg, a kitten, and I'll lick it off and bite the cord, the blood returning to the ground where it belongs; the moon will be full pulling" (p. 191). In this way, Atwood's pre-oedipal, pre-cultural family romance can perpetuate and reproduce itself. The transformation of the father and the attempt to find in Joe a potential father to this new child, parallels the call for shared parenting in feminist psychoanalytic writing, but it seems equally unrealistic. Joe, she says hopefully, "isn't anything, he is only half formed, and for that reason I can trust him" (p. 224).

The novel posits a place outside of language and civilization. There the narrator finds, however, that both indeed are necessary and decides to return, to Joe and the city, to a mythically inflated and ultimately quite problematic vision of her potential child as the "first true human" who "must be born, allowed." She projects a different life, one in which she will "refuse to be a victim." She concretely envisions using language. Still, the ending of the novel is curiously suspended just before the moment of return to civilization and to language. She leans forward but remains waiting, suspended. She is still nameless, still unformed. She can potentially join with Joe, because in her conception he too is "only half-formed," although if we are to believe the novel, we might be more suspicious of the depth of his complicities than the narrator is. With the last sentence, the novel still resides within the dichotomies it has been both building and challenging, dichotomies it finally lets stand and does not resolve. On the one hand, Joe calls her by the name she never revealed to us; on the other, "the lake is quiet, the trees surround me, asking and giving nothing" (p. 224). Language and culture are there, demanding to be transformed; yet, nature still seems to offer an alternative. The narrator rests suspended between these two possibilities. The novel itself remains at that tenuous, liminal point between what Margaret Homans has called "separatism and appropriation" in language, between the will to difference—a belief in an alternative—and the recognition of a deep complicity. Yet, I would argue that this seeming liminality is in itself suspect, perhaps even dishonest. The text has revealed a profound sense of complicity on every level; even the lake was filled with death. To posit, even tentatively, a space outside of ideology and patriarchy is to support and participate in that very ideology, rather than to attempt to undermine it. It is just like raising one's children on a Canadian lake during World War II and encouraging them to draw smiling rabbits. Atwood's narrator perceives her own complicity, which is equal to that of her parents, yet she continues to deny that perception, to suspend herself outside of history, to promise alternatives through myth. Atwood's novel thereby illustrates what I see as the main danger of the feminist family romance in this period: the mystification of a pre-oedipal realm which, in this case, includes not only mother and daughter, but also a transformed father, a transformed lover, and a potentially transformatory child.

Waiting outside the Closed Door: Duras's *The Lover*

"The story of my life doesn't exist," asserts the (again) nameless narrator of *The Lover*. "Does not exist. There's never any center to it. No path, no line" (p. 8). The text begins with a long self-portrait, a reflection of the narrator's aged face, first as it is described to her by a young man she encounters in a public space, then as she herself sees it evolve from the age of eighteen to the present moment of utter devastation. The entire text revolves around an earlier recollection, the moment just preceding that laying to waste: the crossing of the Mekong River on a ferry at the age of fifteen and the visual image (a photograph never taken) of the young girl dressed in a low-cut silk dress, evening shoes, and a man's fedora. This tension between narrative and image, movement and stasis, controls the text, as does the tension between the external objective perception of the narrator by others and her self-perception, between the third and the first person, and between speech and silence.

The Lover is already a revision of a *fabula* which has appeared, in different guises, in several of Duras's works. Both the 1958 novel, *Un Barrage contre le Pacifique (The Sea Wall)*[33] and the 1977 play *L'Eden Cinéma*[34] deal with aspects of the same plot: the young girl's adolescence in colonial Indochina, the broken dreams of her disturbed and impoverished mother, the hated and adored brother(s), and the rich older lover who promises the entire family an escape from hopelessness. But, as Duras explains in *The Lover*, "Before, I spoke of the clear periods, those on which the light fell. Now I'm talking about the hidden stretches of that same youth, of certain facts, feelings, events that I buried" (p. 8). The darkness and silence, the difficulty of telling and the need to retell, again and again, the narrator explains, is connected to the figure of her mother, the figure around whom these texts revolve. "In the books I've written about my childhood I can't remember, suddenly, what I left out, what I said. I think I wrote about our love for our mother, but I don't know if I wrote about how we hated her too. . . . It's the area on whose brink silence begins. What happens there is silence, the slow travail of my whole life. I'm still there, watching those possessed children, as far away from the mystery now as I was then. I've never written, though I thought I wrote, never loved, though I thought I loved, never done anything but wait outside the closed door" (p. 25). In this remarkable passage, the narrator is both mother and child, mother as she stands watching "those possessed children," and child as she enacts the unspeakable primal scene "outside the closed door."

The Lover, then, is but one of several repeated attempts to open that door, to illuminate the area of supreme darkness "hidden in the very depths of my flesh, blind as a newborn child" (p. 25). To tell the story of passionate mother-child attachment and identification, Duras uses images similar to Colette's—mystery, darkness, something hidden beyond view, unavailable to narrative. And, like Colette, Duras identifies this search for the "darkest plots" with the process of what she elsewhere calls "feminine literature," defined as "an organic, translated writing . . . translated from blackness, from darkness."[35] But Duras identifies her "feminine writing" in specific contrast to Colette who, she says, wrote " 'feminine literature' as men wanted it." Whereas, in Duras's view, Colette writes for the enjoyment of men, the feminine literature she herself envisions and practices, is "a violent, direct literature" which aims to "make women the point of departure in judging, make darkness the point of departure in judging what men call light, make obscurity the point of departure in judging what men call clarity" (p. 426).

Interestingly, Duras's judgment of Colette resembles Rich's reading of Woolf—too much attention paid to men, too much compromise and not enough anger and violence. Whereas, unlike Colette's texts, Duras's do indeed present a past full of anger and violence, pain and suffering, her search through "the darkest plots" of mother-daughter attachment is, like Colette's, mediated by a heterosexual love narrative which is also ultimately and radically rejected. If the figure of the mother appears as both the point of departure and the destination of the narrative, the narrative places her in a multiple network of mediations with the male brothers and the lover whom she ultimately displaces in her daughter's passionate and disturbed attachment. Although these male figures function as pre-texts leading to the mother, their presence complicates and confuses the narrative of daughterly desire.

In a post-script to *L'Eden Cinéma*, Duras's adaptation of *The Sea Wall* for the stage, the author apologizes for one particularly disturbing passage of her play, giving license to directors to remove it. The passage is a letter written by the mother to the cadastral agents who had leased her a plot of land which, since it turned out to be totally infertile, robbed her of all her savings and of any possible future livelihood. Providing (like Sido's letters included in *Break of Day*) a glimpse into the mother's own discourse and imagination, this letter is a long and uncontrolled outpouring of rage and complaints, culminating in detailed threats on the agents' lives, with concrete plans for their violent murder. It is this violence, written in the mother's voice, that Duras feared might be unacceptable to the audiences of her play: "I hesitated to keep—in 1977—the murderous threats that the mother's last letter to the cadastral agents contained. . . . Then I decided to leave it in. As inadmissible as this violence may appear, it seemed to me more serious to silence it then to disfigure with it the figure of the mother. This violence existed for us, it cradled our childhood." Continuing in detail to describe the pain, sadness, and despair contained in the letter, Duras concludes: "If the violence of this woman, the mother, is, however, apt to shock or not to be heard at the very point of its greatest legitimacy, then that passage of the letter can be deleted" (p. 150, my translation). The letter in *L'Eden Cinéma* is reprinted from *The Sea Wall*, where Joseph and Suzanne discuss it at length. Joseph also silences the mother's rage—he decides not to mail the letter since he feels it would be more useful to him and his sister than to the insensitive agents. It would teach him to keep alive his own anger, and, for his sister, it would function as a negative example: "You must remember these stories about the Eden cinema [the theater where the mother played piano to accompany silent movies] and you must always do just the opposite of what she did" (p. 224). Maternal identification threatens and unsettles disturbingly the daughter's process of subject-formation; yet the reasons for this threat transcend the patterns of psychology.

In *The Lover*, where no such letter appears, the act of silencing the mother is more comprehensive. Yet the mother does express similar rage in her dialogue and is reported to have done so throughout the narrator's childhood and adolescence. In this last text Duras's narrator focuses on her own relation to the mother's rage and violence, especially on how maternal anger and maternal madness affect and inform her own imagination and her own writing. It is as though the mother's own discourse could be better rewritten, revised, by the daughter if it were excised from the text: "I tell him that when I was a child my mother's unhappiness took the place of dreams. My dreams were of my mother, never of Christmas trees, always just her, a mother either flayed by poverty or distraught and muttering in the wilderness, either searching for food or endlessly telling what's happened to her, Marie Legrand from Roubaix, telling of her innocence, her savings, her hopes" (p. 46). When the mother is present, she only causes fear and anger in the daughter: "There was no longer anything there to inhabit her image. I went mad in full possession of my senses." Faced with the mother's mad alterity, the terrified daughter comes to inhabit the mother's body, herself taking the place the mother has left empty during the attack.

This account and experience of the mother's pain and her madness, her hysterical outbursts, her absences, her radical otherness, terrifying for her children, dominates the pages of *The Lover*, although the mother's own words are absent. Not only does the mother not write, she also discourages, even forbids, the narrator to write. The daughter's text, emerging from that prohibition, can no longer contain the voice of the enraged mother, even though it takes shape around that missing voice in the effort to give it life, to keep it alive, to open the door that might allow her to understand it. This pattern of maternal presence/absence very much resembles that of *Break of Day*, even though the quality of the mother's elided and sought-after subjectivity is radically different. Whereas the memory of "Sido" represents the idealized garden of the narrator's childhood, a paradisiacal realm of which "Colette" is no longer worthy, which she needs to recapture and may never be able to, the memory of Marie Roubaix reflects the hardships of widowhood and single motherhood, the colonial existence of a teacher and her family in Indochina, war, hunger, poverty, and the resulting madness. Nevertheless, the outlook of both protagonists is shaped by their mothers', and Duras's narrator needs the access to and the distance from the mother's madness as much as "Colette" needs access to her mother's plenitude. "Because of what's been done to our mother, so amiable, so trusting, we hate life, we hate ourselves" (p. 55). Here, however, the pre-oedipal world of mother-child union is no Eden to recapture. Not only does it fail to offer an alternative to the violence of civilization, it is very much a product of that violence.

The relationship between the narrator of *The Lover* and her mother is filtered through a complex structure of mediating relationships which include the two brothers, the older Chinese lover, and even a female friend, Hélène Lagonelle. Through each of these figures, the narrator gains access to the others and ultimately seeks to gain access to the mother, the figure behind the closed door. Some significant changes have taken place since *The Sea Wall*, however. The single adored brother Joseph, clearly a "man-who-would-understand," has been replaced by two brothers—a revered younger brother who has all of Joseph's positive and none of his negative qualities, and a despised older brother, the image of an authoritative patriarch who, although powerless in the world, destructively dominates the lives of his family members. The lover has also shifted both in character and plot. No longer French, he is Chinese; although he is rich, he occupies a lower social status than the narrator and her family. It is this shift in power and status, perhaps, that makes it possible for the narrator to desire him sexually, whereas in the earlier text she could barely tolerate his presence. The older brother, revered and preferred by the mother, serves as a repressive object of jealousy and rage, later contempt, throughout the narrative. The younger brother is the narrator's adored twin whose early death nearly causes her own destruction. Vastly different from each other, the three siblings are united only through the passionate love they share for their mother, and through their sorrow for her ruined life. In this family, the primal psychic triangle defining the narrator's individuation does not consist of mother/father/daughter but of mother/son/daughter, with the brother split into two, one good, one bad. Whereas the father is totally absent from the narrative, an object of memory and longing only for the mother, the brothers remain important psychic forces throughout the space of the text. Yet in the course of the plot they also come to be displaced—the younger brother dies and the older brother eventually loses his authority, becoming a traitor, even a thief, before his demise.

It is not the lover, however, who displaces the brothers from the narrator's affection or from the center of the narrative. During her affair with the lover, all three male figures coexist in her forever shifting affections—between her love for the younger brother, the physical passion for the lover, and the murderous hatred for the older brother. The affair does not represent a rupture in her affections, then, but merely another element in the structure of mediation that defines them. From the beginning of their affair, the lover's presence is entangled with the very material being of the mother, the brothers, and Hélène Lagonelle. When they meet and go out to dinner together, the lover and the brothers do not speak. But during the narrator's moments of extreme bodily intimacy and togetherness with the Chinese lover, the brothers are there, approving or disapproving, similar to him or different: "The shadow of another man must have passed through the room, the shadow of a young murderer, but I didn't know that then. . . . The shadow of a young hunter must have passed through the room too, but that one, yes, I knew about, sometimes he was present in the pleasure and I'd tell the lover from Cholon, talk to him of the other's body and member, of his indescribable sweetness" (p. 100). Rather than a simple break from childhood and familial attachments, the lover offers, through mediation, a way to remain embedded in those attachments, even while finding enough distance from them to be capable of describing their intensity. In fact, I would argue that he offers a privileged form of access to her mother: during their passionate scenes of lovemaking, the lover becomes her mother, as she becomes his child. The passion she feels gives her access to the mother's body: "So I became his child. And he became something else for me too. I began to recognize the inexpressible softness of his skin, of his member, apart from himself" (p. 100). As the narration moves from first to third person during the moments of passion, the protagonist gains distance from herself and access to the mother's mad self-abandonment by way of the sexual passion she shares with the lover.

The Lover is the story of the narrator's coming to writing. Even at the moments of greatest childhood and adolescent despair, she knows that she will write and that to do so she must leave behind her family and the lover. It is only when she has left Saigon and is traveling on the boat to France that the narrator understands the depth of her love for the Chinese man from Cholon; it is only after the younger brother dies that she accepts the "unfathomable mystery" of her love for him which also makes her want to die. Even as she separates from the figures of her adolescence, they establish themselves as permanent fixtures in her imagination, to be examined again and again in their complex relations to each other, providing the obsessive themes and images of Duras's oeuvre. The novel ends as, years later, the lover calls her in Paris to tell her that he will always love her, that nothing has changed. It is *his* declaration. For her, for the older woman novelist, love and the lover need to recede into the background of the fiction. Like the brothers, the lover is not the object of nostalgia or longed-for recovery, but an important marker in the shifting structure of mediation which creates not only the space for writing in Duras's work, but also its obsessive preoccupation.

The mother, however, functions as more than such a pre-text; one could argue that she is the ground on which all the other relationships rest and to which they lead. But she is, in many respects, an absent ground. Although she is featured in many of Duras's texts, she often remains silent. The most dramatic staging of her silent presence is in *L'Eden Cinéma*, where the stage directions read as follows:

> *The mother sits on a low seat and the others gather around her. . . . Then they speak about the mother. About her past. About her life. About the love she elicited. The mother will remain immobile on her seat, expressionless, like a statue, distant, separated—like the stage—from her own story. The others touch her, caress her arms, kiss her hands. She allows it: what she* represents *in this play surpasses what she is and she* is not responsible for it. *. . . the mother—object of the narrative—will never speak for herself.* (p. 12; my translation)

The Lover, as do the other texts which tell the same story, presents a version of the feminist family romance that differs from the ones we encountered earlier. If mother-daughter entanglement serves as a narrative focus here, it does so as the privileged relationship in a nexus of shifting attachments, each mediating a series of others. If Duras's text seeks to open a closed door, she can do so only to find that it leads to other doors, each connected to all the others, but none providing an ultimate point of origin. Does the desire for the lover allow her to seek the mother, or is it the reverse? Does the love for her younger brother enable her to recognize her love for the lover or vice versa? How is power distributed in these relationships: does the lover hold the power because he is older, richer, and male, or does the narrator because she is white? Duras overturns and complicates such dichotomies and divisions. No relationship and no point in the process of subject-formation is immune from the struggles of power and from the degradations of a civilization engaged in war and imperial expansion. No alternative can be offered, none can even be envisioned. The process of repeated revisions and shifting mediations allows Duras and her narrators to go over the same ground again and again, making discoveries but reaching no ultimate illumination. As the narrator says: "Sometimes I realize that if writing isn't, all things, all contraries confounded, a quest for vanity and void, it's nothing. That if it's not, each time, all things confounded into one through some inexpressible essence, then writing is nothing but advertisement" (p. 8).

Yet *The Lover* suggests that the figure of the mother is this "inexpressible essence" which confounds all other things into one, thereby making writing possible. She does so not by offering a destination to which to return, but by functioning precisely as "vanity and void"; she may be a privileged point in the nexus of relationships defining the structures of desire, but she is not the "center" which would make the story of the narrator's life "exist" or cohere. She does so not by providing an alternative realm to cultural complicity, but through her very entanglement in the culture and the relationships which define it.

Such a reading lies outside of the confines of a feminist family romance based in psychoanalysis alone. Julia Kristeva's recent article on Duras illustrates the limitations of a psychoanalytic perspective.[36] Interestingly, her reading of Duras's writing is preceded by a reflection on the literature that might best approximate the politics of our age, the psychic pain inflicted by the gas chambers, the bomb, and the gulag. Duras, she feels, possesses the discourse of "blunted pain," the art of "non-catharsis" which brings the reader to the edge of silence and not beyond. After this haunting and suggestive beginning, two related aspects of her reading are particularly striking: her insistence that "political events . . . are internalized and measured only by the human pain they induce," that "public life becomes profoundly unreal, whereas private life is intensified to the point that it invades the real and invalidates all other preoccupation," and in contrast, her identification of maternal abandonment as *the* traumatic structure which lies at the basis of all of Duras's writing, of all the internal pain. In her narrative of this pervasive structure of maternal abandonment, Kristeva represents the mother as other, as the "archaic, uncontrollable" object, the icon of madness whose function it is to disrupt all efforts at identity and sameness. Kristeva's internalization of the political, and her location of its force in the figure of the abandoning, mad, and unfaithful mother, is symptomatic of the moves of psychoanalytic feminism (especially insofar as it is allied with French deconstructive theory, but also in its American object-relations incarnation). In eclipsing the mother's own voice, her own story, and allowing her only the status of object, or of "Other," Kristeva, and to an extent Duras also, eclipse the political dimensions of women's lives, conflating them with the psychological. Here, I believe, lies a major limit of psychoanalytic feminism.

What Kristeva sees as the structure of maternal violence and abandonment, leading to "reduplication" and ultimately stasis and "nothingness," can be read through a lens different from the lens of subjectivity and identity. Another obsessive figure in Duras's work illustrates the need for such a shift in perspective—the beggar woman from Vinlongh or Savannakhet who returns in many of the novels and films from *The Sea-Wall* to *The Vice Consul* to *India Song, Love,* and *The Lover*. Poor, at times pregnant, at other times trying to sell her child to another mother (the somewhat less poor white woman), this figure of lament, whose delirious song and cry punctuate Duras's novels, serves, in Madeleine Borgomano's terms, as the "generative cell" for Duras's entire narrative project and, in Kristeva's terms, as the double of her other characters.[37] In a taped interview, cited by Borgomano, Duras relates the autobiographical incident which constituted the generative cell of this generative cell: "My mother once came back from the market having bought a child . . . a six-month old little girl . . . that she only kept for several days and who died. . . . I still see my mother crossing the garden with this woman who followed her. . . . My mother cried . . . she was always enraged by such misery. . . . I remember this stubbornness, this fantastic will to give away her child. . . . I have tried to transform this monstrous and adorable act into literature but I have not succeeded."[38]

The obsessive and unnarratable nature of this memory emerges quite clearly in this oral account, as it does in the many scenes of her work Duras has devoted to it; what emerges with equal force, however, is Duras's interest in sustaining the irrevocable *strangeness* and *opacity* (these are her terms) of the beggar woman's shocking maternal act. In so doing, Duras can perhaps minimize its monumental threat, a threat so great that in *The Lover* she describes it as the fear of a state worse than death, of entering the beggar woman's madness, or perhaps of becoming the child who is killed by it. The dangers of maternal identification are here.

Yet, the scene Duras describes in that taped interview has obvious significances beyond the psychological, significances which, interestingly, emerge more clearly in the early texts in which the mother screams and speaks than in the later ones in which she remains silent so as to be spoken about. The Indian beggar mother, ostracized by her own mother and reduced to dire poverty, sells her child to the white woman while the white daughter looks on; the white second mother, although she dresses the child in a lace gown, is incapable of keeping her alive; in *The Sea Wall* the white brother buries the child, and the white mother swears she will never care for children again. The white mother herself is too poor to care for her own children. She watches her own children's failure to thrive and all around her she watches many other children die of hunger and disease. She is the colonizer, yet, as a woman, she is also the colonized. Certainly she is the victim of colonialism. She is more and more angry, more and more depressed. A doctor (the text's image of a "psychiatrist") warns that her fits of angry screaming may be fatal. But the third person narrator's voice argues with the doctor's diagnosis: "The doctor traced these attacks of hers to the crumbling of the sea wall. Maybe he was mistaken. So much resentment could only have accumulated very slowly, year by year, day by day. There was more than one single cause: there were thousands, counting the collapse of the sea walls, the world's injustice, the sight of her children splashing in the river . . ." (p. 17). While the doctor sees only one cause, the narrative voice understands the complexity and vastness of the problems faced by the mother. Whereas in a psychoanalytic reading the crumbling of the sea wall represents a psychic disintegration pervasive in Duras's texts, the text itself, I would argue, demands a more multifaceted reading which goes beyond the psychological to the economic and the political and which places the mother's madness in that context. Similarly, the white eight-year-old, terrified of the beggar woman's touch in *The Lover*, is afraid of the touch of poverty as well as of the touch of the madness of mother-child fusion. The fear and the power of "all things confounded into one" need to be traced back not only to their roots in the psyche and their connection to writing, but also to the connections between that psyche and the biological and social body it inhabits. Such contextualization might perhaps make it possible to take the maternal out of the realm of silence and unrepresentability and to include, in the feminist family romance and on the stage of feminist self-presentation, the perspective and the voice of mothers as well as of daughters.

"How Did We Become as We Are Today?"
Wolf's *A Model Childhood*

Christa Wolf's *Kindheitsmuster*, translated both as *A Model Childhood* and as *Patterns of Childhood*, is prefaced by a conventional disclaimer—"All characters in this book are the invention of the narrator, . . ."—which is all the more surprising when we consider the openly acknowledged autobiographical content of Wolf's narrative, underscored by the careful dating and placing of each episode. The second part of the disclaimer does throw some light on this seeming discrepancy: "Anyone believing that he detects a similarity between a character in this narrative and either himself or anyone else should consider the strange lack of individuality in the behavior of many contemporaries. Generally recognizable behavior patterns should be blamed on circumstances." Is Wolf's text autobiography or is it fabulation? As we begin reading *Kindheitsmuster*, this question, which I have posed on several occasions in this book without answering it, gains an additional twist. First, we encounter the epigram by Pablo Neruda which also marks the text as self-reflexive: "Where is the child I used to be,/still within, or far away? . . ." Next, we confront the complicated pronoun arrangements that frame the interrogation of the relation between past and present announced in the first chapter: "What is past is not dead; it is not even past" (p. 3). Most strikingly, the reader is addressed, assaulted even, with the unusual and disorienting pronoun "you" which dominates the narrative. A voice, addressing itself (and, unavoidably, the reader) as "you,"[39] about to begin typing on a fresh sheet of paper, outlines the impossible choice she faces as a writing subject: "to remain speechless, or else to live in the third person. The first is impossible, the second strange" (p. 3). Wolf's narrative shapes itself, awkwardly, uncomfortably, self-consciously, and self-reflexively somewhere between monologue and dialogue, somewhere between past and present, between "I," "you," and "she." If this is an autobiography, it is a group autobiography, the autobiography of a generation who lived its "model" or "monstrous" childhood during World War II in Germany, and whose patterns of behavior have assumed an avowed familiarity. "Generally recognizable behavior patterns should be blamed on circumstances."

The narrative takes place on three carefully dated temporal levels: the present moment of composition, between November 1972 and May 1975, in which the writer-narrator speaks of herself in the second person; the recent past, in 1971, during which the narrator, still "you," takes a trip to her native village, now a part of Poland, accompanied by her husband, her brother Lutz, and her daughter Lenka; and the more distant past, from the early 1930s to 1945 during which the child, named Nelly Jordan and spoken about in the third person, makes her way through that same village and beyond in her wartime childhood and adolescence. What connects the disparate levels and pronominal constructions is one controlling question—"How did we become as we are today?"—a question which seems to suggest that the impulse of the narrative is to find links, to merge and unify the awkwardly separate parts of the narrative and the self, at least to explain the rifts that make the narrative so uncomfortable. Memory and the process of writing itself, it seems to be implied, can find an answer to the question of becoming, an explanatory thread. Throughout the text, the narrator yearns for one voice, and for one pronoun—the "I" which, openly and boldly voiced, might signify self-acceptance and self-forgiveness and the merging of child and adult. But the division between adult and child is not only temporal, it is also fundamentally ideological and therefore unassimilable: "What is past is not dead; it is not even past. We cut ourselves off from it; we pretend to be strangers" (p. 3).

Thus another contrary impulse, against assimilation and reunification, is equally present in the text. Maintaining the rifts between parts of the self could serve to highlight the distortions and to nurse a discomfort which, so profoundly part of the experience of this generation, must also find its way into its narratives. In an interview, Wolf asserts her conviction that literature must try "to show the layers that are lying within us—not so cleanly ordered, not catalogued and nicely mastered as we might like."[40] The multiple pronouns and names used to refer to the protagonist and the text's uneasy situation between autobiography and fiction constitute an experiment with forms that would allow a confrontation with the past whose aim is *not* to come to terms with it. As Wolf says, "And when you ask: Can it be overcome *(bewältigen)?* Then I can only clearly say: No" (Sauer, p. 41, my translation). Like Atwood, Wolf explores the consequences of living part of one's life as a lie and of attempting to determine the existence and status of the "truth."

Where is the writer between past and present, between falsehood and truth? "The two-fold meaning of the word 'to mediate.' To be the mediator between past and present—the medium of a communication between the two. In the sense of reconciliation? appeasement? smoothing out? Or a rapprochement of the two? To permit today's person to meet yesterday's person through the medium of writing?" (p. 164). The break which creates the impetus for the narrative, and which precludes closure, is now within the writing subject and cannot and should not be repaired. It exists as well on a more global scale in the world in which she writes: in fact, she is connected to her world through the experience of multiple fractures and rifts. The rift between the ideology of national socialism and the values Nelly develops as she grows to adolescence, variously at odds with each other at different moments, has now been transformed into the rift between West and East, between Poland and Germany, between the values of capitalism and of Soviet communism. The multiplicity of value structures and ideological systems contributes to the writer's inability to say "I," to pretend to a uniformity that seems forever to have vanished from the universe in which she lives and writes.

Familial structures and experiences, although central, cannot and do not offset these fundamental divisions. Wolf's narrative is embedded in familial affiliations, ranging from Nelly's family—mother, father, brother, aunts, uncles, and grandparents, going through the war and post-war years—to the narrator's present family, husband, two daughters, and brother, who actually facilitate the process of memory and narration. The narrator writes as daughter to Charlotte and Bruno Jordan, as sister to Lutz, and as mother to Lenka. Nelly can only be reached by means of the relationships that formed her early self—her desire to kill her brother, for example, and the guilt of that desire, or her undisputable love for her parents, challenged daily by their beliefs.

The issue of transmission to the next generation is crucial. Lenka also must confront the ideological reality of her mother's past under National Socialism, and she also must try to square that with the mother she knows in the present, with the mother she loves. She must confront, as well, the feelings of jealousy toward a mother who lived through experiences of an intensity her own can never match. The other daughter, Ruth, present in only one sentence of this narrative, must also be connected, if much more obliquely, to the process of transmission that takes place here. At every moment in the text, the personal familial issues are intertwined with public political ones. The family becomes society's primary agent of socialization and subject-formation. Even the activity of writing is a familial gesture: a daughter writing about her parents, a mother writing for her daughter(s). The "I" which remains the text's main question and primary goal can be perceived only within and through its relational contexts. And, it can only emerge within its political definitions. It exists only in the process of memory and writing. Or—to use Wolf's own imagery from her description of the immediate post-war period of defeat and redefinition—the inner landscape is no longer a private introspective one: "What happened was that one's inner sense of time stopped. Yet Nelly maintained her outward appearance. Of course nobody noticed how she felt, since she was behaving in keeping with the circumstances, and nobody is curious about another's inner life when his own life is in danger" (p. 319). This lack of introspection and sympathy is true of all wartime relationships, from the inability to hand bread to the hungry concentration camp survivors, to "the categorical refusal of the children to participate emotionally in their mother's drama" (p. 328).

The familial structures that define Wolf's narrative and the narrator/character's self are distinctly formed by historical experience. Fathers and uncles disappear during the war and are absent in the post-war period. Nelly's family consists of her mother and brother, her aunt and her grandparents. As they are forced to leave their home, fleeing from the approaching Russian troops, Nelly's mother stays behind, unable to make the break with her home and her property. Nelly is separated from her mother for the first time, to be reunited only several weeks later when Charlotte succeeds in finding her family again. During their flight new affiliations form; as people take them in, friends and enemies shift from day to day. Power structures alter as well in the largely female world of the post-war; Nelly herself works as mayor's assistant in the little town where they temporarily settle. The mayor himself, scared and discouraged, takes to his bed and lets a fifteen-year-old girl do his job.

In this war and post-war world, there is no heterosexual love narrative; men are absent, and when they return as conquering troops or freed prisoners, they elicit either fear or pity, not love. The affective life of the growing adolescent is mediated primarily by ideas and ideologies: its primary object is first the national socialist teacher Julia and then the post-war teacher Maria who forces Nelly to reevaluate all that Julia had taught.

The father, once he returns from a Soviet prisoner of war camp, inspires only guilt and the inability to love: visually not himself, he has to eat to try to resemble and reassemble himself again. This reframing of the oedipal romance plot has not changed significantly on the 1970s narrative level. Although the narrator's husband accompanies her research journey and intersperses a few comments, he remains a minor presence. The same could be said of the brother who, after inspiring murderous feelings of sibling rivalry in infancy, remains no more than a distant companion through her journeys. There is no oedipal plot in this novel; there are only echoes of how plots used to be structured.

There is, however, a pre-oedipal narrative, the story of the birth of the "I." The post-war period, the flight and forced ideological and emotional reassessment necessitated by Germany's loss are described as a violent rupture in Nelly's life, as a period of profound alienation and emotional stasis. The illness and breakdown that interrupts this period and enables Nelly to return to herself again, actually to begin to feel again, is described by Wolf as a structural necessity. "Nelly must fall ill, break down. The structure which strictly governs coincidence is evident here" (p. 392). Her convalescence from tuberculosis, at home in the apple orchard and later in the sanatorium, is a period not so much of rebirth, as of re-vision, of rethinking who she is and what she believes in. Some of this takes place through reading—in effect building a structure of selfhood by means of books. Some of it takes place through the relationships she forms in the sanatorium, especially her nurturing of the five-year-old Hannelore who cannot be saved and whose death elicits Nelly's first ability to mourn. As Nelly emerges from her illness, all the relationships in her life have been transformed; for example, she is nursed to health by her father who, resembling himself more closely again, daily brings a nutritious syrup to the hospital. The sanatorium scenes themselves are, of course, a revision of Thomas Mann's story of youth and development, *The Magic Mountain*, which also ends with the release from the sanatorium, but in that case on the eve of World War I. But Wolf's sanatorium fails to offer the hope of Mann's: no great intellectual insights are found here. The patients are more concerned with keeping warm and having enough to eat than with European culture. With her allusion to Mann, Wolf no doubt wants to explore how much has changed in Germany between the eve of World War I and the aftermath of World War II.

Kindheitsmuster ends as Nelly is released from the sanatorium in 1945, as the narrator and her family return from Poland in 1971, and as all the note papers disappear from her desk in 1975. It is three days since the end of the Vietnam war. The personal story is still deeply embedded in its historical context. Yet, closure is only tentative, provisional; the process of memory and revision which motivates this novel is not completed at its end. Even though the "I" does appear on the novel's last page, indicating that perhaps the different parts of the self can be reassembled, at least enough to voice a unified first-person pronoun, the "I" appears in the present only to say "I don't know," thereby disavowing its own existence. It appears again in the future tense, remaining a goal beyond the novel's end. But even this "I" of the future does not represent a reconciliation of the "you" and the "she" we have previously encountered. Instead, it is envisioned as an *eye* which sees, outside of itself, a continually metamorphosing presence, an eye which is only half awake, half dreaming, anticipating a reawakening: "At night I shall see—whether waking, whether dreaming—the outline of a human being who will change, through whom other persons, adults, children will pass without hindrance. I will hardly be surprised if this outline may also be that of an animal, a tree, even a house, in which anyone who wishes may go in and out at will" (p. 407). In this future-oriented moment of only apparent closure, the self has not been unified, the rift between past and present has not been resolved. Yet the capacious shape of a human being who allows others to take shape inside of her—a mother?—looks hopefully toward the future. As she sinks into dreaming, the narrating voice also sinks into silence, enjoying a brief reprieve from the struggles of narration: "I shall not revolt against the limits of the expressible."

In her 1968 essay "The Reader and the Writer," Wolf accounts for the genesis of narrative: "Writing can only begin for those to whom reality is no longer a matter-of-course."[41] As she goes on to develop this observation, it becomes apparent that for her the sources of fiction are epistemological and political, not psychological. When asked why she wrote *Kindheitsmuster*, Wolf speaks about the disjunction between the German Democratic Republic's official memory of the war and post-war period, and her own personal memory, sense of implication, and responsibility.[42] She speaks of her desire to account for the historical experience of her generation rather than to deal with issues of female identity or psychology.

Is it helpful, then, to read this novel in light of psychoanalytic paradigms and the notion of the feminist family romance? I would argue that it is precisely because historicizing the feminist family romance enables us to explore the intersections between the psychological and the political. For example, if men and fathers are displaced from the center of Wolf's plot, it is at least partially because they were away at war or in prison camp. Or if her sense of self is divided, it is so at least partially because of the ideological shifts she had to undergo in rapid succession between the thirties and the seventies. Yet a purely historical reading would ignore important dimensions of Wolf's text visible only through the feminist psychoanalytic lens. The most important of these, perhaps, is the pronominal structure of the text and its complicated structure of address. Who is the "you" that dominates the narrative and what is its relation to the reader? How is the novel's second person related to Lenka and perhaps to Ruth, the daughter(s) for whose benefit the text is written? And the daughters who are alive are related to the dead child Hannelore who, like the aborted fetus in *Surfacing* and the beggar woman's child in *The Lover*, seems to be at the basis of the mother-woman's process of subject-formation.

The issue of transmission transcends the boundaries of the political. The plural voice adopted by the novel's "narrator" is, at least in part, the voice of a mother telling her story of development to her daughter, or to her daughters. And if she does so, she does it at least in part in reference to her own mother, to bridge a personal, generational, and ideological division which has been present during her entire life. As the "I" becomes ever more inclusive, it transforms itself into "we."

Reading (and Writing) as Re-Vision

Christa Wolf's *Kindheitsmuster* presents important challenges to the picture of the feminist family romance emerging from fictional and theoretical writings of the 1970s. Wolf's narrator does not idealize the pre-oedipal period which, by definition, is unavailable to her memory. Her first recollections of Nelly already place her in a state of division: her mother's calling her name reveals their distance from one another; her desire to kill her baby brother increases that feeling of distance. Having no access to the pre-oedipal, she offers instead someone else's account of how she sat in front of her father's store saying "I I I I." If this is a first moment of self-consciousness, it cannot be recalled but must be reported as second-hand information. And it must be relived through every moment of the activity of narration.

This sense of fundamental self-division becomes doubly significant in relation to the issue of transmission. Unlike Nelly, unlike the narrator, unlike all the fictional protagonists I have been discussing in this book, Lenka (and Ruth?) will know her/their own pre-history: she/they will know the mother's story. And because Lenka will have been an interlocutor in its telling, she will know that story "differently than we have ever known it." This knowledge does not necessarily promise change: Wolf's allusions to current events, such as Vietnam and Chile, are convincing reminders of unavoidable repetition. This could explain the total absence of the other daughter from the novel. If Lenka participates in the emergence of the mother's story, her sister Ruth remains either totally ignorant or becomes a more untainted and even more receptive narratee. Not in the text, she promises a move beyond repetition. In reading Wolf's novel, transmitted from mother to daughter(s), we read the narrative of a female voice which has evolved, or which is in the process of evolving, from daughter to mother. Not surprisingly, her fractured and painful narrative transcends the bounds of psychoanalytic frameworks and the feminist family romance.

By supplementing the process of reading the past with the process of writing for the future, Wolf's novel thus comes closest to Rich's figure of re-vision. Although entitled "Writing as Re-Vision," Rich's essay actually outlines a process of reading the texts of the past, of "entering an old text from a new critical direction" (p. 90), a process of reading which promises that a new perspective will lead to a new way to live as a woman. Yet the re-visions examined in this chapter circumscribe certain limitations inherent in the very process of "looking back." Be they the lives of mothers represented in daughters' fictions, be they the frameworks, fictional or theoretical, that have explained and analyzed those lives, the texts of the past may actually hamper the move forward envisioned by Rich. "We need to know the writing of the past, and to know it differently than we have ever known it; not to pass on a tradition but to break its hold over us." It seems to me that only Wolf offers a model for this break, that only Lenka and perhaps Ruth may be able to progress from knowledge to a fresh life.

In taking as their point of departure not only the works and the terms of male theorists such as Freud and Lacan, but also a developed system relying on androcentric assumptions, the revisionary models of Chodorow, Gilligan, Irigaray, Kristeva, and others are necessarily hampered in their process of revision. Psychoanalytic theory and a feminism heavily based in psychoanalytic terminology, cannot, as I will show in the next chapter, present one crucial aspect of women's experience—the voice or the subjectivity of the mother. For such a feminism, looking back is looking to the story of a mother who is defined as subordinate in patriarchy, the backdrop for the child's developing consciousness, the object of the child's subjectivity. Looking back, for the feminist daughter, may permit a form of knowledge, a "sustained quest," but it will not permit a *different* form of knowledge. That difference, that break on the hold of tradition, can only come if the feminist daughter becomes a feminist mother who can tell her feminist daughter about that process of becoming. Adrienne Rich gives us the framework for that process in "When We Dead Awaken" and in its revisions; Christa Wolf begins to outline it in addressing us, her readers, as "you," demanding that we experience her story in a double process of identification with her, the writer, and with her daughter, the listener.

This process of reading as re-vision is a form of interpersonal fusion, but it is a fusion dislocated by the strange mixture of pronouns in which we are "I," "you," and "she." Can we find here perhaps the suggestion of a new form of intersubjectivity, a way out of oedipal and pre-oedipal dualism located in the very practices of reading and writing? I would argue that the constraining oedipal structures which circumscribe the thinking and plotting of this particular feminist generation can be loosened not by stepping outside the family, but by giving voice to those members of the family who have served as silent backdrop to the development of others. Wolf's novel might serve as a model for this restructured family and story.

In her article "The Oedipal Riddle: Authority, Autonomy and the New Narcissism," Jessica Benjamin explores paths to maturity and individuality that might provide an alternative to oedipal and even pre-oedipal models which still rely on the need for attachment and mastery and lead to authority and domination.[43] She suggests, instead, that those needs could be met through a process of mutual recognition, a mutuality in which we recognize both our dependency on others and their dependence on us: "True differentiation involves not only the awareness of the separation between self and other but the appreciation of the other's independent existence as an equivalent center" (p. 207). Reaching this combination of mutuality and autonomy entails a radical change in the representation of the relationship between mother and child: "In the earliest struggle for recognition, the mother must at some point actually remove herself from the child's sense of control, of omnipotence. She must establish her existence as another subject, as a person, that the child too can have a sense of selfhood" (pp. 207–208). For Benjamin, then, the root of our culture's continuing reliance on oedipal psychology lies in the denial of subjectivity to mothers. This denial is perpetuated in what I have called the feminist family romance. So long as mothers remain objects of exploration rather than social, psychological, and linguistic subjects, the hold of tradition cannot be broken, and new stories cannot be told.

The story of female development, both in fiction and theory, needs to be written in the voice of mothers as well as in that of daughters. It needs to cease mystifying maternal stories, to cease making them the objects of a "sustained quest." Only in combining both voices, in finding a double voice that would yield a multiple female consciousness, can we begin to envision ways to "live afresh." Only thus can feminists begin to imagine a form of consciousness and of subjectivity creating, and created by, the social and ideological revolution that feminism has only begun to effect.[44] However, as Adrienne Rich says, we as feminists still "have our work cut out for us" ("When We Dead," p. 49).

5

FEMINIST DISCOURSE/
MATERNAL DISCOURSE

SPEAKING WITH TWO VOICES

> Within the body, growing as a graft, in-
> domitable, there is an other.
>
> —Julia Kristeva

> We always learned to expect sentences to
> have two parts, the second seeming
> to contradict the first, the unity lying
> in our growing ability to tolerate
> ambivalence—for that is what
> motherly love is like.
>
> —Jane Lazarre

> What did it mean for a black woman to be
> an artist in our grandmother's time?
> In our great-grandmother's day? It is
> a question with an answer cruel
> enough to stop the blood.
>
> —Alice Walker

> I am angry nearly every day of my life,
> but I have learned not to show it; and
> I still try to hope not to feel it,
> though it may take me another forty
> years to do it.
>
> —Louisa May Alcott

Sisterhood Is Powerful

In 1978 Robin Morgan, the editor of *Sisterhood Is Powerful* (one of the most influential anthologies of the U.S. Women's Liberation movement), described the conflict she felt between feminist politics and maternal experience during the movement's early days. "Since the patriarchy commanded women to be mothers (the thesis)," she wrote in her autobiography, "we had to rebel with our own polarity and declare motherhood a reactionary cabal (antithesis). Today a new synthesis has emerged; the concept of mother-right, affirmation of a woman's child-bearing and/or child-rearing when it is a woman's *choice*. . . . It is refreshing at last to be able to come out of my mother-closet and yell to the world that I love my dear wonderful delicious child."[1]

The hesitation Morgan felt about speaking as a mother can still be detected in feminist rhetoric today. Feminist writing and scholarship, continuing in large part to adopt *daughterly* perspectives, can be said to collude with patriarchy in placing mothers into the position of object— thereby keeping mothering outside of representation and maternal discourse a theoretical impossibility.

To be sure, the term "mother" and the discourse about/of mothering are objects of sometimes radical division within feminist analysis. The question that needs to be confronted is a question of definition: "What is a mother? What is maternal?" It is a question that situates itself at the breaking point between various feminist positions: between presence and absence, speech and silence, essentialism and constructivism, materialism and psychoanalysis. Is motherhood "experience" or "institution?" Is it biological or cultural? Is the mother present or absent, single or divided, in collusion with patriarchy or at odds with it, conformist or subversive? Can an analysis of motherhood point toward liberation or does it inevitably ensconce feminists in constraining cultural stereotypes?[2]

Obliquely, these and related questions underly the argument of this chapter, which looks at some of the points where feminist discourse establishes itself as separate from the maternal position. Only a probing scrutiny of what separates feminist discourse from maternal discourse can free feminist thinking to define some of the shapes of maternal subjectivity and to study the articulation of specifically *maternal* voices.[3] Only thus might we envision a feminist family romance of mothers *and* daughters, both subjects, speaking to each other and living in familial and communal contexts which enable the subjectivity of each member.

In writing about mothers, I am aware of the dangers of idealizing and mystifying a certain biological female experience and of reviving an identification between femininity and maternity which certainly has not served the interests of women. My intent is precisely the opposite: to make space for differences among women from the perspective not of biology, but of experience. I find useful here Teresa de Lauretis's definition of experience as "a complex of habits resulting from the semiotic interaction of 'outer world' and 'inner world', the continuous engagement of a self, as subject, in social reality."[4] It is most useful, I believe, to look at the mother *as subject* constituted in a particular relation to social reality, to sexuality, to work and historical experience, to subjectivity. Accounting for difference, not only between women and men, but also *among women*, remains an important challenge for feminist analysis and the mother, cast as other, can be used to test the openness of feminist rhetoric toward others. My discussion of the uneasy relation between feminist discourse and maternal discourse is an experiment with bringing a maternal perspective to bear on a series of texts which themselves put such a perspective into play.

Throughout the 1970s, the metaphor of sisterhood, of friendship or of surrogate motherhood has been the dominant model for female and feminist relationships.[5] To say that "sisterhood is powerful," however, is to isolate feminist discourse within one generation and to banish feminists who are mothers to the "mother-closet." In the 1970s, the prototypical feminist voice was, to a large degree, the voice of the daughter attempting to separate from an overly connected or rejecting mother, in order to bond with her sisters in a relationship of mutual nurturance and support among equals. With its possibilities of mutuality and its desire to avoid power, the paradigm of sisterhood has the advantage of freeing women from the biological function of giving birth, even while offering a specifically feminine relational model. "Sisters" can be "maternal" to one another without allowing their bodies to be invaded by men and the physical acts of pregnancy, birth, and lactation. In this feminist family romance, sisters are better mothers, providing more nurturance and a greater encouragement of autonomy. In functioning as mutual surrogate mothers, sisters can replace mothers.[6]

Bell Gale Chevigny's essay, "Daughters Writing: Toward a Theory of Women's Biography," demonstrates the power of this fantasy of reciprocity, whether among sisters or surrogate mothers and daughters, for feminist scholarly discourse. "There is a stage in which author and subject [of the biography] in effect become *surrogate mothers* in that they offer one another 'maternal' nurture. But the fantasy of the surrogate mother differs in several ways from the fantasy of the perfect mother. It is a fantasy of reciprocity; far from being all-powerful, both 'mothers' are engaged in struggle; both nurture not an infant, but a girl or woman; and for both, nurture is a sanctioning of their autonomy" (italics in original).[7] As Chevigny illustrates, the ideal of sisterhood and of reciprocal surrogate motherhood highlights the maternal as function, but rejects and makes invisible the actual mother, who, it is implied, infantilizes the daughter and fails to encourage autonomy.[8] I do believe that in the feminist movement sisterhood has served not only as a fantasy, but also as an ideal of relation and as an actual practice, sometimes emerging in response to complicated interactions feminists had had with their actual and their professional mothers. Yet the effects of its pervasiveness as metaphor for feminist relation, coupled with the metaphor of daughterhood in the academy, have been to separate feminist theorizing from maternal stories and experiences and to suppress the maternal within the feminist.[9] In addition, the notion of sisterhood has had the effect of glossing over other critical differences of assumption, voice, and experience among women who might be able to identify with the feminist movement were feminism capacious enough to include their different voices. I see here the maternal critique of "daughterly feminism" as parallel to the critiques of white feminism by women of color in the Unites States, as well as to the similar critiques of Western feminism by Third World women and the critiques of middle-class feminism by working-class women.

The construction of sisterhood as feminist ideal highlights some of the reasons for the feminist separation from maternal discourse, perspective, and subjectivity. Four areas of avoidance and discomfort with the maternal emerge with particular force in feminist rhetoric.[10] First, the perception that motherhood remains a patriarchal construction and that the mother is an empty function connects the figure of the mother with continued bondage to men and patriarchy. As Adrienne Rich explains: "Matrophobia can be seen as a womanly splitting of the self, in the desire to become purged once and for all of our mothers' bondage, to become individuated and free. The mother stands for the victim in ourselves, the unfree women, the martyr. Our personalities seem dangerously to blur and overlap with our mothers'; and, in a desperate attempt to know where mother ends and daughter begins, we perform radical surgery" (*Of Woman Born*, p. 236). Fran Scoble's recent essay "Mothers and Daughters: Giving the Lie" offers just one of many recent examples of specifically feminist "matrophobia."[11] Mothers in our culture, Scoble says, deny the truth about their own experience of bondage and frustration and lie to their daughters whose growth then is constrained by the perpetuation of mutual deception. Scoble expresses the feminist daughter's anger at the mother who has accepted her powerlessness, who is unable to protect her from a submission to society's gender arrangements. This anger may well be justified in many cases. Essays like Scoble's, however, view the mother as falsely unified, ignoring the possibility of the mother's double or multiple consciousness which would certainly complicate her reading of motherhood. An alignment of feminist with daughterly, such as Scoble's, only perpetuates mystifications of the maternal.

Second, feminist writings are often characterized by a discomfort with the vulnerability and lack of control that are attributed to, and certainly are elements of, maternity. Feminist discourse has set an extremely high value on control—control of women's bodies, of their legal status, their salaries, their choice of life and plot. Nothing challenges a very hard-earned and still enormously fragile sense of control more than the vulnerabilities and dependencies of maternity—dependency on the unpredictabilities of female bodies, on an alienating yet necessary medical establishment, on the men who in one form or another are involved in the production and rearing of children (and this is true even for single or lesbian mothers), on the society which along with women and often in opposition to them shapes children's development and women's own capacities to care for them, and on the children themselves. The image that pervades feminist writing is the image of self-creation—women giving birth to themselves, determining their own course. Yet we need to ask, what happens to actual mothers, and what happens to actual children, when women figuratively become their own "mothers"? With the vulnerabilities of maternity, feminist discourse excludes dimensions of women's consciousness and experience that go beyond reason and control.

Third, Elizabeth V. Spellman has identified "somatophobia"—the fear of and discomfort with the body—as a pervasive discomfort among women and within feminism.[12] Nothing entangles women more firmly in their bodies than pregnancy, birth, lactation, miscarriage, or the inability to conceive. Most areas of feminist analysis have been terribly careful to rule out an identification with biology. The thoroughness with which feminist theorizing, responding to the patriarchal identification of women with body and the need to keep the definition of feminine within the cultural, has done this—what Nancy Miller has recently called "the feminist bugaboo about essentialism"—must be motivated by a discomfort with the body.[13] Certainly, the connection of maternity and sexuality remains a pervasive taboo in feminist analysis.[14] French feminist writing appears to have conquered this taboo and to have constructed a new and liberating discourse of the body—one that is often called essentialist. I would submit, however, that the representation of the female body in French feminist discourse is neither essentialist or experiential. Cixous's mother's milk and menstrual blood, or Irigaray's labia, are figures for feminine writing and speech, just as maternity is Kristeva's figure for poetry. For Hélène Cixous and Luce Irigaray, the body is not matter but metaphor, and their gestures of reconstruction are figural enough not to have to include the mother's literally pregnant body. As Jane Gallop argues, "discourse about the body seems to represent a point of unusually suggestive tension about the referent," but the new, reconstructed, non-phallomorphic body presented in Irigaray's work is not in any sense "real."[15] It could, however, have an effect on "real" bodies, and this writing (about) the body therefore needs to occupy an important place in feminist analysis. I believe that the body must continue to be explored in feminist writing, not only in its relation to writing, but also in its relation to psychology, society, and history.

Fourth, the separation between feminist discourse and maternal discourse can be attributed to feminism's complicated ambivalence about power, authority, and, as I will argue more fully, anger. Dorothy Dinnerstein and others have claimed that women's acceptance of paternal authority stems from deep seated and unconscious fears of what is perceived by the infant as maternal power, that the mother, in fact, is in the position of carrying all human fears and fantasies about power and authority.[16] Nancy Chodorow and Susan Contratto have shown most persuasively that feminist theoretical writing in the U.S. is permeated with fears of maternal power and with anger at maternal powerlessness.[17] Using the language of sisterhood to describe women's relations to one another has the effect of disguising and repressing the rivalries and competitions and the power inequities that form a part of women's relations as much as of any other.[18] Clearly, some of these fears must be confronted and defused before feminists who write can assume a maternal voice or position—and before feminists more generally can claim power—without intense ambivalence.

Unless feminism can begin to demystify and politicize motherhood, and by extension female power more generally, fears and projections will continue. Feminism might begin by listening to the stories that mothers have to tell, and by creating the space in which mothers might articulate those stories. Evelyn Fox Keller concludes: "Few of us ever get to know the real mother, her real power, or the limits of her power. Instead she survives as a specter alternately overwhelming and inconsequential."[19] The redefinition of how power can function in relationship, suggested in Keller's work on gender and science, as well as in the work of Sara Ruddick, Jessica Benjamin, Carol Gilligan, and Luce Irigaray, among others, might make it more possible for feminist theorizing to assume a maternal position and occasionally to speak in a maternal voice. A reconceptualization of power, authority, and anger can emerge only if feminism can both practice and theorize a maternal discourse, based in maternal experience and capable of combining power and powerlessness, authority and invisibility, strength and vulnerability, anger and love. Only thus can the maternal cease to polarize feminists; only thus can it be politicized from within feminist discourse.

Feminisms and Psychoanalyses

One of the barriers to a theory and a practice of maternal discourse is the feminist reliance on psychoanalysis as a conceptual framework and on the psychoanalytic construction of mothering. Insofar as psychoanalytic theories have been helpful to feminism in illuminating the complex ways in which an individual internalizes social forces and their gender paradigms, they have been able to do so only from the point of view of the developing child. In all psychoanalytic writing, *the child* is the subject of both study and discourse.[20] While psychoanalytic feminisms have added the female child to the male, they have not succeeded in inscribing the perspective of adult women. The adult woman who is a mother, in particular, continues to exist only in relation to her child, never as a subject in her own right. And in her maternal function, she remains an object, always distanced, always idealized or denigrated, always mystified, always represented through the small child's point of view.

Moreover, for psychoanalysis, and in a large part even for psychoanalytic feminism, a continued allegiance to the mother appears as regressive and potentially lethal; it must be transcended. Maturity can be reached only through an alignment with the paternal, by means of an angry and hostile break from the mother. As Freud states, "a powerful tendency to aggressiveness is always present beside a powerful love, and the more passionately a child loves its object the more sensitive does it become to disappointments and frustrations from that object; and in the end the love must succumb to the accumulated hostility. . . . it is the special nature of the mother-child relationship that leads, with equal inevitability, to the destruction of the child's love."[21] For Freud, anger between child and mother, anger directed specifically at the mother, fundamentally underlies the sequence of individual maturation; it makes that linear narrative possible. The repression of the initial fusion with the mother is the condition of the construction of the subject. And although the mother herself can desire fulfillment only through her child, if she is a good, or even a good-enough mother (and Winnicott's reformulation does not in any way resolve this problem),[22] she does not resist, but accepts, without visible hostility, an abandonment psychoanalytic writing presents as inevitable.

Within a psychoanalytic framework, the mother's desire can never be voiced because her desire exists only in the fantasy of the child as something the child can never satisfy. Their dyadic desire is broken by reference to the phallus, which is beyond them both in the realm of the father. Both Freud and Lacan attribute to the mother a sole object of desire—the phallus. And since the phallus (as lack) is the tool of representation, and since the mother does not have it (in Lacan's terms, women lack lack), any other articulation of her own becomes an impossibility.[23] The child, coming to language, becomes subject to the name-of-the-father, accepting the exigencies of symbolizing desire in language and thereby transcending the mother's silence. The mother herself is and remains absent even to herself. The place she inhabits is vacant. Although she produces and upholds the subject, she herself remains the matrix, the other, the origin. And the child's own narrative—the narrative of our culture—rests on that "othering."

Freud writes that a woman of 30 is psychically rigid and unchangeable, depleted by the work of becoming-woman. For her, he maintains, "there are no paths open to further development" ("Femininity," p. 135). The adult woman's immature libidinal processes—the unresolved pre-oedipal love for her mother and oedipal attachment to her father—make her particularly attractive to the adult man, who, through her, attempts to relive his own pre-oedipal bliss. But, as Freud says, "one gets an impression that a man's love and a woman's are a phase apart psychologically" ("Femininity," p. 134): the woman's emotional fulfillment, unlike the man's, comes not from her relationship with her husband but from the attachment to her children (actually, Freud privileges the son here), through whom she vicariously gains access to her own earliest moments of infantile plenitude. Only through this mediation can she relate to herself as *mother*.

Freud's narrative, even if we take it entirely on its own terms, contains a profound paradox, one that he does not and cannot see. On the one hand, he insists that female fulfillment lies in the relation between mother and child; on the other, he posits a necessary and hostile rupture of that relation by the child. What he fails to look at, and what he cannot look at, is how the mother herself experiences the rupture on which he insists. If the story of individual development, as Freud tells it, rests on a process of separation from the mother, then the mother's own part in that process remains absent, erased from theoretical and narrative representation.

Feminist revisions of the Freudian plot maintain some of its essential features: a woman's greatest attachment and most fulfilling emotional relationships are still said to be with her children—in this case daughters rather than sons—but those children still need to undergo a process of separation, often motivated by anger and hostility. What has hardly changed, between Freud and the work of Nancy Chodorow or Luce Irigaray, is the presentation of a mother who is overly invested in her child, powerless in the world, a constraining rather than an enabling force in the girl's development, and an inadequate and disappointing object of identification. I would submit, then, that to a large degree feminist theorizing itself still argues from the position of the child or, to a lesser extent, that of the childless adult woman and continues to represent the mother in the terms originally outlined by Freud. The insightful article by Nancy Chodorow and Susan Contratto, "The Fantasy of the Perfect Mother," points to the degree of idealization and projection that shapes much feminist writing about maternity and daughterhood. Feminist analysis, they insist, is still written from the child's primary process perspective: permeated with desires for the mother's approval, with fear of her power, and with anger and resentment at her powerlessness.

Is it possible to tell the untold tale of maternal participation in the psychoanalytic narrative, staying within psychoanalytic terminology? Can we invest with speech the silence that defines maternal experience? There is, as Linda Orr has pointed out, a strange liaison between silence and anger: silence makes us uncomfortable because we tend to suspect that it conceals anger, as in "Are you mad at me?"[24] Faced with maternal silence, we might posit maternal anger. Anger becomes, in fact, a dominant theme in this exploration of maternal subjectivity. Anger, Marilyn Frye has said, is an "instrument of cartography."[25] To be angry is to claim a place, to assert a right to expression and to discourse, a right to intelligibility. "By determining where, with whom, about what and in what circumstances one can get angry . . ., one can map others' concepts of who and what one is" (p. 94). If we see anger as a particularly pointed assertion and articulation of subjectivity, we can use it as an "instrument of cartography" to map the subjectivity of those who are denied it by culture and discourse, in this case mothers.

Exploring maternal anger makes it possible to confront both the cultural construction of motherhood—the angry abandoning or abandoned mother has reached the status of a cultural icon—*and* maternal responses to that construction. I recognize that, in privileging anger, I represent maternal subjectivity from one, limited vantage point, and one that converges with cultural representations of the maternal. Yet I suspect that such a vantage point is unavoidable since anger may well be what defines subjectivity whenever the subjective is denied speech.[26] This formulation points to connections between maternal subjectivity and the subjectivity of oppressed or colonized peoples. Still, inasmuch as women can be subjects at all, the subjectivity of mothers is different. The woman who is a mother was a subject as a daughter. But as a mother, her subjectivity is under erasure; during the process of her daughter's accession to subjectivity, she is told to recede into the background, to be replaced. Inasmuch as that suppression *is* her maternal function, it is reasonable to assume anger as her response, especially if we grant that female subjectivity is already suppressed in relation to male subjectivity.

The projected angry mother of the psychoanalytic narrative, then, would react to the child's so-called inevitable hostility with anger of her own, would feel wronged when, after years of nurturing and care, she is left behind. Should she rebel, however, should she express her own feelings about an enforced and inevitable separation, she would cease to be maternal. For the essence of the maternal in psychoanalytic writing lies in the service to the interests of the child. And to be angry is to assert one's own self, not to subordinate it to the development of another's self. A mother cannot articulate anger *as a mother*; to do so she must step out of a culturally circumscribed role which commands mothers to be caring and nurturing to others, even at the expense of themselves.

To be angry, moreover, is to create a space of separation, to isolate oneself temporarily; such breaks in connection, such disruptions of relationship again challenge the role that not only psychoanalysis, but also culture itself assigns to mothers. Moreover, our culture's conjunction of anger and aggression, that is, of feeling and behavior, makes maternal anger doubly threatening and precludes the expression and perhaps even the experience of it.[27] Those who are heirs to Greek mythology are haunted by the specter of Medea, the woman who turns her anger at her husband into violence against her children, or by the specter of Clytemnestra, whose anger on behalf of her child irremediably perverts her maternity. Furthermore, the cultural separation between care and anger, care and self-interest, makes it as impossible for mothers to integrate anger into their activity of mothering as for mothers to care for themselves even as they nurture their children. Unconscious desires for unconditional maternal love, unconscious beliefs in maternal omnipotence and potential destructiveness—beliefs present even in feminist writings about mother-hood—create irrational, pervasive fears of maternal power and aggression. These fears and needs may well be responsible for the inability to theorize an anger that can coexist with love and that does not turn into aggression, and for the inability to think past anger to a fuller picture of maternal subjectivity. Even as feminist theorizing urges women to shift our political allegiance from fathers back to mothers, even as it urges us to sympathize with mothers' positions in patriarchy, it continues to inscribe the fears and projections of an infantile perspective on the mother.

To tell this part of the psychoanalytic narrative is still to assume that the child's development necessitates a rupture from the mother, that the mother is overly invested in her child and is devastated by the break, that attachment is profoundly endangered by the expression of anger, that maternal subjectivity exists exclusively in response to the child's, and that maternal subjectivity must be erased for daughterly subjectivity to develop. The psychoanalytic plot has not only silenced maternal responses to separation; it also allows only a narrow space in which to fill in what is missing. Investing maternal silence with anger further isolates mothers and mythologizes their destructive power. Suggesting that we posit anger as the content of an untold, an unspeakable maternal experience, and implying, at the same time, that anger is the antithesis of the maternal, psychoanalytic theory actually facilitates separation, placing those who theorize into the position of the child and placing the mother into a position of otherness. Theory thus continues to cover "experience."

Two recent strands in psychoanalytic feminism, one grounded in a Lacanian and one in an object-relations framework, have attempted to challenge this distance between theoretical feminism and maternal experience by highlighting *the maternal*. Although this process of theorizing from the place of the maternal has brought feminism closer to a position in which maternal voices might be voiced and heard, it also reveals the complicated and sometimes self-defeating nature of such revisionary attempts.

In the theoretical discourse of Julia Kristeva, for example, the maternal occupies a central space. Mary Jacobus has called Kristeva's work "the most formidable literary and psychoanalytic elaboration of maternity."[28] The mother as split subject, as locus of the semiotic, as both phallic and castrated, present and absent, omnipotent and powerless, the body before language, unrepresentable, inexpressible, unsettling, has become the privileged metaphor for a subversive femininity. In *Powers of Horror*, she is the "abject," who threatens the tenuous boundary between the not-yet-subject and the not-yet-object; she remains the object who enables or impedes the child's development.[29] In *Tales of Love*, she is the center-piece of the discourses of love ranging from courtly love to psychoanalytic practice, to narcissism, to sublimity.[30] Kristeva's discourse of maternity highlights both the endangering qualities of the undifferentiated space it inhabits and its tremendous potential for subversion. At the same time, maternity remains virtually inaccessible, except by way of a mediation through the symbolic, the paternal, the phallic—a mediation Freud and Lacan also perceived as crucial. Kristeva maintains: "As long as there is language-symbolism-paternity, there will never be any other way to represent, to objectify, and to explain this unsettling of the symbolic stratum, this nature/culture threshold, this instilling the subjectless biological program into the very body of the symbolizing subject, this event called motherhood."[31] Yet Kristeva herself does write in a maternal voice, and of a maternal experience—the birth of her son. In "L'Hérétique de l'amour" (1977), reissued as "Stabat Mater" in *Tales of Love,* she intersperses a "maternal" text into a discursive analysis of the conjunction between maternity and virginity in Christian discourse, actually allowing the bold-faced maternal narrative to disrupt and unsettle the other.[32] Clearly, this doubleness, this mediation and alternation, is necessary for her account of the birth and of the experience of maternity. Clearly also, the space of the maternal is a tentative space of heterogeneity, lack of control, self-alienation, absence. As Kristeva's text insists, the abyss between mother and child, the "permanent parting" of the mother and the permanent division of the flesh and the word, offer an invaluable perspective to the feminist analysis of culture: the ability to recognize otherness and arbitrariness, an ability which unsettles and dismantles all symbolic and philosophical power.

More than anyone else, Kristeva identifies the maternal with the unspeakable. But, what are the implications of this identification? Jacobus herself is right in seeing that "the discourse of maternity gives birth to Kristevan poetics" (p. 170), that it serves as a metaphor for "the symbolic crisis brought about by the disunited, multifold differences and engraftings of poetic language." Adopting the voice of the mother allows Kristeva to theorize and to posit a poetic voice which defines a new avant-garde practice, but that poetic practice then appropriates the force of Kristeva's maternal discourse. Jane Gallop voices a similar criticism when she argues that Kristeva, by viewing the mother as phallic and then de-phallicizing her, posits her as a privileged "dissident," privileged in relation to the continuous disruption of the symbolic by what she has called the semiotic.[33] Gallop quotes a section of Kristeva's "L'Autre du sexe": "The maternal function can be the apprenticeship of modesty and of a permanent calling into question; and if a woman lives maternity and her artist's work thus, far from being a totalizing Mother-Goddess, she is rather a locus for vulnerability, of calling into question of oneself and of language" (cited in *The Daughter's Seduction,* p. 122).

These glosses of Kristeva's analysis of maternity point to important limitations in her project. For Kristeva, the maternal position is still the site of privileged femininity, either the idealized metaphor for "poetic revolution" or a revolutionary poetics, or the denigrated space of horror whose ab-jection is the condition of subject-formation. She privileges the Bellini madonnas over Leonardo's because of the quality of unrepresentability Bellini's contain. Kristeva, speaking as mother, has a mediated relationship to her own maternal voice; her own maternal voice has for her the status of metaphor. Yet, as Domna Stanton has so rightly pointed out in her analysis of the "maternal metaphor" in Kristeva, Cixous, and Irigaray, the very process of metaphorization, which would make the maternal into the unrepresentable capable of shattering the scene of representation, actually leaves the maternal firmly rooted in the very structure of representation these writers wish to escape.[34] Metaphoricity itself is profoundly ontological: "Although the maternal/semiotic is crucial to the Kristevan theory of art as the exemplary subversive practice, the mother remains, as the phallotext defines her, a passive instinctual force that does not speak, but is spoken by the male" (Stanton, p. 167). Stanton's proposed solution, a metonymization of the maternal—a deferral, postponement, putting off— is, as she herself admits, not a significant departure from the posture traditionally imposed on women. For all its experimentation and multiple mediation, Kristevan maternal discourse remains firmly embedded in structures of representation which place the mother outside or on the margin. It thus makes it impossible to distinguish between the discourse *of* the mother and the discourse *about* her.

Similarly, the turn toward the maternal taken by Irigaray in *Éthique de la différence sexuelle* and in *Sexes et parentés* remains limited. Although this turning celebrates a female genealogy and enables a focus on what maternal knowledge might offer Irigaray's project of reconstruction, Irigaray's writings about the maternal do not allow her to adopt a maternal voice or perspective.

Relying on object-relations theory, some American feminist writers have attempted to inscribe the maternal in a different way—by separating the function and the activity of mothering from the female body, by identifying qualities and processes as maternal without necessarily linking them to biological femaleness. They can thereby leave open for men the possibility of participating in the activity of mothering. Based on the work of D. W. Winnicott, Ruth Perry's concept of "mothering the mind," for example, considers mothering essential to artistic creativity, which emerges not in isolation but in a safe, interactive, interpersonal environment, fostered by the nurturance of a "holding mother."[35] Both the artist and the maternal figure can be either male or female, but, as a result of this need for safety trust and care, Perry has envisioned the artist as always being in the position of the child and the mother as always being in the space of selfless supporter. Thus, a maternal art cannot be imagined. In contrast, Barbara Johnson's essay "Mallarmé as Mother" does show, through the figures of Mallarmé and Margaret Mahler, how, regardless of gender, one can write from a maternal position.[36] Issues of separation so fundamental to writing

are, in Johnson's terms, familiar to the mother, whose experience combines separation with indifferentiation, attachment with detachment, and
whose position, therefore, can appear as the privileged space for writing.
In these analyses of the maternal, mothers are both present—as function or
structure—and yet absent—as subjects. As Barbara Johnson cautions, "The
maternal function as it stands is itself but a branch of phallogocentrism" (p.
82).[37] I would add that centering feminist inquiry in the *maternal* does not
necessarily allow feminists to listen to or to speak as *mothers*, just as
thinking about the *feminine* does not mean that we listen to or speak as
women. In limiting its representation of the mother to the "maternal," to
function or metaphor, feminist theorizing glosses over the stories that
mothers are perhaps trying to tell, the stories that the psychoanalytic frame
in which we have been thinking has made us unable to hear. Thus, it
seems to me, feminist analysis can benefit from this discussion of the
maternal as function or metaphor only if it also recognizes maternity as
experience. Julia Kristeva points to the difficulties of such a proposition, by
showing that maternal experience is always already mediated by structures
of representation which shape a particular and narrowly circumscribed
image of maternity. Still, it may be possible to push against those structures, to reshape them enough to make space for various forms of maternal
discourse.

Feminist theorizing has been critical of psychoanalysis in a variety of
ways, but several recent analyses have undertaken this critique specifically
from the perspective of mothers and have focused on the absence of the
mother from psychoanalytic theory. But in reading the illuminating critiques by Nancy Chodorow and Susan Contratto in "The Fantasy of the
Perfect Mother," by Susan Suleiman, Carol Gilligan, Nina Baym, Monique
Plaza, the editors of *The (M)Other Tongue*, Ann Kaplan, Judith Kegan
Gardiner, and Jane Gallop, one wonders to what extent they are all limited
by the very psychoanalytic framework in which and against which they
situate themselves.[38] For example, in her essay "Writing and Motherhood," Susan Suleiman first reveals and then questions the psychoanalytic
assumption that motherhood and authorship are inherently antithetical by
looking at mothers who do write and by examining how these injunctions
inform their writing. It is only at this point in her essay, when leaving a
psychoanalytic framework for a series of suggestive textual analyses, that
Suleiman can challenge, rather than merely criticize, the framework with
which she began. Suleiman shows that, besides being written, mothers do
write *as mothers*, and that their writing can be furthered rather than merely
impeded by their motherhood. According to Suleiman, maternal texts are
often shaped by the fantasy that the writing mother kills her child.[39] The
progression of Suleiman's essay from Freud, Lacan, object-relations
theory, and Kristeva to Rosellen Brown and Chantal Chawaf has become a
classic move of psychoanalytic feminist writing dissatisfied with its own
framework and searching for an "other" perspective. (This chapter, in fact,

also conforms to such a progression.)[40] For within the discourse of psychoanalysis, the mother's story can only be named inasmuch as it is a response to the child's process of separation. And as such, this story, even if we were to try to write it, does not begin with the mother, does not begin to grant her agency, initiative, and subjectivity.

Barbara Johnson's more recent essay, "Apostrophe, Abortion, and Animation," reverses the image of an overly invested mother, angry at being left by her child, and pushes against the limits of a psychoanalytic vantage point. She highlights a crucial aspect in contemporary maternity—the issue of choice and the thinking about abortion—reading abortion as a *figure* for lyric poetry.[41] Anger, potential violence, and destructiveness are still aspects of this reluctant maternity which, in women's poetry, is defined by fearful fantasies. Language, Johnson argues, animates what it addresses, yet for the woman and for the "mother," especially the reluctant mother, the act of animation has a very different inflection than it does for the male lyricist. "It is as though male writing were by nature procreative while female writing is somehow by nature infanticidal" (p. 198). Johnson's explanation for this general impression, like her argument itself, goes beyond figure to a pointed analysis of the cultural and legal constructions of abortion. Whereas the male poet addresses and thereby animates nature, the woman poet addresses, without actually animating, a dead child: "there is something about the connection between motherhood and death that refuses to remain comfortably and conventionally figurative" (p. 198). When Johnson insists that "rhetorical psychoanalytical and political structures are profoundly implicated in one another," she enables a view of the maternal that transcends metaphor and a purely psychoanalytic framework. Still, she reveals the tremendous difficulty in achieving "a full elaboration of any discursive position other than that of child" (p. 199).

Outside of a psychoanalytic framework lies Ann Ferguson's "On Conceiving Motherhood and Sexuality: A Feminist Materialist Approach," and Sara Ruddick's exemplary analysis of "Maternal Thinking."[42] Ferguson coins the useful concept of "sex-affective production" to describe the work of mothering and women's role in the system of productive and reproductive labor. She outlines what she sees as the double consciousness of mothers—their split allegiance to husbands, on the one hand, and children, on the other. She can thereby identify the complex process by which mothers internalize and perpetuate oppressive structures of parenting without recourse to psychoanalytic terminology, yet the absence of a maternal unconscious which mediates this process leaves Ferguson's model less fully elaborated than it might be.

By looking to identify motherhood as practice and work, by describing what mothers *do* rather than what they *are*, Sara Ruddick helps to demystify the mother and to introduce a maternal and a pragmatic perspective into the analysis of motherhood, even while describing it as work that can be performed by men as well as women. Ruddick, in other words, writes about motherhood both as a mother knowledgeable about the experience and as a philosopher able to abstract from it. Yet the reception of her essay illustrates the difficulty of writing about and within the perspective of the maternal. Although Ruddick speaks of both positive and negative aspects of maternal thinking, the "maternal" tone she employs seems to disguise her expressions of ambivalence and to highlight her celebration of this traditionally feminine form of knowledge and relation.[43] As Ruddick has subsequently written: "It may be that any sympathetic account of mothering is heard as 'idealization'; if so that is an indirect testament to the mother-blaming widespread in our society. It may be, too, that my passionate commitment to mothers as a class, seeps through my lines and muddies the argument."[44] Whereas classical and object-relations psychoanalysis has constructed a "good" or a "good-enough" mother content to erase her anger, her desire, and her subjectivity, the insights of Ferguson, Ruddick, Suleiman, Gilligan, Chodorow and Contratto, and Johnson, among others, provide an access to maternal consciousness and discourse, and to the politics of the maternal which is invaluable to feminist analysis.

Speaking with Two Voices:
Morrison's *Sula*

This chapter has argued that feminist discourse has suffered from its "inner splitting" and "radical surgery," from the absence of the mother as subject in favor either of a celebration of women as sisters and friends, or of the maternal as function or metaphor. If maternal voices are not to be found in feminist theoretical writing, is it possible to turn to feminist fiction for an articulation of maternal subjectivity? Do mothers write their own experience *as mothers?* What shapes and plots accommodate those experiences, and what is the relationship of maternal narratives to the cultural projections this book has traced? To what extent do women writers who are mothers co-conspire in their own silence, hesitant to reveal their stories to their children?

In recent years, several women writers have written in specifically maternal voices, though, for reasons not easy to determine, poets and short fiction writers have done so more frequently than novelists. The numbers are few, although the texts are important and need close attention. In the American tradition one might cite, among others, Alicia Ostriker, Adrienne Rich, Tillie Olsen, Grace Paley, Mary Gordon, Rosellen Brown, Sue Miller, Jan Clausen, and Sharon Olds.

In particular, one tradition among the various feminisms that have developed in the last twenty years does feature the mother prominently and in complex and multiple ways—the tradition of black American women writers of the 1960s, 70s, and 80s. As a generation of feminist writing just in the process of defining itself in relation to a maternal, largely oral past, black feminist writing provides a useful locus for the exploration of maternal discourse and points of resistance to it. Unlike so many contemporary white feminist writers who define their artistic identity as separate from or in opposition to their mothers, black writers have recently been insisting on what Mary Helen Washington identifies as the "connection between the black woman writer's sense of herself as part of a link in generations of women, and her decision to write."[45] Alice Walker's "In Search of Our Mothers' Gardens" and "Saving a Life That Is Your Own,"[46] Paule Marshall's "Shaping the World of My Art"[47] and "From in the Kitchen"[48] are conscious and public attempts, as Mary Helen Washington puts it, to "piece together the story of a viable female culture, one in which there is generational continuity, in which one's mother serves as the female precursor who passes on the authority of authorship to her daughter and provides a model for the black woman's literary presence in this society" ("I Sign," p. 147). Paule Marshall and Alice Walker explain that in their families theirs is the first generation to be college-educated, the first generation engaged in writing down the stories handed down orally by their matrilineal heritage. Even when they write in the voices of daughters rather than mothers, the black feminist writers in this tradition tend to find it necessary, much more than white feminist writers, to "think back through their mothers" in order to define themselves identifiably in their own voices as subjects. Walker and Marshall, as well as Toni Morrison, Gloria Naylor, Ntozake Shange, and Toni Cade Bambara belong to a generation whose writing is obsessed with issues of continuity and separation, connection and disconnection.[49] Their public celebration of maternal presence and influence and their portrayals of strong and powerful mothers, combined with the relative absence of fathers, makes this uniquely feminist tradition a particularly interesting one in which to explore issues of maternal presence and absence, speech and silence.[50] If maternal discourse can emerge in a particular feminist tradition, it may not be surprising that it should be in one that is itself marginal and therefore perhaps more ready to bond with women—mothers and daughters—letting go of male, paternal, fraternal, or filial approval.

The issues of connection and separation which pervade this body of writing have political as well as psychological dimensions. Complicated feelings shape the portraits of mothers, in particular the tremendously powerful need to present to the public a positive image of black womanhood. E. Frances White writes in her "Listening to the Voices of Black Feminism": "How dare we admit the psychological battles that need to be fought with the very women who taught us to survive in this racist and sexist world? We would feel like ungrateful traitors."[51] This pressure explains, perhaps, the disturbing disjunction between the celebration of mothers in the essays of black women writers and the much more ambivalent portrayals in their novels. Although mothers are present, even dominant, in the texts of black women writers, maternal discourse suffers from important and symptomatic limitations and constraints. The daughter-writer often has to define herself in opposition to and not in imitation of the maternal figure. Thus, even while Paule Marshall publicly presents herself as the *griot* (Mary Helen Washington's term), preserving the stories she heard and absorbed in her mother's kitchen as she was growing up, she admits privately in an interview that "my mother never directly encouraged me to write. What I absorbed from her was more a reaction to her negativity . . . she disapproved of all my ambitions."[52] Both Marshall and Walker, in fact, situate themselves among three maternal traditions, the black oral invisible lineage in which their own mothers were artistic storytellers and gardeners, the black written tradition of Phyllis Wheatley, Harriet Jacobs, and Zora Neale Hurston, among others, and the white written tradition of Virginia Woolf's *A Room of One's Own*, which does describe the contradictions of the woman writer, but must be revised to include as well the different story of the black writer. Alice Walker asks: "What did it mean for a black woman to be an artist in our grandmothers' time? In our great-grandmothers' day? It is a question with an answer cruel enough to stop the blood."[53] In this fantasied black feminist family romance, daughters and mothers can speak *to* each other, recognizing the painful experiences of racist and sexist oppression which they share. However, if the fantasy is a shared and loving connection rather than separation, the realities of the texts themselves reveal the fantasy to be mixed with ambivalence, fear, and anger. Between these mothers and daughters, whose lives remain intertwined with each other in plots that never lead to separation, much remains unspeakable and indeed unspoken. A focus on this mother/daughter plot may suggest a particular form of the post-modern, deeply rooted in racial history, feminist consciousness, and political engagement.

These ambivalences and contradictions illuminate Toni Morrison's *Sula*[54] and its complicated interaction of maternal and daughterly voices. The stories that the mothers in this novel tell are indeed "cruel enough to stop the blood." I would like to look closely at what happens when the mothers speak in this novel, at how the mothers' stories inform both the text that is structured around them and the lives of the protagonist daughters.

Set between 1919 and 1965, *Sula* is clearly located in the generation of Morrison's mother and grandmother and not in her own. Thus, the novel's very structure depends upon its ambivalent relation to the past. The text presents the lives of the two protagonists, Sula and Nel, as they move from adolescence to old age. Sula and Nel are presented as members of a new generation of black women, eager to construct new lives and new stories for themselves. Yet their development and their friendship, and the text itself, revolve around their relationships to the powerful maternal figures who come to represent a female past and around their attitude to maternity itself. Although the novel is clearly not written from the perspective of the mothers, its generational structure allows it to serve as an emblem for the relation of an emerging feminism (new generation of women) to the maternal (oral tradition of the past).[55]

The novel begins not with these powerful women, however, but with the story of a young man, Shadrack. In the process of a symbolic birth into a violent and racist culture, Shadrack, an army private at the end of World War I, gains his sense of self by facing his mirror image in a toilet bowl: "There in the toilet water he saw a grave black face. A black so definite, so unequivocal, it astonished him" (p. 13). Shadrack knows he is real because he is black, but, as a result of the war and of his underprivileged social status, he has been dispossessed of everything, including his sense of bodily limits. Through the figure of Shadrack and through the communal rituals he invents to survive his utter inadequacy, the community tries to confront the male impotence that defines it, an impotence that is later represented by Eva's son Plum. Shadrack's birth is motherless, and Plum's death is caused by his mother: mothers have ceased to be able to care for sons in the increasingly feminized, though clearly sexual, culture Morrison constructs. Even Ajax's mother, the "conjure woman," cannot keep her son from abandoning her and Sula.[56] And sons and fathers have ceased to be primary forces in female plots.

The dominant maternal presence in the novel is, of course, the matriarch Eva who rules over the enormous house in which Sula and Nel spend a great deal of their childhood. Ironically, Eva's powerful presence is defined by lack, by her amputated leg which, like Shadrack's blackness, becomes the means of her survival and the mark of her distinction from the other poor and abandoned mothers in Medallion. Eva insists on flaunting her missing leg by wearing calf length skirts which display and call attention to the beauty of her other leg. I would argue that Eva's missing leg is the mark of maternal discourse in the novel and the key to its (thematized) ambivalence toward it.

The absent leg functions as a gap in the center of the text, the unspeakable around which Sula and Nel's stories begin to take shape. Following the account of Eva's abandonment by BoyBoy, of her miserable winter attempting to care for three children with no money at all, and of her night in the freezing outhouse helping baby Plum loosen his bowels, there is an ellipsis in the text, a silence surrounding Eva's 18-months' absence from Medallion. This gap gives rise to numerous tales, some told by Eva herself to amuse the children ("how the leg got up by itself one day and walked off"), others invented by the townspeople in their effort to explain her return without one leg, but with a new black pocketbook full of money. The tales are clearly apocryphal: the mother's (self-)mutilation in the service of her own and her children's survival remains, to the end of the novel, unnarrated, and perhaps unnarratable, but the source of endless narration. Maternal speech is sparse in this novel: mothers and daughters never quite succeed in addressing each other directly, mothers fail to communicate the stories they wish to tell. This pattern of missed communication begins when Nel and her mother Helene undertake an exhausting journey south to attend the funeral of Nel's great-grandmother. Here, in the place of maternal origin, Nel cannot understand the Creole she hears her grandmother speak. Barely exchanging a few words with her mother, Helene later admits that she also does not know Creole. As Nel returns home and remembers the painful moments of the trip—her mother's profound humiliation by the white conductor and by the black men in the train, the disgust on her great-grandmother's dead face, and the coldness between her mother and grandmother, she looks into the mirror and begins a new life: "I'm me. I'm not their daughter. I'm not Nel. I'm me" (p. 24). Helene Wright, the mother, emerges as wrong in many ways, wrong in her adoption of middle-class values, wrong in her manipulative control of her daughter's life and in the foolish smile she flashes at the train conductor who has just insulted her, wrong too because she severed the connection with her own mother and failed to learn her mother tongue. Nel's image of her mother as formless custard barely contained by her heavy velvet dress makes it imperative that she identify herself as separate, different from her maternal heritage, as a very definite "me." Filled with "power joy and fear" at this moment of self-creation, she cannot sustain this self-definition alone, but needs a friend to complete her, a friend who can offer reflection and support but who will be free of the heavy suitcases and the orderly house, of the history which encumbers Helene Wright. This friend is the much less conventional Sula.

Sula's family, although more communicative, succeeds no better in bridging the distance between the lives and the perspectives of the three generations. An important exchange occurs between Sula's mother, Hannah, and Hannah's mother, Eva. Although Hannah is herself a mother, her discourse is circumscribed by her daughterly relation to Eva and by conventional and clearly inapplicable conceptions of motherhood and maternal love. "Mamma, did you ever love us? . . . No." Eva answers, "I don't reckon I did. Not the way you thinkin' " (p. 58). Hannah cannot bear to listen to what Eva has to tell: "I didn't mean that, Mamma. I know you fed us and all. I was talkin' 'bout something else. Like. Like. Playin' with us. . . . I know 'bout them beets, Mamma. You told us that a million times. . . . They had to be some time when you wasn't thinkin' 'bout . . ." (pp. 67–69). In response, Eva comes back with the same old stories about the three remaining beets, about the sores in the children's mouths, about their "shitting worms," stories that fail to fit into the mythology of motherhood to which Hannah wants to subscribe.

The exchange between mother and daughter clearly challenges this mythology, especially when Hannah asks Eva why she set fire to her adult son Plum. Eva's response, an interior monologue followed by the longest speech she makes in the novel, contains hurt and pain, anger and love, but fails adequately to explain her inconceivable act. Eva's relation to Plum is so obscenely intimate, it has to be described in the third person: "The last food staple in the house she had rammed up her baby's behind to keep from hurting him too much when she opened up his bowels to pull the stools out. He had been screaming fit to kill but when she found his hole at last and stuck her finger up in it, the shock was so great he was suddenly quiet" (p. 70). In her own voice Eva continues to articulate what she sees as Plum's inadequacy as an adult male ruined by the war, his passivity, his efforts to "crawl back in my womb . . . I had room enough in my heart," she insists, "but not in my womb, not no more" (p. 71). The mutual penetration of bodies signals, perhaps, the limits of what any relationship can sustain and demonstrates the ambiguous status of the mother, whose body has already been penetrated so that this child might be produced. In trying to explain to Hannah an act which is so obviously beyond comprehension, Eva dwells on an intense need for self-protection, a clear drawing of her own boundaries, a definitive expression of the limits of what she has to give, and she insists as well on Plum's boundaries, which, as a mother, she was forced to violate.

The double voice with which Eva delivers her painful explanation— "When Eva spoke at last it was with two voices. Like two people were talking at the same time, saying the same thing, one a fraction of a second behind the other" (p. 61)—suggests her double identity, as an individual subject and as a mother, signalling perhaps the self-division that by necessity characterizes and distinguishes maternal discourse. The text acts out the double voice, as it combines third with first person narration, free indirect discourse with dialogue. The message too is, of course, double; anger is mixed with love, pain with pride, sadness with tenderness, as Eva adds her afterthought: "But I held him close first. Real close. Sweet Plum. My baby boy" (p. 72). The scene between Eva and Hannah, one of the few moments in the novel when mothers speak as mothers, enacts the difficulty of telling and of hearing her story. Later on, Sula will send the grandmother away to an old age home so as to silence her more completely: "Don't talk to me about how much you gave me, Big Mamma, and how much I owe you or none of that" (p. 92).

In her conversation with her mother, Hannah, like everyone else, refrains from addressing the central question of the missing leg, although the questions she asks, however awkwardly, revolve around this untold tale. Like Hannah's, Sula and Nel's very development is determined by it, because the leg becomes for them a very graphic representation of sexual (and perhaps racial) difference, seen as lack.[57] Interpreters of the novel have seen Eva as a kind of phallic mother who assumes God-like powers of control over naming, creation, and destruction.[58] For example, she calls three different boys by the same name, Dewey, and they quickly become indistinguishable. But the stories Eva tells reveal a mixture of power and powerlessness that calls the very notion of phallic mother into question. The phallic mother can exist only as a child's projection. If Eva chooses to flaunt her castration, to assume the logic of the lack that is essential to the male posture in order thereby to gain a semblance of male power, she can only reveal how much *that* power depends on a masquerade. With this term I refer to Lacan's definition of femininity as masquerade, as constructed in reference to male desire.[59] Eva's strategy demonstrates that the male phallic position is also a sham, resting on conventional constructions that are easily overturned. Thus Morrison challenges phallocentrism, even as she shows Eva's manipulation of and complicity with the phallic order.

Sula adopts Eva's powerful strategy. Her first act in the novel repeats Eva's gesture of self-mutilation in the service of survival and her denial of her powerlessness.[60] Threatened by some boys on the way home from school, Sula takes a knife and slices off part of her finger, frightening the boys with "If I can do that to myself, what you suppose I'll do to you?" (pp. 54–55). This act is Sula's own moment of self-recognition, of her affiliation with Eva and the world of her maternal ancestors. Although Sula possesses her birthmark, a stemmed rose, ambiguously phallic and vaginal—a mark of plenitude which distinguishes her from other women—she is forced to recognize the vulnerability she shares with Eva, a vulnerability her act of self-injury, like Eva's, can only disguise but cannot change. It is this recognition which causes Sula's continued and determined rebellion against a traditional womanhood defined for her by maternity and enslavement to the family.

Like Hannah and Eva, Sula and Hannah also share a pivotal moment of (indirect) confrontation around the subject of maternal love. Sula overhears Hannah and her friends discussing their children: "'Well, Hester grown now and I can't say love is exactly what I feel.' 'Sure you do. You love her, like I love Sula. I just don't like her. That's the difference.' 'Guess so. Likin' them is another thing'" (p. 57). This transgressive maternal speech determines the novel's structural progression: this scene is immediately followed by the drowning of Chicken Little. After overhearing what she takes as her mother's rejection, Sula runs off with Nel and, in a vaguely homoerotic moment of tenderness in the grass as well as in their symbolic acting out of heterosexual play with sticks in the ground, they begin to discover their own sexuality. The appearance at this point of Chicken Little, the little boy in whom both girls take a maternal interest ("Your mama tole you to stop eatin' snot, Chicken"), focuses for Sula the conjunction of maternal rejection with her budding sexuality. I read Chicken's death—he quietly slips into the river and the girls don't try to save him—as a signal of Sula and Nel's rebellious, if as yet unconscious, refusal of adult heterosexuality and motherhood as they perceive it, as a clear refusal of the plot written for them. In the novel's terms, this is one in a series of unspeakable murders, significantly parallel to Eva's murder of Plum. Silence and secrecy surround Chicken's death and Sula and Nel's involvement in it; only Shadrack *knows* and only Eva understands this "maternal" guilt.

Sula and Nel's reaction of looking or watching Chicken disappear in the water instead of attempting to save him is later repeated when Sula watches her mother's accidental death by burning, thrilled and wanting "her to keep on jerking like that, to keep on dancing." This contrasts sharply with Eva's unsuccessful attempt to save her daughter: "Eva knew there was time for nothing in this world other than the time it took to get there and cover her daughter's body with her own" (p. 75). Ironically, of course, it is her original maternal act of self-mutilation, her missing leg, which prevents her from succeeding, but not from participating bodily in Hannah's painful death: she jumps out the window, drags herself across the lawn and finally has to be taken to the hospital together with her dying daughter. Sula's complicity in her mother's death is only suggested in the text—she acted crazy on that day, distracting Eva and Hannah from interpreting the dream that foreshadowed the accident, she did not try to save Hannah, and she clearly failed to hear her mother's dying words: "Help me y'all" (p. 77).

Eva's own complicity, even more disguised, complicates the oppositions Sula constructs between watching and helping, and between self-reliance and care, oppositions which underlie her unconditional refusal of a maternal role. As she emphatically declares, silencing Eva's suggestion that she needs babies, "I don't want to make somebody else. I want to make myself" (p. 92). Here Sula conceives of herself as artist, as inventor of alternate plots and bodies for women. As she does so, however, she reinforces another irreconcilable dichotomy—that of mother and artist—a difference she equates with that between saving someone from dying and of watching her die. What looks at first like two contrasting reactions— Eva's and Sula's—however, emerges, more and more, as equal complicity and ambivalence, the mark of maternal discourse in the novel, a discourse from which Sula tries to but cannot escape.

In the economy of this text, Sula's rejection of maternity means an assumption of male freedom. In several published interviews, Morrison has admitted fascination with Sula's choice, although it represents the ultimate evil for a woman as far as the community is concerned. "I guess I'm not supposed to say that. But the fact that they [men] would split in a minute just delights me. . . . that has always been to me one of the most attractive features about black male life."[61] With characters like Sula and later with Jadine in *Tar Baby*, Morrison invents a female character who will not be maternal but will try to get beyond an ideology which identifies woman with nurturing and caretaking. Yet, Nel's warning is prophetic: "You *can't* do it all. You a woman and a colored woman at that. You can't act like a man" (p. 142). Having children represents for Nel the crucial distinction between the masculine and the feminine position. Women, as Eva succeeds in demonstrating, can *act* like men, but, unlike men, they cannot leave their children and get away with it: that plot does not exist. Yet when Sula contemplates the women who stay with their children, she is confronted with emptiness, desperation, and the end of plot: "Those with men had had the sweetness sucked from their breath by ovens and steam kettles. Their children were like distant but exposed wounds whose aches were no less intimate because separate from their flesh. They had looked at the world and back at their children, back at the world and back again at their children, and Sula knew that one clear young eye was all that kept the knife away from the throat's curve" (p. 122). Until her death, Sula is haunted by the fears of the destruction domesticity brings: witness her dream about the baking powder girl who disintegrates into a pile of dust. Whereas for Sula motherhood constitutes a threat of disintegration, for Nel it comes to mean an immutable, inescapable, desperate fusion: "They [her children] were all she would ever know of love. But it was a love that, like a pan of syrup kept too long on the stove, had cooked out, leaving only its odor and a hard, sweet sludge, impossible to scrape off" (p. 165).

The novel proposes women's friendship as an alternative relation, an alternative story, both to heterosexuality and to maternity, but it does not do so unquestioningly. Might her friendship with Nel have saved Sula from the slow erosion which kills her? Who is to be blamed for endangering and impairing this friendship when Sula sleeps with Nel's husband? Other—truly artistic—possibilities of expression are unavailable to Sula in her world and, suffering from an "idle imagination," she remains "an artist with no art form." Although she can assert at the end of her life that she has indeed created herself ("I got my mind. And what goes on in it. Which is to say, I got me." [p. 143]), her lack of attachments robs her of the food for her imagination and creativity. "*I have sung all the songs there are,*" she repeats. Yet, as she retreats totally into the utter aloneness of her head and slips from life to death, Sula longs to speak to Nel, to tell her about what death feels like. Female plot is embedded in affiliation.

Sula's repudiation of motherhood and attachment does not enable her to have an alternate career as an artist. Whether under different economic and social conditions it could have, the text leaves unanswered. The novel concludes with Nel's epiphanic recognition that it is her friend Sula she has missed all these years and not her husband Jude. Nel returns to the fantasy of a perfect sisterhood and recognizes that the heterosexual love plot in which she was engaged merely masked a deeper story. Thus, the plot of sisterhood and female friendship provides an alternative both to the love plot and to the maternal.[62] Nel's cry contrasts sharply with the literal stories told by Eva or Helene: "It was a fine cry—loud and long—but it had no bottom and no top, just circles and circles of sorrow." In her discussion of this cry, Margaret Homans presents it as an assertion of separatism, of a specifically feminine expression in language: "what finally expresses her woman-identified self is of necessity nonrepresentational."[63] It is perhaps understandable that such a moment should lead back to childhood, to a pre-oedipal, pre-separational female past, as yet uncontaminated by social institutions—the feminist family romance discussed in chapter 4. The fusion of Sula and Nel, affirmed in the last scene by the ancient Eva who refuses to distinguish between them, offers such a privileged if dangerous mode of relation and expression, one that in the economy of this novel could never be shared in by the mother. No such fusion or confusion exists between generations of women in this text; the roles and the voices of mothers and daughters are forcibly separated, even within the characters of Hannah, Helene, and Nel who are both. The novel's short circuit, its ultimate return to its own beginnings, only reinforces the two protagonists' inability to transcend the plots of their mothers, *as well as* their inability to repeat them. For women who reject unconditionally the lives and the stories of their mothers, who attempt to perform what Rich called "radical surgery," there is nowhere to go. The novel both suggests and, in its own unfocused second part, actually acts out this rupture and its resultant lack of direction. Holding on to a pervasive belief in the danger of the maternal, and reiterating that danger not only in the deaths of Chicken Little and of Plum, but also in the death of a large part of the town in the half-built, womb-like tunnel at the end of the novel, the text demonstrates the trap that lies within the attempt to escape from the maternal.[64] It thus gives shape to what I have termed a black feminist family romance which at once creates space for maternal voices *and* suppresses them. ·

Maternal discourse (and plot), *when it can be spoken*, is always repetitive, literal, hopelessly representational. It is rooted in the body which shivers, hurts, bleeds, suffers, burns, rather than in the eyes or in the voice which can utter its cries of pain. It is rooted in Eva's fierce bodily love for Hannah, as well as in her anger, aggression, her violence, but not in the unspoken hostility, eventually overcome, between Nel and Sula. The ancient Eva in the old age home, with her aggressive tone and her direct questions, is still a threat to Nel, whose polite visit cannot accommodate the vehement anger that keeps Eva alive. Maternal discourse, the story Eva never tells as well as the stories she repeats obsessively, remains both absent and present in the novel, a mark of difference which does provide the narrative with its dynamic momentum, but which to do so must remain at the edge of the unspoken. Is the novel suggesting, then, that the maternal plot can provide only the point of departure for the text but not its content, that art is primarily based on the child's drama in relation to the mother? Could it be that maternal discourse can exist in the text only on the condition that it remain fragmentary, incomplete and mediated through the perspective of the daughter-writer? Could it be that the novel to some degree depends on the conjunction between the maternal and the unspeakable, thus repeating older plot patterns?

Adrienne Rich says, "For me, poetry was where I lived as no-one's mother, where I existed as myself,"[65] provoking Helen Vendler to ask: "Is there something about the relation with children, in contrast to relations with adults, which makes it unavailable to the writer?"[66] If this chapter has been attempting to define a feminist family romance which focuses on the figure of the mother—which begins there—it has been frustrated precisely by this disjunction between the shapes of plot and the processes and experiences involved in maternity. The plot of *Sula* takes shape around this disjunction.

Writing (Out) the Mother's Anger: Walker's "Everyday Use" and "One Child of One's Own"

Unusual for its maternal perspective, Alice Walker's "Everyday Use" throws a different light on the configurations of maternal subjectivity and maternal narrative exhibited in *Sula*. Walker's short story is the first-person narration of an older black mother awaiting the return of her daughter, Dee. After moving away from their poor rural home to the city, Dee has become successful by breaking with a familial past she has come to view as oppressive. Also waiting for Dee is a sister—Maggie—in every sense her opposite. Shy, homely, nervous, ashamed, Maggie is the daughter who made no break but remained at home. As the story begins, we get a very definite sense of the articulate strength and rich quality of the narrator-mother's voice, a voice all the more remarkable because its possessor assures us that she does not have a quick tongue, that she is uneducated and virtually illiterate, and that she mistrusts words, books, and knowledge. Whereas some critics have viewed the mother's voice as a narrative incongruity or a conceptual flaw in the story, for me this self-disavowing voice *is* the story. What interests me in particular is the process by which the mother's voice evolves to the point of "everyday use"—to the point of being able to articulate both her love and her anger. Tracing the emergence of this maternal voice can shed some light on the connections between oral and written traditions, between maternal and daughterly voices, and between anger and writing.[67]

The misunderstandings that mark the reunion between mother and daughter in this story revolve around Dee's relation to her familial past, a past she has rejected by leaving and by Africanizing her name, but which she now wants to reclaim as fashionable "heritage." She admires the wooden benches, the traditional butter churn, the old quilts she had refused as backward when she went to college, but now wants to own for purposes of interior decoration. For her, heritage is something to be displayed on the coffee table and on the wall; for her sister Maggie, on the other hand, who had been promised the quilts made by her grandmother and aunt out of pieces of old clothing, the past is a living reality in which she participates both by planning to use the quilts on her bed and by learning how to quilt herself. The rich image of the quilt, a patchwork of fragmentary and material representations of the past's survival into the present, delineates these daughters' relation to their matriarchal heritage.[68] The daughter who has left her maternal heritage can only reconnect with it intellectually and aesthetically, in ignorance of its daily reality. The daughter who has remained home knows the reality of the past, but is scared of present and future. The mother who has been abandoned and betrayed by one daughter ends up fostering and protecting the other, more needy one, who has remained loyal to her.

The mother-narrator reports Dee's appearance and that of the man who is accompanying her in a tolerant voice marked by understated humor and subtle irony. Yet, as the story progresses, the two visitors come to look more and more foreign, less and less in touch with the reality of her world. Still she remains calm, openminded, and curious: " 'Well,' I say, 'Dee.' 'No, Mama,' she says. 'Not "Dee." Wangero Leewanika Keemanjo!' 'What happened to "Dee"?' I wanted to know. 'She's dead.' Wangero said. 'I couldn't bear it any longer, being named after the people who oppress me.' 'You know as well as me you was named after your Aunt Dicie.' . . . 'But who was *she* named after?' asked Wangero? 'I guess after Grandma Dee.' I said. 'And who was she named after?' asked Wangero. 'Her mother, I guess.' I said, and saw Wangero was getting tired" (p. 53). The mother quietly goes along with Wangero, with the long-haired Hakim-a-Barber, with all of Dee's requests. Reporting the visit, she presents herself as passive and totally accepting: she quietly takes all of Dee's abuse. Yet her narrating voice demonstrates a different strength: her ability to take pleasure in her daughter's difference without conceding any of her own choices and values. Through irony she is able to modulate her reactions and communicate to the reader/to herself the distance she insists on maintaining from Dee's reality, without visibly rejecting her. Even as she experiences her daughter's strangeness as uncomfortable, she notices and notes every detail about her and is able to delight in her perception of it. Whereas the mother as character is passive, immobile, almost pathetic, the mother as narrator is funny, active, in control. It is the power of this mother-narrator which underscores the acquiescence and defeat of the mother-character, an acquiescence which reveals her consent to her own erasure through much of the story.

The confrontation between mother and daughter occurs over Maggie's modest resigned concession of the quilts to Dee. " 'She can have them, Mama,' she [Maggie] said, like someone used to never winning anything, of having anything reserved for her. 'I can 'member Grandma Dee without the quilts' " (p. 58). Confronted with the necessity of making a choice, the mother chooses Maggie and rejects Dee, and the way in which she asserts her choice, her sudden freedom to act, her sudden transformation from passive object to agent in the narrative, constitutes the crux of the story. It is Maggie's statement that releases the mother's anger and thereby also her love, propelling this women who only moments before felt too heavy to get up from her chair into a rapid series of actions: "When I looked at her like that something hit me in the top of my head and ran down to the soles of my feet. Just like when I'm in church and the spirit of God touches me and

I get happy and shout. I did something I never had done before: hugged Maggie to me, then dragged her into the room, snatched the quilts out of Miss Wangero's hands and dumped them into Maggie's lap. Maggie just sat there on my bed with her mouth open" (p. 58). What is it that provokes this almost religious illumination, freeing the mother to act, to speak out, and, I would argue, eventually to tell her tale?

As we go back over the story, we see that the almost violent abruptness in this scene—snatching, hugging, dragging, dumping—has been present in the mother's voice, if not in her actions, since the story's beginning. The mother's surface serenity barely succeeds in disguising her profound agitation as she waits. Thus, Dee's arrival is preceded by an imaginary meeting on a T.V. talk show, in which Dee hugs a much slimmer and more verbal mother and pins an orchid to her dress. As she fantasizes this happy reconciliation, the mother immediately adds an alternate, much angrier version in parentheses: "(A pleasant surprise of course: what would they do if parent and child came on the show only to curse out and insult each other?)" (pp. 47–48). As she describes herself, the contrast to the imaginary TV mother comes into focus: she is big-boned, rough, manly, she can kill hogs and knock out bull calves, and she can eat their innards. Unlike the TV mother and unlike Dee, she cannot look a white man in the eye or speak with a witty tongue. She cannot be the mother Dee wants her to be.

Other reminiscences add to the atmosphere of expectation, gradually making it more disturbing. Maggie's pathetic gestures and appearance are, we find out, the result of a fire that burned down their old house, a fire in which she was severely injured. As the mother recalls Dee's behavior during the fire, she becomes more visibly angry: "Why don't you dance around the ashes? I'd wanted to ask her. She had hated that house so much. I used to think she hated Maggie too" (p. 50). A greater and greater distance develops in the course of these thoughts between Dee, on the one hand, and the mother and Maggie, on the other. Dee's education appears aggressive, her attitude almost violent: "She used to read to us without pity; forcing words, lies, other folks' habits, whole lives upon us, sitting trapped and ignorant underneath her voice. She washed us in a river of make-believe, burned us with a lot of knowledge we didn't necessarily need to know" (p. 50). The mother recalls Dee's verbal aggression, her "scalding humor that erupted like bubbles in lye," and recalls also her own anger, always contained: "Often I fought off the temptation to shake her" (p. 50). Her reflections end with the speculation that "when Dee sees it [their new house], she will want to tear it down" (p. 51).

Contrary to her own self-assessment, the mother-narrator has succeeded in establishing, through subtle manipulation of imagery and irony, the quality of the rift between her world and her daughter's and has suggested that under the serene surface of the yard lurk anger and simmering violence. References to slaughtered pigs, burned-down houses, hurtful looks, and violent alien words paint feelings and gestures of mutual aggression, even as the mother calmly sits and waits for her daughter's return.

Dee's appearance is in itself felt as aggressive: the loud colors of her dress hurt the mother's eyes. Her first action is to pull out a camera and to snap pictures of mother, sister, cow, and house. Her thoughtless comments, her distance from their lives, only confirm the initial impression. Dee dominates the conversation and controls the plot of the meeting. The mother, however, remains tolerant and interested. Although she turns a rather vicious humor against Hakim-a-Barber ("the barber" as she calls him to the reader), she maintains the connection with Dee, until she is confronted with the necessity of making a choice between the conflicting needs of her two children. I would argue that when the mother hears Maggie's resigned acquiescence, she sees it as a betrayal of the grandmother and aunt from whom Maggie learned to quilt. As Valerie Smith has suggested in "Writing Revolution," the mother sees in Maggie's angerless fear an image of her passive acceptance of Dee's aggression, her own suppressed anger. And then she claims her authority and expresses her anger openly, asserting her value and the value of her life against the rejection of her daughter. Ironically, of course, her action connects her only more firmly to the angry and assertive Dee.

The transformation Maggie undergoes in the story, from the frightened attempt to hide, to her inarticulate, angry sucking in of the breath, to her short concession speech, and finally, to her *real* smile, this transformation charts her competitive relationship with her sister, as well as her own relation to her past and her mother. For if the mother has been angry with the powerful Dee all along, she has also been enraged at the powerless, pathetic Maggie, calling her a "lame animal," describing her "dopey hang-dog look." As with Dee, however, her helpless anger at Maggie has not prevented her from noticing every detail of her appearance, from guessing and understanding her minutest feelings. And this sympathy enables her to identify with Maggie's acquiescence and to find it unacceptable.

Initially, Maggie's helplessness, combined with Dee's contempt, had paralyzed, incapacitated the mother to the point where she was absolutely unable to speak out. Finally freed—by Dee's excessive demand and by Maggie's passive acquiescence—to acknowledge her anger at both daughters, the one who leaves and the one who clings, the mother can develop into someone who resembles much more closely the narrator who manipulates so brilliantly the ironies of this tale. If the story ends in a scene of separation from Dee, it is one provoked by the mother herself, the mother who remains behind, content with her own life, with its quiet stasis. That separation is eased, of course, by Maggie's presence, by Maggie's unconditional acceptance of the female heritage the mother can hand down to her, and by the visibly empowering effect that the gift of the quilts and her acceptance into the female community of quilters have on her: "Maggie smiled; maybe at the sunglasses. But a real smile, not scared" (p. 59). Dee goes with Hakim-a-Barber to the powerful male world (both white and black) of books and television shows in which she has always felt comfortable. As she puts on her sunglasses, she comes to look at the world through their different perspective. Maggie, even if she marries John Thomas, will remain home, loyal to her mother and to her maternal past.

It is important to note that the triangle in this story is not with father (he's totally absent) or husband, but between two sisters and their mother. The male world is there only by implication—in the claims it makes on the daughters, in the separations it effects from the mother. Although the structure is still triangular, no heterosexual intervention is needed for the inception of plot. Creating a plot between mother, daughters, and sisters, Walker's narrative is totally untouched by the plot of heterosexual romance.

Alice Walker wrote this story at the same time as her influential essay on black women's creativity, "In Search of Our Mothers' Gardens." In the essay Walker connects black women's artistic creativity very firmly to a maternal past; although the creative spirit of the mothers was thwarted by oppression and abuse, much can be learned from their hidden spirituality. Their artistic expression took unconventional forms: storytelling, quiltmaking, gardening, singing. Her own voice as a writer, Walker maintains, derives from her mother whose oral stories she can translate into writing, whose manner of telling them she has absorbed, whose gardening she admires. In the essay, Walker insists on the connection between her maternal heritage and her identity as a writer, but unlike the story, the essay is written entirely in the voice of the daughter who finds her own voice as she revises the story of two mothers—her own and her adopted literary mother, Virginia Woolf.[69]

"Everyday Use" constitutes an interesting, though oblique, comment and fictional illustration of the essay. The mother's remarkable voice, we assume, derives from the generation of Walker's mother—she states in the essay that she often writes about characters who are older. If we assume that Walker imagines a mother, her mother, confronted with two daughters whose relation to their common past is vastly different, we wonder where in the story Alice Walker would situate *herself*. With Dee, the verbal city daughter, or with Maggie, the scared rural daughter?[70] Clearly, Walker and her generation of women writers need to find a position between Maggie's (staying home and not changing) and Dee's (leaving home and rejecting it or turning it into artifact). In writing the mother's anger, is not Walker trying to understand, to empathize with the maternal response to her own distance and closeness, her own rejection and acceptance of her maternal heritage? For Walker, *writing* itself constitutes a form of distance, a distance she modulates and reduces by writing about the past, by using it as a way back to establishing closeness. Thus, she can convert the mother's non-verbal violence—snatching, hugging, dumping—into the uniquely verbal expression that characterizes the story itself. In so doing, Walker has granted *the mother* a voice with which to tell that story, but has also made *herself* vulnerable to becoming the object of that voice and of maternal anger, *to* being rejected in the person of the bad daughter Dee, even while she is nurtured in the persona of the good daughter Maggie. Yet in her dedication, "for your grandmama," we see that Walker addresses her own daughter in the story, placing herself in the position of link between grandmother and granddaughter, in the position of mother and daughter both. This particular doubleness of the narrative voice may be the key to its unusual and seemingly incongruous quality—it is the product of both mother and daughter, of both oral tradition and written tradition, of both internal authenticity and external projection, of both extraliterary strength and literary strength, of both anger and love.

As she writes the story of maternal anger, Walker imagines a mother who is tolerant and generous, even as she is angry; a mother who can feel and express her anger without doing devastating damage; a mother who is able to combine anger with attentive love;[71] but a mother whose power is limited by her circumstances, who knows that one child needs her more than the other. Although Walker's story is the result of the daughter-writer's attempt to imagine the mother's story, *and* the result of the mother-writer's attempt to articulate her experience of motherhood and daughterhood, it is not free from the fearful projections of maternal anger we have seen before.

Anger in this story does ultimately create a rift between mother and daughter: the effects on Dee are suggested only in the distancing gesture of putting on her sunglasses and covering her face. If Dee loses as much in power as Maggie gains by the mother's choice, we can begin to understand why the maternal voice in the story is a creation of the daughter's imagination and of her guilt. We can begin to understand why the mother herself would hesitate to write her own version of this story as long as her child can read it, why the mother continues to conspire to perpetuate her own silence, and why Walker must, at each point, act as a daughter and as a mother both. Walker's story does not and ultimately cannot resolve the differences between the three female voices and the positions it explores—there are, after all, only two old hand-made quilts and, as some women in the family leave home, their capacity to reproduce their traditions by producing more quilts is lost. At a moment of radical social change, and in an economy of scarcity, divisions and the anger they evoke can find no easy resolution.

Walker's later essay, "One Child of One's Own: A Meaningful Digression within the Work(s)," represents a further elaboration of her position in relation to anger and the maternal.[72] The obvious references to Woolf, as well as Walker's allusions to Tillie Olsen's *Silences,* and to George Eliot, Jane Austen, the Brontës, Sylvia Plath, and also to Nella Larsen, Lorraine Hansberry, and Zora Neale Hurston, seem to underscore a commonality between black and white women writers when it comes to the cultural opposition between writing and motherhood. Walker, in this essay, writes in the voice of a young black mother who traces her progress through the white patriarchal and feminist world of the sixties and seventies. She articulates her own maternal voice through a radical break from her own non-writing mother who, as a representative of "women's folly," counsels her to have more than one child. Angrily, Walker's speaker rejects her mother's voice and, in a strong alliance with her own daughter, she boldly sets *herself* up as the mother, exploring, in great detail, the insights that a *maternal* perspective on the world offers her. That perspective is filled with anger: at "women's folly" which has imprisoned previous generations of black women, at the white pediatrician who won't make a housecall, at the white feminist who erases the words of black women and fears their bodies, at the black women who identify with their men and therefore abandon their responsibilities to women across the world. Her ability to write her anger forcefully makes it possible to strengthen the voice she has adopted; it enables her to see that in "the racism and sexism of an advanced capitalist society" which would "deny [her] the untrampled blossoming of [her] existence" her child is "the very least of her obstacles in her chosen work" (p. 371).

In reading and re-reading this essay, I puzzled for a long while over this particular formulation, which seemed to reveal the existence of a great deal of unacknowledged anger at her daughter Rebecca. The suppression of the speaker's anger at her child emerged with greater clarity as I thought over other details of the essay: the speaker's memories of her own harassed mother as she tried to get five children ready for church, her own memories of the unpleasantness of pregnancy and the excruciating pain of childbirth, her discomfort with the changes in her body caused by pregnancy and birth, her fear that having a child had changed her irrevocably, that it would prevent her from writing, and, most powerful, her actual experience of the child as "a giant stopper in [my] throat" (pp. 381–382). I concluded that not only was Walker's speaker unable to write as a mother without separating in anger from her own mother and her "women's folly," that is, without making the break that Freud's classic psychoanalytic plot demands of daughters, but also that she adhered to a pervasive cultural taboo: her own anger could never be openly and directly aimed *at* her child. Its very existence must be repressed.

A question by Mary Helen Washington prompted me to attempt to rethink this conclusion to my reading of Walker's texts. When I read this analysis as a paper in the fall of 1986 at the Boston Area Colloquium on Feminist Theory at Northeastern University, Washington asked why I focused my analysis on only one aspect of Walker's essay, her anger at her mother and her possible anger at her daughter, thereby ignoring "what the essay was really about," her anger at white feminists. Was I in fact ignoring "what the essay was really about" or was there another question I should have asked: why the particular conjunction of these two themes in this essay? Why frame an essay about black women's anger at white feminists with suggestions for the optimal reproductive choices open to women writers? And why interrupt her discussion of ways to resolve the opposition of writing and motherhood with an analysis of the absence of black voices and bodies from the important monuments of the (white) feminist movement?

Re-reading Walker's essay with these questions in mind reveals meaningful repressions in the psychoanalytic feminist methodology and the privatized familial ideology this chapter discusses. Specifically, psychoanalysis glosses over the political dimensions of the anger expressed in Walker's essay and of motherhood itself. Is it significant, for example, that the speaker conceived a child so that her husband might be able to avoid being drafted before he turned 26, so that they might not have to move to Canada? Is it important that her pregnancy was dominated by feelings of rage against the Vietnam war, by feelings of anxiety, depression, and violence? Is it important that her writing constituted the only possible protection against her violent anger? "When I didn't write I thought of making bombs and throwing them. Of shooting racists. Of doing away—as painlessly and neatly as possible . . . —with myself. Writing saved me from the inconvenience of violence" (p. 369). The essay documents how Walker's speaker moves from the depression that comes with the suppression of anger to the forceful expression that makes anger into an effective political force. And that move, that transformation is intimately connected to her motherhood.

In an essay entitled "The Politics of Anger: On Silence, Ressentiment and Political Speech," Peter Lyman asserts that "anger becomes a political resource only when it is collective."[73] In isolation, anger is privatized and neutralized, unrecognizable. This is the problem with an exclusively psychological approach to anger, Lyman suggests, and he envisions a psychology more attuned to the historical reality of our century: "A psychology of suffering would have to understand guilt, anxiety, depression, or hysteria as suppressed social relations. Psychology without this sense of social relations 'mythologizes' human suffering, treating it as essentially individual and as a problem of 'personality.' Psychology serves the interests of the hegemony when it strips human experience of its collective and active character, and conceals oppression by blaming the victim for their symptoms" (pp. 58–59).

Throughout her essay, Walker's speaker explores the possibilities of turning her anger into a political force by finding the collective that would recognize its legitimacy. This search constitutes a complex and tortuous process of subject-formation. And throughout this process, throughout what she refers to as her pilgrimage, the speaker finds it necessary to separate in anger from the groups she encounters and with whom she tries to bond. She finds she has to reject her maternal ancestry, the representatives of women's folly, even while she feels the pain of that rejection. She rejects the feminists who are incapable of seeing her as both a black and a woman, and she rejects the black women and men who are incapable of seeing her as both black and female. How, in the face of her ensuing isolation, does Walker's speaker manage to avoid the internalization of her anger and its resultant depression?

Possibly what allows her to speak her anger instead is her unquestioned alliance with her child. Walker's is a journey of forever changing allegiances, charting a heterogeneous, shifting, and often self-contradictory identity.[74] In conceiving of identity in this manner, we move beyond a Freudian model of a family romance in which the developing individual shifts her cathexes from mother, to father, to husband, and then to her own child; we also move away from revisionary family romances which reverse or modify this progression without ultimately challenging it. If we confront, beyond the family, the claims of racial, class, linguistic, ethnic, gender, and cultural affiliations and assimilations, and the clash between culturally hegemonic and subordinate groups, and if we grant, to members of each of these groups, the right to subjectivity and the access to the symbolic, we need to develop a more complicated model of identity and self-consciousness. Such a model would have to reflect a more tortuous process of adopting, and continually refining and redefining a sense of selfhood. That sense of selfhood would have to balance the personal with the political, the subjective experience with the cognitive process of identification with various group-identities. It would have to include a consciousness of oppression and political struggle. It would have to be *both* familial and extra-familial. As such, it would be post-modern in a political rather than merely an aesthetic or epistemological sense.

If Walker is tracing in this essay the process of identity as a strategy of shifting affiliations, she may be suggesting that in the course of such a process one bond, at least, would need to remain unproblematic and thereby consistently empowering. "I began to see," Walker's voice suggests," . . . that her birth and the difficulties it provided us, joined me to a body of experience and a depth of commitment to my own life hard to comprehend otherwise" (p. 369). It is perhaps this sense of commitment and self-regard that makes it possible for the speaker to develop the sense of righteousness, self-protection, and self-assertion that is the precondition of a forcefully political anger. And the alliance with Rebecca may well give her both a personal sense of affirmation and a collective sense of identity. "It is not my child who has purged my face from history and herstory and left mystory just that, a mystery; my child loves my face and would have it on every page, if she could, as I have loved my own parents' faces above all the others, and have refused to let them be denied, or myself to let them go" (p. 382).

The speaker's refusal or inability to acknowledge her anger at her child may well corroborate a pervasive cultural taboo to which all women, whether white or black, are subject, as I suggested above. Yet, clearly, more is at stake here. Taking Marilyn Frye's suggestion and viewing Walker's anger as an "instrument of cartography" which could help us to chart who, in this essay, she represents herself as being, we can begin to appreciate difference—the specificity of her situation as a black woman writer, writing at a particular moment of feminist consciousness. We can see her anger, her various forms of anger, as strategies of self-assertion. And the self she asserts may be multiple in its adherences and divided in its alliances, but, Walker seems to suggest, it cannot be isolated: "We are together, my child and I. Mother and child, yes, but *sisters* really, against whatever denies us what we are" (p. 382). Such a formulation suggests, as well, that this model of identity as process and strategy is not, for Walker, an antihumanist, post-Lacanian one of an alienated subject divided in language and against itself. Neither is it defined by plenitude or transcendence, however. Walker asserts the need for affiliation, affirmation, and connection, as well as a sense of duality or multiplicity, as basic to the process of identity.

After finding in Walker's essay a model of identity and a form of anger that moves beyond a privatized psychology to political significance, I find I cannot close my reading here, but have to place it, once again, under analytic scrutiny. In particular, I am still bothered by what I have referred to here as the speaker's unquestioned, unproblematic bond with her child and by the place of the child in the essay. "One Child of One's Own"—the possessive in the title is in itself disturbing. And so is, finally, the erasure of the child, as person, as subject, from the entire body of the essay. Rebecca is not a barrier to writing; on the contrary, she is presented as an asset, as the child who "by the age of seven, at the latest, is one's friend, and can be told of the fears one has, that she can, by listening to one . . . help allay" (p. 382). When the daughter becomes "the sister" in political struggle, I worry that she disappears as daughter, as child, as person. As she loves her mother's face and would have it on every page, I worry that her own face disappears from the pages of the essay. Could this perhaps be the form that the speaker's unacknowledged anger at Rebecca takes—the form of erasure? Does anger in getting diverted from the personal and psychological to the political erase love and recognition of the individual child?

In answer to these questions, I might suggest that Walker's speaker makes, in the essay, not a definitive but a provisional bond with her child, a bond motivated at the time by pragmatism and need—by the child's dependence on her and, conversely, by her need for one bond that will allow her to call the other allegiances in her life into question. In another context, other bonds may remain unquestioned and this one may emerge as problematic. Of all the relationships in her life, it makes eminent sense at *that* moment to choose *this* one as the one that provides the background for all the others. Yet in suppressing her anger at her child, in leaving it in the realm of the unnarratable, Walker runs the risk of idealizing motherhood, of idealizing her child, and thereby of erasing her. She runs the risk of simply reversing an all too familiar relationship, that is, of turning the child into an adoring nurturing "maternal" figure, the object who enables the growth of *her* subjectivity. Most important, perhaps, through this gap in her text, she runs the risk of going backwards, from the political back to the personal and psychological. A feminist family romance that begins with mothers, that grants voice to mothers as well as to daughters, is embedded in these risks and contradictions. As a transforming structure it is in continual need of being formed and transformed.

Teresa de Lauretis has suggested that, in feminist analysis, the personal and the political must be allowed to coexist, in tension, without being combined (*Feminist Studies/Critical Studies*, p. 9). Walker's painful, fractured, and self-contradictory essay provides an opportunity to understand how difficult and tenuous that coexistence is and perhaps has to be. Reading Walker, we can begin to define the contours of maternal anger and maternal subjectivity in such a way as to demystify its power without weakening its force. Doing so, we can begin to claim a place for mothers and for maternal plots. In that place we can begin to imagine the conjunction of anger and love, to describe more than one dimension of maternal subjectivity, and to imagine plots that transcend familial models. We can explore the historical, economic, and political circumstances that have profound effects on familial interactions, contextualizing the relationship of love and anger, anger and aggression, subjectivity and anger, and sorting out issues of desire, competition, and identification. And, we can begin to map the topography of a subjectivity based not on autonomy but on a fundamental connectedness.[75]

Maternal Feminisms

These texts from the tradition of black American women writers thematize some of the ambivalences about maternal discourse more broadly present in other feminist traditions and chart some ways of nevertheless articulating maternal subjectivity. As *Sula* and Walker's texts suggest, an acknowledgment of the specificity of maternal experience could offer a perspective crucial to feminist discourse. Until feminists can find ways to speak as mothers, feminism as a social and intellectual movement will be unable to account for important experiential differences among women.

Inasmuch as a mother is simultaneously a daughter and a mother, a woman and a mother, in the house and in the world, powerful and powerless, nurturing and nurtured, dependent and depended upon, maternal discourse is necessarily plural. And, as these works demonstrate, maternal discourse is intimately tied to and tied up in social and political reality, as well as to biological and psychological structures. Maternal knowledge, moreover, can enlarge a feminist analysis and reverse traditional conceptions of love and anger, of power and knowledge, of self in relation to other, of femininity and maturity, of sexuality and nurturance. Mothers who must work to raise children to be acceptable members of their society can reveal a great deal about the functioning of ideology and the processes of assimilation and interpellation.

In studying the relationships of mothers, daughters, and narrative plots, this book has only been able to initiate a study of the representation of maternal subjectivity. Further consistent exploration of maternal discourse—whether in theoretical, fictional, or autobiographical writing—would reveal, I believe, notions of identity and subjectivity that correspond neither to the unified ego of ego-psychology, nor to the fluid boundaries of object-relations theory, nor to a subjectivity split against itself as outlined by Lacanian psychoanalysis. What model or definition of subjectivity might be derived from a theory that begins with mothers rather than with children? Can we conceive of development as other than a process of separation from a neutral, either nurturing or hostile, but ultimately self-effacing "holding" background? I would suggest that if we start our study of the subject with *mothers* rather than with *children* a different conception of subjectivity might emerge. Although it might be difficult to define, we might try to envision a culturally variable, mutually affirming form of interconnection between one body and another, one person and another, existing as social, legal, and psychological subjects. Similarly, we might ask whether it is possible to conceive of a narrative that does not depend on maternal "othering," on triangulations, on separation and death. We might ask what shapes such plotting might take.

In calling for a more focused study of maternal subjectivity, I am not suggesting that the maternal story is *the* female story or that it offers a privileged access to femininity. But I am arguing that it is one, in itself multiple, story among others, and that excluding it causes particular blindnesses. The implications of such a conceptualization of a maternal subject which is more than an object in relation to the child's process of subject-formation are enormous. Rather than daughters having to "speak for" mothers, mothers would be able to speak for themselves, perhaps "with two voices." Only thus can mothers and daughters speak to one another. Only thus could the plots of mothers and daughters become speakable.

Morrison's *Beloved*, with which I began this book, explores just such a maternal voice. Sethe's story—her life under slavery, the conception and care of her children in the most dire conditions, her escape and liberation, and her desperately violent and loving act of infanticide—provides, in a sense, the background for the unspoken anger of Eva and of Walker's maternal characters. When Sethe tries to explain to Beloved why she cut her throat, she is explaining an anger handed down through generations of mothers who could have no control over their children's lives, no voice in their upbringing. *Beloved* suggests why that anger may have to remain unspeakable, and how it might nevertheless be spoken. In fact, the mother-daughter conversations that do occur in *Beloved* are conversations from beyond the grave; if Sethe is to explain herself, she has to do so to a ghost. When Sethe tentatively says, at the end of the novel, "Me? Me?", she begins for the first time to speak *for herself*. However, she can do so only in the context of another human bond; she can do so only because Paul D. is holding her hand. Is this a reversion to oedipal mediations and triangulations, a return to the always already read? Or is it an affirmation of a subjectivity which, even when it is maternal, can only emerge in and through human interconnection? Could this be the construction of a new plot which nevertheless emerges out of a reconstruction of old structures? With Paul D. males return to the plots of mothers and daughters, this time, however, to participate in a reconstructed family which is part of a greater community and culture, part of a renewal in which both mother and daughter, both Sethe and Denver, will be able to engage mutually. Yet the double death of Beloved points to the cost of familial reconstruction and of maternal subjectivity in patriarchy. With this painful and fractured novel, Toni Morrison has done more than to shift the direction of her own work and of feminist theorizing: she has opened the space for maternal narrative in feminist fiction.

For me, writing this book in the voice of the daughter of my mother and my father, the mother of my sons, the companion of my husband, the feminist theorist, and the reader of novels by women, the "daughter" and "mother" in the academy, the "sister" of my feminist colleagues, and the "mother" of my students and younger colleagues, for me many questions remain unanswered, perhaps unanswerable. How can I combine the voices that are writing this book, or how can I continue to live out the contradictions that shape it—contradictions between writing and mother-hood, between the concrete, literal, material work of the mother combined with the practical fights for child care policies, parental leaves, reproductive freedom, reform of custody laws, and the theoretical discourses feminists are trying to forge?

I believe that feminists are in the process of inventing new theories and new fictions that might be maternal without falling into essentialism, that might act out the mother's contradictory double position. Such fictions, such theories, will have to be grounded in the material and repetitive work of mothers in culture even as they account for the structures of language and representation. They will have to build the most sophisticated models of individual and group relations to language and will have to affirm a necessary polyvocality, even as they recognize the political power women can derive from speaking, and from speaking with one voice. They will have to account for women's and for mothers' collusion with patriarchy even as they imagine ways of overcoming that collusion. Such fictions, such theories, will have to be supple enough to respect and reflect the vast differences among mothers who mother in vastly different social and cultural conditions. Such theories will have to relinquish their exclusive dependence on psychoanalytic models and will have to integrate psychoanalysis with other perspectives—historical, social, economic. They will have to refuse the split between theory and practice and will have to integrate the perspectives of those who fight for better policies with those who invent better theories; they will have to respond to the practical needs of women's, men's, and children's lives. They will have to include aggression, ambivalence, contradiction, even as they wish for connection, support, and affiliation. They will have to include the body even as they avoid essentialism. They will have to imagine ways that, in spite of repeated conflicts and disappointments, women and men can parent together, and ways for women and men to parent alone. And they will have to oppose, as rigorously as possible, mystifications of maternity and femininity, by creating ways to theorize adult, maternal as well as paternal, experience and by transcending the limited perspective of the developing child.

The greatest tragedy that can occur between mother and daughter is when they cease being able to speak and to listen to one another. But what if they inhabit the same body, what if they are the same person, speaking with two voices?

NOTES

Introduction

1. See Susan Gubar's discussion of the poem in "Mother, Maiden and the Marriage of Death: Women Writers and an Ancient Myth," *Women's Studies: An Interdisciplinary Journal* 6(1979): 301–315. See also Rachel Blau DuPlessis, *Writing beyond the Ending: Narrative Strategies of Twentieth-Century Women Writers* (Bloomington: Indiana University Press, 1985), p. 130.

2. Teresa de Lauretis, *Alice Doesn't: Feminism, Semiotics, Cinema* (Bloomington: Indiana University Press, 1984), p. 109.

3. Hélène Cixous, *Le Nom d'Oedipe: Chant du corps interdit* (Paris: des femmes, 1978). Music by André Boucourechliev.

4. In Muriel Rukeyser, *The Green Wave* (New York: Doubleday, 1948). I am grateful to Kate Daniels for bringing this poem to my attention.

5. Sophocles, *Oedipus Rex*, trans. E. F. Watling (New York: Penguin Books, 1947).

6. See Hans Licht, *Sexual Life in Ancient Greece* (London: Routledge and Kegan Paul, 1932).

7. "Jocasta's Crimes," *International Journal of Psychoanalysis* 42(1961): 424–430. See also George Devereux, "Why Oedipus Killed Laius," *International Journal of Psychoanalysis* 34(1951): 132–141; Sandor Goodhart, "Oedipus and Laius's Many Murderers," *Diacritics* 8 (Spring 1978): 55–71; Jean-Pierre Vernant, "Ambiguity and Reversal: On the Enigmatic Structure of *Oedipus Rex*," *New Literary History* 9(1978): 475–501; Cynthia Chase, "Oedipal Textuality: Reading Freud's Reading of Oedipus," in *Decomposing Figures* (Baltimore: Johns Hopkins University Press, 1986); Iza Erlich, "What Happened to Jocasta?" *Bulletin of the Menninger Clinic* 41(May 1977): 280–284; Jim Swan, "Mater and Nannie: Freud's Two Mothers and the Discovery of the Oedipus Complex," *American Imago* 31(1974): 1–64; and Coppélia Kahn, "The Hand that Rocks the Cradle: Recent Gender Theories and their Implications," in Shirley Nelson Garner, Claire Kahane, and Madelon Sprengnether, eds., *The (M)Other Tongue: Essays in Feminist Psychoanalytic Interpretation* (Ithaca: Cornell University Press, 1985).

8. See Iza Erlich, "What Happened to Jocasta?": "Whatever the reason, the 'oedipal mother' in Freud's early works is a static figure, a Jocasta who unknowingly plays out her destiny while Laius springs back to life" (p. 284).

9. See "Hymn to Demeter," *The Homeric Hymns*, trans. and ed. Apostolos N. Athanassakis (Baltimore: Johns Hopkins University Press, 1976). To read the works of Afro-American writers within the contexts of a tradition shaped by the texts of Greek mythology is indeed to make very large claims for the influence of this tradition. I discuss this methodological problem in this book's Prelude. Yet, I am convinced that in *Beloved* Morrison uses Oedipus and Demeter as intertexts which serve to confront a Western notion of family with the realities of a slave economy which served both to support and to distort that notion. Other intertexts come to mind, as well—the separation of Iphigenia and Clytemnestra, or the closeness of Ruth and Naomi which parallels the connection between Sethe and her mother-in-law, Baby Suggs.

10. See C. G. Jung and C. Kerényi, *Essays on a Science of Mythology: The Myths of the Divine Child and the Divine Maiden* (New York: Harper Torchbooks, 1963); C. Kerényi, *Eleusis: Archetypal Image of Mother and Daughter* (New York: Schocken, 1977); and Marylin Arthur, "Politics and Pomegranates: An Interpretation of the Homeric Hymn to Demeter," *Arethusa* 10(1977): 7–47. Helene Foley has been an invaluable resource in relation to all my discussions of classical texts.

11. Toni Morrison, *Beloved* (New York: Alfred A. Knopf, 1987).

12. Carol Gilligan argues that women tend to construct moral dilemmas more contextually than men do. See Carol Gilligan, *In a Different Voice: Psychological Theory and Women's Development* (Cambridge: Harvard University Press, 1982).

13. The term is Patricia Yaeger's in *Honey-Mad Women: Emancipatory Strategies in Women's Fiction* (New York: Columbia University Press, 1987).

14. The strategies Miller labels as feminist are: the self-consciousness about women's identity both as cultural fiction and as a process of social construction; the claim for the heroine's singularity; the contestation of available plots of female development and their revision; and the figuration of the existence of other subjective economies. See Nancy K. Miller, *Subject to Change: Reading Feminist Writing* (New York: Columbia University Press, 1988), p. 8. Elaine Showalter uses the terms *female*, *feminine*, and *feminist* to mark a historical progression. See Elaine Showalter, *A Literature of Their Own: British Women Novelists from Brontë to Lessing* (Princeton: Princeton University Press, 1977). See also DuPlessis, *Writing beyond the Ending* for a definition closer to Miller's: "These writers are 'feminist' because they construct a variety of oppositional strategies to the depiction of gender institution in narrative" (p. 34).

15. Following the constraints of the English language, I use the term *female* throughout this book and I connect it to cultural construction and not just to biology; I reserve the term *feminine* for more conventional notions of *femininity*, however.

16. This is what Sandra Gilbert and Susan Gubar have called the "complex female affiliation complex." See " 'Forward into the Past': The Female Affiliation Complex," in Sandra M. Gilbert and Susan Gubar, *No Man's Land: The Place of the Woman Writer in the Twentieth Century* (New Haven: Yale University Press, 1988).

17. Louis Althusser, *For Marx*, trans. Ben Brewster (London: New Left Books, 1977), p. 233. See also "Ideology and Ideological State Apparatuses (Notes toward an Investigation)" in Louis Althusser, *Lenin and Philosophy and Other Essays*, trans. Ben Brewster (London: New Left Books, 1971) and Catherine Belsey, "Constructing the Subject: Deconstructing the Text," in Judith Newton and Deborah Rosenfelt, eds., *Feminist Criticism and Social Change* (New York: Methuen, 1985).

18. For an analysis of this dominant plot, see Joseph Allen Boone, *Tradition Counter Tradition: Love and the Form of Fiction* (Chicago: University of Chicago Press, 1987).

19. See "Family Romances" ("Der Familienroman der Neurotiker"), (1908) in *The Standard Edition of the Complete Works of Sigmund Freud*, ed. and trans. James Strachey, vol. 9 (London: Hogarth Press, 1953), pp. 237–241. I discuss this essay in detail in chapter 1.

20. Julia Kristeva, *Powers of Horror: An Essay on Abjection*, trans. Léon Roudiez (New York: Columbia University Press, 1982), p. 165.

21. For a different feminist reading of the novel as family romance, see Christine van Boheemen, *The Novel as Family Romance: Language, Gender and Authority from Fielding to Joyce* (Ithaca: Cornell University Press, 1987). Van Boheemen argues against the possibility of female or feminist transformations of family romance patterns, asserting that "the novel is the instrument of patriarchy, giving presence to its predominance in the act of utterance" (p. 33).

22. Gilles Deleuze and Félix Guattari, *Anti-Oedipus: Capitalism and Schizophrenia*, trans. Robert Hurley, Mark Seem, and Helen R. Lane (Minneapolis: University of Minnesota Press, 1983) identify and criticize the "imperialism of Oedipus," arguing that the familial triangle has reached the status of the dominant signifying structure in Western thinking. Their far-reaching critique of familial ideologies is not, however, based on a gender analysis.

23. Althusser says that "the individual is *interpellated as a (free) subject in order that he shall . . . (freely) accept his subjection*," in *Lenin and Philosophy*, p. 169 (italics in original).

24. For a concise introduction to that debate see the discussion between Nancy K. Miller and Peggy Kamuf in *Diacritics* 12(Summer 1982): 42–53.

25. See Phyllis Chesler, *Sacred Bond* (New York: Times Books, 1988).

26. Ann Dally, *Inventing Motherhood: The Consequences of an Ideal* (New York: Schocken, 1983), p. 17. See also Elisabeth Badinter, *Mother Love: Myth and Reality* (New York: Macmillan, 1981); Barbara Ehrenreich and Deirdre English, *For Her Own Good: 150 Years of the Experts' Advice to Women* (Garden City, N.Y.: Anchor, 1978); Phillippe Ariès, *Centuries of Childhood* (London: Cape, 1962); Mary O'Brien, *The Politics of Reproduction* (London: Routledge and Kegan Paul, 1981); and Heather Jon Maroney, "Embracing Motherhood: New Feminist Theory," in *The Politics of Diversity*, ed. Roberta Hamilton and Michèle Barrett (London: Verso, 1986).

27. In Cherríe Moraga and Gloria Anzaldúa, eds., *This Bridge Called My Back: Writings by Radical Women of Color* (New York: Kitchen Table Press, 1981 and 1983), pp. 14–15.

28. See Adrienne Rich, "Notes Toward a Politics of Location," in *Blood, Bread and Poetry* (New York: Norton, 1986) and Nancy K. Miller, "Introduction: Writing Feminist Criticism," in *Subject to Change*. See also Biddy Martin and Chandra Talpede Mohanty, "Feminist Politics: What's Home Got to Do with It?" in *Feminist Studies/Critical Studies*, ed. Teresa de Lauretis (Bloomington: Indiana University Press, 1986) and Chandra Talpede Mohanty, "Feminist Encounters: Locating the Politics of Experience," *Copyright* 1, 1(1988): 30–44.

29. This may seem paradoxical, but I was fortunate to have a three-months maternity leave from teaching, and like many women I know, I experienced this first pregnancy as a time of self-nurturing.

30. This collaborative effort resulted in the following two articles: "A Conversation with Christiane Rochefort," *L'Esprit Createur* 19, 2 (1979): 107–120 and "Godard and Rochefort: Two or Three Things about Prostitution," *French Review* 41, 3(1979), 440–448.

31. Adrienne Rich, *Of Woman Born* (New York: Norton, 1976), pp. 225–226.

32. Dorothy Dinnerstein, *The Mermaid and the Minotaur* (New York: Harper Colophon Books, 1977).

33. See the critique of Dinnerstein, among others, by Nancy Chodorow and Susan Contratto, "The Fantasy of the Perfect Mother," in Barrie Thorne and Marilyn Yalom, eds., *Rethinking the Family* (New York: Longman, 1982).

34. Juliet Mitchell, *Psychoanalysis and Feminism* (New York: Vintage, 1975), p. xiv.

35. Nancy Chodorow, *The Reproduction of Mothering* (Berkeley: University of California Press, 1978) and Hester Eisenstein and Alice Jardine, eds., *The Future of Difference* (Boston: G.K. Hall & Co., 1980).

36. Elizabeth Abel, Marianne Hirsch, and Elizabeth Langland, eds., *The Voyage In* (Hanover, N.H.: University Press of New England, 1982).

37. Marianne Hirsch, "Mothers and Daughters: A Review Essay," *Signs: Journal of Women in Culture and Society* 7, 1(Autumn 1981): 200–222.

38. Quoted from my original prospectus for this book. Colleagues in literature

working along similar lines at the time were Elizabeth Abel, Judith Kegan Gardiner, Joan Lidoff, Sharon O'Brien, and Jane Lilienfeld, among others.

39. See Juliet Mitchell and Jacqueline Rose, eds., *Feminine Sexuality: Jacques Lacan and the 'école freudienne,'* trans. Jacqueline Rose (New York: Norton, 1982), pp. 48–50.

40. Cathy N. Davidson and E. M. Broner, eds., *The Lost Tradition: Mothers and Daughters in Literature* (New York: Frederick Ungar, 1980).

41. Judith Lorber et al., "On *The Reproduction of Mothering:* A Methodological Debate," *Signs* 6, 3 (Spring 1981): 501.

42. Ruddick's essay appeared in *Feminist Studies* 6, 2 (Summer 1980): 342–367 and Rich's in *Signs* 5, 4 (Summer 1980): 631–660, and has since been revised and republished in Rich's *Blood, Bread and Poetry* (New York: Norton, 1986).

43. My collaborators were Colette Gaudin, Mary Jean Green, Lynn Higgins, Vivian Kogan, Claudia Reeder, and Nancy J. Vickers.

44. For a somewhat different emphasis, see Nancy K. Miller's influential "Emphasis Added: Plots and Plausibilities in Women's Fiction," *PMLA* 96 (1981) rpt. in Elaine Showalter, ed., *The New Feminist Criticism: Essays on Women, Literature, Theory* (New York: Pantheon, 1985). For more recent feminist rereadings of Lafayette's novel, see Peggy Kamuf, "A Mother's Will" in *Fictions of Feminine Desire* (Lincoln: University of Nebraska Press, 1982); Joan de Jean, "Lafayette's Ellipses: The Privilege of Anonymity," *PMLA* 99(October 1984): 884–902; Dalia Judovitz, "The Aesthetics of Implausibility: *La Princesse de Clèves,*" *Modern Language Notes* 99(1984): 1037–1056; Elizabeth Richardson Viti, "The Princesse de Clèves: The 'Euphoric' Dysphoric Heroine," *Wascana Review* (1986): 3–16; and Naomi Schor, "The Portrait of a Gentleman: Representing Men in (French) Women's Writing," *Representations* 20(Fall 1987): 113–133.

45. Jane Gallop, "The Monster in the Mirror: The Feminist Critic's Psychoanalysis," in *Feminism and Psychoanalysis,* ed. Richard Feldstein and Judith Roof (Ithaca: Cornell University Press, forthcoming).

46. Some of the regular members of the group were Teresa Bernardez, Gail Reimer, Valerie Smith, Ann Bookman, Judith Lewis Herrmann, Susan Strasser, Irene Sosa Vasquez, Jaimie Gordon, Kate Daniels, Helena Lewis, Patricia Frazier Lamb, Margaret Carroll, Elaine Spatz-Rabinowitz, Pamela Coxson, Mary Roth Walsh, Barbara Hooley. I am grateful to Gail Reimer and Valerie Smith for helping me to formulate some of the aspects of this retrospective analysis.

47. Readings which proved especially helpful on the issue of race and gender were: Gloria Anzaldúa and Cherríe Moraga, eds., *This Bridge Called My Back: Writings by Radical Women of Color;* Ginny Apuzzo and Betty Powell, "Confrontations: Black White," *Quest: A Feminist Quarterly* 3, 4(Spring 1977): 34–45; Bonnie Thornton Dill, "Race, Class, and Gender: Prospects for an All-Inclusive Sisterhood," *Feminist Studies* 9, 1(Spring 1983): 131–150; Bernice Fisher, "Guilt and Shame in the Women's Movement: The Radical Ideal of Action and Its Meaning for Feminist Intellectuals," *Feminist Studies,* 10, 7 (Summer 1984): 185–209; Bev Fisher, "Race and Class: Beyond Personal Politics," *Quest: A Feminist Quarterly* 3, 4(Spring 1977): 2–14; Marilyn Frye, "Who Wants a Piece of the Pie?" *Quest: A Feminist Quarterly* 3, 3(Winter 1976–77): 28–35; Bell Hooks, *Feminist Theory: From Margin to Center* (Boston: South End Press, 1984); Audre Lorde, *Sister Outsider: Essays and Speeches* (Trumansburg, N. Y.: The Crossing Press, 1984); Maria Lugones and Elizabeth V. Spelman, "Have We Got a Theory for You! Feminist Theory, Cultural Imperialism and the Demand for 'The Woman's Voice,' " *Women's Studies International Forum* 6, 6(1983): 573–581; Roslyn Terborg-Penn, "Discrimination against Afro-American Women in the Women's Movement," in *The Afro-American Woman: Struggles and Images* ed. Sharon Harley and Roslyn Terborg-Penn (Port Washington, N.Y.: Kennikat Press, 1978); Elizabeth V. Spelman,

"Theories of Race and Gender: The Erasure of Black Women," *Quest: A Feminist Quarterly* 5, 4(1982); E. Frances White, "Listening to the Voices of Black Feminism," *Radical America* 18 (1984): 2–3; and Bell Hooks, *Ain't I a Woman* (Boston: South End Press, 1982).

48. Joan Scott "Critical Tensions," review of *Feminist Studies/Critical Studies* in *The Women's Review of Books* 5, 1(October 1987): 18.

49. See Denise Riley, "Does Sex Have a History: 'Women' and Feminism," *New Formations* 1(1987): 35–45 and Chandra Talpede Mohanty, "Under Western Eyes: Feminist Scholarship and Colonial Discourses," *boundary 2/xii, 3/xiii*(Spring/Fall 1984): 333–358.

50. Its members were Gail Reimer, Evelyn Fox Keller, Amy Lang, Teresa Bernardez, Susan Rubin Suleiman, Ruth Perry, Carol Gilligan, Mieke Bal, and myself.

51. See Catherine McKinnon, "Feminism, Marxism, Method and the State: An Agenda for Theory," *Signs* 7, 3(Spring 1982), 515–544, and Teresa de Lauretis, *Alice Doesn't* (chap. 6) on consciousness raising as the "critical method" for a feminist analysis of social reality.

Prelude

1. Luce Irigaray, *Le corps-à-corps avec la mère* (Montréal: les éditions de la pleine lune, 1981) p. 15, my translation. Reprinted in a revised edition in *Sexes et parentés* (Paris: Minuit, 1988). All subsequent references are to the earlier edition.

2. For an illuminating analysis of the varieties of family structures in a black working-class community, see Carol B. Stack, *All Our Kin: Strategies for Survival in a Black Community* (New York: Harper and Row, 1974).

3. *The Eumenides,* ll. 657–659 in Aeschylus, *The Oresteian Trilogy*, trans. Philip Vellacott (London: Penguin Books, 1959), p. 169. I shall also refer to Sophocles' *Electra* in *Electra and Other Plays*, trans. E. F. Watling (New York: Penguin, 1953) and Euripides' *Electra* in *Euripides V*, ed. David Grene and Richmond Lattimore, trans. Emily Townsend Vermeule (Chicago: University of Chicago Press, 1959).

4. In a paper delivered at the conference on "The First Decade: Ten Years of Coeducation at Dartmouth," Dartmouth College, 1981, Christian Wolff suggests how Sophocles resolves this paradox by radically privatizing Electra's heroism. Sophocles' play, Wolff suggests, is successful to the extent that it suppresses its matricide as a public issue (how else could Electra be praised for her filial piety?), depoliticizes Electra's heroism, and closes off any reference to future consequences of the murder, either for Electra or Orestes.

5. See the analysis of Electra's paternal allegiance in Julia Kristeva, *About Chinese Women*, trans. Anita Barrows (New York: Urizen Books, 1977), pp. 31–32.

6. Virginia Woolf, *A Writer's Diary* (New York: Harcourt Brace Jovanovich, 1954), p. 5.

7. Christina Sorum argues that Electra persists in an "unseasonable childhood with neither husband nor child." Christina Sorum, "The Family in Sophocles' *Antigone* and *Electra*," *The Classical World* 75, 4(1982): 209.

8. Mary O'Brien, *The Politics of Reproduction* (London: Routledge and Kegan Paul, 1981), pp. 150–158. O'Brien rightly points out that, in *The Oresteia*, Clytemnestra's divine parentage is never mentioned; she is, after all, the daughter of Zeus as much as Athena is, but because of her rebelliousness she must be ostracized.

9. George Eliot, *Essays of George Eliot*, ed. Thomas Pinney (New York: Columbia University Press, 1963), pp. 263–264. See also Gerhard Joseph, "The *Antigone* as Cultural Touchstone: Matthew Arnold, Hegel, George Eliot, Virginia Woolf and Margaret Drabble," *PMLA* 96,1(January 1981): 22–35, and George Steiner, *Antigones* (Oxford: Oxford Univeristy Press, 1984).

10. See Hegel, *The Phenomenology of Mind*, trans. J. B. Baillie, rev. 2d ed. (London: Allen and Unwin, 1949), pp. 456–506.

11. Sophocles, *Antigone*, in *The Theban Plays*, trans. E. F. Watling (London: Penguin Books, 1980), ll. 905–910. See Irigaray's discussion of Antigone in Luce Irigaray, *Speculum of the Other Woman*, trans. Gillian C. Gill (Ithaca: Cornell University Press, 1985) and Josette Féral, "Antigone or the Irony of the Tribe," *Diacritics* (September 1978): 2–14. For a critique of these feminist readings, see Page du Bois, "Antigone and the Feminist Critic," *Genre* 19, 4(Winter 1986): 371–382.

12. In an analysis of patterns of brother-sister incest, Elizabeth Abel suggests that for the sister, incest is most often motivated by political concerns, while for the brother, the motivation tends to be erotic. "The Sister's Choice: Antigone, Incest and Fiction by Women," Paper delivered by Elizabeth Abel at the 1982 Convention of the Modern Language Association.

13. Teresa de Lauretis, *Alice Doesn't: Feminism, Semiotics, Cinema* (Bloomington: Indiana University Press, 1984).

14. *The Homeric Hymns*, trans. and ed. Apostolos N. Athanassakis (Baltimore: Johns Hopkins University Press, 1976).

15. Peter Brooks, *Reading for the Plot: Design and Intention in Narrative* (New York: Alfred A. Knopf, 1984), p. 103.

16. Euripides, *Orestes and Other Plays*, trans. Philip Vellacott (London: Penguin Books, 1980).

17. See Bennett Simon, "Tragic Drama and the Family: The Killing of Children and the Killing of Storytelling," in *Discourse in Psychoanalysis and Literature*, ed. Shlomith Rimmon-Kenan (London: Methuen, 1987) for some fascinating reflections on familial plots in classical and modern tragedy.

1. Female Family Romances

1. See esp. Luce Irigaray, *Ethique de la différence sexuelle* (Paris: Minuit, 1984) and some of the essays in Luce Irigaray, *Sexes et parentés* (Paris: Minuit, 1988).

2. Sandra M. Gilbert and Susan Gubar, *The Madwoman in the Attic* (New Haven: Yale University Press, 1979).

3. Adrienne Rich, *On Lies, Secrets and Silence: Selected Prose, 1966–1978* (New York: Norton, 1979), p. 91.

4. Elaine Showalter supports this contention when she emphasizes the pervasiveness of paternal identification as constitutive of Victorian women's self-presentation as writers. See Elaine Showalter, *A Literature of Their Own: British Women Novelists from Brontë to Lessing* (Princeton: Princeton University Press, 1977), pp. 61ff. Susan Peter McDonald finds in the suppression of maternal influence the key to the daughter's maturation in realist fiction: "The good supportive mother is potentially so powerful a figure as to prevent her daughter's trials from occurring, to shield her from the process of maturation, and thus to disrupt the equilibrium of the novel. But if she's dead or absent, the good mother can remain an ideal without her presence disrupting or preventing the necessary drama for the novel." See "Jane Austen and the Tradition of the Absent Mother," in Cathy Davidson and E.M. Broner, eds. *The Lost Tradition: Mothers and Daughters in Literature* (New York: Frederick Ungar, 1980), p. 58. See also Judith Kegan Gardiner, "A Wake for Mother: The Maternal Deathbed in Women's Fiction," *Feminist Studies* 4,1(February, 1978): 146–165.

5. Many of these fictional patterns do, of course, have roots in biography. Elaine Showalter quotes some revealing statistics: "About 50 percent of the women writers born in the nineteenth century married; in the general population, the figure was about 85 percent. Of the married women writers, about 65 percent had children, although they tended to have families well below the Victorian norm of

six children" (*A Literature of Their Own*, p. 65). Or as Tillie Olsen has shown in *Silences* (New York: Delta, 1979) "Almost no mothers—as almost no part-time, part-self persons—have created enduring literature . . . so far" (p. 19).

6. Nina Auerbach, "Artists and Mothers: A False Alliance," *Women and Literature* 6,1(Spring 1978): 3.

7. Margaret Homans, *Bearing the Word: Language and Female Experience in Nineteenth-Century Women's Writing* (Chicago: University of Chicago Press, 1986), p. 27. See also Gail Reimer on Mrs. Oliphant, "Revisions of Labor," *Life/Lines: Theorizing Women's Autobiography*, Bella Brodzki and Celeste Schenck, eds. (Ithaca: Cornell University Press, 1989). Susan Rubin Suleiman has shown that the Victorian belief in the incompatibility of creativity and procreativity is transformed into a fact of nature and thereby institutionalized in the early writings of psychoanalytic theory. She quotes Helene Deutsch: "The urge to intellectual and artistic creation and the productivity of motherhood spring from common sources, and *it seems very natural that one should be capable of replacing the other*" (p. 358) in her article, "Writing and Motherhood," in *The (M)Other Tongue: Essays in Feminist Psychoanalytic Interpretation* ed. Shirley Nelson Garner, Claire Kahane, and Madelon Sprengnether (Ithaca: Cornell University Press, 1985). See also Susan Stanford Friedman's excellent analysis of male and female poets' invocations of metaphors of (pro)creativity in "Creativity and the Childbirth Metaphor: Gender Difference in Literary Discourse," *Feminist Studies* 13, 1(Spring 1987): 49–82.

8. Accepting, and even applauding the heroine's motherlessness, previous critics have concentrated on the heroine's relationship to other constraints, particularly the marriage plot, the Victorian ideology of propriety and true womanhood, and the nineteenth-century woman writer's anxiety of authorship. They have pointed out how women authors and their heroines manage, in complex and often tenuous ways, to evade the constraints and prescriptions to which these structures subject them: through palimpsestic constructions which inscribe their rebellion in the subplots and the margins of their texts, and which subvert the text's overt ideological commitments, through the use of popular forms, and through participation in communal and demonic myths. See among others, Sandra M. Gilbert and Susan Gubar's *The Madwoman in the Attic*, Nina Auerbach's *Communities of Women: An Idea in Fiction* (Cambridge: Harvard University Press, 1978) and her *Woman and the Demon: The Life of a Victorian Myth* (Cambridge: Harvard University Press, 1982), Mary Poovey's *The Proper Lady and the Woman Writer: Ideology as Style in the Works of Mary Wollstonecraft, Mary Shelley, and Jane Austen* (Chicago: Chicago University Press, 1984), Mary Jacobus's *Reading Woman: Essays in Feminist Criticism* (New York: Columbia University Press, 1986), Nancy K. Miller's "Emphasis Added: Plots and Plausibilities in Women's Fiction," *PMLA* 96, 1(January 1981): 36–48, Joseph Allen Boone, *Tradition Counter Tradition: Love and the Form of Fiction* (Chicago: University of Chicago Press, 1987), and Gillian Beer, *Darwin's Plots: Evolutionary Narrative in Darwin, Eliot and Nineteenth-Century Fiction* (London: Routledge and Kegan Paul, 1983).

9. In posing these questions, my inquiry into nineteenth-century novels in this chapter parallels and complements Homans' *Bearing the Word* (see n. 7 above) to a degree. Whereas Homans concentrates on women's relation to language and the structures of the symbolic, I focus primarily on women writers' manipulations of the period's pervasive structures of plotting and on their relation to familial structures. This different point of view leads me to be more guarded about making claims for a specifically feminine relation to language and plot than Homans is. Thus, as I see it, the emergence of the revisionary plot structure which I call a female family romance still rests on pervasive patterns of maternal absence and on the avoidance of maternity.

10. Joan Manheimer suggests that "the failure of mothers as often reflects a

problem with the institutions the woman is expected to serve as it reflects a problem with the woman herself" ("Murderous Mothers," *Feminist Studies* 5, 3(1979): 534).

11. Jane Austen, *Emma*, ed. Stephen Parrish (New York: Norton, 1972), p. 23.

12. Charlotte Brontë, *Shirley*, ed. Herbert Rosengarten and Margaret Smith (Oxford: Oxford University Press, 1979), p. 438.

13. George Eliot, *The Mill on the Floss*, ed. Gordon S. Haight (Boston: Houghton Mifflin, 1961), p. 424.

14. An abbreviated version of this section and the next appeared in *Literature and Psychology* 23, 4(1986): 37–47.

15. Patricia Drechsel Tobin, *Time and the Novel: The Genealogical Imperative* (Princeton: Princeton University Press, 1978), p. 7.

16. Edward W. Said, *Beginnings: Intention and Method* (Baltimore: Johns Hopkins University Press, 1975), p. 93.

17. Peter Brooks, *Reading for the Plot: Design and Intention in Narrative* (New York: Alfred A. Knopf, 1984), p. 146.

18. George Levine, *The Realistic Imagination: English Fiction from Frankenstein to Lady Chatterley* (Chicago: University of Chicago Press, 1981), p. 4, and Leo Bersani, *A Future for Astyanax: Character and Desire in Literature* (Boston: Little Brown, 1976), p. 63. See also Elizabeth Deeds Ermarth, *Realism and Consensus in the English Novel* (Princeton: Princeton University Press, 1983).

19. Naomi Schor, *Breaking the Chain: Women, Theory, and French Realist Fiction* (New York: Columbia University Press, 1985), p. xi. See also Christine van Boheemen's parallel argument about maternal repression as a basis for the coherence of fictional structure in her *The Novel as Family Romance: Language, Gender and Authority from Fielding to Joyce* (Ithaca: Cornell University Press, 1987).

20. Catherine Gallagher suggests a historical reason for this in her response to Neil Hertz's analysis of a certain nineteenth-century pattern of male hysteria. Whereas Hertz sees the Medusa's head as a representation of the fear of castration, and therefore loss and lack, Gallagher interprets it as the fear of plenitude, that is, reproduction uncontrolled by law: "It is precisely this possibility of seemingly disorganized reproduction (of children, of goods, of money, of value) that ignites . . . fear." The threat is to the patriarchal family, weakened by the revolutionary violence following 1789. See Gallagher's essay in Neil Hertz, *The End of the Line: Essays on Psychoanalysis and the Sublime* (New York: Columbia University Press, 1985), pp. 194–196.

21. Sigmund Freud, "Creative Writing and Daydreaming" ("Der Dichter und das Phantasieren") (1907), *The Standard Edition of the Complete Works of Sigmund Freud*, ed. James Strachey, vol. 9 (London: Hogarth Press, 1953), pp. 143–153.

22. Roland Barthes, "Introduction to the Structural Analysis of Narratives," in *Image/Music/Text*, trans. Stephen Heath (New York: Hill and Wang, 1977), p. 124.

23. Roland Barthes, *The Pleasure of the Text*, trans. Richard Miller (New York: Hill and Wang, 1975), p. 47.

24. Margaret Homans cites Terry Eagleton's elaboration of the specifically gendered vision of a writing which emerges from lack: "All desire springs from a lack. . . . Human language works by such lack: the absence of the real objects which signs designate. . . . We are severed from the mother's body. . . . We will spend all our lives hunting for it." Terry Eagleton, *Literary Theory* (Minneapolis: University of Minnesota Press, 1983), pp. 167–168, quoted in Homans, *Bearing the Word*, p. 8.

25. Several feminist responses to Brooks's argument have pointed to the gender bias of his narratology. See Marianne Hirsch, "Ideology, Form and 'Allerleirauh': Reflections on *Reading for the Plot*," *Children's Literature* 14(1986): 163–168, and Susan Winnett, "Coming Unstrung: Women, Men, Narrative and (the) Principle of Plea-

sure," forthcoming. See also Brooks's more recent "The Idea of a Psychoanalytic Criticism," *Critical Inquiry* 13, 2(Winter 1987): 334–348.

26. In her illuminating article "Oedipal Textuality: Reading Freud's Reading of Oedipus," in *Decomposing Figures: Rhetorical Readings in the Romantic Tradition* (Baltimore: Johns Hopkins University Press, 1986), Cynthia Chase elaborates on the metaleptic nature of oedipal textuality where a "first scene" is, after a certain time lag, invariably followed by a "second scene" in which its meaning is clarified to the subject. One example is the murder of the father in the Oedipus story; another might be any scene of infantile sexuality which acquires sexual meaning only from an adult vantage point. Chase makes no gender distinctions in her argument.

27. For the relationship of feminism and narratology, see Susan Snaider Lanser, "Toward a Feminist Narratology," *Style* 20, 3(Fall 1986): 341–363 and Maria Minich Brewer, " 'A Loosening of Tongues': From Narrative Economy to Women's Writing," *MLN* 99(1984), 1141–1161. Outside of the scope of this argument lies a related question: is there space for male difference in Brooks's model—difference imposed by class, race, nationality, sexual preference?

28. Sigmund Freud, "Family Romances" ("Der Familienroman der Neurotiker")(1908), *The Standard Edition*, vol. 9, pp. 237–241.

29. Patricia McKee in *Heroic Commitment in Richardson, Eliot and James* (Princeton: Princeton University Press, 1986) suggests that the plots of nineteenth-century realism can be read through the lens of Freud's work by invoking the notion of "reality principle": "the organization of a self-controlled human being is implied in the organization of realistic novels" (p. 18). The reality principle, she argues convincingly, requires the same kind of delay and postponement as the structure of realistic plot.

30. Luce Irigaray, *Speculum of the Other Woman*, trans. Gillian C. Gill (Ithaca: Cornell University Press, 1985), p. 11.

31. Marthe Robert, *Origins of the Novel*, trans. Sacha Rabinowitch (Bloomington: Indiana University Press, 1980).

32. Freud, "Creative Writers and Daydreaming" (1907), *The Standard Edition*, vol. 9, pp. 143–153. This formulation is a curious reversal of the earlier statement in "Family Romances" that erotic motives predominate for boys as well. I suspect that, whereas Freud obviously wants to privilege eros, he must turn from eros to ambition if he is to account for the structures of male plotting. See Nancy K. Miller's discussion of this conflict in "Emphasis Added: Plots and Plausibilities in Women's Fiction."

33. Phyllis Chesler has suggested that we can see in father-daughter incest a paradigm for marriage: "Women are encouraged to commit incest as a way of life. . . . As opposed to marrying our fathers, we marry men like our fathers . . . men who are older than us, have more money than us, more power than us, are taller than us . . . our fathers." Phyllis Chesler, "Rape and Psychotherapy," in Noreen Connell and Cassandra Wilson, eds., *Rape: The First Sourcebook for Women* (New York: New American Library, 1974), p. 76.

34. Judith Lewis Herman and Lisa Hirschman, *Father-Daughter Incest* (Cambridge: Harvard University Press, 1981), p. 57.

35. In Dianne Sadoff's terms, the daughter needs not only to please and obey the father in order to bind herself to the law, but also to replace her mother in his affections. See Sadoff's *Monsters of Affection: Dickens, Eliot and Brontë on Fatherhood* (Baltimore: Johns Hopkins University Press, 1982).

36. Sigmund Freud, "Negation" (1925), *Standard Edition*, vol. 19, p. 235.

37. Sigmund Freud, "Female Sexuality" (1931), *Standard Edition*, vol. 21, pp. 225–246; and "Femininity" (1933), *Standard Edition*, vol. 22, pp. 112–135. I discuss these essays at greater length in chapter 3.

38. On the function of chatter in Austen's fiction, see D. A. Miller, *Narrative and Its Discontents* (Princeton: Princeton University Press, 1981), pp. 30ff.

39. See Bersani, *A Future for Astyanax* for an analysis of specific strategies of containment in realist narrative, pp. 51–88.

40. Jane Austen, *Mansfield Park* (New York: Penguin, 1987).

41. See Bersani on Fanny's "fear of desire" in *A Future for Astyanax.*

42. Cross and chain surely could not be arbitrary metaphors here.

43. Ellen Moers, *Literary Women* (Garden City, N.Y.: Anchor, 1977), p. 160.

44. George Sand, *Valentine*, trans. George Burnham Ives (Chicago: Cassandra Editions, 1978).

45. Nancy K. Miller, "Writing (from) the Feminine: George Sand and the Novel of the Female Pastoral," in Carolyn Heilbrun and Margaret Higonnet, eds., *The Representation of Women in Fiction* (Baltimore: Johns Hopkins University Press, 1983).

46. We see the same kind of recovery in a novel like Eliot's *The Mill on the Floss*, where Maggie and Tom embrace in the Floss, "living through again in one supreme moment the days when they had clasped their little hands in love,and roamed the daisied fields together"(p. 456).

47. As Gilbert and Gubar argue in *The Madwoman:* "All the heroines who reject inadequate fathers are engaged in a search for better, more sensitive men who are, nevertheless, still the representatives of authority. . . . the happy ending of an Austen novel occurs when the girl becomes daughter to her husband, an older and wiser man who has been her teacher and her advisor, whose house can provide her with shelter and sustenance and at least derived status, reflected glory" (p. 154).

48. Kate Chopin, *The Awakening*, ed. Margo Culley (New York: Norton, 1976). This reading is based on my earlier article: "Spiritual Bildung: The Beautiful Soul as Paradigm," in Abel, Hirsch, and Langland, eds., *The Voyage In: Fictions of Female Development* (Hanover: University Press of New England, 1983). See also Susan Rosowski's "The Novel of Awakening" in the same volume.

2. Fraternal Plots

1. Excerpt from George Eliot's unpublished poem "Erinna" used as an epigram to chapter 51 of *Daniel Deronda*, ed. Barbara Hardy (London: Penguin Books, 1967).

2. Margaret Cavendish, *Poems and Fancies* (Scolar Press, 1972), p. 2, cited in Sandra M. Gilbert and Susan Gubar, *The Madwoman in the Attic: The Woman Writer and the Nineteenth-Century Poetic Imagination* (New Haven: Yale University Press, 1979), p. 525. See pp. 520–526 for an analysis of sewing and spinning in Eliot's work. See also Gillian Beer, *Darwin's Plots: Evolutionary Narrative in Darwin, George Eliot and Nineteenth-Century Fiction* (London: Routledge and Kegan Paul, 1983), pp. 149–180, for a discussion of the image of the web in Victorian writing.

3. See Nancy K. Miller, "Arachnologies: The Woman, the Text and the Critic," in *The Poetics of Gender*, ed. Nancy K. Miller (New York: Columbia University Press, 1986) and Patricia Klindienst Joplin, "The Voice of the Shuttle is Ours," *Stanford Literature Review* 1, 1(Spring 1984): 25–53.

4. See Miller, "Arachnologies," p. 288.

5. A. S. F. Gow and D. L. Page, eds., *The Greek Anthology: Hellenistic Epigrams* (Cambridge: Cambridge University Press, 1965). See also Marilyn Arthur, "The Tortoise and the Mirror: Erinna PSI 1090," *Classical World* 74(1980): 53–65 and Sarah Pomeroy, "Supplementary Notes on Erinna," *Zeitschrift für Papyrologie* 32(1978): 17–21; I am grateful to Helene Foley for these references.

6. Marilyn Arthur alludes, in this connection, to the myth of Chelone who did not want to attend Zeus's marriage because of her disdain for the institution of marriage and, in punishment, was turned into a tortoise by Hermes.

7. This part of Erinna's story is mentioned by Gillian Beer in *George Eliot* (Bloomington: Indiana University Press, 1986), pp. 23 and 207–208, but it is not documented. Erinna's own fragment, *The Distaff*, does not mention her mother but does present some children's games where the girls act out the complex role of mother.

8. Ellen Rosenman points out that the novel's title reflects this ambivalence: it carries Daniel's name, yet Daniel was named by his mother in a radical break from her own paternal lineage. See "Women's Speech and the Roles of the Sexes in *Daniel Deronda*," *Texas Studies in Language and Literature*, 31, 2(Summer 1989).

9. See Catherine Gallagher, "George Eliot and *Daniel Deronda*: The Prostitute and the Jewish Question," in *Sex, Politics and Science in the Nineteenth-Century Novel*, ed. Ruth Bernard Yeazell (Baltimore: Johns Hopkins University Press, 1986), for an analysis of the complex patterns of prostitution that pervade this novel.

10. Dianne F. Sadoff sees Lydia and Grandcourt as the parents in the oedipal triangle where Gwendolen is the daughter. See Dianne F. Sadoff, *Monsters of Affection: Dickens, Eliot and Brontë on Fatherhood* (Baltimore: Johns Hopkins University Press, 1982), p. 100.

11. See Nina Auerbach, *Woman and the Demon: The Life of a Victorian Myth* (Cambridge: Harvard University Press, 1982), p. 205, for a discussion of the Alcharisi as Eliot's self-portrait.

12. Neil Hertz, *The End of the Line* (New York: Columbia University Press, 1985), pp. 224–233. See also Elizabeth Langland, "Patriarchal Ideology and Marginal Motherhood in Victorian Novels by Women," *Studies in the Novel*, 19, 3(Fall 1987), 381–394.

13. See Julia Kristeva, *Powers of Horror: An Essay on Abjection*, trans. Léon S. Roudiez (New York: Columbia University Press, 1982).

14. As Ellen Rosenman points out, Mirah and the Princess also never meet; their relationship is mediated through Daniel who is supposed to deliver his mother's portrait to Mirah.

15.Deirdre David, in *Fictions of Resolution in Three Victorian Novels: North and South, Our Mutual Friend, Daniel Deronda* (London: Macmillan, 1981), pp. 176–204, argues that Gwendolen's development is arrested at the narcissistic stage of mother-love.

16. This extra-verbal relation corroborates Margaret Homans's distinction between the literal and the symbolic in the myth of language. See Margaret Homans, *Bearing the Word: Language and Female Experience in Nineteenth-Century Women's Writing* (Chicago: University Press of Chicago, 1986).

17. See Dianne Sadoff, *Monsters*, pp. 65–118, for an extensive discussion of father-daughter relationships in Eliot's work, and see Nancy Pell, "The Fathers' Daughters in *Daniel Deronda*," *Nineteenth-Century Fiction* 36, 4(March 1982): 424–451 for a discussion of the disastrous effects of paternity in the novel.

18. In the days before the talking cure was perfected, analysis included the laying on of hands. Breuer cared for the ailing Anna O. in much the way Daniel does for Gwendolen in Venice—he fed her, sat by her bed, massaged her body. As Jacqueline Rose points out, *Daniel Deronda* was published only ten years before Freud's earliest writings and Gwendolen could almost be defined as "the original literary hysteric"; see Jacqueline Rose, *Sexuality in the Field of Vision* (London: Verso, 1986), pp. 115–116.

19. I am indebted here to Gail T. Reimer's research into Eliot's discourse of confession. See also Michel Foucault on confession as the discourse of sexuality in the nineteenth-century, esp. his *The History of Sexualtiy, Volume I: An Introduction*, trans. Robert Hurley (New York: Vintage, 1980).

20. According to Ellen Rosenman, "women come to stand for the claims

of self and the casual valuing of human life" in this novel; they are figured as "dangerous and anarchic" and the novel itself cannot quite make space for their disruptive stories.

21. Rose argues in *Sexuality in the Field of Vision* that the novel constructs the reader as spectator and the woman as spectacle, as object of intense and ceaseless scrutiny and investigation.

22. As Terry Eagleton says, "Realism, as Eliot conceives of it, involves the tactful unravelling of interlaced processes, the equitable distribution of authorial sympathies, the holding of competing values in precarious equipoise," in *Criticism and Ideology: A Study of Marxist Literary Theory* (London: New Left Books 1976), p. 114. From this point of view, Daniel is the epitome of Eliot's realist narrator, and Eliot herself, I would argue, privileges him while shortchanging Gwedolen.

23. George Levine, in "George Eliot's Hypothesis of Reality," *Nineteenth-Century Fiction* 35, 1(1980): 1–28, argues that, in Eliot's vision, an openness and receptiveness to the vast and inextricable relations in external reality necessitates an erasure of self and personality. In this view, Daniel is much better prepared for Eliot's ideal vision than Gwendolen.

24. In Rosenman's reading Mirah's own self-lessness is the other side of the Princess's self-assertion.

25. Carol Gilligan, *In A Different Voice: Psychological Theory and Women's Development* (Cambridge: Harvard University Press, 1982), 128–150.

26. See Joseph Boone, *Tradition Counter Tradition: Love and the Form of Fiction* (Chicago: University of Chicago Press, 1987), pp. 174–193.

27. The novel's imbalance has by now become a critical commonplace, especially since F. R. Leavis suggested that Daniel's half of the novel could easily be eliminated. See F. R. Leavis, *The Great Tradition* (London: Chato & Windus, 1948), pp. 79–125. See also Patricia McKee, *Heroic Commitment in Richardson, Eliot and James* (Princeton: Princeton University Press, 1986), pp. 208–269, for a discussion of the novel's "uneasy relations." It is my attempt to account for the imbalances and uneasy relations that mark this novel's structure by looking at the gender differences it seems on the surface to repress.

28. For a discussion of the wedding night as a motif in women's fiction, including this novel, see Nancy K. Miller, "Writing (from) the Feminine: George Sand and the Novel of Female Pastoral," in *The Representation of Women in Fiction* ed. Carolyn G. Heilbrun and Margaret R. Higonnet (Baltimore: Johns Hopkins University Press, 1983), esp. p. 134.

29. On anger in Eliot's fiction, see Carol Christ, "Aggression and Providential Death in George Eliot's Fiction," *Novel: A Forum on Fiction* 9, 2(Winter 1976): 130–140.

30. Jacqueline Rose, in *Sexuality*, pp. 105–107, compares the tableau scene to the moment of Gwendolen's arrival in the Venice harbor: two horror scenes in which the spectacle of the crazed woman is presented to the male spectator—Klesmer and Daniel.

31. See Joseph Boone's analysis of the novel's overturning of conventional expectations of the marriage plot (see n. 26 above).

32. See Margaret Homans on the male usurpation of reproduction in the fiction of this period, especially her analysis of *Frankenstein* in Homans, *Bearing the Word*.

33. See Cynthia Chase, "The Decomposition of the Elephants: Double-Reading *Daniel Deronda*," in *Decomposing Figures: Rhetorical Readings in the Romantic Tradition* (Baltimore: Johns Hopkins University Press, 1986), p. 167, for an interpretation of this moment not as reproductive generation but as verbal creation. In her terms, Daniel's Jewish identity is the "product of a coercive speech act." That verbal power is reserved for males in Eliot's fiction. In *The Realistic Imagination*, George Levine distinguishes between two kinds of dream in Eliot's realist fiction, the "gossamer

dreaming of an inexperienced, egoistic Gwendolen and creative dreaming based in 'the stored up accumulation of previous experiences' " that characterize Mordecai's "visionary and creative wisdom," p. 24.

34. Cynthia Chase, *Decomposing*, brilliantly describes the deconstruction of causality in the novel.

35. Gillian Beer poses this and similar questions in *Darwin's Plots;* see esp. pp. 184–207.

36. Edward W. Said views the novel's Zionist plot as an integral part of imperial expansion. See his analysis of Zionism and homelessness in Edward Said, *The Question of Palestine* (New York: Vintage, 1980), pp. 60–68.

37. Charlotte Brontë's Lucy Snowe is a notable exception, but unlike Grandcourt's death, Monsieur Paul's has not been definitively established.

38. Carol Christ sees providential death as the means by which Eliot both protects her characters from actual guilt, and induces in them a psychological guilt which furthers their moral education. For Gwendolen, Grandcourt's providential death not only liberates her from guilt, but it opens for her an uncharted future, enabling her not to find in death the only solution to her plot.   •

39. See U. C. Knoepflmacher, "Unveiling Men: Power and Masculinity in George Eliot's Fiction," *Women and Literature,* 2(1981): 130–146.

40. How are we to read Eliot's own participation in this gender asymmetry? Jacqueline Rose eloquently suggests that Eliot's position can best be described in terms of "masquerade," rather than as either complicity or transcendent judgment (*Sexuality,* p. 120).

3. The Darkest Plots

1. Virginia Woolf, *A Room of One's Own* (New York: Harcourt Brace Jovanovich, 1929), p. 4.

2. In *Alice Doesn't: Feminism, Semiotics, Cinema* (Bloomington: Indiana University Press, 1984), Teresa de Lauretis uses Woolf's distinction between *instinct* and *reason* to develop an extremely useful way of theorizing female *experience*. See esp. pp. 158–160, 182–186.

3. *Oscillation* is a term also used by Rachel Blau DuPlessis in relation to Woolf and other modernist writers. See her *Writing beyond the Ending: Narrative Strategies of Twentieth-Century Women Writers* (Bloomington: Indiana University Press, 1985) and "For the Etruscans: Sexual Difference and Artistic Production—The Debate Over a Female Aesthetic," in *The Future of Difference,* ed. Hester Eisenstein and Alice Jardine (Boston: G. K. Hall & Co., 1980).

4. Jane Marcus, *Virginia Woolf and the Languages of Patriarchy* (Bloomington: Indiana University Press, 1987), p. 184.

5. Peggy Kamuf, "Penelope at Work: Interruptions in *A Room of One's Own,*" *Novel* 16, 1(Fall 1982): 5–18; see also Toril Moi, *Sexual/Textual Politics: Feminist Literary Theory* (London: Methuen, 1985) for a deconstructive reading of Woolf and a strong argument in favor of the exclusive validity of such readings.

6. See Naomi Schor's "Reading Double: Sand's Difference," in *The Poetics of Gender,* ed. Nancy K. Miller (New York: Columbia University Press, 1986), for a suggestive exposition of this feminist strategy.

7. Adrienne Rich, "When We Dead Awaken: Writing as Re-Vision," in *On Lies, Secrets and Silence* (New York: Norton, 1979), p. 37.

8. John Burt, "Irreconcilable Habits of Thought in *A Room of One's Own* and *To the Lighthouse,*" *English Literary History* 49(1982): 893.

9. On brothers and sisters in Woolf see Sara Ruddick, "Private Brother, Public World," in *New Feminist Essays on Virginia Woolf,* ed. Jane Marcus (Lincoln: University of Nebraska Press, 1981). In *The Years* and *The Pargiters,* Woolf does a more

devastating critique of the gender arrangements which train brothers for war and sisters for domestic life.

10. For readings of androgyny in Woolf, see Carolyn Heilbrun, *Toward a Recognition of Androgyny* (New York: Norton, 1964) and Nancy Topping Bazin, *Virginia Woolf and the Androgynous Vision* (New Brunswick: Rutgers University Press, 1973). I disagree here with Elaine Showalter, *A Literature of Their Own: British Women Novelists from Brontë to Lessing* (Princeton: Princeton University Press, 1977), who describes Woolf's stance as a "flight" into androgyny. Rather than a flight, I prefer to see it as a momentary solution, not granted any ultimate validity. See also Jane Marcus's discussion of this moment in *A Room*, in her *Virginia Woolf and the Languages of Patriarchy*, pp. 159–162.

11. See Elizabeth Abel's brilliant analysis of hunger and food in *A Room*, in her *Virginia Woolf and the Fictions of Psychoanalysis* (Chicago: University of Chicago Press, 1989).

12. Reprinted in Michèle Barrett, ed., *Women and Writing* (New York: Harcourt Brace Jovanovich, 1979).

13. Mary Jacobus, *Reading Woman: Essays in Feminist Criticism* (New York: Columbia University Press, 1986), p. 39.

14. See Sandra M. Gilbert and Susan Gubar, *The Madwoman in the Attic* (New Haven: Yale University Press, 1979), chap. 1, and Elaine Showalter, "Feminist Criticism in the Wilderness," in *The New Feminist Criticism* (New York: Pantheon, 1985).

15. That she sees literature as changing in similar ways is obvious from her celebrated essay on modern fiction, "Mr. Bennett and Mrs. Brown" (1924) in which she asserts, prophetically, that "on or about December 1910 human character changed." *Collected Essays*, vol. 1 (New York: Harcourt, Brace & World, 1967), p. 320.

16. Ellen Moers, *Literary Women* (New York: Anchor, 1977), p. 354.

17. On the female artist novel during this period, see DuPlessis, *Writing beyond the Ending*, and Susan Gubar, "The Birth of the Artist as Heroine: (Re)production, the *Künstlerroman* Tradition, and the Fiction of Katherine Mansfield," in *The Representation of Women in Fiction*, ed. Carolyn G. Heilbrun and Margaret R. Higonnet (Baltimore: Johns Hopkins University Press, 1983). On Cather, Woolf, and Colette, see Jane Lilienfeld, "Re-entering Paradise: Cather, Colette, Woolf and Their Mothers," in *The Lost Tradition: Mothers and Daughters*, ed. Cathy N. Davidson and E. M. Broner (New York: Frederick Ungar, 1980).

18. Colette, *Break of Day*, trans. Enid McLeod (New York: Farrar, Straus, and Giroux, 1961), p. 62.

19. Virginia Woolf, *The Common Reader*, 1st series, 1923.

20. Susan Gubar, "The Birth of the Artist as Heroine." See also Barbara Ehrenreich and Deirdre English, *For Her Own Good: 150 Years of the Experts' Advice to Women* (Garden City, N.Y.: Anchor, 1978) and Linda Gordon, *Woman's Body, Woman's Right: A Social History of Birth Control in America* (New York: Penguin, 1977).

21. In her notebooks, Woolf uses the term elegy to describe *To the Lighthouse*. For a feminist analysis of the elegy, see Celeste M. Schenck, "Feminism and Deconstruction: Re-Constructing the Elegy," *Tulsa Studies in Women's Literature* 5, 1(Spring 1986): 13–27.

22. Adrienne Rich, "Compulsory Heterosexuality and Lesbian Existence," *Signs* 5, 4(Summer 1980): 631–660.

23. Sigmund Freud, "Female Sexuality" (1931), *Standard Edition*, vol. 21, p. 226; Rachel Blau DuPlessis's use of the image of the Etruscans is similar.

24. See Robert Briffault, *The Mothers: A Study of the Origins of Sentiments and Institutions* (New York: Macmillan, 1927); J. J. Bachofen, *Myth, Religion and Mother-*

Right, trans. Ralph Manheim (Princeton: Princeton University Press, 1967); Erich Neumann, *The Great Mother: An Analysis of the Archetype*, trans. Ralph Manheim (Princeton: Bollingen, 1955). For contemporary feminist analyses of these theories and of their impact on the novel, see Evelyn Reed, *Women's Evolution* (New York: Pathfinder Press, 1975) and esp. Elizabeth Abel, *Virginia Woolf and the Fictions of Psychoanalysis* as well as Sandra M. Gilbert and Susan Gubar's *No Man's Land* (New Haven: Yale University Press, 1988).

25. See Sandra M. Gilbert's discussion of male modernism in relation to matriarchy theories, esp. in "Potent Griselda: 'The Ladybird' and the Great Mother," in *D. H. Lawrence: A Centenary Consideration*, ed. Peter Balbert and Phillip L. Marcus (Ithaca: Cornell University Press, 1985).

26. In chapter 5, I return to this moment in Freud and examine the motivations Freud posits to explain this shift in the girl's developmental journey, in particular, the motivation of anger.

27. De Lauretis, *Alice Doesn't*, esp. chapter 5, "Desire in Narrative."

28. Elizabeth Abel, "Narrative Structure(s) and Female Development: The Case of *Mrs. Dalloway*," in *The Voyage In: Fictions of Female Development*, ed. Elizabeth Abel, Marianne Hirsch, and Elizabeth Langland (Hanover: University Press of New England, 1983), p. 171.

29. See Melanie Klein, *Love, Guilt and Reparation and Other Works, 1921–1945* (New York: Dell, 1975) and Phyllis Grosskurth, *Melanie Klein: Her World and Her Work* (New York: Alfred A. Knopf, 1986). For a much fuller account of Melanie Klein's work in relation to modernist narrative see Elizabeth Abel's *Virginia Woolf and the Fictions of Psychoanalysis*.

30. See Karen Horney, "The Flight from Womanhood: The Masculinity Complex in Women as Viewed by Men and by Women" (1926) in Jean Strouse, *Women and Analysis* (New York: Dell, 1974).

31. Luce Irigaray pushes insights such as these much further, wondering why Freud fails to posit just such a primary femininity, characterized by vulval, vaginal or uterine stages, in addition to phallic ones. This failure renders Freud guilty of the "blind spot of an old dream of symmetry," she claims. See Luce Irigaray, *Speculum of the Other Woman*, trans. Gillian G. Gill (Ithaca: Cornell University Press, 1985), pp. 29, 59, 60. On Irigaray's "impertinent questions" to Freud and Lacan, see Jane Gallop's *The Daughter's Seduction: Feminism and Psychoanalysis* (Ithaca: Cornell University Press, 1982), pp. 80–91.

32. Helene Deutsch, *The Psychology Of Women*, vol. 1 (New York: Grune & Stratton, 1944), p. 116. See also Nancy Chodorow's excellent analysis of all these issues in reference to mother-daughter relationships in her *The Reproduction of Mothering: Psychoanalysis and the Sociology of Gender* (Berkeley: University of California Press, 1978).

33. Abel's "Narrative Structures and Female Development" is based on similar assumptions.

34. On contradiction and duplicity as elements of the feminine unconscious, see Michèle Montrelay, *L'ombre et le nom: sur la féminité* (Paris: Minuit, 1977), esp. the section entitled "Recherches sur la féminité." Translated as "Inquiry into Femininity," *m/f* 1(1978).

35. Peter Brooks, *Reading for the Plot: Design and Intention in Narrative* (New York: Alfred A. Knopf, 1984), p. 92.

36. Marilyn Yalom, *Maternity, Mortality and the Literature of Madness* (University Park: Pennsylvania State University Press, 1985).

37. Nancy K. Miller, "Women's Autobiography in France: For a Dialectic of Identification," in *Women and Language in Literature and Society*, ed. Sally McConnell-Ginet, Ruth Borker, and Nelly Furman (New York: Praeger, 1980) and in *Colette: The Woman, The Writer*, ed. Erica Eisinger and Mari McCarty (Pittsburgh: Pennsylvania

State University Press, 1981); Germaine Brée, "Le Mythe des origines et l'autoportrait chez George Sand et Colette," in *Symbolism in Modern Literature: Studies in Honor of Wallace Fowlie*, ed. Marcel Tétel (Durham: Duke University Press, 1978). See also Elaine Marks, *Colette* (New Brunswick: Rutgers University Press, 1960); Jane Lilienfeld, "The Magic Spinning Wheel: Straw to Gold—Colette, Willy, and Sido," in *Mothering the Mind: Twelve Studies of Writers and Their Silent Partners*, ed. Ruth Perry and Martine Watson Brownley (New York: Holmes and Meier, 1984); and Susan D. Fraiman, "Shadow in the Garden: The Double Aspect of Motherhood in Colette," *Perspectives on Contemporary Literature*, 11(1985): 46–53.

38. These textual incongruities might explain why it apparently was so difficult for Colette to complete. Motivated by financial difficulties she repeatedly had to force herself to sit down to write, only to report, time after time, that she had to break off without having finished. "My novel fights me like a demon," she wrote to a friend. See Letter to Léopold Marchand, Sept. 27, 1927, cited by Claude Pichois in the Preface to *La Naissance du jour* (Paris: Garnier-Flammarion, 1969), p. 22 (my translation).

39. Michelle Sarde, *Colette*, trans. Richard Miller (New York: William Morrow, 1980), p. 286. See also *Sido: Lettres à sa fille* (Paris: des femmes, 1984).

40. See the preface to *Sido: Lettres à sa fille* by Jeannie Malige, p. x.

41. Nancy K. Miller, "D'une solitude à l'autre: vers un intertexte féminin," *French Review* 54, 6(May 1981): 797–803.

42. Just as she was writing about renouncing the love of Vial, Colette was herself in the process of marrying for the third time.

43. Such a letter is not included in the des femmes edition; it is obviously Colette's textual construction.

44. Cited by Pichois, *La Naissance*, p. 23.

45. Colette, *My Mother's House and Sido*, trans. Una Vicenzo Troubridge and Enid McLeod (New York: Farrar, Straus and Giroux, 1953), p. 194.

46. Jane Marcus, *Virginia Woolf and the Languages of Patriarchy*, p. 8.

47. *The Diary of Virginia Woolf*, vol. 3, ed. Anne Olivier Bell (New York: Harcourt Brace Jovanovich, 1980), May 14, 1925.

48. Virginia Woolf, *Moments of Being*, 2d edition, ed. Jeanne Schulkind (New York: Harcourt Brace Jovanovich, 1985), p. 80.

49. To write about *To the Lighthouse* as a mother-daughter text is to situate oneself within a ten-year tradition of feminist readings which have featured this novel as the central mother-daughter text in women's writing and have featured the mother-daughter thematics as central to any understanding of the text. Among these readings, see esp. Sara Ruddick, "Learning to Live with the Angel in the House," *Women's Studies*, 4 (1977): 181–200; Jane Lilienfeld, "The Deceptiveness of Beauty: Mother Love and Mother Hate in *To the Lighthouse*," *Twentieth-Century Literature* 23(1977): 345–376; Elizabeth Abel's chapters on *To the Lighthouse* in *Virginia Woolf and the Fictions of Psychoanalysis*; Ellen Bayuk Rosenman, *The Invisible Presence: Virginia Woolf and the Mother-Daughter Relationship* (Baton Rouge: Louisiana State University Press, 1986); Joan Lidoff, "Virginia Woolf's Feminine Sentence: The Mother-Daughter World of *To the Lighthouse*," *Literature and Psychology* 32, 3(1986): 43–59; Claire Kahane, "The Nuptials of Metaphor: Self and Other in Virginia Woolf," *Literature and Psychology* 30, 2(1980): 72–82; Susan Squier, "Mirroring and Mothering: Reflections on the Mirror Encounter Metaphor in Virginia Woolf's Works," *Twentieth-Century Literature*, 27, 3(Fall 1981): 272–288; Gayatri Spivak, "Making and Unmaking in *To the Lighthouse*," in *Women and Language in Literature and Society*, ed. Sally McConnell-Ginet, Ruth Borker, and Nelly Furman (New York: Praeger, 1980); Carolyn Williams, "Virginia Woolf's Rhetoric of Enclosure," *Denver Quarterly* 18, 4(Winter 1984): 43–61; Carolyn Heilbrun, "Virginia Woolf's *To the Lighthouse*," paper delivered at the 1986 MLA Convention.

50. Helen Storm Corsa, *"To the Lighthouse:* Death, Mourning and Transfigura-
tion," *Literature and Psychology* 21, 3(1971): 115–132; Sharon Wood Proudfit, "Lily
Briscoe's Painting: A Key to Personal Relationships in *To the Lighthouse," Criticism*
13, 1(1971): 26–38; Jean O. Love, *Virginia Woolf: Sources of Madness and Art* (Berkeley:
University of California Press, 1977); Maria di Battista, *Virginia Woolf's Major Novels:
The Fables of Anon* (New Haven: Yale University Press, 1980).

51. Jane Lilienfeld aptly points out that Lily is the figure of the Victorian orphan
reframed as surrogate daughter, passionately attached to the mother. See "Deceptiveness."

52. In his study of Lily's painting in relation to contemporary artistic conventions, Thomas Matro also argues against the achievement of balance in the novel;
see his "Only Relations: Vision and Achievement in *To the Lighthouse," PMLA* 99,
2(March 1984): 212–224.

53. In *Moments of Being,* Woolf describes her parents' bedroom: "the bedroom—
the double bedded bedroom on the first floor was the sexual centre; the birth
centre, the death centre of the house" (p. 118).

54. See Lilienfeld's analysis of food and ritual in the novel in "Deceptiveness."

55. On the novel's critique of the Victorian ideology of marriage, see Joseph A.
Boone, *Tradition Counter Tradition: Love and the Form of Fiction* (Chicago: University of
Chicago Press, 1987), pp. 201–214.

56. In "Making and Unmaking," Gayatri Spivak argues that Mrs. Ramsay is in
the position of predicate rather than subject; she sees Lily's creation as a form of
uterine plenitude developing a thematics of womb-envy in the novel, but one in
which Mrs. Ramsay cannot participate.

57. This is what Spivak calls the copula, identified in her argument with the
"Time Passes" section, which, like the line, occupies the space in the center. She
reads "Time Passes" as the discourse of madness, war, and undecidability. See also
Matro's focus in "Only Relations" on effort rather than achievement and his
emphasis on the "to" in the novel's title.

58. Abel's reading of Cam's silence diverges radically from Homans's. For Homans, Cam is not the silent sister and paternal daughter, but the representative of a
different, non-figurative, mother-daughter language of presence. See the last chapter in Margaret Homans, *Bearing the Word: Language and Female Experience in
Nineteenth-Century Women's Writing* (Chicago: University of Chicago Press,
1986).

59. 1929 *Diary,* cited in *Women and Writing,* ed. Michèle Barrett, p. 3.

60. Spivak defines the novel as "an attempt to articulate, by using man as an
instrument, a woman's vision of a woman" ("Making and Unmaking," p. 326).

61. Sandra M. Gilbert and Susan Gubar, *The Madwoman in the Attic,* p. 50. See
also Gilbert and Gubar's much more detailed discussion of male modernism in
relation to the emergence of female writing and to the anxiety about female
precursors in the first volume of *No Man's Land,* esp. chap. 3, "Tradition and the
Female Talent: Modernism and Masculinism."

62. Edith Wharton, *The Mother's Recompense* (New York: Scribners, 1925).

63. Interestingly, society and Anne were willing to forgive Kate the first
lover with whom she ran away, even though he caused her to abandon her
child; the unforgivable breech was the sexual pleasure she experienced with
Chris.

4. Feminist Family Romances

1. *College English, XXXIV,* 1 (October 1972): 18–25, rpt. in *Adrienne Rich's Poetry,*
ed. Barbara Charlesworth Gelpi and Albert Gelpi (New York: W. W. Norton, 1975),
pp. 90–98. Page numbers will refer to this latter reprinting.

2. Adrienne Rich, *On Lies, Secrets and Silence: Selected Prose 1966–1978* (New York: W. W. Norton, 1979), p. 33. This is a citation from Rich's preface to the revised version of her essay, reprinted here.

3. Elaine Showalter, "Toward a Feminist Poetics," in her *The New Feminist Criticism: Essays on Women, Literature, Theory* (New York: Pantheon, 1985), p. 135.

4. I am grateful to Brenda Silver for calling my attention to these revisions.

5. Adrienne Rich, *Of Woman Born: Motherhood as Experience and Institution* (New York: W. W. Norton, 1976).

6. Luce Irigaray, *Le corps-à-corps avec la mère* (Montreal: les éditions de la pleine lune, 1981), p. 61.

7. Juliet Mitchell, *Psychoanalysis and Feminism: Freud, Reich, Laing and Women* (New York: Vintage, 1975).

8. Nancy Friday, *My Mother/My Self: A Daughter's Search for Identity* (New York: Delacorte Press, 1977),

9. Marie Cardinal, *The Words to Say It*, trans. Pat Goodheart (Cambridge, Mass: Van Vactor & Goodheart, 1983). *Les Mots pour le dire* (Paris: Bernard Grasset, 1975).

10. Cardinal's novel is dedicated to "the doctor who helped me be born."

11. Nancy Chodorow, *The Reproduction of Mothering: Psychoanalysis and the Sociology of Gender* (Berkeley: University of California Press, 1978). See Jane Gallop, "Reading the Mother Tongue: Psychoanalytic Feminist Criticism," *Critical Inquiry* 13, 1(Winter 1987): 314–329. Whereas Gallop speaks of Chodorow's psychoanalysis as "mother-centered," I focus, in this chapter and the next, on the child-centered biases of object-relations theories, where the mother may be more present than the father, but where she is present not as subject, but only as the child's object. See also the essays in *The (M)Other Tongue*.

12. See especially Luce Irigaray, *This Sex Which Is Not One*, trans. Catherine Porter and Carolyn Burke (Ithaca: Cornell University Press, 1985); "And the One Doesn't Stir Without the Other," trans. Hélène Vivienne Wenzel, *Signs* 7, 1 (Winter 1981): 60–67.

13. See Julia Kristeva, *Polylogue* (Paris: Seuil, 1977); *Desire in Language: A Semiotic Approach to Literature and Art*, ed. Léon Roudiez and trans. Thomas Gora, Alice Jardine, and Léon Roudiez (New York: Columbia University Press, 1980). See also, Hélène Cixous and Catherine Clément, *The Newly Born Woman*, trans. Betsy Wing (Minneapolis: University of Minnesota Press, 1986).

14. In "Compulsory Heterosexuality and Lesbian Existence," *Signs* 5, 4(Summer 1980): 631–660, Adrienne Rich discusses these implications of Chodorow's argument, although she insists that "mothering-by-women is [not] a 'sufficient cause' of lesbian existence," p. 638.

15. Dorothy Dinnerstein, *The Mermaid and the Minotaur: Sexual Arrangements and Human Malaise* (New York: Harper Colophon, 1977).

16. Irigaray, *Le corps-à-corps avec la mère*, pp. 20, 21.

17. Jane Flax, "The Conflict between Nurturance and Autonomy in Mother/Daughter Relationships and within Feminism," *Feminist Studies* 4, 1(February 1978): 171–89, and "Mother-Daughter Relationships: Psychodynamics, Politics and Philosophy" in *The Future of Difference*, ed. Hester Eisenstein and Alice Jardine (Boston: G. K. Hall, 1980); Jessica Benjamin, "The Bonds of Love: Rational Violence and Erotic Domination," *Feminist Studies* 6, 1(Spring 1980), 144–174.

18. See Sara Ruddick, "Preservative Love and Military Destruction: Some Reflections on Mothering and Peace," in *Mothering: Essays in Feminist Theory*, ed. Joyce Trebilcott (New York: Rowman and Allenheld, 1984), 231–262.

19. Carol Gilligan's argument in *In a Different Voice: Psychological Theory and Women's Development* (Cambridge: Harvard University Press, 1982) is especially suggestive in this regard, as is the work of Sara Ruddick. It needs to be emphasized that neither argument is essentialist.

20. Adrienne Rich, "Sibling Mysteries," *Dream of a Common Language* (New York: Norton, 1978), p. 48.

21. My brief discussion in the Prelude and chapter 1 of Irigaray's more recent work, esp. *L'Ethique de la différence sexuelle* and *Le corps-à-corps avec la mère* should indicate how much her work has evolved in the 1980s toward a greater understanding and acceptance of the maternal, toward a recognition that her project—the redefinition of the subject in philosophy and psychoanalysis as well as the reconstruction of the female body and its discourses—cannot take place without an intense engagement of the intergenerational relations among women. Irigaray's oeuvre traces a classic feminist pattern—the rejection of the mother in favor of other female relationships and a return to the maternal, no longer as the basis for an idealized separate realm, but as the space for a different, adult subjectivity.

22. Elaine Showalter continues her discussion of the "sustained quest," by saying: "As the death of the father has always been an archetypal rite of passage for the Western hero, now the death of the mother as witnessed and transcended by the daughter has become one of the most profound occasions of female literature" (*The New Feminist Criticism*, p. 135). Showalter's examples are Lisa Alter's *Kinflicks* and Margaret Atwood's *Surfacing*.

23. Margaret Atwood, *Surfacing* (New York: Popular Library, 1976).

24. Marguerite Duras, *The Lover*, trans. Barbara Bray (New York: Pantheon, 1985). Translation of *L'Amant* (Paris: Minuit, 1984). Page numbers refer to the Bray translation except where indicated.

25. Christa Wolf, *Kindheitsmuster* (Berlin und Weimar: Aufbau Verlag, 1976), translated as *A Model Childhood* by Ursule Molinaro and Hedwig Rappolt (New York: Farrar, Straus and Giroux, 1980). The English title was later changed to *Patterns of Childhood*. Page numbers refer to the Molinaro and Rappolt translation except where indicated. I could have chosen among numerous other novels to illustrate some of these trends, for example: Rosellen Brown's *The Autobiography of My Mother*; Simone Schwartz-Bart's *Pluie et vent sur Telumée-Miracle (The Bridge of Beyond)*; Maxine Hong Kingston's *The Woman Warrior*; Marilynne Robinson's *Housekeeping*; Karin Struck's *Die Mutter*; Katja Behrens's *Die dreizehnte Fee*, etc. The next chapter deals with works by black women writers in the U.S. which illustrate some similar patterns.

26. Jacques Lacan, "The Agency of the Letter in the Unconscious or Reason in Freud," *Ecrits*, trans. Alan Sheridan (New York: W. W. Norton, 1977).

27. Andreas Huyssens, "Mapping the Post-Modern," in his *After the Great Divide: Modernism, Mass Culture, Post-Modernism* (Bloomington: Indiana University Press, 1986) and Craig Owens, "The Discourse of Others: Feminists and Post-Modernism," in *The Anti-Aesthetic: Essays on Postmodern Culture*, ed. Hal Foster (Port Townsend, Washington: Bay Press, 1983). For the most accepted definition of the post-modern see Jean-François Lyotard, *The Postmodern Condition: A Report on Knowledge*, trans. Geoff Bennington and Brian Massumi (Minneapolis: University of Minnesota Press, 1984) and the counterargument of Jürgen Habermas in "Modernity vs. Postmodernity," *New German Critique* 22(Winter 1981): 3–14.

28. Hal Foster, "Post-Modernism: A Preface," *The Anti-Aesthetic*, p. xv.

29. See also Edward W. Said's historicized definition of the post-modern in relation to the post-colonial moment in "Representing the Colonized: Anthropology and its Interlocutors," *Critical Inquiry* 15, 2(Winter 1989): 205–225, and in his forthcoming *Culture and Imperialism*.

30. For a brilliant analysis of the uneasy relationships between feminism and modernity (the equivalent, in some sense, of what here I am calling postmodernism), see Alice Jardine, *Gynesis* (Ithaca: Cornell University Press, 1985).

31. F.e. Adrienne Rich in *Of Woman Born*, pp. 240–242, sees the novel as a modern version of the Demeter-Kore myth. Carol P. Christ, in *Diving Deep and*

Surfacing: Women Writers on Spiritual Quest (Boston: Beacon, 1980) and in "Margaret Atwood: The Surfacing of Women's Spiritual Quest and Vision" *Signs* 2, 2(Winter 1976): 316–330, reads Atwood's novel as a paradigmatic example of the feminist quest novel, illustrating the three stages of the quest—death, rebirth and integration. See also Judith Plaskow's response to Christ, "On Carol Christ on Margaret Atwood: Some Theological Reflections" *Signs* 2, 2(Winter 1976): 331–339. For Margaret Homans, *Surfacing* exemplifies the alternatives of appropriation and separatism in feminist writing confronting the dominant language and culture. See, " 'Her Very Own Howl': The Ambiguities of Representation in Recent Women's Fiction," *Signs* 9, 2 (Winter 1983): 186–205.

32. Margaret Atwood, *Life Before Man* (New York: Simon and Schuster, 1979). Atwood's novel about a paleontologist explores different forms of pre-history; "man" needs to be read both specifically and generically.

33. Marguerite Duras, *Un Barrage Contre le Pacifique* (Paris: Gallimard, 1958). *The Sea Wall* trans. Herma Briffault (New York: Perennial Library, 1986).

34. Marguerite Duras, *L'Eden Cinéma* (Paris: Mercure de France, 1977).

35. Susan Husserl-Kapit, "An Interview with Marguerite Duras," *Signs* 1, 2 (Winter 1975): 425.

36. "The Pain of Sorrow in the Modern World: The Work of Marguerite Duras," *PMLA* 102 (March 1987): 138–152. Also in *Soleil Noir: Dépression et Mélancolie* (Paris: Gallimard, 1987). Marcelle Marini offers an opposite reading of Duras, which highlights Duras's political writings and involvements in a talk given at Dartmouth College, April 1987.

37. Madeleine Borgomano, "L'"Histoire de la mendiante indienne: Une cellule génératrice de l'oeuvre de Marguerite Duras," *Poétique* 8(November 1981): 479–493. See also Madeleine Borgomano, *Duras: Une lecture des fantasmes* (Paris: Cistres Essais, 1987).

38. Marguerite Duras parle: "Elle a vendu un enfant," *Coll. Francais de notre temps*, no. 37. (Alliance Francaise), cited in Borgomano, p. 491 (my translation).

39. Michel Butor's novel *La Modification (Change of Heart)* (Paris: Minuit, 1957) offers one of the few examples of a novel written in the second person. See also Butor's *Essais sur le roman* (Paris: Gallimard, 1964) for a discussion of this structure of address.

40. "Diskussion mit Christa Wolf," (Okt. & Dec. 1975), in *Christa Wolf: Materialienbuch*, ed. Klaus Sauer (Darmstadt und Neuwied: Hermann Luchterhand Verlag, 1979), p. 44 (my translation).

41. In Christa Wolf, *The Reader and the Writer: Essays, Sketches, Memories*, trans. Joan Becker (New York: International Publishers, 1977), p. 202.

42. The GDR position is to place blame on the other side and to identify only with the resistance forces in the Nazi era. See Norbert Schachtsiek-Freitag, "Vom Versagen der Kritik: Die Aufnahme von *Kindheitsmuster* in beiden deutschen Staaten," in Sauer, pp. 117–130.

43. Jessica Benjamin, "The Oedipal Riddle," in *The Problem of Authority in America*, ed. John P. Diggins and Mark E. Kann (Philadelphia: Temple University Press, 1981).

44. Both Catherine A. MacKinnon in "Feminism, Marxism, Method and the State," *Signs* 7, 3(Spring 1982) and Teresa de Lauretis in *Alice Doesn't: Feminism, Semiotics, Cinema* (Bloomington: Indiana University Press, 1984) name the practice of consciousness-raising as an important formative factor in the emergence of what de Lauretis calls "the female subject of feminism." It would be interesting to study the participation of mothers in consciousness-raising groups during the 1970s. I suspect that the consciousness-raising movement was dominated by emerging

feminists who thought of themselves primarily as daughters. That certainly was my experience: although one of the members of my group was a mother, all of us spoke only of our experience as daughters. In part, of course, this was a generational issue.

5. Feminist Discourse/Maternal Discourse

1. Robin Morgan, *Going Too Far: The Personal Chronicle of a Feminist* (New York: Vintage, 1978), p. 8; *Sisterhood Is Powerful: An Anthology of Writings from the Women's Liberation Movement* (New York: Vintage, 1970).

2. Some related questions with which I cannot deal here but which are of crucial importance are: Can women be mothers if they have not given birth to children, or if they are not engaged in the work of child-rearing? Can/should men be mothers? Should the term *mothering* be replaced by *parenting* or *nurturing*?

3. When I use the term *feminist* in this chapter, I refer primarily to the United States feminist movement, including black American feminism, and to Western European feminisms. My aim is to uncover dominant trends and distinctions; I am aware, however, that in revealing these, I may be glossing over others.

4. Teresa de Lauretis, *Alice Doesn't: Feminism, Semiotics, Cinema* (Bloomington: Indiana University Press, 1984), p. 182.

5. These metaphors are often used interchangeably.

6. I discuss this progression from pre-oedipal mother-daughter closeness to identification and affiliation with sisters in chapter 4.

7. Bell Gale Chevigny, "Daughters Writing: Toward a Theory of Women's Biography," *Feminist Studies* 9, 1 (Spring 1983): 95–96. Also rpt. in *Between Women*, ed. Carol Ascher, Louise de Salvo, Sara Ruddick (Boston: Beacon Press, 1984).

8. See Jane Flax, "The Conflict between Nurturance and Autonomy in Mother/ Daughter Relationships and within Feminism," *Feminist Studies* 4, 1(February 1978): 171–189, for an analysis of some of these assumptions.

9. See, for example, Elaine Showalter: "We are both the daughters of the male tradition, of our teachers, our dissertation advisers, our publishers—a tradition which asks us to be marginal and grateful; and sisters in a new women's movement which engenders another kind of awareness and commitment, which demands that we renounce the pseudo-success of token womanhood, and the ironic masks of academic debate," "Towards a Feminist Poetics," in *Women Writing and Writing about Women*, ed. Mary Jacobus (London: Croom Helm, 1979), p. 39, also rpt. in Elaine Showalter, ed., *The New Feminist Criticism* (New York: Pantheon, 1986). In Showalter's "family," the feminist is both daughter and sister, she is never the mother. Similarly, Jane Gallop describes feminism as the seductive daughter of psychoanalysis, and herself as both the daughter and the grand-daughter of Lacan and Freud (grand-daughter by way of their other daughters and her mothers, Kristeva and Irigaray). See Jane Gallop, *The Daughter's Seduction: Feminism and Psychoanalysis* (Ithaca: Cornell University Press, 1982).

10. Here, of course, there are significant ethnic and cultural variations: matrophobia, for example, is stronger among white feminists than among black, just as one's relation to anger and one's ambivalence about authority varies with cultural and ethnic heritage. The identification of feminist consciousness with a desire for control seems more broadly applicable.

11. Fran Scoble, "Mothers and Daughters: Giving the Lie," *Denver Quarterly* 18, 4 (Winter 1984): 126–133.

12. Elizabeth V. Spellman, "Theories of Race and Gender: The Erasure of Black Women," *Quest: A Feminist Quarterly* 5, 4(1982): 36–62.

13. Nancy K. Miller, "Changing the Subject: Authorship, Writing and the Reader," in *Feminist Studies/Critical Studies*, ed. Teresa de Lauretis (Bloomington: Indiana University Press, 1986), p. 115. See also Adrienne Rich, *Of Woman Born*, p. 284, for a persuasive call for women to begin to *"think through the body,"* as well as Jane Gallop's *Thinking Through The Body* (New York: Columbia University Press, 1988).

14. See, for example, the analyses of Susan W. Contratto, "Maternal Sexuality and Asexual Motherhood," *Signs* 5, 4 (Summer 1980): 766–782 and Jane Gallop, *The Daughter's Seduction*.

15. Jane Gallop, *"Quand nos lèvres s'écrivent:* Irigaray's Body Politic," *Romanic Review* 74, 1(1983): 83.

16. See Dorothy Dinnerstein, *The Mermaid and the Minotaur: Sexual Arrangements and the Human Malaise* (New York: Harper & Row, 1976) and Jessica Benjamin, "The Bonds of Love: Rational Violence and Erotic Domination," *Feminist Studies* 6, 1 (Spring 1980): 144–174.

17. Nancy Chodorow and Susan Contratto, "The Fantasy of the Perfect Mother," in *Rethinking the Family*, ed. Barrie Thorne and Marilyn Yalom (New York: Longman, 1982).

18. For an effort to examine some of these more uncomfortable aspects of women's relationships, see Valerie Miner and Helen Longino, eds. *Competition: A Feminist Taboo?* (New York: The Feminist Press, 1987), in particular the essay by Evelyn Fox Keller and Helene Moglen, "Competition: A Problem for Academic Women," where the metaphors of mother-daughter and sister-sister relations are used to describe the interaction of academic women. See also the critique of Helena Michie, "Mother, Sister, Other: The 'Other Woman' in Feminist Theory," *Literature and Psychology* 32, 4(1986): 1–10.

19. Evelyn Fox Keller, *Reflections on Gender and Science* (New Haven: Yale University Press, 1985), p. 111.

20. See Susan Rubin Suleiman, "Writing and Motherhood," in *The (M)Other Tongue: Essays in Feminist Psychoanalytic Interpretation*, ed. Shirley Nelson Garner, Claire Kahane, Madelon Sprengnether (Ithaca: Cornell University Press, 1985) for an illuminating discussion of the child-centered bias of major psychoanalytic theories and of the incompatibility of *writing* and *motherhood*.

21. Sigmund Freud, "Femininity," (1933), *Standard Edition*, vol. 22, p. 124.

22. See D. W. Winnicott's definition: "The good-enough 'mother' (not necessarily the infant's own mother) is one who makes active adaptation to the infant's needs, an active adaptation that gradually lessens, according to the infant's growing ability to account for failure of adaptation and to tolerate the results of frustration." "Transitional Objects and Transitional Phenomena," in *Playing and Reality* (New York: Basic Books, 1971), p. 10.

23. See Juliet Mitchell and Jacqueline Rose, eds., *Feminine Sexuality: Jacques Lacan and the 'ecole freudienne'* (New York: Norton, 1982).

24. Linda Orr, "The Rage to Write," paper delivered at the The *Poetics of Anger* Colloquium, Columbia University, November 1985.

25. Marilyn Frye, *The Politics of Reality: Essays in Feminist Theory* (Trumansburg, N.Y.: The Crossing Press, 1983), p. 94.

26. I owe this formulation to Mieke Bal.

27. See Jean Baker Miller, "The Development of Women's Sense of Self," and "The Construction of Anger in Men and Women," *Work in Progress Series*, Stone Center for Developmental Services and Studies, Wellesley College, 1984; Judith Lewis Herman and Helen Block Lewis, "Anger in the Mother-Daughter Relationship," in *The Psychology of Today's Woman: A Psychoanalytic Perspective* ed. T. Bernay and D. Cantor (Boston: The Analytic Press, 1985); and Teresa Bernardez-Bonesatti, "Women and Anger: Conflicts with Aggression in Contemporary Women," *Journal of the AMWA* 33, 5(1987): 215–219.

28. Mary Jacobus, *Reading Woman: Essays in Feminist Criticism* (New York: Columbia University Press, 1986), p. 145.

29. Julia Kristeva, *Powers of Horror: An Essay on Abjection*, trans. Léon S. Roudiez (New York: Columbia University Press, 1982).

30. *Tales of Love*, trans. Léon Roudiez (New York: Columbia University Press, 1986).

31. Julia Kristeva, "Motherhood According to Giovanni Bellini," in *Desire in Language: A Semiotic Approach to Literature and Art*, ed. Léon S. Roudiez (New York: Columbia University Press, 1980), pp. 241–242.

32. Julia Kristeva, "L'Hérétique de l'amour," *Tel Quel* 74(Winter 1977): 30–49; "Stabat Mater" in *Histoires d'Amour* (Paris: Denoel, 1983); published in English translation in Susan Rubin Suleiman, ed., *The Female Body in Western Culture: Contemporary Perspectives* (Cambridge: Harvard University Press, 1986). See also "Un nouveau type d'intellectuel: le dissident," *Tel Quel* 74(Winter 1977), trans. in Toril Moi, ed., *The Kristeva Reader* (New York: Columbia University Press, 1986).

33. Gallop, *The Daughter's Seduction*. See also Ann Rosalind Jones, "Kristeva on Femininity: The Limits of a Semiotic Politics," *Feminist Review* 18(November 1984); Jacqueline Rose, "Julia Kristeva: Take Two," in her *Sexuality in the Field of Vision* (London: Verso, 1986); and Alice Jardine, "Opaque Texts and Transparent Contexts: The Political Difference of Julia Kristeva" in *The Poetics of Gender*, ed. Nancy K. Miller (New York: Columbia University Press, 1986).

34. Domna Stanton, "Difference on Trial: A Critique of The Maternal Metaphor in Cixous, Irigaray and Kristeva," in *The Poetics of Gender*.

35. See "Introduction," *Mothering the Mind: Twelve Studies of Writers and Their Silent Partners*, ed. Ruth Perry and Martine Watson Brownley (New York: Holmes and Meier, 1984).

36. Barbara Johnson, "Mallarmé as Mother: A Preliminary Sketch," in *A World of Difference* (Baltimore: Johns Hopkins University Press, 1987).

37. Johnson expresses particular caution about the male appropriation of the maternal position and its implications for the more effective silencing of women. See also Alice Jardine's reading of the "writing couple" where she shows how Simone de Beauvoir, allowing Sartre to perform a maternal role, has more thoroughly suppressed her actual mother: "Death Sentences: Writing Couples and Ideology," in *The Female Body in Western Culture* ed. Susan Rubin Suleiman.

38. See Nina Baym, "The Madwoman and Her Languages: Why I Don't Do Feminist Literary Theory," *Tulsa Studies in Women's Literature* 3, 1/2(Spring/Fall 1984): 45–59, for a critique of feminist literary theory as written from a daughterly perspective: "There is no future for a commonality of women if we cannot traverse the generations." See also Carol Gilligan and Eve Stern, "The Riddle of Femininity and the Psychology of Love," unpublished paper; Monique Plaza, "The Mother/ The Same: Hatred of the Mother in Psychoanalysis," *Feminist Issues* 2, 1(September 1982): 75–100; Garner, Kahane, and Sprengnether, eds., "Introduction," *The (M)Other Tongue*; E. Ann Kaplan, *Motherhood and Representation in Literature and Film, 1830–1960* (New York: Routledge, 1989); Judith Kegan Gardiner, "Maternal Metaphors, Women Readers and Female Identity," unpublished paper; Jane Gallop, "Reading the Mother Tongue: Psychoanalytic Feminist Criticism," *Critical Inquiry* 13, 2(Winter 1987): 314–329.

39. See also Suleiman's elaboration of this argument in "The 'Other Mother': On Maternal Splitting (a propos of Mary Gordon's *Men and Angels*)," *Signs* 14, 1(Autumn 1988), 25–41.

40. For another recent example, see Christine Froula, "The Daughter's Seduction: Sexual Violence and Literary History," *Signs* 11, 4(Summer 1986): 621–644.

41. In Johnson, *A World of Difference*.

224 Notes for pages 175-179

42. Ann Ferguson, "On Conceiving Motherhood and Sexuality," in *Mothering: Essays in Feminist Theory*, ed. Joyce Trebilcott (Totowa, N.J.: Rowman and Allanheld, 1983). Sara Ruddick, "Maternal Thinking," *Feminist Studies* 6, 2 (Summer 1980): 342–367. Shorter versions in Thorne and Yalom, eds., *Rethinking the Family* and in Trebilcott, ed., *Mothering: Essays in Feminist Theory*.

43. The same has been true of the reception of Carol Gilligan's *In a Different Voice* (Cambridge: Harvard University Press, 1982); writing in the tone of the ethic of care demands a generosity which can disguise, sometimes too effectively, the anger and ambivalence that are part of that ethic. Gilligan's book, especially the chapters analyzing her abortion study, offers important insights into women's relation to maternity. The women Gilligan studies all struggle to redefine a convention that equates goodness with self-sacrifice and to reconcile morality with a refusal of maternity. What is at issue is maturity and the search for a voice that would be capable of encompassing both "femininity and adulthood, in relationships and in work." See also Katherine Hayles, "Anger in Different Voices: Carol Gilligan and *The Mill on the Floss*," *Signs* 12, 1(Autumn 1986): 23–39.

44. Sara Ruddick, "Thinking about Mothering and Putting Maternal Thinking to Use," *Women's Studies Quarterly* 11, 4(Winter 1983): 5–6.

45. Mary Helen Washington, "I Sign My Mother's Name: Alice Walker, Dorothy West, Paule Marshall," in Perry and Brownley, eds., *Mothering the Mind*, p. 161.

46. Both in Alice Walker, *In Search of Our Mothers' Gardens* (New York: Harcourt Brace Jovanovich, 1983).

47. Paule Marshall, "Shaping the World of My Art," *New Letters* 40(Autumn 1973): 97–112.

48. Paule Marshall, "From in the Kitchen," *New York Times Book Review* (January 9, 1983), 3, 34–35.

49. Valerie Smith, "Writing Revolution: The Sixties as Text in Contemporary Black Women's Literature," paper delivered at the Conference of the School of Criticism and Theory at Dartmouth College on "Literature and History," April 1986. Smith argues that these writers use maternal voices as figures for their own ambivalence about the radical activism of the 1960s.

50. I continue to use the term "feminist" here although I am aware that it has been attacked by some women of color for its appropriation by white middle-class women. Alice Walker, for example, prefers the term "womanist" for black feminists.

51. E. Frances White, "Listening to the Voices of Black Feminism," *Radical America* 18, 2–3(Spring 1984). Mary Helen Washington pointed out to me that contemporary black women writers are responding to a powerful tradition of maternal praise going back to the times of slavery and the celebration of the resilience of the slave mother. For recent explorations of mother/daughter relationships in Afro-American culture, see Gloria I. Joseph and Jill Lewis, *Common Differences: Conflicts in Black and White Feminist Perspectives* (New York: Doubleday, 1981) and a special issue on mothers and daughters of *Sage: A Scholarly Journal on Black Women* 1, 2(Fall 1984).

52. Cited by Mary Helen Washington, "I Sign," p. 156.

53. Walker, "In Search of Our Mothers's Gardens," p. 233.

54. Toni Morrison, *Sula* (New York: New American Library, 1973).

55. Hortense J. Spillers, in "A Hateful Passion, A Lost Love," *Feminist Studies* 9, 2 (Summer 1983): 293–323, stresses the radical departure of Sula in relation to the tradition of black female writing. In its novelty *Sula* is representative of its generation, she says: "The black woman as artist, as an intellectual spokesperson for her own cultural apprenticeship, has not existed before, for anyone" (p. 297).

56. For a different view of the novel's representation of heterosexual relations, see Houston A. Baker, Jr., "When Lindbergh Sleeps with Bessie Smith: The Writing

of Place in Toni Morrison's *Sula*," Colloquium Paper, School of Criticism and Theory, Dartmouth College, 1987.

57. For an interesting discussion of lack as a figure for the experience of racial otherness, see Susan Willis, "Eruptions of Funk: Historicizing Toni Morrison," in *Black Literature and Literary Theory*, ed. Henry Louis Gates, Jr. (New York: Methuen, 1984).

58. Mary Helen Washington, in *Midnight Birds: Stories of Contemporary Black Women Writers* (Garden City, N.Y.: Anchor, 1980), pp. 153–155, calls Eva the "creator and sovereign" who "gives and takes life." Hortense Spillers says that "Eva behaves as though she were herself the sole instrument of divine inscrutable will," "A Hateful Passion," p. 314.

59. See Jacques Lacan, "The Meaning of the Phallus," in *Feminine Sexuality: Jacques Lacan and the 'école freudienne,'* Mitchell and Rose, eds., as well as "Introduction II" in the same volume, for a discussion of the notions of "phallic mother" and "masquerade." See also Joan Rivière, "Womanliness as Mascarade," *IJPA*, 10(1929): 303–313, and Michèle Montrelay, "An Inquiry into Femininity," *Semiotext(e)* 10, vol. 4, 1(1981): 228–235.

60. See Susan Willis's discussion of self-mutilation as a literary figure of black confrontation with white domination, "Eruptions," p. 277. Willis sees Sula's gesture as a more radical rebellion than I do.

61. Robert Stepto, " 'Intimate Things in Place': A Conversation with Toni Morrison," *The Massachusetts Review* 18(1977): 487.

62. For a discussion of the implications of the novel's celebration of female friendship, see Elizabeth Abel, "(E)Merging Identities: The Dynamics of Female Friendship in Contemporary Fiction by Women," *Signs* 6, 3(Spring 1981): 413–435, and Judith Kegan Gardiner, "The (Us)es of (I)dentity: A Response to Abel on '(E)Merging Identities,' " *Signs* 6, 3 (Spring 1981): 436–444. See also Adrienne Rich's reading of this novel as a representative of what she calls the "female double life," in "Compulsory Heterosexuality and Lesbian Existence" (1980) in *Blood, Bread and Poetry* (New York: Norton, 1986).

63. Margaret Homans, " 'Her Very Own Howl': The Ambiguities of Representation in Recent Women's Fiction," *Signs* 9, 2(Autumn 1983): 193.

64. Whereas critics like Hortense Spillers see in Sula's rejection of traditional womanhood a "radical alternative" and a "radical freedom," I find that the novel thematizes a much more ambivalent attitude toward the maternal, showing both its dangers and the dangers of rejecting it.

65. Adrienne Rich, *Of Woman Born*, p. 31. See also, Mary Gordon, "On Mothership and Authorhood," *The New York Times Book Review* (February 19, 1985): 1, 34–35, and Susan Rubin Suleiman, "Writing and Motherhood."

66. Helen Vendler, *Part of Nature, Part of Us* (Cambridge: Harvard University Press, 1980), p. 266.

67. My reading of *Everyday Use* is heavily influenced by discussions with Gail Reimer and Valerie Smith.

68. On quilting as an image for female writing in the American tradition, see Elaine Showalter, "Piecing and Writing," in *The Poetics of Gender*, ed. Miller, and Houston A. Baker, Jr. and Charlotte Pierce-Baker, "Patches: Quilts and Community in Alice Walker's 'Everyday Use,' " *The Southern Review* 21, 3 (July 1985): 706–720.

69. Walker has always insisted on a broadly defined female heritage. Thus *In Love and Trouble* is dedicated to Muriel Rukeyser, Jane Cooper, Zora Neale Hurston, Nella Larsen, and Jean Toomer. See Dianne F. Sadoff, "Black Matrilineage: The Case of Alice Walker and Zora Neale Hurston," *Signs: Journal of Women in Culture and Society* 11, 1(Autumn 1985): 4–26, and Deborah McDowell, " 'The Changing Same': Generational Connections and Black Women Novelists," *New Literary History* 18, 2(Winter 1987): 281–302.

70. See Walker's poem, "My Sister Molly Who in the Fifties," in *Revolutionary Petunias and Other Poems* (New York: Harcourt Brace Jovanovich, 1973) which suggests that she herself is Maggie.

71. For a discussion of "attentive love" see Sara Ruddick, "Maternal Thinking."

72. Also in Walker, *In Search of Our Mothers' Gardens*.

73. Peter Lyman, "The Politics of Anger: On Silence, Ressentiment and Political Speech," *Socialist Review* 11, 3 (1981): 69. See also Naomi Sheman, "Anger and the Politics of Naming," in *Women and Language in Culture and Society* ed. Sally McConnell-Ginet, Ruth Borker and Nelly Furman (New York: Praeger, 1980), and Elizabeth V. Spelman, "Anger and Insubordination," unpublished paper, Smith College.

74. For a helpful discussion of such a notion of identity derived from feminist self-consciousness and practice, see Teresa de Lauretis, "Feminist Studies/Critical Studies: Issues, Terms, Contexts," in her volume *Feminist Studies/Critical Studies*.

75. A slightly different version of my analysis of the Walker texts appeared in a special issue of the *minnesota review* on "Feminism, Psychoanalysis and Social Change," N.S. 29(Fall 1987): 81–87.

BIBLIOGRAPHY

Included in this bibliography are general texts in literary theory, feminist theory, and psychoanalytic theory used in this book. All primary and secondary texts of individual authors can be found in the notes to particular chapters.

Abel, Elizabeth. "(E)Merging Identities: The Dynamics of Female Friendship in Contemporary Fiction by Women." *Signs: Journal of Women in Culture and Society* 6.3 (1981):413–435.
———. *Virginia Woolf and the Fictions of Psychoanalysis.* Chicago: University of Chicago Press, 1989.
Abel, Elizabeth, Marianne Hirsch, and Elizabeth Langland, eds. *The Voyage In: Fictions of Female Development.* Hanover: University Press of New England, 1983.
Arcana, Judith. *Our Mothers' Daughters.* Berkeley: Shameless Hussy Press, 1979.
Ascher, Carol, Louise de Salvo, and Sara Ruddick, eds. *Between Women.* Boston: Beacon, 1984.
Atwood, Margaret. "What Is a Woman's Novel? For That Matter, What Is a Man's?" *MS.* August 1986:98.
Auerbach, Nina. "Artists and Mothers: A False Alliance." *Women and Literature* 6.1 (Spring 1978):3–15.
———. *Communities of Women: An Idea in Fiction.* Cambridge: Harvard University Press, 1978.
———. *Woman and the Demon: The Life of a Victorian Myth.* Cambridge: Harvard University Press, 1982.
Bachofen, J. J. *Myth, Religion and Mother-Right: Selected Writings.* Trans. Ralph Manheim. Princeton: Princeton University Press, 1967.
Badinter, Elisabeth. *Mother Love: Myth and Reality.* New York: Macmillan, 1981.
Bakhtin, M. M. *The Dialogic Imagination: Four Essays.* Trans. Caryl Emerson and Michael Holquist. Ed. Michael Holquist. Austin: University of Texas Press, 1983.
Balmary, Marie. *Psychoanalyzing Psychanalysis: Freud and the Hidden Fault of the Father.* Trans. Ned Lukacher. Baltimore: Johns Hopkins University Press, 1982.
Baym, Nina. "The Madwoman and Her Languages: Why I Don't Do Feminist Literary Theory." *Tulsa Studies in Women's Literature* 3.1/2 (1984):45–59.
Beer, Gillian. *Darwin's Plots: Evolutionary Narrative in Darwin, George Eliot and Nineteenth-Century Fiction.* London: Routledge and Kegan Paul, 1983.
Benjamin, Jessica. "Authority and the Family Revisited, or, a World without Fathers?" *New German Critique* 13 (1978):35–58.
———. *The Bonds of Love: Psychoanalysis, Feminism, and the Problem of Domination.* New York: Pantheon, 1988.
Bennett, Paula. *My Life A Loaded Gun: Female Creativity and Feminist Poetics.* Boston: Beacon, 1986.
Bernard, Jessie. *The Future of Motherhood.* New York: Dial, 1974.

Bernardez-Bonesatti, Teresa. "Women and Anger: Conflicts with Aggression in Contemporary Women." *Journal of the AMWA* 33.5 (1978):215–219.

Bernheimer, Charles, and Claire Kahane, eds. *In Dora's Case: Freud, Hysteria, Feminism*. New York: Columbia University Press, 1985.

Bernikow, Louise. *Among Women*. New York: Harper, 1981.

Bersani, Leo. *A Future for Astyanax: Character and Desire in Literature*. Boston: Little Brown, 1976.

Boone, Joseph Allen. *Tradition Counter Tradition: Love and the Form of Fiction*. Chicago: University of Chicago Press, 1987.

Boose, Lynda E. and Betty S. Flowers, eds., *Daughters and Fathers*. Baltimore: Johns Hopkins University Press, 1989.

Brewer, Maria Minich. " 'A Loosening of Tongues': From Narrative Economy to Women's Writing." *MLN* 99 (1984):1141–61.

Briffault, Robert. *The Mothers: A Study of the Origins of Sentiments and Institutions*. New York: Macmillan, 1927.

Brooks, Peter. "The Idea of a Psychoanalytic Literary Criticism." *Critical Inquiry* 13.2 (1987):334–348.

———. *Reading for the Plot: Design and Intention in Narrative*. New York: Alfred A. Knopf, 1984.

Brownstein, Rachel M. *Becoming a Heroine: Reading about Women in Novels*. New York: Penguin, 1984.

Burck, Frances Wells. *Mothers Talking: Sharing the Secret*. New York: St. Martin's Press, 1986.

Burke, Carolyn. "Report from Paris: Women's Writing and the Women's Movement." *Signs* 3.4 (1978):843–855.

Cahill, Susan. *Motherhood: A Reader for Men and Women*. New York: Avon, 1982.

Caplan, Paula J. *Between Women: Lowering the Barriers*. Toronto: Personal Library, 1981.

Carruthers, Mary. "Imagining Women: Notes toward a Feminist Poetic." *Massachusetts Review* 20 (1979):281–307.

Chase, Cynthia. *Decomposing Figures: Rhetorical Readings in the Romantic Tradition*. Baltimore: Johns Hopkins University Press, 1986.

Chernin, Kim. *The Hungry Self: Women, Eating, and Identity*. New York: Harper & Row, 1986.

Chesler, Phyllis. *Mothers on Trial: The Battle for Children and Custody*. Seattle, Washington: Seal, 1987.

———. *Sacred Bond: The Legacy of Baby M*. New York: Times Books, 1988.

Chevigny, Bell Gale. "Daughters Writing: Toward a Theory of Women's Biography." *Feminist Studies* 9.1 (1983):79–102.

Chodorow, Nancy. "Feminism and Difference: Gender, Relation and Difference in Psychanalytic Perspective." *Socialist Review* 46 (1979):51–69.

———. "Mothering, Object-Relations and the Female Oedipal Configuration." *Feminist Studies* 4.1 (1978):137–138.

———. *The Reproduction of Mothering: Psychoanalysis and the Sociology of Gender*. Berkeley: University of California Press, 1978.

Chodorow, Nancy, and Susan Contratto. "The Fantasy of the Perfect Mother." *Rethinking the Family*. Ed. Barrie Thorne and Marilyn Yalom. New York: Longman, 1982.

Christian, Barbara. *Black Feminist Criticism: Perspectives on Black Women Writers*. New York: Pergamon, 1985.

Cixous, Hélène, and Catherine Clément. *The Newly Born Woman*. Trans. Betsy Wing. Minneapolis: University of Minnesota Press, 1986.

Contratto, Susan. "Maternal Sexuality and Asexual Motherhood." *Signs* 5.4 (1980):766–782.

Coward, Rosalind. *Patriarchal Precedents: Sexuality and Social Relations.* London: Routledge and Kegan Paul, 1983.

Culler, Jonathan. *On Deconstruction: Theory and Criticism after Structuralism.* Ithaca: Cornell University Press, 1982.

Culley, Margo, et al. "The Politics of Nurturance." *Gendered Subjects: The Dynamics of Feminist Teaching.* Ed. Margo Culley and Catherine Portuges. Boston: Routledge and Kegan Paul, 1985.

Dally, Ann. *Inventing Motherhood: The Consequences of an Ideal.* New York: Schocken, 1983.

Davidson, Cathy N., and E. M. Broner, eds. *The Lost Tradition: Mothers and Daughters in Literature.* New York: Frederick Ungar, 1980.

Davis, Robert Con, ed. *The Fictional Father: Lacanian Readings of the Text.* Amherst: University of Massachusetts Press, 1981.

de Lauretis, Teresa. *Alice Doesn't: Feminism, Semiotics, Cinema.* Bloomington: Indiana University Press, 1984.

————, ed. *Feminist Studies/ Critical Studies.* Bloomington: Indiana University Press, 1986.

————. *Technologies of Gender: Essays on Theory, Film and Fiction.* Bloomington: Indiana University Press, 1987.

Deleuze, Gilles, and Félix Guattari. *Anti-Oedipus: Capitalism and Schizophrenia.* Trans. Robert Hurley, Mark Seem, and Helen R. Lane. Minneapolis: University of Minnesota Press, 1983.

Derrida, Jacques, and Christie V. McDonald. "Choreographies." *Diacritics* 12 (1982):66–76.

Dill, Bonnie Thornton. "Race, Class and Gender: Prospects for an All-Inclusive Sisterhood." *Feminist Studies* 9.1 (1983):131–150.

Dinnerstein, Dorothy. *The Mermaid and the Minotaur: Sexual Arrangements and Human Malaise.* New York: Harper Colophon Books, 1977.

Downing, Christine. *The Goddess: Mythological Images of the Feminine.* New York: Crossroad, 1981.

DuPlessis, Rachel Blau. *Writing beyond the Ending: Narrative Strategies of Twentieth-Century Women Writers.* Bloomington: Indiana University Press, 1985.

Duras, Marguerite, and Xavière Gauthier. *Les Parleuses.* Paris: Minuit, 1979.

Eagleton, Terry. *Criticism and Ideology: A Study of Marxist Literary Theory.* London: New Left Books, 1976

Edwards, Lee R. *Psyche As Hero: Female Heroism and Fictional Form.* Middletown, Connecticut: Wesleyan University Press, 1984.

Ehrenreich, Barbara, and Deirdre English. *For Her Own Good: 150 Years of the Experts' Advice to Women.* Garden City, N.Y.: Anchor, 1978.

Eichenbaum, Luise, and Susie Orbach. *Understanding Women: A Feminist Psychoanalytic Approach.* New York: Basic Books, 1983.

Eisenstein, Hester, and Alice Jardine, eds. *The Future of Difference.* Boston: G. K. Hall & Co., 1980.

Ellmann, Mary. *Thinking about Women.* New York: Harcourt, 1968.

Erikson, Erik H. *Identity: Youth and Crisis.* New York: Norton, 1968.

Ermarth, Elizabeth Deeds. *Realism and Consensus in the English Novel.* Princeton: Princeton University Press, 1983.

Fairbairn, W. R. D. *An Object-Relations Theory of Personality.* New York: Basic Books, 1952.

Feit-Diehl, Joanne. " 'Come Slowly Eden': An Exploration of Women Poets and Their Muse." *Signs* 3.3 (1978):572–587.

Felman, Shoshana. "Beyond Oedipus: The Specimen Story of Psychoanalysis." *Lacan and Narration: The Psychoanalytic Difference in Narrative Theory.*

Ed. Robert Con Davis. Baltimore: Johns Hopkins University Press, 1983.

Firestone, Shulamith. *The Dialectic of Sex: The Case for Feminist Revolution.* New York: Bantam, 1971.

Fisher, Berenice. "Guilt and Shame in the Women's Movement: The Radical Ideal of Action and Its Meaning for Feminist Intellectuals." *Feminist Studies* 10.7 (1984):185–212.

Fisher, Bev. "Race and Class: Beyond Personal Politics." *Quest* 3.4 (1977):2–14.

Flax, Jane. "The Conflict between Nurturance and Autonomy in Mother/Daughter Relationships and within Feminism." *Feminist Studies* 4.1 (1978):171–189.

Flynn, Elizabeth A., and Patrocinio P. Schweickart, eds. *Gender and Reading: Essays on Readers, Texts, and Contexts.* Baltimore: Johns Hopkins University Press, 1986.

Foster, Hal. *The Anti-Aesthetic: Essays on Postmodern Culture.* Port Townsend, Washington: Bay Press, 1983.

Foucault, Michel. *The History of Sexuality. Volume 1: An Introduction.* Trans. Robert Hurley. New York: Vintage, 1980.

Freud, Sigmund. *The Standard Edition of the Complete Psychological Works of Sigmund Freud.* 24 vols. Ed. and trans. James Strachey. London: Hogarth, 1953–74.

Friday, Nancy. *My Mother/My Self: The Daughter's Search for Identity.* New York: Delacorte, 1977.

Friedman, Susan Stanford. "Creativity and the Childbirth Metaphor: Gender Difference in Literary Discourse." *Feminist Studies* 13.1 (1987):49–82.

Frye, Marilyn. *The Politics of Reality: Essays in Feminist Theory.* Trumansburg, N.Y.: The Crossing Press, 1983.

————. "Who Wants a Piece of the Pie?" *Quest* 3.3 (1977):28–35.

Gallagher, Catherine. *The Industrial Reformation of English Fiction: Social Discourse and Narrative Form, 1832–1867.* Chicago: University of Chicago Press, 1985.

Gallop, Jane. *The Daughter's Seduction: Feminism and Psychoanalysis.* Ithaca: Cornell University Press, 1982.

————. "Monster in the Mirror: The Feminist Critic's Psychoanalysis." *Feminism and Psychoanalysis.* Ed. Richard Feldstein and Judith Roof. Ithaca: Cornell University Press, 1989.

————. *Reading Lacan.* Ithaca: Cornell University Press, 1985.

————. "Reading the Mother Tongue: Psychoanalytic Feminist Criticism." *Critical Inquiry* 13.1 (1987):314–329.

————. *Thinking Through The Body.* New York: Columbia University Press, 1988.

Gardiner, Judith Kegan. "The New Motherhood." *North American Review* 263.2 (1978):72–76.

————. "A Wake for Mother: The Maternal Deathbed in Women's Fiction." *Feminist Studies* 4.1 (1978):146–165.

Garner, Shirley Nelson, Claire Kahane, and Madelon Sprengnether, eds. *The (M)other Tongue: Essays in Feminist Psychoanalytic Interpretation.* Ithaca: Cornell University Press, 1985.

Gates, Henry Louis, Jr., ed. *Black Literature and Literary Theory.* New York: Methuen, 1984.

Gerson, Kathleen. *Hard Choices: How Women Decide about Work, Career, and Motherhood.* Berkeley: University of California Press, 1985.

Giddings, Paula. *When and Where I Enter: The Impact of Black Women on Race and Sex in America.* New York: Bantam, 1985.

Gilbert, Sandra M., and Susan Gubar. *The Madwoman in the Attic: The Woman Writer and the Nineteenth-Century Literary Imagination.* New Haven: Yale University Press, 1979.

———. *No Man's Land: The Place of the Woman Writer in the Twentieth Century, Vol. 1, The War of the Words.* New Haven: Yale University Press, 1988.

Gilligan, Carol. "The Conquistador and the Dark Continent: Reflections on the Psychology of Love." *Daedalus* August 1984:75–95.

———. *In A Different Voice: Psychological Theory and Women's Development.* Cambridge: Harvard University Press, 1982.

Girard, René. *Deceit, Desire, and the Novel: Self and Other in Literary Structure.* Trans. Yvonne Freccero. Baltimore: Johns Hopkins University Press, 1969.

Gordon, Linda. *Woman's Body, Woman's Right: A Social History of Birth Control in America.* New York: Penguin, 1977.

Gordon, Mary. "On Mothership and Authorhood." *New York Times Book Review* 19 February 1985: 34–35.

Greene, Gayle, and Coppélia Kahn, eds. *Making a Difference: Feminist Literary Criticism.* London: Methuen, 1985.

Griffin, Susan. *Woman and Nature: The Roaring Inside Her.* New York: Harper, 1980.

Grosskurth, Phyllis. *Melanie Klein: Her World and Her Work.* New York: Alfred A. Knopf, 1986.

Guntrip, Harry. *Psychoanalytic Theory, Therapy, and the Self: A Basic Guide to the Human Personality in Freud, Erikson, Klein, Sullivan, Fairbairn, Hartmann, Jacobson, and Winnicott.* New York: Basic Books, 1973.

Hall, Nor. *The Moon and the Virgin: Reflections on the Archetypal Feminine.* New York: Harper & Row, 1980.

Hamilton, Roberta, and Michèle Barrett, eds. *The Politics of Diversity: Feminism, Marxism, and Nationalism.* London: Verso, 1986.

Hammer, Signe. *Daughters and Mothers: Mothers and Daughters.* New York: New American Library, 1976.

Haraway, Donna. "A Manifesto for Cyborgs: Science, Technology, and Socialist Feminism in the 1980s." *Socialist Review* (1985):65–107.

Harding, M. Esther. *The Way of All Women: A Psychological Interpretation.* New York: Harper & Row, 1975.

———. *Woman's Mysteries, Ancient and Modern: A Psychological Interpretation of the Feminine Principle as Portrayed in Myth, Story, and Dreams.* New York: Harper & Row, 1976.

Harley, Sharon, and Roslyn Terborg-Penn, eds. *The Afro-American Woman: Struggles and Images.* Port Washington, N.Y.: Kennikat, 1978.

Heath, Stephen. *The Sexual Fix.* New York: Schocken, 1984.

Hedin, Raymond. "The Structuring of Emotion in Black American Fiction." *Novel* (1982):35–54.

Heilbrun, Carolyn G. *Writing a Woman's Life.* New York: W.W. Norton, 1988.

———, and Margaret R. Higonnet, eds. *The Representation of Women in Fiction: Selected Papers from the English Institute, 1981.* Baltimore: Johns Hopkins University Press, 1983.

Herman, Judith Lewis, and Lisa Hirschman. *Father-Daughter Incest.* Cambridge: Harvard University Press, 1981.

Herman, Judith Lewis, and Helen Block Lewis. "Anger in the Mother-Daughter Relationship." *The Psychology of Today's Woman: A Psychoanalytic Perspective.* Ed. T. Bernay and D. Cantor. Boston: Analytic, 1985.

Herrmann, Claudine. *Les Voleuses de langue.* Paris: des femmes, 1976.

Hertz, Neil. *The End of the Line: Essays on Psychoanalysis and the Sublime.* New York: Columbia University Press, 1985.

Hirsch, Marianne. "Incorporation and Repetition in *La Princesse de Clèves.*" *Yale French Studies* 62 (1981):67–87.

——. "Mothers and Daughters: A Review Essay." *Signs* 7.1 (Autumn 1981):200–222.

——. "Ideology, Form and 'Allerleirauh': Reflections on *Reading for the Plot*." *Children's Literature* 14 (1986):163–168.

Homans, Margaret. *Bearing the Word: Language and Female Experience in Nineteenth-Century Women's Writing*. Chicago: University of Chicago Press, 1986.

——. " 'Her Very Own Howl': The Ambiguities of Representation in Recent Women's Fiction." *Signs* 9.2 (1983):186-205.

——. *Women Writers and Poetic Identity: Dorothy Wordsworth, Emily Brontë, and Emily Dickinson*. Princeton: Princeton University Press, 1980.

Hooks, Bell. *Feminist Theory: From Margin to Center*. Boston: South End Press, 1984.

Horney, Karen. *New Ways in Psychoanalysis*. New York: Norton, 1966.

Huyssens, Andreas. *After the Great Divide: Modernism, Mass Culture, Post-Modernism*. Bloomington: Indiana University Press, 1986.

Irigaray, Luce. "And the One Doesn't Stir Without the Other." Trans. Hélène Vivienne Wenzel. *Signs* 7.1 (1981):60–67.

——. *Ce sexe qui n'en est pas un*. Paris: Minuit, 1977.

——. *Le corps-à-corps avec la mère*. Montréal: Les éditions de la pleine lune, 1981.

——. *Et l'une ne bouge pas sans l'autre*. Paris: Minuit, 1979.

——. *Éthique de la différence sexuelle*. Paris: Minuit, 1984.

——. *Speculum of the Other Woman*. Trans. Gillian C. Gill. Ithaca: Cornell University Press, 1985.

——. *This Sex Which Is Not One*. Trans. Catherine Porter and Carolyn Burke. Ithaca: Cornell University Press, 1985.

——. "When Our Lips Speak Together." Trans. Carolyn Burke. *Signs* 6.1 (1980):69–79.

Jacobus, Mary. *Reading Woman: Essays in Feminist Criticism*. New York: Columbia University Press, 1986.

——, ed. *Women Writing and Writing about Women*. London: Croom Helm, 1979.

Jameson, Fredric. *The Political Unconscious: Narrative as a Socially Symbolic Act*. Ithaca: Cornell University Press, 1982.

Jardine, Alice A. "Death Sentences: Writing Couples and Ideology." *Poetics Today* 6.1/2 (1985):119-131.

——. *Gynesis: Configurations of Woman and Modernity*. Ithaca: Cornell University Press, 1985.

Johnson, Barbara. *A World of Difference*. Baltimore: Johns Hopkins University Press, 1987.

Joplin, Patricia Klindienst. "The Voice of the Shuttle Is Ours." *Stanford Literary Review* 1.1 (1984):25–53.

Joseph, Gloria. I., and Jill Lewis. *Common Differences: Conflicts in Black and White Feminist Perspectives*. New York: Anchor, 1981.

Jung, Carl G., and C. Kerényi. *Essays on a Science of Mythology: The Myths of the Divine Child and the Divine Maiden*. New York: Harper Torchbooks, 1963.

Kahn, Coppélia. "Excavating 'Those Dim Minoan Regions': Maternal Subtexts in Patriarchal Literature." *Diacritics* 12 (1982):32-41.

Kamuf, Peggy. *Fictions of Feminine Desire*. Lincoln: University of Nebraska Press, 1982.

Kaplan, E. Ann. *Motherhood and Representation in Literature and Film, 1830–1960*. New York: Routledge, 1989.

Keller, Evelyn Fox, *Reflections on Gender and Science*. New Haven: Yale University Press, 1988.

Kelly, Mary. *Post-Partum Document*. London: Routledge and Kegan Paul, 1985.

Kerényi, C. *Eleusis: Archetypal Image of Mother and Daughter*. Trans. Ralph Manheim. New York: Schocken, 1977.

Klein, Melanie. *Love, Guilt and Reparation and Other Works, 1921–1945*. New York: Dell, 1975.

Kofman, Sarah. *The Enigma of Woman: Woman in Freud's Writings*. Trans. Catherine Porter. Ithaca: Cornell University Press, 1985.

Kolodny, Annette. "A Map of Rereading: Or, Gender and the Interpretation of Literary Texts." *New Literary History* 11.3 (1980):451–467.

Koppelman, Susan. *Between Mothers and Daughters; Stories Across a Generation*. Old Westbury, N.Y.: Feminist Press, 1985.

Kristeva, Julia. *About Chinese Women*. Trans. Anita Barrows. New York: Urizen Books, 1977.

———. *Desire in Language: A Semiotic Approach to Literature and Art*. Ed. Léon S. Roudiez and trans. Thomas Gora, Alice Jardine, and Léon S. Roudiez. New York: Columbia University Press. 1980.

———. *Histoires d'amour*. Paris: Denoël, 1983.

———. *Polylogue*. Paris: Seuil, 1977.

———. *Powers of Horror: An Essay on Abjection*. Trans. Léon S. Roudiez. New York: Columbia University Press, 1982.

———. *La révolution du langage poétique: l'avant-garde à la fin du XIXe siècle: Lautréamont et Mallarmé*. Paris: Seuil, 1974.

———. *Tales of Love*. Trans. Léon S. Roudiez. New York: Columbia University Press, 1986.

Kuhn, Annette, and AnnMarie Wolpe, eds. *Feminism and Materialism: Women and Modes of Production*. London: Routledge and Kegan Paul, 1980.

Lacan, Jacques. *Écrits: A Selection*. Trans. Alan Sheridan. New York: Norton, 1977.

———. *The Language of the Self: The Function of Language in Psychoanalysis*. Trans. Anthony Wilden. New York: Dell, 1968.

Lanser, Susan Snaider. *The Narrative Act: Point of View in Prose Fiction*. Princeton: Princeton University Press, 1981.

———. "Toward a Feminist Narratology." *Style* 20.3 (1986):341–363.

Lazarre, Jane. *The Mother Knot*. Boston: Beacon, 1986.

Lemoine-Luccioni, Eugénie. *Partage des femmes*. Paris: Seuil, 1982.

Leonard, Linda Schierse. *The Wounded Woman: Healing the Father-Daughter Relationship*. Boulder, Colorado: Shambhala, 1983.

Lerner, Harriet Goldhor. *The Dance of Anger: A Woman's Guide to Changing the Patterns of Intimate Relationships*. New York: Harper & Row, 1986.

Levine, George. *The Realistic Imagination: English Fiction from Frankenstein to Lady Chatterley*. Chicago: University of Chicago Press, 1981.

Lorber, Judith, et al. "On *The Reproduction of Mothering*: A Methodological Debate." *Signs* 6.3 (1981):482–514.

Lorde, Audre. *Sister Outsider*. Trumansburg, N.Y.: Crossing Press, 1984.

Lugones, María C., and Elizabeth V. Spelman. "Have We Got a Theory for You! Feminist Theory, Cultural Imperialism and the Demand for 'the Woman's Voice'." *Women's Studies International Forum* 6.6 (1983):573–581.

Lukács, Georg. *Studies in European Realism*. New York: Grosset, 1964.

Luker, Kristin. *Abortion and the Politics of Motherhood*. Berkeley: University of California Press, 1985.

MacKinnon, Catherine. "Feminism, Marxism, Method and the State: An Agenda for Theory." *Signs* 7.3 (1982):515–544.

Mahler, Margaret, Fred Pine, and Anni Bergman. *The Psychological Birth of the Human Infant*. New York: Basic Books, 1975.

Manheimer, Joan. "Murderous Mothers: The Problem of Parenting in the Victorian Novel." *Feminist Studies* 5.3 (1979):530–546.

Marks, Elaine. "Women and Literature in France." *Signs* 3.4 (1978):832–842.

Marks, Elaine, and Isabelle de Courtivron, eds. *New French Feminisms: An Anthology*. Amherst: University of Massachusetts Press, 1980.

Masson, Jeffrey Moussaieff. *The Assault on Truth: Freud's Suppression of the Seduction Theory*. New York: Penguin, 1985.

McBride, Angela Barron. *The Growth and Development of Mothers*. New York: Harper & Row, 1973.

McConnell-Ginet, Sally, Ruth Borker, and Nelly Furman, eds. *Women and Language in Literature and Society*. New York: Praeger, 1980.

McDowell, Deborah E. "New Directions for Black Feminist Criticism." *Black American Literature Forum* 14 (1980):153–158.

Meese, Elizabeth A. *Crossing the Double-Cross: The Practice of Feminist Criticism*. Chapel Hill: University of North Carolina Press, 1986.

Michie, Helena. "Mother, Sister, Other: The 'Other Woman' in Feminist Theory." *Literature and Psychology* 32.2 (1986):1–10.

Miller, D. A. *Narrative and Its Discontents*. Princeton: Princeton University Press, 1981.

Miller, Jean Baker. "The Construction of Anger in Men and Women." *Work in Progress Series*. Stone Center for Developmental Services and Studies, Wellesley College, 1984.

———. "The Development of Women's Sense of Self." *Work in Progress Series*. Stone Center for Developmental Services and Studies, Wellesley College, 1984.

———, ed. *Psychoanalysis and Women*. New York: Penguin, 1978.

———. *Toward a New Psychology of Women*. Boston: Beacon, 1977.

Miller, Nancy K. "Emphasis Added: Plots and Plausibilities in Women's Fiction." *The New Feminist Criticism: Essays on Women, Literature, Theory*. Ed. Elaine Showalter. New York: Pantheon, 1985.

———. *The Heroine's Text*. New York: Columbia University Press, 1980.

———, ed. *The Poetics of Gender*. New York: Columbia University Press, 1986.

———. *Subject to Change: Reading Feminist Writing*. New York: Columbia University Press, 1988.

Miner, Valerie, and Helen Longino. *Competition: A Feminist Taboo?* New York: Feminist Press, 1987.

Mitchell, Juliet. *Psychoanalysis and Feminism: Freud, Reich, Laing and Women*. New York: Vintage, 1975.

Mitchell, Juliet, and Jacqueline Rose, eds. *Feminine Sexuality: Jacques Lacan and the 'école freudienne.'* Trans. Jacqueline Rose. New York: Norton, 1982.

Moers, Ellen. *Literary Women*. Garden City, N.Y.: Anchor, 1977.

Mohanty, Chandra Talpede. "Feminist Encounters: Locating the Politics of Experience." *Copyright* 1.1 (1988):30–44.

———. "Under Western Eyes: Feminist Scholarship and Colonial Discourses." *boundary* 2/xii, 3/xii. (1984):333–358.

Moi, Toril. *Sexual/Textual Politics: Feminist Literary Theory*. London: Methuen, 1985.

Montrelay, Michèle. *L'ombre et le nom: sur la féminité*. Paris: Minuit, 1977.

———. "An Inquiry into Femininity." *Semiotext(e)* 10 4.1 (1981):228–235.

Moraga, Cherríe, and Gloria Anzaldúa. *This Bridge Called My Back: Writings by Radical Women of Color*. New York: Kitchen Table Press, 1981 and 1983.

Neumann, Erich. *The Great Mother: An Analysis of the Archetype*. Trans. Ralph Manheim. Princeton: Bollingen, 1974.

Newton, Judith, and Deborah Rosenfelt, eds. *Feminist Criticism and Social Change: Sex, Class, and Race in Literature and Culture*. New York: Methuen, 1985.

O'Brien, Mary. *The Politics of Reproduction*. London: Routledge and Kegan Paul, 1981.

Olivier, Christiane. *Les Enfants de Jocaste*. Paris: Denoël, 1980.

Olsen, Tillie. *Silences*. New York: Delta, 1979.

Ostriker, Alicia Suskin. *Stealing the Language: The Emergence of Women's Poetry in America*. Boston: Beacon, 1986.

Payne, Karen, ed. *Between Ourselves: Letters Between Mothers and Daughters 1750–1982*. Boston: Houghton, 1983.

Perry, Ruth, and Martine Watson Brownley, eds. *Mothering the Mind: Twelve Studies of Writers and Their Silent Partners*. New York: Holmes and Meier, 1984.

Plath, Sylvia. *Letters Home: Correspondence 1950–63*. Ed. Aurelia Schober Plath. New York: Bantam, 1977.

Plaza, Monique. "The Mother/The Same: Hatred of the Mother in Psychoanalysis." *Feminist Issues* 2.1 (1982):75–100.

Pomeroy, Sarah B. *Goddesses, Whores, Wives, and Slaves*. New York: Schocken, 1976.

Poovey, Mary. *The Proper Lady and the Woman Writer: Ideology as Style in the Works of Mary Wollstonecraft, Mary Shelley, and Jane Austen*. Chicago: University of Chicago Press, 1984.

Poston, Carol. "Childbirth in Literature." *Feminist Studies* 4.1 (1978):18–31.

Pratt, Annis, et al. *Archetypal Patterns in Women's Fiction*. Bloomington: Indiana University Press, 1981.

Pryse, Marjorie, and Hortense Spillers, ed. *Conjuring: Black Women and Literary Tradition*. Bloomington: Indiana University Press, 1985.

Reiter, Rayna R., ed. *Toward an Anthropology of Women*. New York: Monthly Review, 1975.

Rich, Adrienne. *Blood, Bread and Poetry: Selected Prose, 1979–1985*. New York: Norton, 1986.

———. *Of Woman Born: Motherhood as Experience and Institution*. New York: Norton, 1976.

———. *On Lies, Secrets and Silence: Selected Prose, 1966–1978*. New York: Norton, 1979.

Riley, Denise. "Does Sex Have a History: 'Women' and Feminism." *New Formations* 1 (1987):35–45.

Rimmon-Kenan, Shlomith. *Discourse in Psychoanalysis and Literature*. London: Methuen, 1987.

Rivière, Joan. "Womanliness as Mascarade." *IJPA* 10 (1929):303–313.

Rosaldo, Michelle Zimbalist, and Louise Lamphere, eds. *Woman, Culture, and Society*. Stanford: Stanford University Press, 1974.

Rose, Jacqueline. *Sexuality in the Field of Vision*. London: Verso, 1986.

Ruddick, Sara. *From Maternal Thinking to Peace Politics*. Boston: Beacon, 1989.

———. "Maternal Thinking." *Feminist Studies* 6.2 (1980):342–367.

———. "Preservative Love and Military Destruction: Some Reflections on Mothering and Peace." *Mothering: Essays in Feminist Theory*. Ed. Joyce Trebilcott. New York: Rowman and Allenheld, 1984.

Russ, Joanna. *How to Suppress Women's Writing*. Austin: University of Texas Press, 1983.

———. *Magic Mommas, Trembling Sisters, Puritans, and Perverts: Feminist Essays*. Trumansburg, New York: Crossing, 1985.

Sadoff, Dianne F. "Black Matrilineage: The Case of Alice Walker and Zora Neale Hurston." *Signs* 11.1 (1985):4–26.

———. *Monsters of Affection: Dickens, Eliot and Brontë on Fatherhood*. Baltimore: Johns Hopkins University Press, 1982.

Said, Edward W. *Beginnings: Intention and Method*. Baltimore: Johns Hopkins University Press, 1975.

———. *The World, the Text, and the Critic*. Cambridge: Harvard University Press, 1983.

Sayers, Janet. *Sexual Contradictions: Psychology, Psychoanalysis, and Feminism*. London: Tavistock, 1986.

Schenk, Celeste M. "Feminism and Deconstruction: Re-Constructing the Elegy." *Tulsa Studies in Women's Literature* 5.1 (1986):13–27.

Schor, Naomi. *Breaking the Chain: Women, Theory, and French Realist Fiction*. New York: Columbia University Press, 1985.

Sedgwick, Eve Kosofsky. *Between Men: English Literature and Male Homosocial Desire*. New York: Columbia University Press, 1985.

Sheman, Naomi. "Anger and the Politics of Naming." *Women and Language in Literature and Society*. Ed. Sally McConnell-Ginet, Ruth Borker, and Nelly Furman. New York: Praeger, 1980.

Showalter, Elaine. *The Female Malady: Women, Madness, and English Culture, 1830–1980*. New York: Pantheon, 1985.

———. *A Literature of Their Own: British Women Novelists from Brontë to Lessing*. Princeton: Princeton University Press, 1977.

———, ed. *The New Feminist Criticism*. New York: Pantheon, 1986.

———. "Women Who Write Are Women." *New York Times Book Review* 16 December 1984.

Silverman, Kaja. *The Acoustic Mirror: The Female Voice in Psychoanalysis and Cinema*. Bloomington: Indiana University Press, 1988.

———. *The Subject of Semiotics*. New York: Oxford University Press, 1983.

Slater, Philip E. *The Glory of Hera: Greek Mythology and the Greek Family*. Boston: Beacon, 1971.

Smith-Rosenberg, Carroll. *Disorderly Conduct: Visions of Gender in Victorian America*. New York: Oxford University Press, 1986.

———. "The Female World of Love and Ritual: Relations Between Women in Nineteenth-Century America." *Signs* 1.1 (1975):1–29.

Snitow, Ann, Christine Stansell, and Sharon Thompson, eds. *Powers of Desire: The Politics of Sexuality*. New York: Monthly Review, 1983.

Spacks, Patricia Meyer. *The Female Imagination*. New York: Avon, 1976.

Spelman, Elizabeth V. "Theories of Race and Gender: The Erasure of Black Women." *Quest* 5.4 (1982):36–62.

Spinner, Stephanie, ed. *Motherlove: Stories by Women About Motherhood*. New York: Dell, 1978.

Spivat, Gayatri Chakravorty. *In Other Worlds: Essays in Cultural Politics*. New York: Methuen, 1987.

Stack, Carol B. *All Our Kin: Strategies for Survival in a Black Community*. New York: Harper & Row, 1974.

Stiller, Nikki. *Eve's Orphans: Mothers and Daughters in Medieval Literature*. Westport, Connecticut: Greenwood, 1980.

Strouse, Jean, ed. *Women and Analysis: Dialogues on Psychoanalytic Views of Femininity*. New York: Dell, 1974.

Suleiman, Susan R., ed. *The Female Body in Western Culture: Contemporary Perspectives*. Cambridge: Harvard University Press, 1986.

Tanner, Tony. *Adultery in the Novel: Contract and Transgression*. Baltimore: Johns Hopkins University Press, 1979.

Tate, Claudia, ed. *Black Women Artists At Work*. New York: Continuum, 1983.

Thorne, Barrie, and Marilyn Yalom, eds. *Rethinking the Family*. New York: Longman, 1982.

Todd, Janet. *Women's Friendship in Literature*. New York: Columbia University Press, 1980.

Trebilcott, Joyce, ed. *Mothering: Essays in Feminist Theory*. Totawa, N.J.: Rowman and Allenheld, 1983.

Van Boheemen, Christine. *The Novel as Family Romance: Language, Gender and Authority from Fielding to Joyce*. Ithaca: Cornell University Press, 1987.

Washington, Mary Helen. *Invented Lives: Narratives of Black Women 1860–1960*. New York: Doubleday, 1987.

———, ed. *Midnight Birds: Stories by Contemporary Black Women Writers*. Garden City, N.Y.: Anchor, 1980.

———. "New Lives and New Letters: Black Women Writers at the End of the Seventies." *College English* 43.1 (1981): 1–11.

Wasson, R. Gordon, Albert Hofman, and Carl A. P. Ruck, eds. *The Road to Eleusis: Unveiling the Secret of the Mysteries*. New York: Harcourt Brace Jovanovich, 1978.

Weinstein, Phillip M. *The Semantics of Desire: Changing Models of Identity from Dickens to Joyce*. Princeton: Princeton University Press, 1984.

White, E. Frances. "Listening to the Voices of Black Feminism." *Radical America*, 18.2/3 (1984).

Winnicott, D. W. *The Child, the Family, and the Outside World*. Harmondsworth, England: Penguin, 1976.

———. *Playing and Reality*. New York: Basic Books, 1971.

Wolf, Christa. *The Reader and the Writer: Essays, Sketches, Memories*. Trans. Joan Becker. New York: International Publishers, 1977.

Woolf, Virginia. *Granite and Rainbow: Essays*. London: Hogarth, 1958.

———. "Modern Fiction." *English Critical Essays: Twentieth Century*. Ed. Phyllis M. Jones. London: Oxford University Press, 1933: 388–399.

———. *Moments of Being: Unpublished Autobiographical Writings*. Ed. Jeanne Schulkind. 2nd ed. New York: Harcourt Brace Jovanovich, 1985.

———. *A Room of One's Own*. New York: Harcourt Brace Jovanovich, 1957.

———. *Women and Writing*. Ed. Michèle Barrett. New York: Harcourt Brace Jovanovich, 1980.

Wright, Elizabeth. *Psychoanalytic Criticism: Theory in Practice*. London: Methuen, 1984.

Yaeger, Patricia. *Honey-Mad Women: Emancipatory Strategies in Women's Fiction*. New York: Columbia University Press, 1987.

Yalom, Marilyn. *Maternity, Mortality and the Literature of Madness*. University Park: Pennsylvania State University Press, 1985.

Yeazell, Ruth Bernard, ed. *Sex, Politics, and Science in the Nineteenth-Century Novel: Selected Papers from the English Institute, 1983–84*. New Series 10. Baltimore: Johns Hopkins University Press, 1986.

INDEX